COLONIALISM AND CULTURE

COLONIALISM AND CULTURE

Hispanic Modernisms and
the Social Imaginary

IRIS M. ZAVALA

INDIANA UNIVERSITY PRESS

Bloomington and Indianapolis

The paper used in this publication meets the minimum requirements of American
National Standard for Information Sciences—Permanence of Paper for Printed
Library Materials, ANSI Z39.48-1984.

Manufactured in the United States of America

Library of Congress Cataloging-in-Publication Data

Zavala, Iris M.
    Colonialism and culture : Hispanic modernisms and the social
imaginary / Iris M. Zavala.
        p.   cm.
    Includes bibliographical references and index.
    ISBN 0-253-36861-8 (cloth)
    1. Modernism (Literature)—Latin America.   2. Spanish American
literature—History and criticism.   3. Literature and history—Latin
America.   4. Comparative literature—Spanish American and European.
5. Literature, Comparative—European and Spanish American.   6. Latin
America—Civilization.   I. Title.
PQ7081.Z38   1992
860.9'98—dc20   91-31785

1 2 3 4 5 95 94 93 92

To 2000
and Adrienne Rich
and Michelle Cliff

A national culture is the whole body of efforts made by a people in the sphere of thought to describe, justify and praise the action through which the people has created itself and keeps itself in existence. A national culture in under-developed countries should therefore take its place at the very heart of the struggle for freedom which these countries are carrying on.

—Frantz Fanon, *The Wretched of the Earth*

There is neither a first nor a last word and there are no limits to the dialogic context (it extends into the boundless past and the boundless future). Even *past* meanings, that is, those born in the dialogue of past centuries, can never be stable (finalized, ended once and for all)—they will always change (be renewed) in the process of subsequent, future develop-ment of the dialogue.

—M. Bakhtin, "Methodology for the
Human Sciences"

[They] all participated completely or in part in the movement of moral and intellectual reform . . . that modern man [*sic*] can and should live without religion. . . . This seems to me even today the most important contribution to world culture that we modern intellectuals have given; it seems to me a civil accomplish-ment that should not be lost. . . .

—Antonio Gramsci, *Lettere dal Carcere*
(1931)

By *relativizing* all that was externally stable, set and ready-made, carnivalization with its pathos of change and renewal . . . proved remarkably productive as a means for captur-ing in art the developing relationships under capitalism, at a time when previous forms of life, moral principles and beliefs were being turned into "rotten cords" and the previously concealed, ambivalent, and unfinalized nature of man and human *thought* was being nakedly exposed. . . . Capitalism, similar to that "pan-der" Socrates on the market square of Athens, brings together people and ideas.

—M. Bakhtin, *Problems of Dostoevsky's
Poetics*

CONTENTS

ACKNOWLEDGMENTS

Some of the material in this book was first presented as lectures at various universities in the United States, Puerto Rico, Germany, Italy, and Spain. Earlier versions of two essays were published in the following journals, to which I express my appreciation: "Turn of the Century Lyric: Rubén Darío and the Sign of the Swan," *Hispanic Issues* 3 (1988):279–305; "The Social Imaginary: The Cultural Sign of Hispanic Modernism," *Critical Studies* 1:1 (1989):23–41. The essays have been revised for this book. I also express my gratitude to the Monthly Review Foundation for allowing me to quote from José Martí. Reprinted by permission are excerpts from *Inside the Monster*, copyright 1975; *Our America*, copyright 1977; *On Art and Literature*, copyright 1982.

COLONIALISM AND CULTURE

INTRODUCTION

THE OPEN-ENDED TEXT OF MODERNITY

> "What are we?" is the mutual question, and
> little by little they furnish answers. When a
> problem arises in Cojímar, they do not seek its
> solution in Danzig. The frockcoats are still
> French, but thought begins to be American.
>
> —Martí, *Our America* (1891)

I have always been inclined to think that the colonial and postcolonial eye is anatropic; that we see the colonialist metropolitan space in an epistemologically inverted image. This inversion is not a misrecognition; on the contrary, the upside-down perception reveals a cognitive theory focusing on the specific mechanisms which have served to dominate. Its inner logic is a devaluation of all external positions and hierarchical worldviews. Therefore, the valiant hero, the dashing soldier, the adventurous navigator, the learned scientist, the zealous and pious monk become, through this anatropic perception, their opposite. It is in this way that Aimé Césaire (1972) so rightly saw the adventurer, the pirate, the gold digger, the merchant, since colonization is neither evangelization nor a philanthropic enterprise, nor a project for the glory of democracy, or progress or freedom or God. The metropolitan hero in the colony is the tyrant, or the murderer, or the exploiter, at best the humanitarian equalizer. One could think of many historical events that justify such inversions of the cognitive eye.

Modernism is an appropriate subject to examine in connection with the procedure of anatropic inversion I have just described, since its development in Latin America in the nineteenth century could never have been brought about without turning the European world upside down. Latin American modernity still dramatizes the aporias of imperial Europe, and its emergence in the nineteenth century manifested the historical discontinuity and the crises. What represented the emancipation of Latin America after the wars of independence and later Cuba's liberation, although contradictory and accidental, was perceived by the colonialists as "the disaster" (*el desastre*). The unmasking of bourgeois humanism—brilliantly developed by Franz Fanon—by the Latin American proved to be the modern crisis of language in the metropolis, and the suspension of hierarchical precedence in the modernist space, the event in which people were "reborn for new" relations. In this space, the "utopian ideal and the realistic merged"—in what Bakhtin calls the carnival spirit, but which I prefer to call an anatropic inversion—to create a "third world," which was neither the past nor a satisfying present, but an open possibility which would be neither European nor North American.

The significance accorded to the anti-colonial and the resistance strife which erupted in Cuba in 1895, culminating in the *Maine* incident, the subsequent American recolonization of Puerto Rico and the Philippines in 1898, and the intervention of the North American government in Cuba are the historical events which inaugurated the dialogical/polemical discourse of modernity in the Hispanic world. It represented a rearrangement of social organization in a hegemonic dialogic relation including the colonial, the postcolonial, and the ex-colonial empire. The turn of the century brought not only the struggle in the Caribbean but also the imperialist restructuring in 1900 of the Ottoman Empire, divided into fragments by European powers. In the Hispanic world, this date marked the appropriate political role of involvement and imaginative resistance for the modern Latin American intellectual, whose understanding of emancipatory struggle had crystallized since the 1880s in the Antilles and in the rest of the continent, specifically in Mexico during the Porfiriato, after the imposed reign of Maximilian (1864–1867).

The first step was a conscious desire for national and cultural identity against the holism of "sameness," using an experimental imaginary to create distance and a world of equals within the postcolonial cultures.

At the heart of the method of these reflections was the construction of the marks of identity and difference between Latin Americans and European colonialism on the one hand, and North American "instrumental reason" or the "institutionalization of rationality" and the authoritarian technologies of power on the other.[1] These were supported by a geographical violence involving North American "moving West," or what in 1845 editor John Louis Sullivan labeled "our manifest destiny." In the spirit of "manifest destiny" there were invasions and interventions in the Spanish Antilles, Central America, and Mexico. The problems of territorial (national) expansion of frontiers became all too apparent with the invasion of Mexico in 1846—what is known as the Mexican War, when a battalion of Marines reached Mexico City, occupying "the halls of Montezuma"—which led to an alignment between Spain, France, and England to counteract North American influence in the continent. This war provoked a surge of national pride, and Walt Whitman gloated about it as a triumph which brought "true self-respect [to] the American people."[2] Other nations were less satisfied with the wars of conquest and expansionism of James Knox Polk's presidency, and tried to emulate. France took the opportunity to invade the country in 1861, and a new war of independence broke out, headed by Benito Juárez. In the Caribbean, since the 1860s there had been an awareness among some moderns of a new capitalist type of imperialism, and its different cultural system. At this point, there fully emerged the new historical poetics of modernism as sustaining narrative of anti-colonial struggle, as well as an emergent concept of culture which helped reposition identities and relationships to language.

What I will call the chronotope of this historical poetics was actualized with the first modernity, in its liberationist imaginary toward independence from Spain, whose rule of direct domination came to an end (except in Cuba, the Philippines, and Puerto Rico, then still ruled by the Spanish monarchy). By 1898, the "manifest destiny" arose again, and the first giant leaps toward world power were taken, following the example of the new imperialism of European powers in Africa and Asia since the 1870s. "The splendid little war," as the future secretary of state John Hay called it, included an invasion force of 17,000 American troops commanded by Lt. Col. Theodore Roosevelt (called the "Rough Riders") in Cuba, the taking of Manila at the end of April, and the annexation of Puerto Rico (what is called the Treaty of Paris). Giant steps in the Pacific started to be taken at that time, while at home, North Americans worried about the prospect of incorporating so many aliens into American life; as one senator exclaimed, "Bananas and self-government cannot grow on the same piece of land."

These events prompted a second moment of anti-imperialist struggle against North America in a pan-Hispanic alliance, as a result of its continuous interventions on geographical and territorial grounds. This led to what I will call a distinctive "second moment of modernity," grounded on a shared strategy of construction of a new order of the social fabric to reformulate a hegemonic project, this time within a dialogical configuration including Spain itself, as a culture of opposition, a sense of modernness, calling forth a problem of identity.

Clearly, what I am suggesting is that construction of the concept of modernism and modernness proceeded at a rapid pace during the 1890s, and two idioms describe the same dialogical alliance: modernism and the so-called Young Generation of 1898. The linguistic code of a common symbolic geography produced modernism/modern as a social category, which included as an important point a narrativity of the self, a cultural identity, and cultural nationalism, as well as what could be identified as a "calling of a nation." The question of language at that point was political, cultural, and literary in its most material sense, since a defense of language by the Latin Americans, and specifically by the Caribbeans, was a choice of identity.[3] This new terrain supposed a transformation of the symbolic level, and new forms of the social.

Quite consciously, the distance from both Spanish culture as part of imperialism and North American instrumental reason gave way to a cultural imagination, a social imaginary, as a double bind of distancing and decolonization. These recoveries, identifications, and social imagining were literally grounded on different phases or moments of modernism. A close look at the cultural texts of these modernisms reveals that the rejection of the idea of violent progress conceived among the Anglo-Americans not only contrasted with their own idea of collective destiny but revealed different modes of knowledge and of being. As a discursive episteme, the structure of thought of modernism refers to a set of relations questioning the degrees of complexity of the mode of being of language, nature, and self.

I will stress the common features in the variables involved in Latin American societies—which ranged from the "feudal" to a specific mode of capitalism, as E. Laclau (1977) argues; however, we must consider the differences which affected two discourses simultaneously: a postcolonial discourse with specific kinds of subject positions, and an anti-colonial, anti-imperialist phase of national independence in Cuba and Puerto Rico, which were still negotiating independence. Both stages of struggle divided Latin American modernity. This last phase is inscribed in the discourse which emerged against instrumental reason in the form of imperialism, originally in the Caribbean (Cuba and Puerto Rico), and which became hegemonic around 1898.

The trajectory and periodization of Latin American modernisms are contained in the following: in the historical temporalities of the region's emerging nation-states; in its transition from a colonial to a modern social type in the process of economic liberalization; in its process of political independence, and the incorporation of the former colonial society into the world economy; and also in the forms of social change through the relations of production that were created.[4] When I equate these modern states with modernness and modernization, it should be clear that the historical project was not modernization in the form of dependency theory or capitalist world system. This fact is well known. On the contrary: the struggles both to become modern nation states and to reach technological modernization were part of an alternative revolutionary program for emancipation.

Simultaneously, and this is the objective of my inquiry, there emerged a concept of culture connected to these new political and emotional loyalties by the accentuations of new shared terms. Since culture had been previously articulated through the language of the empire and the war of independence which had been fought around it, there was a strengthening alternative definition in the field of ideological interpellation (in the Althusserian sense) against imperialist connotations of culture. The new idioms on group, ethnicity, and class helped constitute new subject positions within an emancipatory ideological discourse, and to reposition identities and relationships to language. They were forms of critical thinking about culture and power which prompted the repoliticization of many spheres of life as a result of the awareness that politics was cultural. Cultures were theorized in their internal differences and their heterogeneity, even within their hybridity. The novelty was in the diversity of forces and sites in emancipatory struggles. It could be said that it is a local which claims its identity from global (mis)representation.

The reader will rightly conclude that I suggest there is no typical "modernism," that there are no universals or essences. Basing my inquiry on a Gramscian theory of hegemony and Bakhtinian dialogism, I hope to avoid the essentialism and "centrisms" that define modernism as an illusory whole, which includes only parts of Europe and North America. Within a broadly conceived field of cultural studies, I will explore the theoretical essentialisms which claim globalizations to represent particular local experiences. Since I am concerned with the legitimacy of the functional differentiation of modernity, I try to avoid the tendency both to universalize modernism and modernity and to dissolve the particularities in either a domesticated sameness or a muted difference. At the same time, I hope to provide an explanation of the process of becoming modern and the patterns of modernity away from a teleological and Eurocentric view.

In this endeavor I am in good company. Lately, Rey Chow (1986–87) has demystified Jameson's globalizations and totalizations, and has called attention to Chinese modernism (around 1919), whose main features included the controversial advocacy of the vernacular and myriad experimentations with "Western" literary forms. On similar grounds, Neil Lazarus (1986–87) has spoken about the rational humanism of South African modernism, and the particular situation of an intelligentsia silenced by social circumstances in which violence and repression are endemic and institutionalized. For the same reasons, Afro-American modernism had its own critical voice, as Baker (1987) has lucidly proven, and Césaire is better understood now as a modernist poet of liberation (Arnold 1981). Furthermore, Eisenstadt (1987) endeavors to explain the reception of modernism in non-Western cultures.

The tendency toward universals—"Modernism is . . . ," or "Hispanic *modernismo* is different . . ."—has led to widespread generalizations about the ideologies of modernism(s), and about their political role in other cultural domains which are irreducibly different, with few exceptions.[5] My aim is to reinforce and re-accentuate the relation between modernism, modernity, and modernization in Latin America—and partly the Hispanic experience—with the subjective transformation of individual life and human collective practice at the turn of the century.[6] I insist on these relations, which have been partly explored from other perspectives, to signal the nonfixation or openness of the discursive positions and the ensemble of social practices which produced modernism as a category of dialogical modern thinking interwoven with capitalism. The focus of my reading consists in the following points:

1. That modernism is not a set of formal features in a given text, but a chronotope including both literary discourse and social life.

2. That modernism is better understood as a narrative of liberation, and also as an exercise in social theory.

3. That a dialogical approach to the epistemological and cultural, and a Gramscian hegemonic approach to the social, represent a promising point of view to understand these historical and cultural coordinates, and societal changes.

4. That in that framework, in the Hispanic world, the contested field of modernism became an organic ideology at the turn of the century, creating a hegemony of cultural formalization founded in the logic of identity, while bringing into question modern forms of capitalist expansion.

5. That modernism—in its plurality and differences—became a historical

mode of textual organization, and a mode of organizing experience within a heteroglotic world.

6. That as a discursive formation, in the chronotope of modernism, time and space are fundamental axiological elements as they help us understand the situatedness of language as encounters of evaluative utterances that constitute subjects.

7. That this dialogism was a new form for expressing time, space, self, and was related to the uncovering of social contradictions. Such uncovering pushed time into the future, through enthymemic forms of discourse.

8. That the time/space relation of Hispanic modernist texts should be perceived in the context of the larger time/space relation of the turn of the century, as a situated evaluation, judged from a particular point of view.

9. That a dialogical reading allows for an understanding of the heteroglossia inherent in modernism, the elements of carnivalization, and the struggle for the sign, which constitutes not only metaphoricity but also subjectivity.

10. That dialogism, as a method of historical poetics, with its emphasis on time, space, and value, offers a method to posit the complex of economic, political, and historical forces as a combination of ideologies which conglomerate within capitalism.

The evaluative event which created the dialogical organic alliance was the rejection of North American capitalist expansionism, which finally was confronted in the juncture of 1898. With this situatedness in mind, it is not surprising that this historical juncture of the 1890s of the Anglo-Spanish struggle over the Caribbean hastened a critical modernism, as well as strengthened postcolonial identities.[7] With this contingency and in this conjuncture, an analysis of Hispanic modernism(s) as a historical narrative in the shape of alliances must be evoked, both the narrative of emancipation for Latin America and a narrative of a critical self-reflexivity among the "organic intellectuals" (the Gramscian organizers) in the Peninsula, who were renovating and making critical older hegemonic institutional formations, among them that of institutionalized culture.

This organic bloc was composed of a seemingly contradictory corpus of anarchists, socialists, and bohemians—described in 1873 by Mikhail Bakunin as an "intellectual proletariat." The bohemians made up, according to Bakunin, a new social class composed of people from different strata and different intellectual levels of society (1977:47). Decisive battles were fought by the positional alignments of moderns as much in civil society as in the economy or state. The new notion here, the episteme of modernism and the sense of modernness, may be understood within a "situated" convention of signification. If in the Peninsula the moderns were dismantling hegemonic knowledges, the Latin American modernities/modernisms can be described as rearranging a new configuration of modern knowledge, politics, and culture to enable a new subjectivity to develop. In this sense, modernism is far from being an "alienated," "nonpolitical," "conservative," "imitative," or at best "culturalist" apoliticized literary movement. Culture cannot be removed from ideology if ideology, like language—in Bakhtin's suggestions—is an effect that a subject assumes for its own cause.

From the perspective of a historical poetics, modernism linked disparate conjunctural social forces which retained their identities, interests, and aspirations in the higher synthesis of the organic collective will, in Gramsci's sense of "organic" (see Laclau and Mouffe 1985:66–67). Thus, no single model or articulation is appropriate. As ideological discourse, modernism is a practice that acts upon language with its social contexts (Bakhtin's "situated utterance") and points toward a future that would radically alter its own relation to reality. Implicit were forms of knowledge which produced discourses on moral and ethical beliefs, emotional orientations, and subjectivities. As a condition of these modern culture(s), different relations to traditions and/or heritages were constructed, and in such competing constructions ideological differences of interpretation took place simultaneously within several potentially conflicting cultural practices within multiple fronts of struggle.

If European modernity in the first years of this century was still caught between a classical past, an indeterminate technical present, and an unknown future, and was divided between a semi-aristocratic order, a semi-industrialized capitalist economy, and a semi-emergent labor movement (Anderson 1988:326), it could be said that a Latin American contesting modernity shares few of these characteristics. In reality, it presents an alternative to all of them.

When I equate modernism and modernity, I refer specifically to four dimensions: a cultural/philosophical discourse, a historical discourse, a theory of progress, and a writing and readerly discourse with a utopian function based on a critical hermeneutics to appropriate and (re)define heritage and anticolonialism. Cultural texts present alternative definitions in the field of ideological interpellation to the readers toward resistance. Their potential—like that of many of the "creolized" hybrid myths—constituted a horizon for the future, in the responsiveness and answerability of the dialogical word. The rustle of modernist discourse is thus a heterology, anticipating the discourses to come from the situational horizon from which they were directed.

The theoretical assertion which emerged with the postcolonial Spanish cultural claim revolved around the notion of a new concept of culture as a whole, and the positivity of the subject as agent of history in enthymemic discourses of a responsive nature; this was designed to help create a cultural polyphony of freedom to blend the different worlds against the social and cultural enclosures produced throughout the long journey from conquest and colonization. In a crusade for cosmopolitanism, the idea of open cultural and political space was frequently counterposed to the asphyxiating colonial atmosphere. Such emancipatory projections take shape through strategic creativity combining feeling, knowledge, and political strategy aimed at producing versions of the colonial antagonism, which in 1898 took the form of a cultural offensive to express the rejection of North American culture and expansionist politics, designating the invasion as an extrusion of evil while affirming a collective identity.

I will employ the spatial metaphor of *dialogical social imaginary* to describe this strategic creativity as the medium for a counterdiscourse and a practice of symbolic resistance. This ideological imagining projects virtual reality through words as an objective form of dreams to share in the collective conscious. Such experimental imagining indicates how discourses can find their meaning by reference to ideological positions through the mechanism of identification and disidentification with the antagonistic invader with opposing (and even violent) imperatives of utility, morality, and modernity. Accordingly, my analyses propose a dialogue between the individual texts of some of the founders of this narrative, and the complex collective formation to which that discourse is a primary contribution. In short, we will explore how literary texts are interconnected to the flux of the social world.

It should be understood that when I use the concept *narrative,* it is meant not as a literary category but as one of the major forms of discourse structuring. It is not specifically an aesthetic category, and should be understood in the contemporary sense given to "narratives," as historical accounts of the past and correlative anticipations of a people, nation, or community which perform functions of social integration and political legitimation.[8]

Against this background, I argue for Latin American modernism at the turn of the century as the inscription of a "master narrative" or "master plot" of decolonization and anti-imperialism. This inscription grew out of different forms of struggle against subordination, which included different subject positions traversing class and ethnic sectors, whose intention was to generate a cultural capital belonging to the whole society. The challenge of the new decolonized modern subject, with its own national identity in the postcolc.nial and colonial—of which it was so organically a part—was originally a polemic against the domesticated reductive sameness of colonialism. As proposed in a different context in Said's "Orientalism," the representation of the Spanish colonial America was a science of incorporation and inclusion by virtue of which this "New World" was constituted and then reintroduced into Europe. The experience can be traced to 1492, the advent of the world market, which stands for interior colonialism and imperialism in the history of Spanish (and European) hegemonies: the publication of the first imperialist grammar, the conquest of Granada, the expulsion of the Jews, and the conquest of the so-called New World. All are examples of simultaneous and multidirected subcontraries as modes of imperial inscription.

The emergence of a modern narrative at the end of the century as the projection of a decolonized social discourse is particularly suitable for an analysis of the imaginary as a potential creator of sustaining fictions and emancipatory projections through the mediation of human and historical agency. This liberating imaginary gives voice to what had remained unexpressed—what Voloshinov/Bakhtin call the enthymeme—in the social or the individual within an anatropic atmosphere of heterologic liberation or emancipation. This led modernists to a rejection (in the Bakhtinian sense) of the imaginary relations of the master-slave dialectic, since the dialogical transforms the mirror metaphor into the boundary of speaking subjects in interacting evaluations. Modernist discourse is a process whereby heteroglossic social groups struggle to establish their intellectual, cultural, and moral influence, consequently redefining the social map itself.

This collective master narrative should not be understood as a fundamental, essentialist way of organizing the world, but rather as a heteroglotic construct of a collective subject and its new national identities. The situation of speech communication, with all its individual circumstances, was meant to erase the essential boundaries in order to maximize the "active responsive position" of the participants. Within this critical historical conjuncture, however great the diversity, the common enterprise ("Our America," to use José Martí's term) was shared by many Latin American moderns from different geographical points at different times—Argentina, Bolivia, Chile, Colombia, Costa Rica, Cuba, Guatemala, Nicaragua, Peru, Puerto Rico, San Salvador, Venezuela—as the embodiment of dynamic relationships of struggle. The process of self-assertiveness and sovereignty as the principle of modernity and as a *third way* out between European colonialism and North American imperialism was developed via a narrative reconstruction projected mainly (but not exclusively) by Martí. This specific event of 1898 compels the work of "genealogists"—in the meaning given to this term by Foucault in his essay on Nietzsche (1977)—who will push the masquerade to its limit and prepare the great carnival of time where masks constantly reappear. At this high point of the process, there is a natural association with the anarchist movement, a historically bounded practice also common among French symbolists and many Italian and English modernists.

The sovereignty of the subject, which Latin American moderns had previously shared with the romantics—along with, I suggest, an emancipatory conception of art, a poetics of dialogical negation, and the organizing epistemological logic of the allegorical—crystallized in the fulfillment of the modern age. The social utopian content of literature already present was re-accentuated and reconstituted with the pragmatic experience of the North American invasion. Space and time were stirred by the confrontation with Latin America's (and the Hispanic) absolute Other.

The intellectual climate or "literary field" (in Bourdieu's term [1966, 1984]) was strongly marked by a tendency to seek political unity in the newly fragmented geographical space, and to search for a comprehensive theoretical, democratic, and republican model of unity and coherence for a future and solidary history. Thus understood, modernism emerged as an attempt to produce a theory of a modern society with the potential for a humane collective life. José Martí (1853–1895) led the way after 1882 through his anti-colonial and liberatory discourse, and in an aesthetics of commitment. The modernist understanding of the aesthetic was also a commitment to the political and its conception of the nature of a cultural literary avant-garde which, in the Hispanic world, the Nicaraguan poet Rubén Darío (1867-1916) defined as *modernismo* in 1888.[9]

The nonconformist stance of the turn-of-the-century *modernistas* has been historically modified with time, and the contemporary reader must be sensitive both to the failures of modernism and to its achievements. But a minimum direct knowledge of the cultural texts themselves would indicate the legitimizing nature of their negativity, and the active presence of a critical stand against "instrumental reason" with its existing division of intellectual labor, its primacy of economics and economic motives, and its culture limited by the interests of the capitalist society. The crisis energized a set of rhetorical tropes with referential value: "minotaurs," "buffaloes," "clowns," "barbarians," the nation "which allowed Edgar Poe to die in misery," "haters of the ideal [poetry]." Marx made use of similar metaphors in *Capital* against utilitarianism, as he deepened his hostility toward capitalism. In his words: "Franklin's definition of man as a tool-making animal is characteristic of Yankeedom" (I:358).

My purpose here is to recuperate the "cultural polyphony" of Latin American modernity, its newly constructed subject, and its adversarial cultural counterdiscourse in what remains powerful; to re-accentuate and recombine the quality of carnival, of heteroglossia, of polyphony that occupied this modernity and which continue to have meaning, even within every new situatedness. This modernist dialogical discourse exhausted its potential around the First World War; however, the cultural meanings remain in a semantic political underground and call for a constant process of redefinition. Next, I want to insist that this polyphony included the young Spanish moderns, in their meaningful alliance with anarchists and socialists, around the 1890s. Thus, in ethicopolitical terms, both were moments of modernity and, simultaneously (the Bakhtinian both/and), its critics. Finally, this is an attempt to reconstitute that double dialogical alliance which was constituted around the Anglo-Spanish struggle of the Caribbean, as an articulation of cultural values, and the fundamental problem of cognition as mediated through the rustle of modernist language. What this book is *not* is a history of Latin American literature, or Caribbean literatures, or Spanish literature. What I hope to do is to indicate the moment in which the contested space of modernity called for this "relative" alliance.

Throughout this book I use the dominant modern term *Latin America* instead of *Spanish America;* some readers will notice, however, that the nineteenth-century quoted texts say *America.* The latter should not be confused with Anglo-America. It should be clear, however, that I refer only to Spanish America, since Brazil offers yet another set of challenges.

The present book has been written as a continuation of previous inquiries. It is intended as a critical contribution to the question of modernism and the understanding of the dynamics of modernity and decolonization, as well as an exploration of the modern urban working-class creativity in light of popular allegiances and democratic re-accentuations and rereadings of "elite" traditions. There is a vast amount of interfacing between the two discourses; they feed and enrich each other in multiple ways. My approach is to establish a set of contrasts between Latin American (and Peninsular or Hispanic) modernism and the themes of modernism as a whole. I have used a variety of approaches relevant to Marxism and Critical Theory, as well as to Foucault's concern with power, knowledge, and authority. The whole of my elaboration is based on a re-accentuation of critical modernists: Marx himself as a modernist, the Bakhtin circle's theories on language as communication and the dialogical, and Gramsci's concepts of hegemony, common sense, organic crisis, and organic intellectual.[10]

The open-ended theorized nature of their work as an interaction which consequently makes the "viewer" also a participant seems a fruitful counter to the monologic character of many theories.[11] I do not wish to remain outside these observed worlds, but to be a constituent part. I also borrow from their work hoping to establish a nonreductive and more differentiated concept of knowledge in turn-of-the-century Hispanic modernism, which will account for its emancipatory potential while at the same time securing the legitimate function of its differentiated narrative.[12]

This book is the result of a five-part project on the dialogics of modernism and modernity in the Hispanic experience comprising already published books on Darío, Unamuno, Valle-Inclán, and theories of modernity (in press). I have translated all the Spanish quotations, unless otherwise stated, and must confess to taking great pleasure in answering the challenge of rendering a comprehensible version of boleros, tangos, anarchist songs, and cuplés. Unless otherwise stated, all translations of texts are my own. I also want to thank my colleague Myriam Díaz-Diocaretz for her reading of this text and for her suggestions and insights, and my editors Joan Catapano and Jane Lyle, without whose patient and thorough editing this book would never have found its final form.

I

THE DIALOGICAL SOCIAL IMAGINARY AND SELF-REPRESENTATION

> Without *one's own* questions one cannot cre-
> atively understand anything other or
> foreign. . . . Such a dialogic encounter of two
> cultures does not result in merging or mixing.
> Each retains its own unity and *open* totality,
> but they are mutually enriched.
>
> —M. Bakhtin, "Response to a Question
> from *Novy Mir*"

The Bakhtin Circle and the Dialogical

A significant point in the current discussion of modernity (and postmodernity) is the way in which subjectivity has been explored within the Western philosophical tradition, and its ethical questions. With this in mind, I hope to open *out* the discussion toward different intellectual and political traditions in order to inquire about the relations between discursive systems, the imaginary, and symbolic introspection as modes of cultural knowledge. I will draw on recent theories of the sign and theories of interpretation, and will link them to social analyses to explore the symbolic resistance of discursive practices, through the use of what I have called the dialogical social imaginary. My intention is to suggest a nonreductionist conceptualization of modernism, and of both the imaginary and the symbolic, by reversing the terms of the problem to produce an account of a specifically social form of imagining. I hope it is clear that I am not valorizing the symbolic over material appropriations. What I suggest is that through the symbolic, ideological interpellations are projected.

In order to further reconstruct the turn-of-the-century modernist emancipatory narrative, I will specify the difference between what I propose as a dialogical social imaginary which projects and monitors a critical reflection of liberation from the symbolic, and the mainstream psychoanalytical (and poststructuralist) notions of social subjects trapped in the mesh of the symbolic. To convey this objective, I will return to the polemical/dialogical alliance of various currents of thought on the configuration of ideology, the imaginary, the symbolic, and representation to broaden the frame of reference needed to grasp their logic within a revolutionary practice to create a perceptual metalepsis or ideological inversion. If in describing the dialogical social imaginary as an operative concept, and as a creative "consciousness raising" (in Critical Theory's term), I privilege Lacan, it is because his influence has emerged in the current debates concerning self, language, and ideology, specifically the notions of the imaginary and the symbolic, and his description of the subject's entry into the symbolic order of language.

Without adhering to Lacanian theses, I will understand both the imaginary and the symbolic as directly concerned with the question of the production of subjects and the multiple unconscious categories which enable the emergence of forms of subjectivity, and with the construction of subject positions from which the repertoire of ideological interpellations arise. Through "condensed connotation" (to use E. Laclau's term [1988]), the imaginary positions connote one another in a chain of linked interpellations. However, these imaginary positions and relations should be understood also in the Bakhtinian nondialectical transformation of the "mirror" metaphor in the dialogical boundary of interacting evaluations. Therefore, situational ideologies alter and transform signification through language, taking shape in antagonistic relations. In this direction, I will rely on the Bakhtin/Voloshinov theory of language and subjectivity grounded on the construction of the self by forces external to it—language as *used,* as communication, thus a social system, not autonomous from cultural and social institutions. Each group, or each situated utterance, uses the linguistic-semiotic system in different ways to shape its own meaning; there is a polemic over meaning, and situational experiences provoke people to re-accentuate speech genres in order to project each evaluative position over the situation. It is here that we connect the force of literature as a source of human consciousness.

A few references will help us clarify our position on the ideological character of the sign and the socialization of language. According to the Bakhtin circle, language orients the social destiny of utterances in the intersection between language as a refraction (not "mirror" reflection) of social class, and subjective conscience as an internal utterance with a specific socio-historical orientation. From this Bakhtinian dialogical historical poetics, one can deduce that every utterance is determined "by its time in history, its social environment, its speaker's class status and the actual specific circumstances of the utterance" ("What is Language?" *BSP* 105). The collective receptor/interlocutor of the utterance reorganizes the stylistic structure; class ideology is refracted through intonational elements and choice and disposition of words: "Every verbal construction and, not only by its content, but in its very form expresses and realizes the relationship of the speaker to the world and other people, the relationship to the situation and the given audience" ("The Word and Its Social Function," *BSP* 140).

As an *ideological sign,* discourse represents not only a point of view but "an evaluating point of view," in interaction with a social auditory which, in its turn, will confer meaning. A strong support for this theory of language is Marx's powerful insight that "language is practical consciousness, as it exists for other men," and like consciousness it arises only "from the need, the necessity, of intercourse with other men" (1985:173). I will argue about the social orientation of the sign and consciousness, the creative activity of the imaginary, and the potential social force of representations to formulate the politics of signification of modernism, with the background of some Bakhtinian concepts, specifically the *ideologeme,* the *chronotope,* and the *dialogical.* The integration of these categories will allow us to give particular attention to modernism as a historical poetics which prepared the groundwork for a dialogical social imaginary which monitors an imaginary "representation" of social relations based on a collectivity in solidarity with its values and its collective project. This dialogical social imaginary, which took shape at the turn of the century, provides the basis for two related problems: first, how a heterogeneous community organized itself into a collective "I" and "another"; second, how cultural texts forged a tentative wholeness through the discursive position of national and cultural identity.

These Bakhtinian concepts and the circle's theory on social discourses will be our point of departure to question the space of configuration and the subject positions of textual representations within their dialogical relationship with the collectivity. A brief explanation of the productive meaning of these concepts is necessary. The ideologeme, a notion referred to by Medvedev/Bakhtin since 1928, will allow us to posit the interrelation between the ideological horizon and its refraction in the unity of the artistic work (*FM* 22–25). As a starting point, the notion of ideologeme suggests the possibility of relating images, experiences, and discourse, and allows us to abandon the traditional thematic concept and to capture content from an ideological perspective which is part of class struggle. Each narrative, or each thematic construct, incorporates new meanings as it is recontextualized.

The ideologeme is the basis for the content or for new contents, and is inseparable from the ideological horizon of social classes. It should not be confused with Julia Kristeva's reappropriation of the term from a textual, less socialized framework as an "intertextual function read as materialized" at the different structural levels of each text. . . . The concept of text as ideologeme determines the very procedure of a semiotics that, by studying the text as intertextuality, considers it as such . . . (1969, in 1980:36–37). Jameson reactualizes, in another direction, its implications of social and class struggle (1981:87–88). For our purpose it should be kept in mind that the modernist dialogical social imaginary I propose is related to the ideologeme, since it is the space of the inscription of historical utterance and discursive enunciation.[1]

The chronotope is a spatial-temporal indicator representing the image of the human being. It allows us to evaluate the capacity for representation and problematization of the collective space from which literary production comes (literally time-space, and a unity of analysis for textual understanding). The chronotope suggests the heteroglotic space which breaks down not only the enclosing walls between popular and elite culture, or the text and context, or the inside and outside, but also the time/space of confrontation of differently oriented social languages in the shared territory of the utterance. It suggests an optic for reading texts and actualizing the productive forces of the cultural system from which they came (*DI* 84–85). The chronotope is, in fact, a way of perceiving the world as an emerging event, the form-shaping ideology of a genre.[2] From our perspective, modernism is a chronotope with a particular axiological meaning in a specific situation, whose earliest embodiments emerged in the nineteenth century (roughly during the wars of independence), and which continues to organize later texts, up to and in a way including those of the present day.

Finally, the dialogical is not only an interaction of voices in which the utterances of others are projected and prolonged with their different codes and idiolects at the same time, but it should also be understood in its social accent and its pluridiscursive and heteroglossic direction. This dialogue of voices in the social arena is both multiple and simultaneous and is always oriented toward other utterances, both of the same subject and of other authors: "Thus the printed verbal performance engages, as it were, in ideological colloquy at large scale: it responds to something, objects to something, affirms something, anticipates possible responses and objections, seeks support, and so on" (*MPL* 95).[3] Dialogics suggests an ethics, the simultaneity of the also/and of a perception of coexistence and interaction, which provides the possibility to represent open-endedness.

More quotations and examples could be added, all pointing to the social/semiotic interchange (or social intercourse) between the speaker, society, and history. In Bakhtin/Medvedev's words:

> There is no meaning outside of the social communication of understanding, i.e., outside the united and mutually coordinated reactions of people to a given sign. Social intercourse is the medium in which the ideological phenomenon first acquires its specific existence, its ideological meaning, its semiotic nature. (*FM* 9)

Bakhtin's reflections on the questions of language which I have mentioned are the connecting tissue to argue for a dialogical social imaginary of modernism, since the circle stresses that in the social production of the message, the "internal discourse" and the "external discourse" are brought in contact with ideological forms from both the past and the present. Intonation gives meaning to the utterance and "represents," "gives voice" to, "refracts" ideology in the discursive interchange within the space of its textual configuration. Such a linguistic model will allow us to interrogate the social function of writing and to propose the "imaginary" as a social space of potential revolutionary symbolic practice which can change the text of history, the scene or theatrical space of ideology. Within this area, the semantics and syntaxis of the empirical and speculative functions of ideology take place.[4]

From the Bakhtin circle's development of the dialogical, what I intend to do specifically is to situate the "dialogical social imaginary" in terms of the strategic site of organization of the representational bond between a referent and its expression and "ideological fantasy." It is the locus of the monitoring images for the transformation of reality, where representation constitutes the responsiveness of the social being it represents. As a social/collective construct it is inseparable from the revolutionary consciousness that historically some social groupings project from their private subjectivity, through identification and/or estrangement. With respect to the symbolic, I am aware I am advancing in a direction which is risky, since it is also basic to the constitution of the self via Lévi-Strauss and Lacan; however, we have argued that language is social communication, and fundamentally heteroglotic. Furthermore, neo-Kantians have underlined not only that linguistic interchange is economic, but also that representations have a symbolic effectiveness in the construction of reality (see Bourdieu 1982:99). Communication itself is a symbolic exchange, highly dependent on *who* employs language (on its use), and which social group (or groups) supports its performative force.[5] The methodological problems of this ample field of analysis may help shed some light on ideological codes, on their mental representations in textual inscription, on the political function of the imaginary and the social force of the symbolic within the order of signification and communication.

The Imaginary and the Symbolic

This is not the place to go into poststructuralism in any detail, but certain aspects of it will help us grasp the Bakhtinian concepts I am using to reinforce what I propose as the social imaginary. I will use these poststructuralist literary models as suggestive material, and will adapt concepts from other disciplines in order to propose other possibilities, as a way of assessing the organization and materialist topology of the imaginary and the symbolic as a field of study. The usefulness of some of these models lies in the reintroduction of collective and historical preoccupations, while others are contemporary debated approaches which will allow us to argue that the imaginary is a producer of meaning of social and political representation, understanding literature as an imaginary construct.

It will perhaps help us to appreciate the concern with mental and imaginary structures if we remember the most rigorous attempts that have been made to define the power of the imagination. Of course, *imagination, imagining,* and *the imaginary* are not synonyms, but they are notions which raise questions about the relationships between the subject and ideology. The potential of both imagination and imagining is connected to the history of the Western world (much like the opposition *ancien/moderne*). Such critical force was disclosed by Breton in his Surrealist Manifest (1924). The active property of imagination (or imagining) is its doubly oriented aesthetic and political dimension. Needless to say, the avant-garde also heightened its aesthetic and praxis, a dimension energized by the Frankfurt School (Adorno, Benjamin, Horkheimer, Lowenthal, Marcuse, and now Habermas). Marcuse insists that "without phantasy, all philosophical knowledge remains in the grip of the present or the past and severed from the future, which is the only link between philosophy and the real history of mankind" (1968:155). Sartre, in turn, analyzed philosophically *l'imaginare,* understood as a productive force of the imagination. However, contemporary arguments on the imaginary center on theories of the unconscious, as reservoirs of repressed emotion which reduce its social emancipatory force as active resistance.

The new (master) readings of Freud limit the imaginary and the symbolic, the unconscious, the mirror structure, and the specular to psychoanalytical speculations. In Lacan's formulations, both the imaginary and the symbolic are the bases of a schema for the structure of the subject which rests in the dual relation between the Ego and the Other. His model was grounded on the structuralist Lévi-Straussian outlook, for which society is an ensemble of symbolic systems (language, economic relations, art, science, religion); in the analysis of such systems, significance is secondary and derivative. The sets of imaginary relations of ego to ego are a hermeneutic circle of illusions and an endless mirror-play of meaning. Consequently, Lévi-Strauss's emphasis that the signifier precedes and determines the signified is extended into the view that social life is constituted and determined by universal rules.

According to this view—and I draw from Dews (1988)—the explanations of social phenomena "do not have reference to individual or collective experience or affectivity, since the content of experience is itself determined by an unconscious system of shared categories" (78). The imaginary develops in Lacanian theory associated with misleading intersubjective identifications, based on his adoption of Saussurean terminology and the structuralist idea of the arbitrary relation between signifier and signified (Dews 1988:73). On this account, the imaginary is chiefly a misconception and a remoteness from truth on the part of the subject. It is linked to the unconscious as constituent of a theory of desire, a self constructed by language severed from any reality beyond that which it creates itself.

As a logical extension of these imaginary functions, a mapping of the field allows the distinction of a recent tradition which finds sustenance in definitions of ideology based on Lacan. We are required in this context to begin with Althusser's well-known "Ideology and Ideological State Apparatuses" (1971:162), a debatable account of ideology as the unconscious collective representations as well as the activities and rituals in which these representations are embedded: "a representation of the imaginary relationship of individuals to their real conditions of existence." His argument is that ideology interpellates individuals as subjects through the mechanism of recognition. It calls individuals into place and confers upon them their "identity" (163). Althusser's critique, which emphasizes that our consciousness is constructed and that the subject is not the center humanism supposes, has been an important challenge. The same critique is reactualized by Coward and Ellis and by

Jameson from another direction, but the former return to the discursive figure of inversion (1977). In this constellation, Louis Marin's definition is also basic: "L'idéologie [est] une philosophie moyenne des idées-représentations mais, aussi d'une représentation spéculaire et médiée des autres circuits d'échanges" (1975:59).

Althusser's and Marin's theories of ideology tend to identify the aesthetic as imaginary relations, a phantasmatic form of inversion (Marx's *camera obscura*) which constitutes the subject in its relation to objective reality. Ideology is a language, and subjection comes from the interior of the individual: the subjection of society and that of the individual "depend on each other and reject each other." They are specular categories, a double-mirror structure. Ideology is thus equivalent to a network of representations which induce the subject to an imaginary relation with objective/material reality. Consequently, identifications and/or distancings are largely based on cultural factors, through the mediation of human history, of society and language.

To Lacan, the signifier represents a subject to another signifier. The syntactic chain of signifiers assigns a position to the subject, identifying him/her at a certain point of the chain. This mechanism of differential identification is none other than "the effect" of society whose dissymmetries find their cause here. The Imaginary Order is that of identification and duality, and the Symbolic (culture) is that of language, discourse, narratives.[6]

With Lacan's psychoanalytic subject, the Symbolic Order is related to the qualitative difference between *désir* and *demande*. The first is characterized by need (*le manque*) and belongs to the order of the imaginary; the demand is the claim to fulfill desire or to be gratified by (an)other and belongs to the order of the symbolic, where, in consequence, it is inverted into active desiring, a demand posed to the other. Finally, the canonical Freudian psychoanalytical unconscious is an atemporal space; historical time is nonexistent, and as a consequence its social function of creating collective attitudes toward the past, the present, and the future is minimized. Incidentally, this critique of Freudianism and the notion of the social component of the unconscious were put forward by the Bakhtin circle in 1927.

Lacan's psychoanalytical conceptualization of the imaginary and the symbolic, prevalent in most current poststructuralist theoretical constructs, has modified corresponding concepts: representation, ideology, mirror, mediation. Thus, much of the work of French theory after 1960–1963 bears the mark of the Lacanian model of the imaginary inseparable from a misleading and deceptive misrecognition. Lacan's emphasis on the symbolic (adopted from Lévi-Strauss) is the new order which determines the relation between the ego and intersubjectivity, while in his theory of fantasy it is defined as a nonreflexive form of interiority. This problem is central to Roland Barthes (*S/Z* 1970), in many of the metaphors in which the argument is played out. He pursues the same ambiguity when he states: "L'idéologie serait au fond l'Imaginaire d'un temps, le Cinéma d'une société" (1975).

The impact of this model is also felt in philosophy and the social sciences.

Jean Baudrillard rearticulates Lacan's mirror stage from the vantage point of the postmodern as a directive model of indeterminacies and simulations and the delegitimation of master narratives. The argument of his post-Marxist discourse is an increasing incredulity centered against the mirror of production (1973), which would be "humankind consciousness within the *imaginary*" (emphasis added; see Jay 1987–88). Discourse of production and discourse of representation are to him "that mirror where the system of political economy comes to reflect in the imaginary, and reproduce itself there as determining instance" (13). This is, to the French poststructuralist and post-Marxist, the critical illusion of historical materialism.

Finally, Cornelius Castoriadis (1975, trans. 1987), a psychoanalyst by profession and member of the group Socialisme ou Barbarie, within the Lacanian heritage, is largely responsible for a notion of "social imaginary" and the "imaginary institution of society" grounded on desire (lack). He defines it as follows: "The social imaginary is, primordially, the creation of significations and the creation of the images and figures that support these significations. The relation between a signification and its supports (images or figures) is the only precise sense that can be attached to the term 'symbolic'—and this is the sense in which we are using the term here" (238, 356). Castoriadis highlights a slightly different conception which stresses desire to dislocate and disrupt symbolic and social order, in similar orientation to Lyotard's *Discours, Figure* (1974) of libidinal economy.

As we have seen, to Castoriadis and the philosophers of desire who were briefly mentioned, ideology is a language. It is a privileged expression of current notions of the primacy of language. Language, however, is the expression of the individual subject, since institutions by the other ("l'institution par l'autre")—God, history, or nature—designate no philosophical or real social change. Society lacks a "radical imaginary dimension, as revealed in the indivisible unity of social action and the simultaneous elaboration of the universe of meaning, history is neither possible nor conceivable" (265).[7] Both the imaginary and the symbolic I refer to are not only historical but axiological, as experienced by subjects.

The Dialogical Social Imaginary

This brief, descriptive analysis of the foundations of the archeology of contemporary modes of thought and formulations on the imaginary and the symbolic has been necessary to provide a precise discursive location from which to embark. A critical method of anatropic inversion of those theories, by contrast, would inevitably lead to the conclusion we have been pursuing: that as a space, the imaginary constitutes an ideological and practical discourse. From Voloshinov/Bakhtin's argument, we can have a sharper sense of the relations which discourses have with ideological practices, and the political dimension of each use of words. They propose what could be described as a "politics of meaning" or "signification": language consists mainly of "situational utterances," and thus they change their meaning according to the positions held by the users. In short, utterances are part of a "politics of signification," for the creative consti-tution of self and other; therefore, a subject's situatedness can be a decided position from which to rebel against the identity and affiliations granted by hegemonies and domination. This dialogic conception helps explain how ide-ologies take shape in connection to each other, antagonistically, as means of resistance.

The argument I have outlined thus far makes proposals to reposition the "imaginary" and the "symbolic," and reinstate the collective revolutionary praxis of the imaginary as a mediating space where new world visions can be represented and in which symbolic forces are liberated through performatives. Working against the poststructuralist conceptualizations briefly described, and drawing from socialized models, I intend to designate a materialist topology of the imaginary, neither as a symbolic act which mainly privileges nonsocialized language constructs, nor as an untroubled utopian fictional region which affords consolation, but as the site where mental representations may trigger the transforming power of the symbolic through the performative force of emancipatory narratives.

If language as communication is the medium of intersubjectivity and self-consciousness, realized by mutual recognition of subjects as social, concrete others in language, dialogicality serves as a recognition of the other, since every word wishes to be "heard" and "responded to." What the Bakhtin circle has taught us is the multiplicity and heterogeneous nature of modern cultural texts, and it invites us to think of the socialization of every area of life and the openness in the ground of ideology, which constitutes a space in which to work. Dialogism implies that meaning results from the relation between at least two consciousnesses in active participation, and that there is a connection between language and self, and meaning, a process of creation, bending toward the future. That language addresses response in the open event of existence; this version of future response and openness is implied in what I have called a dialogical social imaginary, interpellating from the modernist texts to construct a collective subject position against imperialist exploitation and centralized forms of domination. The organic crisis of 1898 endowed a specific, clearly defined enemy.

In the dialogical social imaginary, meaning is dependent on the response of the interlocutor, and tropes, forms, figures, words, language, like con-sciousness, arise only from the need, the necessity, of interaction with the other. As internal speech—in the Bakhtinian sense—such an imaginary is culturally productive, and represents itself through selective and combinatory operations as part of a collective project. This activated representational ideological con-struct is inscribed as an icon with actualized significations.

To illustrate this Bakhtinian point of the dynamics of the psyche and the social and semantic content of the unconscious, we can posit the social horizon of the imaginary, and the political and social revolutionary possibilities of inner speech to become a performative force and delegitimize the authority of domination and its official ideology. This would correspond to a theory of imagination and its social function. Since social structures cannot be viewed as static systems of symbolic exchange (in Bourdieu's [1979] critique of Lévi-Strauss), they can be invested with opposition and a commitment to deconstructive techniques. To paraphrase Voloshinov/Bakhtin, such a performative realizes in the present a future effect. This suggests that in specific conjunctures the identity and identification set up in dominant ideology can be transformed and displaced, and a new imaginary signification against concrete forms of subordination may be produced embodied in emancipatory narratives.

Following the Bakhtinian lead in suggesting the question of historical agency as the open, nonfinalized construction of self and collectivity, and grounding it in the situational time of the 1880s and 1890s, and more specifically in 1898, we can then contextualize an artistic expression identified with a collective foundation. The Latin American modernist work achieves its critical task of renewal through a symbolic victory. The imaginary and the symbolic become the strategic locus of resistance. The modernist discourse is constituted to construct a center, one could say, and create a relational identity of collectivity against the new forms of subordination represented by the invasion. Cultural texts project a social imaginary of democratization and transformation of political power as a strategy to construct a new order.

From this point of view, then, the symbolizing function of language is regulated for a transformation of the subject of communication by means of the shared patterns of knowledge and belief of the cultural speech community. As theories of hermeneutics have shown, all interpretation necessarily involves a dialogue between reader and text; thus, the social imaginary monitors a symbolic resistance positioning cultural discourse toward anti-colonial struggle. The social function inscribed in the sign itself could help us trace the distinctive feature of, for example, Darío's series of poems *The Swans,* written in 1898, as signs which refract dialogically a specific axiological horizon for the collective.

This leads us to another objective—to localize what is involved in cultural texts which give primacy to contradiction and struggle, and undertake to specify which are the general mechanisms for discursive thought, which can be said to sustain antagonism. Voloshinov/Bakhtin supply the basis for the revolutionary potential of the unconscious or "inner speech," notwithstanding the breach between the official and the unofficial conscious. Inner speech is actualized into outer expression which is "directly included into an unverbalized behavioral context and in that context is amplified by actions, behavior, or verbal responses of other participants in the utterance" (*MPL* 39). In short, the inner world implements the meaning of the sign; exchange of semiotic activity is the process of inner and outer verbal life. To pursue these relations, Bakhtin recognizes the question of how the individual relates to the social, and questions the unconscious.

Voloshinov's/Bakhtin's critique of Freud, *Freudianism: A Marxist Critique* (1927 [in 1976]), seems to be the earliest history of a political unconscious—

which is called "political underground"—in which the text of history is recognized as having a potential for producing a revolutionary change. We do not need to refer in detail to the main dimensions of this questioning, as its critical moments—Adorno, Horkheimer, and Marcuse—are well known. They reintroduced the subterranean dimension of the unconscious, and delved into the drives and demands for happiness toward a Marxian social theory (on this last point see Whitebrook 1985). Let us now bring together several links in our argument. Intellectual and moral leadership constituting what Gramsci called a "collective will," which through ideology becomes organic and widely diffused, becomes the basis for "common sense." This sedimentation and its core conceptions form a tradition, sustain a logic of thought, and "connote and condense each other," as E. Laclau puts it.[8]

What Gramsci argues as arenas of ideology has been a permanent questioning, and has served as background to many socialist and Marxist debates since the nineteenth century. In short, it is the question of how to mobilize collectivities and how to fashion a subjectivity for the emergence of a common project, and how these social identities are addressed through fantasies and imaginary social communities. This "organic"—ideas becoming cultural movements, faiths, collective wills—can be transformed through fantasies in a positionality in relation to language. As a dynamic space, the unconscious has the potential to create counterimages. Its symbolic power lies in the possibility to form and re-form mental structures and project collective emancipatory objectives. The political role of the (organic) intellectual has been to reconstruct subjectivity toward mobilizing popular forces to a collective will. In Voloshinov's words: "Only at first a motive of this sort will develop within a small social milieu and will depart into the underground—not the psychological underground of repressed complexes, but a salutary political underground. That is exactly how a *revolutionary ideology* in all spheres of culture comes about" (*Freudianism: A Marxist Critique* 90).

This quotation traces the distinction between a socialized unconscious and its political projection, in contrast to the storage of repressed content basic to a contemporary Marxist theorization of the subject. This has been reclaimed lately by Jameson, who has also underscored Kenneth Burke's conception of the symbolic as act or praxis (1978), which gives unity to subject and object, thing and language, context and projected action even within its ambiguities. However, since "political unconscious" is now a common concept among North American Marxist scholars, I re-accentuate the fundamental differences with the political identifications sedimented in the unconscious by the dialogical social imaginary I propose, by extrapolating from Bakhtin.

There are basic and crucial differences between the Bakhtin circle's concept of "political underground" and Jameson's *The Political Unconscious,* which I cannot fully develop now. However, two points should be emphasized here. The latter historicizes the Lacanian topology through Althusser's definition of ideology to project a politicized unconscious and history as a socially symbolic act. To Jameson ideology equals the Imaginary, while the Symbolic equals the synchronic network of society, and the Real, the diachronic evolution of history. This model seems to be in dialogue with that of the Frankfurt School (particularly Marcuse), although Jameson does not refer to it; however, in his model, human agency (the responsive coparticipant of the utterance) is missing, or is modeled as inherent in the text. To transform history is to Jameson to bring "to the surface of the text the repressed and buried reality of this fundamental history" (19–20). For Jameson the traces of history are embedded in the text as its unconscious, in much the same way that Pierre Macheray (1966) speaks about the text's unconscious, in the line of Lacan.

In this way Jameson aligns himself with the legacy of both structuralism and formalism, since one cannot take for granted that the human agency is the social. This last point is decisive, since what remains unclear in Jameson's "political unconscious" is what he understands by collective, which seems closer to a universal identification with a system of ideas and with the false consciousness of social agents. In that case, there would be no subject positions traversing discourse, no struggle of discourses depending on the nature of the ideological interests at stake. Briefly, in a basically Lukácsian stand, history is the expressive unity of consciousness and practice, and the subject is constructed through the ideological mechanisms of a text.

We can thus see the central points which demarcate the dialogical social imaginary I propose formulated within the logical extension of Bakhtin's and Gramsci's analyses. My position is that the "political underground"—understood as the sediment of fantasies and imaginary identities—is collective, since the cultural being of the subject is instantiated only in the situational interaction between self and other. The ideological position of the Bakhtinian "third" closes the enunciatory gap through the act of "comprehension" and of "responsiveness," a dialogical truth which builds counterpositions in its own progress. The "third" points to the responsive character of understanding. What elsewhere I have called the enthymemic, or "unuttered formulations of the third," are the categories of knowledge which do not evolve into a final individual truth (Zavala 1989a, 1990b, 1990c). The other maintains its otherness in the collective subject.

Truth, then, or responsiveness, is not individual, "it is born *between people* collectively searching for truth, in the process of their dialogic interaction" (*PDP* 110). A "political underground," based on these premises, is not an *agreement;* therefore it is neither inherent to texts nor universal. The dialogical is a unity in difference, an openness in the ground of ideology.

Given this understanding, the originality of Voloshinov/Bakhtin's "unconscious" is making it coextensive with boundaries and domains of discourses.[9] At this point it is clear now how we may define the terrain of a dialogical social imaginary and its radicalization in a conjuncture where there is a generalized struggle for a redefinition of social identities.

Sustaining Fictions

It should be apparent that my remarks have been addressed to the modernist creation of sustaining fictions as examples of narratives which participate in the constitution of the self. In questioning emancipatory narratives and the subject's resistance to colonialism and domination, I draw broadly upon the theoretical notions of the linguistic constitution of the subject within and outside social practices, and upon the unconscious and the social domain of communication. Therefore, within the contemporary context of literary and cultural theory, I work with the usefulness and applicability of the Bakhtinian idea of the dynamics of the psyche and the social content of the unconscious. From this perspective the social potential of the imaginary becomes prominent, as opposed to a limited theory of desire.

My purpose now is to proceed in another direction—through the power of metalepsis, to go one step further and challenge poststructuralist and post-Marxist arguments through a critique of their essentialist and globalizing practice. As a "resisting reader," I will invert poststructuralist (and postmodern) critical practices so as to oppose the lure of totalization, and to be able to recognize the operations of subjectivity, collectivity, and ideology as oppositional movements. Against the current radically conservative character of much contemporary thought, we can then infer other alternatives within a reflection on power and power structures; specifically, we will consider the link between the ideological horizon and the social emancipatory projection of the imaginary.

We must now return to Baudrillard, who categorically affirms that the imaginary is an absent discourse. One lacks, he affirms, the "revolutionary imaginary" (37). Even though he is analyzing the symptoms of the postindustrial age, he tacitly dismisses any cultural-political project both in the past and at the present time, and explicitly negates any temporal or logical anteriority. In his words, no group has *ever* imagined itself as social, "that is, solidary with its own values and coherent with its collective project; in sum, there has *never* been even the possibility or embryo of a responsible collective subject, and not even the slightest possibility of such an objective" (79, my translation and emphasis).

Although he is giving here a concrete explanation of the nature of multinational capitalism, of its mode of production and its cultural dominants, our anatropic inversion will help underline what is powerful in contemporary emancipatory narratives through the overt example of modernist legitimation of a sustaining anti-colonial, anti-imperialistic narrative. It is necessary to broaden the domain of such grim arguments if we are concerned with the question of the internal organization of experience through language and the link between social practices and historical processes.

The dialogical linguistic and literary model of this liberating narrative was lyrically structured in a dialectics between inner (subjective, personal) and outer (nature, objective reality) spaces—in Martí's terms—which relativizes these fixed references and corresponds to a cultural practice where subjectivity is the source of a collective emancipatory narrative. In polemics with imperialism, which was at its peak in 1898, Latin American modernist cultural production legitimates its own right of self-representation as a collective subject in solidarity with its own real and potential fictions. In marked contrast to the epistemological configuration of the colonial past, modernists inscribe their own ideologeme in a chronotope which constitutes a collective social project.

This modern episteme was conceptualized and defined by the three dimensions of political (and philosophical) reflection, linguistic and cultural productivity, and the economic and social sciences. The cultural field is the extension of a new mode of socialization based on the formation of new national identities. These arguments on the importance of self-representation and self-consciousness suggest the possibility of creating collective attitudes toward the past and the present. As the subject re-appropriates his/her own representation, the possibility is left open for the creation of an emancipatory narrative, and its legitimation is implicit in the structuring of the imaginary (fiction) and the ideological horizon of any concrete social auditory.

This epistemological practice is transmitted from the interior of language (inner speech), in the positioning of the semiotic subject toward the receptor/ interlocutor collective, which reorganizes and reconstitutes the narrative (or the fiction) according to its own inner speech in favor of or against its legitimation. The dividing line is not between the imaginary and the real, but between one collectivity and another within the historical ideological horizons. As a social conceptualization, it does not remain the same. The dialogical social imaginary I propose as emerging with modernists, changes not only its position but also its character.

Fashioned by active subjects, it is continually remade, and hence is capable of being undone or redone, since it is organized through the responsiveness of the future. What marks its still unfolding presence now is a specification of the even more fundamental distinction of difference of the subject positions as sites of enforced silence, constructed by the realities of global capitalism, postindustrial societies, and imperialism. This imaginary is embodied in the conflict between global patterns of history and the local demands or localized versions of a history of much of Latin American literature, from Gabriela Mistral, Octavio Paz, and Pablo Neruda, to Julia de Burgos, Gabriel García Márquez, and Severo Sarduy, to Brazilian Clarice Lispector.

From different subject positions and evaluative points of view, modernists produced in the "organic crisis" of 1898 a *mise en scène* and an imaginary cognitive projection of their concrete social existence within the collective and its historical text. By a process of identification and its opposite of estrangement in the dialogical social imaginary, the reader identifies with a *symbolic victory*. A recognition of Martí's and Darío's politics of meaning within the modernist themes—which I will stress—makes it impossible to deny this concrete social situation of the utterance. The imaginary signification rests on identification, in an emotive/intellectual reception of the signs which in turn induces the reader/

hearer to question these signs in a critical way. Simultaneously, however, the dynamic negative "estranged" references against the invader represent in the social imaginary the reciprocal mirror of the object and its antithesis through anti-values and negations. The double-oriented tropes are equivalent to the object/thesis and antithesis which confront each other in a critical way with the power of a revolutionary ideology.

The practices of Martí and Darío are in this context an exemplary illustration of modernism's anti-colonial narrative (a social project which still remains collectively powerful), and also of the imaginary understood as a cognitive faculty generating the symbolic as a power capable of transforming collective mental structures or mental images. The cognitive value of imagining resides in generating these operations, and through a process of identification it incorporates the social auditory into a collective mobilization.[10]

In moving from the subjective to the collective, the writer functions as an "organic intellectual," in the subtle distinction proposed by Gramsci (1966). One could redirect Gramsci's reflections to analyze the verbal constructs of Spanish American modernists at the turn of the century. This emancipatory narrative is organized through diverse combinations in order to present a conjunctural unitary front based on geographical, ethnic, and social *diversity*, in a truly heteroglossic construct. Within this multiple social formation, the past is questioned through both negations and affirmations, which in turn raise new questions about representation and reality. Sign and referent dissociate and distance themselves from the past, its norms and institutions, against the belief of a reliable, fixed, unproblematic reality. The subject position is both interrogative and affirmative of the project.

As a historical poetics of negation constituted through the allegorical, modernism—as I suggest here—was shaped as a chronotope in relation to both an intratextual world and an extratextual reality. All the contested meanings that can be assumed by the category of modernism were embodied since the wars of independence, and continued to organize later texts in later re-accentuations at subsequent times. We will now give attention to its production, undertaken in the light of a historical poetics, to argue that the time/space relation of its emergence was to coordinate and organize a multiplicity of expectations and beliefs of a postcolonial experience, which also took shape at the level of language activity.

From the time of the romantics (Fichte, for example), language was understood as having a spirit which formed the national character of its users. Although the idea is considered naive today, language acquired for the modernists great importance as the process of inner and outer verbal life to pursue a culture-specific national identity. This was precisely what the event of 1898 engendered, and what triggered the "culturalism" of many modernists. It is best represented in Darío's swan remythologization, and the troublesome question on the future raised by the poet to his audience: "And we, so many millions of people, shall speak English?" (¿Y tantos millones de hombres hablaremos inglés?). The chronotope of modernism is thus period-specific and peculiar to specific culture systems, and determined the speech genre to make the questions meaningful. As a chronotopical formation, modernism made a radical commitment to the historical particularity of the experience of a common language and culture from the unique place of a postcolonial perception. Language and culture, as developed during the wars of independence, provided a basis for giving the appearance of stability to a world which was in flux.

II

TO BE MODERN AT THE TURN OF THE CENTURY

> The creoles prefer to be called Americans.
>
> —Alexander von Humboldt

> But no matter how great is this land, or how anointed the America of Lincoln may be for the free men of America—for us, in our very heart of hearts where nobody dares to challenge or take issue with our secret feelings, the America of Juárez is greater because it has been more unhappy, and because it is ours.
>
> —José Martí, *Mother America* (1889)

The Postcolonial and the Problem of Culture

Modernity was an issue of particular urgency in regard to culture and politics, and it emerged in a variety of designations which still leave the term ill-defined and somewhat misleading. The modern cannot simply be equated with any specific method or country, though one must agree that it was inseparable from progress, from technology, and (at the end of the eighteenth century) from industrialization. This process was determined by what I have called in earlier work an *industrial imaginary*, which tends to articulate the cultural texts, and is discernible in a more advanced locus of capitalist expansion (in Spain, most definitely in the Catalan area). The industrial imaginary conveys an optimism for the mode of production which leaves its mark in symbolization, thus giving rise to themes, ideologies, and social meanings which introduce a modern semiotic practice by calling into question restrictions on teleological universals: the texts question not only tradition, heritages, religion, and the promise of civilization but also what was addressed as an opposition between barbarism and nature.

What I will address as modernism as a historical poetics now is an attribution of a reliable, or even exemplary, cognitive and ethical emancipatory function assigned to literature. What it establishes is a new organic and relational whole, articulated through forms of collective identities and narratives of subjectivity to meet history and to re-create culture. It gave strong support for regional authority against imperialist globalizations in an interplay of voices, of positioned utterances to remap landscapes. As a chronotope it emerged with the nineteenth-century romantics, and in its turn-of-the-century expression, modernism not only is linked to modernity, as may have been argued from varying positions by other interpreters, but becomes an organic whole, embodied in cultural and literary apparatuses, which weld together the historical bloc around core articulatory principles. Modernists reposition culture, literature, social relations, identities, inner speech as civic discourses for socializing future communities through a euphoric optimist key.

This said, we must observe that the chronotopes of modernity and modern in the early part of the nineteenth century (most notably after the wars of independence in South America in 1834 and the First Carlist War of 1834–37) were linked to a utopian process allegorized in progressive romanticism, and a tradition of civic literature which emphasized social need.[1] As a complex discursive formation, the term *modern* was assigned in a contesting way to both a liberal and a socialistic conception of the state. In metropolitan Spain, both Mariano José de Larra and José de Espronceda convincingly identified literary representation with an ethical, liberatory (also read liberal) writing engaged in problems resulting from the search for an equitable distribution of capital. This articulated the kind of modern narrative that came into being at this moment, and is also the main concern of what I elsewhere have addressed as the "first socialists" or "socialist romantics," after the death of Ferdinand VII (1834).

To think about the chronotope of modernism is necessarily to speak in terms of historical periods and historical periodization. It is important, however, to place the emergence of these new collective identities and historical subjects in the situation which made that emergence possible, to relate the new social and political categories—modern, nation, the social, "American"—to the new collective voice which is first heard on the world stage. Here, in any case, the chronotope in question lends itself to the current transitory stage of a cultural space and a situational social practice of the new generation impelling an alternative culture through open-ended discourses. The first dialogical models challenged the past with the promise of a democratic government which would ensure civil liberties and an unprivileged redistribution of cultural capital, as well as the assurance of the basic freedom of creed, so blatantly trampled throughout the long history of the Spanish modern empire since Charles V. This possibility was heralded by the *new,* thus releasing the polyphonic force of dialogism and carnivalesque discourses; dialogism here exteriorizes political and ideological conflicts. It is practical discourse in polemic against theology, against law, against authoritarian states.

Two further key events need to be noted. These Hispanic romantic moderns and their peers associated modernity with democracy, republicanism, and an acceleration of social processes through either an alternative (democratic and liberal) discourse or a revolutionary anti-monarchical and socialist change. What was palpable was that revolution was not just a word but seemed real and achievable. It became possible for radical intellectuals to conceive of revolutionary work in combination with the artisan classes, and inside workers' organizations. This "new age" (a term also used conceptually by Hegel and Marx) was inscribed around the 1830s and took oppositional significance emphatically as a new modern/modernized state. It expressed—in the discourse of the first democrats and socialists—the conviction that the future had begun; and being open to novelty meant having a new reflective awareness of history as a whole, a new beginning for social reform and distribution of capital, which took many forms. The common program also announced civic engagement, which was evidenced during the 1830s and the commune of 1848. Democratic discourse articulated the different forms of resistance and subordination; it became what Laclau and Mouffe call a "nodal point."

This new beginning was felt as a totalizing dynamic force through persuasive key concepts provided by the Fourierists, Cabetians, and Owenites which were either legitimized or delegitimized, claimed or disclaimed in the various field forces at work. For the moderns (also called *young* or *jóvenes*) the new age was meant to accomplish a radical break with the past, without the nostalgic aura of lost traditions and heritage. The first democratic and republican parties in Spain attempted to institute a newly structured social interaction; they also made an effort to instill uncoerced and uncoercive activity through association, and to impart the organization of industrial capitalist society with a utopian expectation about a radically egalitarian industrial or agrarian society. They share these claims with their contemporaries.

Democratic and egalitarian ideas traverse all forms of social discourse. These romantics believed literature could give practical efficacy to emancipation as an element of public life, and art was thought to have the power of a reconciliation open to the future. Larra and Espronceda and the "first socialists" (Fernando Garrido, Sixto Cámara) brought together and developed many of these themes; Larra's journalism was particularly concerned with the present. If Hegel (as Habermas 1990 reminds us) understood early that romantic art was congenial to the spirit of the age through its subjectivism—the true spirit of modernity—this same spirit was recognized in the 1830s by both the Peninsular and the Latin American romantics, whose claim to first republicanism and democracy was a model to conceptualize the modern world. The romantic democrats established an alternative to aristocratic values, and messianism was, generally speaking, active in romantic cultures. The "modern" romantic emerged as a way of making creative space.

This struggle to liberate the world from univocal objectivity through questioning and testing began in the 1820s with the first wave of republican romantics in the Peninsula, and became externalized with the return of the liberal romantics in 1834, a date which coincided with the reception of the different socialist schools in the urban centers of Madrid, Catalonia, and Cadix but also in Latin America (Buenos Aires and Mexico, among the best known). What we witness here are the different forms of modernizing liberalism, and its contested space, and how the variants of liberalism enter and shape the practical consciousness of society, and the internal coherence of its core conceptions.[2] This coherence implies a relational conjoining of different elements.

The situated utterance of the moderns tended to promote a language which serves to communicate national identity, democracy, egalitarianism, and freedom. Modern writing reveals several striking examples of the new and the old, of law and order reanimating and re-accentuating literary thought, orienting it toward new perspectives. An important issue was the fusion of aesthetics and politics to reconcile society and revolutionize the conditions of freedom and understanding, and to dissolve the monologism of the state and of rhetoric. It could be said that the contending discourses of the romantics inaugurated the discourse of modernity: being "modern" specifically posited an optimism about industrialization and technology, monitoring an industrial-technological imaginary, conveying democratic ideals in its metalanguage. The signifying practices inscribe the egalitarian doctrine of what Fourier called "le nouveau monde industriel," which the Catalan romantic writer Andrés Fontcuberta broadly interpreted to include access to culture within the egalitarian and socializing field of the democratic myth: "The great advance of science; the portentous wonders of industry and the community of ideas disseminated by a literature which aspires to be universal" (*El Vapor*, 3 Apr. 1837).

Another Catalan romantic, Antonio Ribot y Fontseré, speaks in the egalitarian and universalistic spirit of bourgeois humanism about society as a totality, each part depending on the other, working together in a kind of harmony, which he compared to the delicate mechanism of a clock (1846). The metonymical imaginary of a harmonious society is the basis for his assurance of what he addresses as a "cosmopolitan literature," a universal literature which will secure the basis for peace: "cosmopolitan literature unites all nations, and perhaps the wars of conquest are ready to shoot their last bullet" (*Poesías escogidas* 1846:56–59).

Republican, democratic, and socialist journals and periodicals embraced these ideals giving potential relevance to aesthetic production; within this horizon of expectations, literature provided a concrete egalitarian utopia. The literary field summarized the symbolic organization of the contesting utopias through newspapers, serials, "engaged" poetry and theater, and translations (particularly Eugène Sue) which communicated the unmasking of oppression. Prophecy and messianism became social agitation; the imaginary was re-accentuated as an actual and potential element of political consciousness. Poems about the poor, or about social injustice, the laborer, the squalor of cities; antislavery narratives; novels against the power of the church or against the Inquisition, or about realist working-class descriptions abounded in this wave of what I have called previously "first realists." The urban space became the protagonist, not only in Balzac and Dickens but also in the "mysteries" surrounding great capitals, such as the *Mysteries of Paris* (1845) by Sue, or in Hugo's situational *Hunchback of Notre Dame*. The voices of suffering, the pain of the oppressed, the cry in the streets were actively projected to announce the modern apocalypse, while civil (state) censorship became axiomatic in the social space (Zavala 1972, 1989b).

The themes may vary, but by elevating contemporary reality and cultural and political fantasies to the ranks of poetry, fiction, and philosophy, the discourses of modernity are introduced as variants of emancipatory aesthetics, what Bakhtin would later call "art and responsibility." Literature becomes a carrier of various discourses that converge to produce specific modes of liberal (modern) behavior. In fact, what is exchanged in society are polyvalent expressions of how the public and the private come together, including, of course, sexual ideologies and gender constructs. A no less powerful industrial and technological imaginary emerged in postcolonial Latin America with the generation of socialist romantics and the positivists. Each Latin American country had its own specific version: *gauchesco* poetry, anti-slavery narratives, or novels projecting anti-colonialism through positive representations of mulattos, Indians, or creole society (the signifiers working out new national constructs throughout the region, from the gaucho, to the *jíbaro* in Puerto Rico, to the *mulato* in Cuba).

The anti-slavery idioms are invoked in the Caribbean from different perspectives, from the national novel *Cecilia Valdés* (1839) by Cirilo Villaverde, to one of the major anti-slavery narratives, *Sab* (1841), produced by Cuban-born Gertrudis Gómez de Avellaneda, herself an abolitionist (see S. Kirkpatrick 1989); the anti-slavery sociogram was, however, cultural practice fostering social equality and solidarity, as well as collective identity and race equality, particularly in Cuba. In Argentina, from the Generation of 1837, a powerful document called *Socialist Dogma* (Dogma socialista) emerged, written by Esteban Echeverría and Juan Bautista Alberdi, which typified republican policies and social concerns (Miliani 1963). On different grounds, Domingo Faustino Sarmiento (president of Argentina and author of *Facundo: Civilization and Barbarism* [1845]) established a program for universal progress, and although he favored American and European capitalism, he warned of the consequences of a global mercantilism; machinery could become the "enemy of ignorant and backward countries," as had been evident in the depressions which followed an apparent Mexican and Chilean prosperity (qtd. in Halperín Donghi 1985:377).

Although this liberal "Catch 22" situation of bringing foreign capitalism to the new Latin American economies had disastrous effects, it should be remembered that in the 1850s even Marx was inclined to emphasize the progressive role of Western capitalism against stagnation (in his case Oriental stagnation).[3] Progress through foreign capitalism and industrialization to disrupt traditional societies was emphasized by Mexican intellectuals as well. The leading figures, unified under the name of positivists, were also advocating a democratic industrial imaginary; the relevance of the positivist epistemology created the myth of science to assert authority. Roughly, this empiricism corresponds to naturalism and the projecting of factual beliefs for scrutiny—economic, social, intellectual, and moral. This literature is concerned with the present and the acquisition of values.

What is more important in the present context is that as the new nations emerged, these first postcolonial territories negotiated national liberation, independence, and modernity in different and uneven ways. In general, however, this generation also sketched an aesthetic program which attributed to art a social-revolutionary role. Art was heralded as a unifying power, a medium for education toward true political freedom, an expressive form to secure identity; even an ambiguous conception of culture surfaced as a separate realm in the idealist philosophical tradition.

Of equal importance was a truly heterological and heteroglossic understanding of language grounded in the principle of subjectivity, which was the core of the well-known polemic between the Argentinian Sarmiento and the Venezuelan Andrés Bello. Bello was one of Latin America's leading intellectuals in his plural role as philologist, legislator, and poet. He represents what I will call a "resisting modern," for he favored classicism (and *castizo* language), as well as a sort of unifying "sameness" with Spain as a model for the modern age. However, Bello was also the author of a poem considered to be the founding discourse of Latin America's reality—*Silvas to Agriculture in the Torrid Zone* (Silvas a la agricultura en la zona tórrida)—combining Virgilian meter as an expressive form to convey national identity through a parallel between nature and the collective.

Whereas the competency of the new and the old—like the old *Querelle of Anciens and Modernes*—was the point of reference for a critical self-reflection on the part of the modern Latin American master narrative, some, such as Bello, followed the conviction that the substance of religion, language, and classicism could be mobilized for the creation of the new states. The appeal to language as vehicle of identity received classic formulations in Fichte's well-known *Addresses to the German Nation*, where he bases national identity on both language and soil. Bello, in turn, combined an Americanist interpretation of modern society with a functionalist legitimation of tradition. Bello, who could be defined as an organic conservative, idealized custom and tradition, and saw in them the repositories of true social authority. What we witness in cultural texts are the competing variants of liberalism, from the conservative to radical individualism. Both projects were simultaneous, and both conceptualizations promoted the process of modernity, since liberalism generated different positions and combinations, including arguing for the social functionality of culture itself.

The essential point here, however, is that this characteristic break of the romantic impulse in the nineteenth century coincided with the beginning of a global industrial revolution. Modernity's self-consciousness of time and space developed as a self-legitimating discourse which took its orientation from the models supplied by high romanticism (in the sense given to this term by M. H. Abrams), on the one hand, and the romantic "aesthetic utopia" (in Habermas's term) of the socialist-republicans, on the other, which attributed to art a social-revolutionary role. These were the first moments of the modern cultural production itself.

The preceding section aimed at making the dynamic terrain of modernism visible. By the end of the nineteenth century it penetrated culture itself through a re-accentuation of three discourses: (1) emancipatory romanticism, (2) poetics of negation, and (3) allegorical writing. It did not become, however (as we shall specify later), the symbolist organicist mystification of romanticism (as defined by Miller, de Man, and Hartman), nor did it fall into the argument that the whole historical enterprise was based on the power of poetry, the visionary pathos, to raise above the commonplace antinomies of subject and object, mind and nature, language and the world of sensory experience, common not only to the English romantics (according to Abrams) but also to the French visionaries, as specified by Paul Bénichou (1973, 1977, 1989). The high romantics argued that poetry can achieve states of mind that transcend everyday perceptual experience. This argument also addresses the determination of a fundamental aspect of human nature (Barzun 1961; A. Berman 1988), the retreat from political action and social thought into the potential of the mind and creativity. It was, and I borrow McGann's (1989) title, a literature in search of knowledge, a writing which illustrates how truth and knowledge are sought in the practice of poetic expression.

For all the distinctions I have just recalled, what really distinguished the emancipatory romanticism I am describing was the established core conceptions which connoted and condensed each other within the discursive chain of meaning. The associative meaning was established as a relationship between art, democracy, and revolution. These moderns relativized the notion of values and a univocal truth by inscribing negation. When I suggest a poetics of negation (which we will examine in greater detail), I do not mean the negativity that, through Kristeva (1980, 1984), is believed to embody the avant-gardist ethical ambiguity and a reductive heterogeneous subject position, but a dialogical polemical interaction (both simultaneous and contiguous) of self-affirmation through heteroglossia, and a negation of imposed representations. This poetics of negation projects the individual's creative construction of self, collectivity, and reality in dialogical relation to others.

The reference point of modernity I address is a self-consciousness which encompasses an understanding of time and space as intersections (the Bakhtinian chronotope). These moderns project a reconceptualization of space itself in the creative time of the new social identities. They remap their space through new cartographies of open boundaries. As cartographers, they revisualize the exclusions and hierarchical arrangements of the social organization created by imperialism and colonialism. This cognitive mapping is a required instrument for heteroglossia and for the situational responsive interaction. In this way, these projections differ from European modernity's consciousness—as it is believed to emerge in Baudelaire, for example—which was based on the kinship of *mode* or fashion, the transient and fleeting, a belief Baudelaire shared with the Italian

Giacomo Leopardi, in particular in the well-known *Zibaldone* (1834, Miscellany). Contemporaneity, in their ironic perception, was circumstantial, a fashion, and consumed itself in actuality.

Latin American modernists, on the contrary, through the optics of metalepsis (a basic perceptual perspective to both Nietzsche and Foucault), inverted this perception by creating an anatropic visualization and reappropriating the term—*new, romantic*—to emphasize the emancipatory self-consciousness. Modernity was not a *mode* or fashion (as understood by Baudelaire), it was the time/space chronotope of the moment of emergence of a radically authentic emancipatory projection, both political and cultural. Such discourse does not consume itself in actuality or in the momentaneous longing for beauty, since actuality is the intersecting point between a surpassed past and an emergent, future present.

The name modern/modernity served the prophets of industrialism and progress, the gospel of social reform, the utilitarians, the socialists, the protectionists, since it was *not* solely the ideology of unifying the ruling class. It is nearer to what Frank Manuel called "the prophets of Paris" (1962), and others, the writers of unbelief—those who, like Fourier (and somewhat before Saint-Simon), hoped to establish affinities with artists and writers, who could manage to change society through linguistic and symbolic material.[4] This situated social practice was anti-authoritative, anti-hegemonic, and anti-repressive, even feminist—Flora Tristan is only one privileged example, but there were more women socialists after the 1830s (Zavala 1989b). America—which had been the fantasized "city of the sun," the Arcadia, the site of the Fountain of Youth—became the site to be remapped in new cartographies from the perspective of new national identities. However, modern and modernity were multireferential, and there was a struggle over their meanings, since both triggered conflicting associations.

The discourse of modernity in the postcolonial and the still-colonial worlds was an agency to accomplish progress, development, emancipation, or revolution and a potential to vindicate the labor movement through the first workers' associations. In the 1830s this modern discourse, as I have suggested, was often linked to the first socialists—Fourierists, Cabetians, and Proudhonians, among others. The lines of argument of emancipation and egalitarianism were often ambiguously intertwined with inherent aporias; the emphasis on the individual, even voluntaristic, dimension of social transformation or the harmonious coexistence between classes objectified its socialist idealism and failure. These were evidenced in the plurality of 1868 revolutions—the Spanish *Septembrina*, the Cuban *Grito de Yara*, Puerto Rico's *Grito de Lares*—in which republicanism failed, and the Bourbon monarchy was restored to the throne in 1874. In the Caribbean, the failure of a concerted effort with Spanish republicans was inevitable because the last colonies' self-legitimizing claims were not reconciled with the universal historical solidarity which constituted the decentering force of republicanism in the Peninsula. Spanish republicanism also received a major blow (until 1931, when the courts voted a "Republic of

Workers") after the short-lived experience of the First Republic, which lasted only thirteen months, with four presidents.

The Puerto Rican José María de Hostos voiced, at that time, the colonies' predicament of dependence on Spanish republicans for their own emancipation. In 1868, Hostos was naively confident that freedom and independence would come to Cuba and Puerto Rico (the Dominican Republic had finally regained its independence in 1865, only to be reoccupied later by American troops), since he had received promises of autonomy from his comrades-in-struggle in Spain. He saw how the problem of the two Antilles was ignored and postponed; he then broke with Spain in an impassioned speech in the Madrid Atheneum, where he declared himself American above all and a federalist: "Colonist, product of colonial despotism" (in Zavala and Rodríguez 1980). By 1871, with the First Spanish Republic, it was clear to the anti-colonialist that no help would come to the weaker partner; Hostos wrote then that it was a "republic of charlatans," a "child's game."

José Martí, who was in Spain in 1871—after his release from imprisonment in Cuba for liberationist activities—wrote against the Spanish Republic on similar grounds, disclosing its contradictions: "A Republic that did these things would be a Republic of ignominy" (1975:21). It became clear that while the Antilleans legitimized autonomy, Spanish republicanism still maintained its colonial interests. What the Cuban and the Puerto Ricans Eugenio María de Hostos and Ramón E. Betances (1827–1898) experienced with the First Republic was what after Gramsci we now call *subaltern subjectivity*. What is important to stress is that the two Antilles—what still remained of the old empire—became aware of the new expanding north at the same time they were still struggling for independence.[5] This process of growing social complexity will help us identify the discursive conditions for the emergence of the collective alliance. We enter here into the ensemble of discourses which impose themselves as the new matrix of the dialogical social imaginary. With this we shall designate the key moments in the establishment of a new legitimacy which introduced a truly novel concept of cultural identity at the level of the social imaginary. It could be described as a synecdochal reintegrative moment in an attempt to project a unification. This is the context in which the power of this symbolic action can best be appreciated.

At this point, we must move on to consider the context of the 1880s, which inscribes three important cultural texts which determined the emergent cultural imaginary: Martí's book of poems *Ismaelillo* (1882), his journalism, and Darío's prose and poetry. Both writers designated the positive content of the original sensibility toward selfhood and language of what was understood as "modernism," especially with Darío in 1888. The wide field of national reconstruction and a unified cultural system is made evident in this juncture, while the event of 1898 helps to connect discourse to the emotional registers and the concrete experiences against a strong emerging imperial power. The event unfolds dialogism in an intimate connection between the larger historical narrative, the project of selfhood, and the project of language.

The 1880s Turn-of-the-Century Genealogists

However great the diversity, the irregularity, the disparity, and the force of the collective idea of modernism from the 1880s, there was a vigorous opening out toward alternative intellectual and political traditions as a means of access to political and ethical questions. It was finally concretized in 1898, centered mainly around Cuba, which became the symbolic site of struggle. I shall associate these cultural texts both with decolonization and resistance and with the existing alternatives offered to the modernist impulse. Given this emphasis, modernism was part of the struggle over identity, over alternative definitions to dismantle the language of the empire, and comprised an internal reference system, a set of core conceptions (e.g., political, economic, moral) connoting and condensing each other to create national states and cultures. The event produced a situational ideology, which strengthened its distinctive core concepts by the associative meanings conferred on them by the cultural practice of concrete social agents. As an organic and relational whole, this social imaginary welded together a historical bloc around a number of basic articulatory principles.

The complex collective will of the modernist political subject position presupposed the attainment of a cultural-social unity through which the multiplicity of dispersed wills interlocked on a single aim. It was indeed taking the power to "narrate" in a collectively intended social act (using in reverse the problem discussed by Said [1984]). Modernism could conjoin modernity and revolution through a coherent discourse for an experience of decolonized, independent modernization and progress that would create the material conditions for the satisfaction of basic human needs. It was an intersection of different historical temporalities brought about as a collective anti-colonial interpellation constructed in alliances between different sectors and social forces clustered around 1898, with North American imperialism as the common adversary. Gramsci's concept of hegemony I have been using is pertinent here. It indicates the directness of the address and its "popular consent."[6]

The openness of the social and political horizon after the wars of independence was constitutive of a movement of collective importance which was operative across more than one culture (nationality) and art form with common features in a struggle for identity. Martí's term *Nuestra América* (Our America) was a concrete ideological interpellation connoting a decolonized and self-determined "birth of a nation." As such it cross-cut class in an effort to combine heterogeneous identities and selves into an organic unity. Martí's emphasis on joint identity suggests that the openness of such a venture was greater and more challenging than the differences which could divide the various postcolonial and colonial nations. He thus enlarged the Bolivarian "Latin American fatherland" (*patria*), which had been projected against the fragmentation and division brought about by the colonial empire. The Puerto Rican Ramón Emeterio Betances had been using an equivalent strategy since 1869 while working toward the utopia of a Confederation of the Antilles. Both con-

ceptions—Bolivar's and Martí's—pointed to Latin America as a socially produced category grounded on a historical and linguistic code of a common
symbolic geography.

As a discursive entity, "Our America" designates the production of the
subject on the basis of the chain of its discourses, in the openness of the social,
and therefore by the unfixed or unfinalized nature of the national and identity
construct. This dialogism came from diverse "situational utterances" which had
been voiced at least since the last quarter of the century. The conditions for
creating meaning, if we follow Bakhtin's epistemology, "extend into the deepest
past and the most distant future. Even meanings born in dialogues of the
remotest past will never be finally grasped once and for all, for they will always
be renewed in later dialogue" (*Speech Genres*, 146). Modernism was constructed as a polyphonic dialogue, and we can sense the struggle of opinions
and ideologies on ultimate questions. Its opposite were those who dealt with
issues that had been resolved within the epoch. The moderns were raising
questions of power, resistance, and emancipation, which also included a symbolic dimension, as they embraced an imaginative vision of the society of the
future.[7]

As an aesthetic discourse the dialogics of modernism became a critique of the
aporias of high modernization and industrialization, inasmuch as both concealed the instrumental mastery of imperialism. On the one hand, the first Latin
American modernists unmasked the subordinating mastery of European (Spanish) modernity after the "discovery." On the other, they monitored the rebellion
against a subjugated subjectivity through a cultural (political) project focusing
on the reappropriation of those discourses which coupled modernity with
European values; the relations were intertextual rather than mimetic modes of
reference. By way of rhetoric and innovative language, the modernists optimized
the cultural process to redirect the fundamental ideas in terms of which we
constitute ourselves as subjects and objects of knowledge. The general consensus was that behind the facade of universality (and humanist culture), the
oppressive and violent operation of more modern techniques and domination of
the self were concealed. Thus the heterological was inscribed as a suspicion of
systems of totalization to resist any model of authority, including that of
language.

The proposal I will explore is that as a cultural discourse, modernism was a
program to explore a heteroglossic constitution of self, and to master speech
genres in a responsive interaction with social change: both Martí's and Darío's
projects, which will be fully discussed, were provoked by this necessity. Their
creative heteroglossia is an indication of the ways in which experience organizes
expression. To universals, modernists opposed the plurality of the lifeworlds
and forms of life, the heterogeneity of master narratives and cultures, the
conditional character of truths.[8] Modernist chronicles and poetry unmasking
"yanquism" and its technocratic myth in the Antilles and Central America
before 1898, as well as the questions of cultural tradition and heritage, were
reconstructed from the point of view of national identities, which rejected both

the cultural hegemony of Spain and the new hegemony embodied in the North American invasion.

Ultimately, of course, this new antagonism in the Caribbean represented a strong threat to the lived unity of the projected society. Far more significant is that both the sense of culture (heritage, language) and sovereignty were implicitly endangered. A really concrete solution in this determinant historical conjuncture was the ideological choice to structure a whole range of strategies to restore a unity. Such an eventuality became synecdochal, as a reintegrative moment and the indication of an attempt to set forth a new unification. This strategic field is an appropriate point to analyze the multiplicity of forms of resistance which were then conceived in terms of cultural and "spiritual" relationships between the postcolonial collective agents and the previous empire. What had been "othered" during the wars of independence became in the juncture of 1898 an articulatory point under the new hegemonic pressure, and common bonds with the Hispanic world were re-accentuated (a pan-Hispanism).

The consequence of this argument is that in its application to the texts, Latin American modernism turned out to designate two things at once. On the one hand, it named the inner logic of the symbolic process itself, as well as the immediate aims and objectives. Writing became identified with a critique of the mastery of reason and rationalization—"instrumental reason"—which, although it can be traced back to thinkers such as Nietzsche and Schopenhauer, who unmasked the rhetorical dimension of language, at this juncture became a powerful incentive and a shrewd diagnosis of the cultural and ideological conflicts of capitalist expansion. In the concreteness of the North American intervention, the constitution of such a discourse became a fully theorized discourse of decolonization and anti-imperialism; these were the focal points of Betances, who since 1869 had been warning his fellow Antilleans of the expansionist North (see Zavala and Rodríguez 1980).

In reassessing these forms of modernism, it seems impossible to overlook this dimension, as well as that of an ethico-political discourse challenging through ironic treatments monolithic notions of values and progress. Hostos, Betances, Martí, Casal, Silva, Nájera—among the first modernists—through varying lenses recognized the need for modern democratic societies in actual conditions of change. By 1888 Martí, while "living inside the monster," clearly saw that the "cult of wealth" had devastated the North American democratic myth, and had created "in the freest democracy of the world the most unjust and shameful of oligarchies" (1975:35). In that same year, from Chile, Darío recognized the condition of a modern culture—"our emerging literature"—while advocating a cultural text which would combine the greatness and splendor of ideas with a writing practice: "not to write as parrots talk, but to speak as eagles silence" (1888; in Zavala, ed. 1989:31).

Such a description luminously articulates the conceptual horizon in which modernism arose. In the 1880s it was an epochal concept which conformed to the new experience of advancing and accelerating historical events; it corresponded to a new epistemic discourse aimed at creating its own normativity. It formed a unity by virtue of the following:[9]

1. Discourse refers to a common object of analysis.
2. There is a preference for a specific enthymemic mode of statement.
3. There is a deployment of a system of permanent and coherent concepts.
4. There is a recurrent articulation of an identity and a persistence of theoretical themes.

In seeking the basis of the unity and the style, what stands as the common and the conceptualized object, and even the thematic choice in politics, economics, literature, and philosophy, is encompassed in the horizon of modernity and modernization. The dimensions of hermeneutics are a tacit understanding that arises from a context of shared opinions and values, in pulling things together within and for a project. As a discourse not yet institutionalized, it represents the social through dialogism and responsiveness.

The 1880s were, in this respect, a rich and conflictual historical conjuncture, in which the "ideological structures" (in Frossaert's term [1989]), as well as the cultural practices and their symbolic interchanges, were resemanticized as the distinctive features of class antagonism split up into hostile camps as a driving force for social change. Intellectuals became active in political life; if in Europe, especially England, France, Italy, and Spain, this historical juncture was accompanied by a more dynamic industrialization and by technological gains—of which the Eiffel Tower, built for the World Trade Fair (1889), is a conspicuous example—the date also marked the strong development of socialism and anarchism. The conflictual 1880s in Europe were a time of social struggle in the form of propaganda by the deed (Russian terrorism as represented by Nechaev, and Kropotkin's impact in the International from London), as well as the cosmopolitan development of the great European capitals (Baron Haussmann's transformation of Paris). The hegemonies also inscribed the advancement of imperialism and empire states after 1875 (see Hobsbawm 1987). Both in the synchrony of events and in their historical continuity, the democratic myth which had supported the bourgeois states was critically being rejected as a delusion.

The Latin American angle of vision and line of interpretation of the moderns favor the assumption that as knowers, it was necessary for them to insert themselves and their perspectives into the domain of the discourse and become self-reflective. They aspired to live in an age of open responsiveness, of renovated social relations, and to theorize about it with no traditional attachment to genres or traditions. Among the first to give voice to a new, modern way were— besides Martí and Darío—Manuel Gutiérrez Nájera (Mexico, 1859–1895), Salvador Díaz Mirón (Mexico, 1853–1928), Julián del Casal (Cuba, 1863– 1893), and José Asunción Silva (Colombia, 1865–1896), who helped redefine Hispanic literary modernity. What we can discover are common concerns regarding the cosmopolitan as open possibilities for new social relations away from the asphyxiating local (a point which distinguishes Latin American modernists, since much Spanish cultural perspective was local and provincial, which prompted Ortega to say that "Spain was purely a province").

A Latin American Modern Conception of An-otherness

We have been arguing that modernism evolved around the question of identity, at the point where the grand story of subjectivity meets the narrative of history and of culture.[10] It was an attempt to connect the alterities outside the colonial (and local) systems of relation, and the positions they had assigned to subjects' identities. In this sense, we are privileging not the local but a historical situatedness which did not fall in the oppression of exclusionary logic, the fixity of either/or. Modernist dialogics was an attempt at a conceptually grounded situatedness from which demystification could be undertaken in openness, against the entrenched condition of subjection to the metropolis. Only through fragmentation of the totality could the modern condition of difference be legitimated.

A starting construct was a displacement of the desacralized space of nature into collective transformation and emancipatory energies of self. Nature is rematerialized in arguments against the system of selfishness and the expansionist power games of capitalism. In this enclave, nature becomes both the concrete material landscape and a poetic symbol in the production of new imagery.

Rhetorical liberation constitutes a strategy of selves immersed in the facticity of history and nature, trying to demystify habitual perceptions and illusions. The modern subjectivity seeks to master both inner and outer nature, a mastery which is not a repetition of the traditional liberal vision of individual freedom. The dialogical force of Martí's cultural text is not based only in the production of a self-absorbed poetic language of "universal values" aimed at the symbolic domination of tropes and idioms, but in bringing together self-understanding and an imaginative vision of the society of the future. His expressed project is open to future responsiveness, for example, his confidence in lyrical poetry as the convergence of both understandings of nature. An optimism based on social and moral grounds becomes the energy giving support to the novel use of symbolic capital, aimed at structuring a coherent vision linking politics, society, art, philosophy, and science. The American modern celebrated a cultural production that would intensify and generate a virtual new world of a free civil society.

The vivid experience of crisis in the 1880s brought about the opposition between modern art as an act of freedom and of reflection, and the classical (and thus European) imitation of nature. Modern art, in this first phase, was understood as mediated unity with its newly regained emancipated nature to affirm autonomous values. Such is the course outlined by the Mexican Gutiérrez Nájera, who ascribed to the new aesthetics in 1885 more than a local or national character, defining an imagined autonomy conjoining self and symbol: "Of course, I declare I disagree with the name of national literature. . . . In my humble belief, we must use, instead of 'national,' the nomenclature of our 'own' "(*Indice* 1968:31). Literature is not only national, he adds, since it communicates with the whole "modern world." Martí had voiced similar distinctions stressing the semantic relation between "national" and "our own," adding, "To know different literatures is the best way to liberate oneself from the tyranny of some of them" (1882; in Zavala, ed. 1989:19). A few years later, the Mexican Juan de Dios Peza would insist on decolonization and revolutionary nationalism: "We are fighting in order to have our own literature" (*Indice* 1968:31). All these perceptions of language in action belong to a double system of transformation: of identity values and of an anti-local dimension, against the "realistic" (mimesis) provincialism of Spanish literature. They aimed, instead, not at mimesis but at semiosis.

The modern seemed to the newly formed societies an unprecedented modernity, but one which could develop its criteria only in accordance with the principle of subjectivity or self-consciousness in order to conceptualize national identity. This lesson was learned from Hegel as the first philosopher for whom modernity became a problem (as Habermas [1990] reminds us), and from Schiller's and Schlegel's programmatic aesthetic critique, as well as from the complex perspectives opened by the first socialists. The utopian element of style (and speech genres) became the basis on which to disclose the heteroglossic and dialogical cultural being for the creative constitution of self and other.[11]

In scientific, technological, and cultural texts, the potential for emancipation was also an effective means of expression for the Latin American "Generation of 1880" of positivists and naturalists. There emerged a complex set of idioms on the the same grounds of redefining the local, such as gauchesco literature, *criollismo,* and *antillanismo.* They were all worked out as social cartographies of the individual situated in nature, and are a central element for understanding national identity constructs throughout the region; nature became a protagonist by way of sketches, cameos of typical characters. These cartographies also recorded the speech of the various ethnicities and social classes. They succeeded in conveying fads, neologisms, various tones of voice, accents, ways of being and dressing, inscribing, in this way, a well-defined heteroglossia. The modern self-consciousness emerged against an orphic look to the past, against a return to colonial origins, although it would make contact with the past, using a *virtual memory* to optimize the monitoring process. The restitution of the subject's wholeness also took the form of restoration of the past, as well as a reappropriation of history through a rewriting of past emancipatory narratives, and not in the form of archeological excavations, which, according to Leenhardt (1989), were frequent in French turn-of-the-century texts.

As a social construction, the discourse of modernism was empowered by the encounter of the two Americas, pulling the writer toward affirming autonomous values. These were measured against the totalizing economic system of the United States and the expansionist power games of American capitalism, moving more strongly toward the Spanish Caribbean and Central America. These projects of imperial expansionism had been common, and the experiential horizon and social subtext of four invasions of Nicaragua, and one of Mexico in 1846, provoked an increasingly negative stance and cultural resistance. In Mexico, the modernist ethico-political organic ideology gained its force on the alien ground of the post-Maximilian monarchy and the gallicized cultural atmosphere of the elite. What we see is a contrast and a polemics against two opposite uses of an industrial and technological imaginary, and of cultural fantasies of progress, equality, and freedom. Technology not only was a fiction, but as such it created the dichotomy of what C. P. Snow called the "two cultures."[12] It also gave impetus to an ideal of democratic technology with its opposite of authoritarian technics, in the lucid division established by Lewis Mumford (1970). By the 1880s the prospect of conflict between the two systems arose, especially after the American technological myth was soon linked to an expanding capitalism and imperialism by means of the corporate and political monopolization of "the very technology which was supposed to preserve the people's liberty."[13]

After the Civil War was won by the North, many Latin American texts reveal that the industrialist and technocratic society was perceived as a menace, since it had gradually turned into an effective means of repression with the frontier expansion against the indigenous population and Mexico. The last Apache frontier was closed in 1886 with the death of Geronimo, and the United States had already annexed Texas and California. That year also saw the silencing of alternative discourses of working-class consciousness within North American society, with the repression against anarchists—i.e., the Chicago martyrs about whose trials Martí wrote extensively. This is the North America Martí described to his Latin American readership, covering every aspect of North American life. From 1880 to 1895 he was a lucid critic of American society, analyzing the stratification of classes and the transformation of the economy to monopoly capitalism, and the dangers this held for Latin America. From an admirer of democratic institutions, he became a critic of the bitter realities, and went on to unmask the instruments of power behind racial prejudice against blacks and oppression of the Indians. He reviewed American history in a powerful article published in 1885 on Ulysses S. Grant, eighteenth president of the United States, in which he uncovered political corruption, fraud, and mismanagement (1975:71–122).

If Martí gained force through a modernist discourse that conjoined tropes with self in collective associations of an oppositional stand to American society, others introduced the national need to demystify acts of imagery. It could be said that this wide mapping of a "Spanish American dream" attracted different personalities, from the political to the tormented, cultivating an estrangement of a lost self.

This exalted sense of a modern culture was detailed in shifts of mood and internal contradictions by Casal (1979), who equated the modern with anti-utilitarian values and moral instrumentality. His chronicles emerged as a response to the doxographers of public opinion (newspapers and journalists) and their *yanquismo:* "Havana's press, that great mercenary which lives in the most repugnant complicity with commerce and industry, offering its shameful favors at a low price" (I:305). Casal developed a critique of the modern spirit of capitalist wealth and utilitarian dogmas, of the worn-out rhetoric on love, politics, and religion, and elevated art as an alternative discourse (1890; I:89). The new "artistic socialism"—he wrote enthusiastically about the young Darío—was against bourgeois values (1891; I:104), and this opposition against functionalism defined the new generation. Casal's stance against pragmatism became central for what has been taken as a literary modernist vocation, measured against systems of trade and systems of selfishness. He invoked a whole spiritual family which included Baudelaire, Swinburne, Leconte de Lisle, Leopardi, Carducci, Richepin, Vigny, Sully-Prudhomme, Paul Bourget, Banville, José María de Heredia, Poe, Villiers de l'Isle-Adam, Catulle Mendès, Alejandro Parodi, Heine, and Mallarmé (I:301). Casal's fantasized Paris is not the bourgeois Paris of Gambetta, Tiers, and the Eiffel Tower, but the cultural text designed by the Parnassians, and the symbolists (I:161). We will return to this.

If in the 1890s being modern was an alternative to *yanquismo,* another functional definition took "modernity" to be a form of consciousness expressing both the birth of a newly gathered Latin American national identity and its culture. If, as suggested by economic historians and developmental economists, the attempt to modernize and industrialize Latin American societies brought about commerce with the aggressive expansionist North, including Porfirian Mexico, then it could be argued that the yanquismo and "utilitarianism" Mexican moderns refer to were a real material and objective menace. The semiotic production of ethico-political principles, symbols, and ideals contends against conflicts and engagements of concrete social history. The social imaginary incorporates the idioms of capitalism as exploitation of living labor and production, and technological and organizational competitiveness for profit. Thus understood, the anti-utilitarianism, anti-technological, and anti-progress modernist discourses are not nostalgic for the past but the projection of a future. These idioms reveal the confrontation between the two camps which divided the political space. The antagonism occupies a precise location in a system of relation with other elements, fortifying the charge of negativity. The discursive construction of the antagonism was constituted within the ensemble of practices and discourses against the monopolization of economic power and its various forms of subordination. Conceived in this manner, the idioms aimed at revealing the extreme exteriority of the antagonisms in a symbolic construction of a national space.

It is worth noting that Martí called into question the achievements of North American authoritarian modernity. His first uses of the word *modern* (modern spirit) and *new* (new age) were related to a series of short articles on painting and sculpture that he published in Mexico (*Revista Universal*) in 1875–76, New York (*The Hour, América*), and Buenos Aires (*La Nación*) in 1885–86 on

Mexican, Spanish, and French impressionist painters. As he developed the concept of "modern" and its political and aesthetic dimensions, Martí accounted for a parallel between art and national liberation, framing it in a cultural valuation of the sculptor Francisco Dumaine. Martí emphasized then an important aspect of modern art which would remain a normative principle: "He merits the posthumous praise which the enthusiastic lovers of national liberty render to his energetic talent, for national liberty encourages every belief of the modern spirit and every form of the new life" (1982:68).

Martí was well acquainted with the concept "modern," which he had been using since his collaborations in *Revista Universal;* "new," "modern" meant a national literature, and now he was seemingly reappropriating it to bind it to his emancipatory discourse. In this context, both *modern* and *new* are radically bound to the moment of their emergence as a contact with historical actuality. The modern work of art is valued as beautiful when it legitimizes emancipation and a national and cultural consciousness. This is the concrete use of Martí's term in his article on the fifty-fifth exhibition at the Academy of Design in New York (1880), where he links art with the traditional "classic" vs. romantic debate: the first gives way to "intelligence," the second to the imagination; thus the romantics are the impressionists and the classics the academics.

His reflection is carried further as he states that Americans (he implies both Spanish and Anglo) often imitate European models of both painting and literature: "While this servile admiration dominates us, we shall never be able to produce anything worthy of the New Continent" (81). This idea is advanced in his article about the Catalan modernist painter Mariano Fortuny, as he addresses his reader with the warning that the American painter must not imitate him. "If we are obliged to imitate," he adds, "instead of asserting our own originality, let us wait for someone who can represent the majestic side of the character of our age" (1880; 1982:94). By 1893, in his article on Casal, he asserts that there is no imitation, but that even the gallicized is re-accentuated by what he calls "creole wisdom." Martí's term is close to what Bakhtin understands by "re-accentuation": when a cultural text is read in different historical circumstances, or a specific situatedness, different aspects or meanings emerge. It is also part of "heteroglossia," and becomes an important element in the struggle for signs. What Martí suspects is that in the universe of discourse, new contexts create different meanings, that a different string of signs is built upon the text being read, as its intertext; that signs (or meanings) are never fixed.

Martí confidently does not read through Eurocentric eyes or adopt the point of view of cultures as fixed essences. He addresses beauty as a meeting place between the larger question of life and art. He is not unlike many romantics in their central concern about aesthetics and political life. This link is emphasized many times; however, he insists on the importance of "novelness." This question is apparent in his comments on an exhibition of French impressionist painters in New York (1886). He draws relations between modern art and French painting while lamenting that the "world's art is being emptied upon New York in the odor of wealth" (119). As he develops his commentaries on Corot,

Manet, Monet, Pissarro, and Renoir, he establishes a correspondence between modern art and the fleeting and transitory representation of beauty. However, he adds that the human spirit is never futile but is essentially transcendental: "All rebellion of form carries with it a rebellion of essence" (121). I should like to call attention to the fact that his understanding of the transcendental does not affirm autonomous values and realms; it does not read as the myth of transcendental agency of a neutralizing idealism. Rather, he suggests the power emerging from a political and creative dialogic structure of consciousness.

Beauty shows itself in harmony between man and nature, and art monitors a distinction between true and false, good and evil, in an aesthetic utopia similar to, but different from, Schiller's program, since for Schiller aesthetic education was an end in itself.[14] In Martí's modern discourse as well as in this emergent modernism, beauty was dialogical, for it was considered a revolutionary force toward mutual understanding and a new society of liberated individuals.

In the domain of intersubjectivity, literary discourse was part of a self-consciousness existing for others (in the spirit of Hegel's *Phenomenology,* in Kojève's reading [1980]). After its emergence, as we have argued, the modernists stressed the importance of language in the self-formative process, while simultaneously (at least with Martí) focusing attention against political usurpation, leaving the colonial subject in bondage, or else to the predominance of utility and the power of money. However, the modernists placed great emphasis on the relation between speaking subjects and nature. They began to make more explicit statements of social and cultural criticism against technology and bureaucracy and their dangers. It not only was a counterposition; it was also a critique of imperialism in its entirety, and of the reality out of which technology operated by distorting it. These dialogical critics considered themselves an avant-garde that promoted and legitimized the process of modernity, venturing into the future. In this sense, no distinction should be made between a political text and a "fictive" or literary text from the point of view of a genre theory based on rhetorical models.

Turn-of-the-century modernists called into question the doxae (opinions) opposed to answerable truth, against the adepts of the accepted views who are able to pass as experts to appeal to credulous minds. Thus, their cultural texts were rhetorically structured in ways that cut across all conventional generic boundaries. Rhetoric cannot be divorced from the interests of epistemological critique, because aesthetics is not independent of epistemology; the acting subject and the knowing subject converge at this point. As a cultural and speech community, modernism was a diachronic set of concretely pronounced discourses, grounding their experience in an intersubjective agreement. The meanings sedimented in language to designate modernity were inseparable from the shared patterns of knowledge and belief. Martí called attention to the fact that the individual/subjective self could emancipate itself from a traditional/colonial way of life; therefore, he proposed an *alternative:* neither colonial European values nor North American authoritarian and expansionist modernization, but a third way out (what Che Guevara called the Third World in 1950, charging the term with connotations of economic disparity), a democratic modernity which would secure self-knowledge and autonomy against a dependency theory. The optimism of this liberatory imaginary was without doubt the most active articulatory point in the ensemble of social practices produced by modernism.

From this emerged the tendency to conjoin the self and nature; the philosophy of the subject was connected to the modernization of society with an increasingly effective exploitation of natural resources. Martí shared with Marx the belief that the achievement of modernization would be to release the potential of society through the direct experience of modern techniques and industrial labor; but while Marx stressed the rational potential, Martí (and Hispanic modernists in general) emphasized the human (and humanitarian) constellation against the instrumentalization of human labor and capital.

This is comprised in the well-known opposition between Ariel and Caliban—an allegory widely used by Latin American modernists at the turn of the century to oppose their humanism (and spiritualism) to the materialistic greed of the North, and which has been contested lately. In his time, it was meant as a rejection not of modernity altogether, but of the tyranny and debasedness of the modern machine-serving age, of the sacrificing to Moloch. The symbolic correspondence between thought and perception (the symbolic art preferred by Hegel) invites here the allegorical reading that de Man suggests for Hegel's *Aesthetics* (1982; 1971 in 1983): to distinguish between experience and the representation of this experience. As figural language, such allegory is not a universal truth but a representation; with modernists, it becomes a projection of the dialogical social imaginary calling individuals to the antagonistically constructed meanings by reference to ideological positions. This experimental imagining should not be understood as realistic, else we fall into the realist fallacy and realistic illusion of reading cultural texts as if they represented material reality; the allegories become ideological interpellations for ethical readings which demand that the reader take responsibility. The premise is to give a historical responsibility and an understanding of the modern scene, in order to make contemporary social life a problem through which to analyze the development of modernity and its effects on freedom and domination.

Between 1880 and 1895, for Martí the whole of the modern technological imaginary was an object of scrutiny: the alienation of the labor force, the stratification of economic classes, the transformation of technology from a democratic use to a monopoly of capitalism. At the same time, he voiced confidence in North American modern aesthetics: Emerson, Whitman, Longfellow, Mark Twain, Louisa May Alcott, which most modernists would later share.[15] He simultaneously monitored a relationship between form and socioeconomic forces; moreover, both these dimensions required cultural valuation to express a different modern project which would undermine the totalization of an uncritical understanding of the world. Martí defiantly insisted on the need to expose the violence of a social modernity which adhered tenaciously to wealth, gains, and exploitation. It was in this context that he undertook to reassess the power of literature—specifically through lyrical poetry—to call into question the achievements of the unifying power of wealth and reification.

That lyrical poetry would express both social and individual conflicts was to him the real challenge for the new poetry. In Martí's words, as he eulogized Walt Whitman, modern literature "announces and spreads the ultimate happy agreement between apparent contradictions. . . . Poetry is more necessary to a people than industry itself, for while industry gives men the means of subsistence, poetry gives them the desire and courage for living" (1887, in 1982:174–75). "The ultimate religion is freedom, and the new cult is the poetry of freedom" are the exact words of his aesthetic utopia, which he had previously sketched in his prologue to a book by the Venezuelan modernist poet Juan Antonio Pérez Bonalde in 1882.

Martí—and with him modernists—departed from and socialized the single most persistent and seductive of romantic tropes: the organicist idea of art as a kind of second nature, a "heterocosm" where all evil antinomies fall away and the imagination achieves a perfect union of subject and object, inner and outer worlds. This had been the legacy of Kant, Rousseau, Hegel, and much German idealism, as well as the Left Hegelians (on this point, cf. Norris 1988). The Cuban questioned how the autocratic power and potential violence of the imagination might seek to secure their claims without a free state which would guarantee equal rights and participation of the collective political will through its civil laws, since the islands of Cuba and Puerto Rico were engaged in an anti-colonial struggle.

This modernist cultural text was reconceptualizing autonomous reflections in an irreversible process, drawing new cartographies of emergent states and cultures. The impulse was toward opening the future as a virtual memory of the past, and not toward unearthing mythical pasts or origins. Far from teleological pasts equating origins and goals, modern anti-colonial times were the medium to contact the past which reaffirmed a culturally revived public sphere to overcome the colonial appropriated historical culture. To Martí, imaginative vision was transcendent, but not in autonomy from the social, and through its synthesizing powers it was possible to deconstruct the idea of colonization and to show the violence of technocratic industrial modernization.

I have refrained from equating modern time consciousness with rationalization, especially since most contemporary discourse connects a theory of modernity with the concept of reason or with northern European (German) rationalization. In my reading, turn-of-the-century Latin American—and very specifically Antillean—modernism comprised a skepticism toward reason in its form of the will to power, which Goya was among the first to reveal, in his famous *capricho:*: "El sueño de la razón produce monstruos" (The dream of reason produces monsters). Such a rejection prompted a definite critique of instrumental reason and an unmasking of bourgeois humanism in its concrete situatedness of colonial violence.

The specific event of 1898 gave meaning to this dialogism. Modernism was a product of the particular values dominating the Hispanic community at a particular point in its history, and the result of the questioning took form through a cultural fantasy of emancipation. Modernism emerged as a complex discursive formation: a philosophical discourse, a historical discourse, a theory of progress, a writing and readerly discourse which arises simultaneously against the universal and global European (colonial) discourse as well as against the authoritarian, capitalist expansive imperialism of the North. What seems evident at this juncture is the potential of the cultural uses that were made of a critique of an imperialistic political economy extended to the critique of the economy of signification.

The insurgent intellectual—at this specific historical crossroads—placed emphasis on human will to create a new collective narrative voice of a yet-unrealized historical possibility. Central to the formation of such an identity was the political emancipation of the America which was still colonial. Poetry was replenished with critical and utopian content and became an agency for the construction of new subjectivities and positions, effected from a distantiated standpoint which should not be confused with the distant postmodern observer. Theirs was a semantic approach; their particular approach to culture and communication was revealed in their conscious rebuilding of meanings, and also in their self-awareness of the necessity to change the ways in which those meanings were reproduced. They sought to project solidarity through symbolic representations, since what was clearly understood is that behind the meaning of the same word—*modern*—lie antagonistic ideologies, comprised in the uses and misuses of modernization.

It is in this movement, from the political to the creative and moral plane, that the decisive projections of the social imaginary helped create the hegemony, so that an ensemble of ideas and values could be shared by a heterogeneous community. In many cases, modernist negation was based on a humanist reading, rather than on a social-theoretical reading of modernity, since modernism fused many relational sectors. We have already noted some of the major points of resistance of this historical poetics through carnivalized language, and the play of voices to articulate the time and space of self and other, the subject positions, and the heteroglossic cultural and linguistic expressions. This experimental imagining stresses openness in contrast to the ideological stratification and dogmatism of closed, finished, terminated social or discursive systems—the monological, authoritarian. In its concrete social event, it invited the *responsive* character of understanding to share the optimism to create a new social world.

III

LYRIC POETRY AND THE CONSTITUTION OF THE SELF

> The object of literature is not for amusement, but to channel leisure to keep spirits high, in the cult of the extraordinary and of what belongs to us. . . . Every word is meant to disclose an act. . . . The word is not to hide truth but to say it.
>
> —José Martí (1875)

> The fact is that in America the new people are in full bloom. . . . They want effort and reality in politics and in literature. . . . This literary generation in America is like a family, for it began with the imitative quest, and is now in the freed and concise elegance, the sincere and artistic expression, brief and chiseled, of personal feeling, and direct, creole wisdom.
>
> —Martí, "Julián del Casal" (1893)

Dialogicality and the Inner Word

By now we have become familiar with the sustaining fiction, a potential mode of thought and literary projection monitored by a dialogical social imaginary. Central to the formation of identity as emancipation was the experience of the self.[1] The rejection of the signifier of colonial institutions was accompanied by a rejection of the "already given" literature and of nineteenth-century moral(istic) and literary conventions. The process needed to legitimize the new narrative led to the socialization of nature and the renaturalization of the self through cultural practice and the lyric experience. The emphasis on process and the radical newness of the situation lent themselves to accent the position of the observer, and the formal means for expressing subjectivity. The "I," that shifter which moves the situatedness of discourse from one subject to another (in

50

Jakobson's influential suggestion), becomes the ground to measure all axiological spatial operations: here/there, now/then. The lyrical "I" is located at
the center of social life, and of language itself.

My central point is that in the last quarter of the nineteenth century (from
around 1880), lyric poetry operated in a complex dialogical interaction with the
political event. The social function of the lyric experience to which I refer is
constructed by a double system of connections, namely:

1. Internal and external discourses are traversed by the ideological
(Bakhtin); language is the medium of representation, and as a form of "practical
consciousness"—in Marx's term—it arises from the need for communication.
The speaker's individuality interacts with the external or social structure that
models heteroglossia. Subjective conscience is understood as an internal utterance with a specific social-historical orientation, as a "situated utterance."

2. Modernist textual strategies are often represented through anatropic perceptions to disclose conflicts and struggles within a carnivalesque atmosphere,
encoded in a parade of masks. Metalepsis and carnival aim to communicate a
new democratic conception of the world through the formation of new meanings, a new narrativity of history. I understand as carnivalesque the essence of
the genre, not the stratification of canons.[2]

My point of departure rests on two premises: First, I use the working concept
of modernism as an epistemic metaphor to redefine the meaning of a venture
oriented toward projecting a political, social, and aesthetic program. As such,
modernism is a discursive practice, a polemical dialogical discourse (an
"organic hegemony," in Gramscian terms) defining the constitution of self in
relation to others, whose situational exigencies were adapted and adopted in
diverse ways in the emerging world of differences and asynchronies called Latin
America (or Spanish America). Second, modernism is a progressive anti-institu-
tional instrument against old canons, a discourse which can be understood as
the result of a differentiated identity, which distinguishes itself from both its
European past and its North American present. This "third way" is constructed
through the new experience of the self and the unmasking of symbols. The
opening of this "third way" through heterology and heteroglossia was aimed at
redefining Latin American identities, and consequently the nations themselves.

The double system that I suggest—dialogical and carnivalesque—generates a
pair of concepts which organize spatial structure (a structure noted in another
context by Walter Benjamin and Iurii Lotman). The typology of internal space is
semiotically formalized in a movement from inside and outside—or from Man
[*sic!*] and Nature, among other oppositional axes—conveyed through the evoc-
ative power of signifiers toward the social horizon of collective expectations (on
this in modern poetry see Jauss 1982). Neither combination is exclusive. On the
one hand, the carnivalesque chronotope can be expressed through the verbal
distancing and interindividual territory of the "culture of folk humor" in a
critical and satirical vein; it creates ratios of otherness. On the other hand, it
uncovers competing languages and discourses, and unmasks veiled morality
and dogmatism through the "estranged" references of overly encoded motifs

and lexicon—swans, fairies, fountains, Greco-Roman mythologies—as we have seen, thus operating in a kind of literary and formal revolution, rearticulating traditions, clichés, and conventions of the past in new semantic fields and, therefore, in new or distinct social universes.

The poet invites the readers/listeners to reconnect themselves with the mythical past (e.g., Casal's antiquity and gallicized "creolized" myths, Darío's and Gutiérrez Nájera's Hellenic "creolization"), which serves as a familiar model to create an imaginary world. The poetic text combines the elegant phraseology of the past with touches of dialectal and conversational language, thus combining the *intertextual* with the *interdiscursive,* making cultural texts *heteroglossic,* as different languages intervene.

As a peculiar medium of communication, poetic discourse once more becomes clearly a carrier of new meaning and knowledge through its methods of transmitting and preserving information about this historical period. In a Humboldtian way, all individual expression was thought of as fundamentally poetic, and culture was a form of social "underground" (as embodied in the carnivalesque, for example). The innovative mastering of genres (prose and poetry in all its speech genres) was an integral part of what Voloshinov/Bakhtin call the "immediate social situation" (*Marxism and the Philosophy of Language,* 86). This new or modern poetics is achieved by the production of performatives and conveys specific processes for the acquisition, preservation, and transmission of "truth." Poetic discourse proved remarkably productive as a means of capturing the developing relationships under capitalism and the unfinalized nature of humankind and human thought. This experience of the self revealed that the world was open and free, and that everything was still in the future.

This understanding of rapidly changing times and the dynamism of historical events of the modern age were combined in the form of an internal dialogizing process "voiced" by the individual and/or collective. Martí's own poetry (*Ismaelillo* [1882] and his prologue to "The Poem of the Niagara" by the Venezuelan J. A. Pérez Bonalde [1882]) supports my proposal. Both discourses ground and figure at once the urgent questions of the modern art of free nations, which Martí had been emphasizing for some time: "The poetry of free nations, of sovereign countries, of our American land, is the one which goes to the bottom and deep down into man [*sic*] and the reasons for life, into nature and the seed of being" (in Esténger 1971 I:32).[3] There is no "national life without national literature," he concluded, while he proposed literature as a performative (the word stands for action). By 1882, when he had renewed his struggle for Cuban independence, this time from New York, he was quite clear about the double bind between personal freedom and the appropriation of the natural world to human requirements. Martí defined the new modernist poetry thus:

> Poets today can neither be lyrical nor epic with any naturalness or calm; nor is there any lyric poetry other than that which each one takes out of himself, as if his own being were the only thing whose existence he did not doubt, or as if the

problem of human life had been challenged with such courage, and investigated with such eagerness, that there is no better objective—nor one more moved by profundity and greatness—than the study of oneself. (1982:310)

What characterizes Martí's modernity is the realization and problematization of the present as movement and change, modernness and novelness. The feeling was well-known to Baudelaire, and to the citizens of "Paris—Capital of the Nineteenth Century," to quote Benjamin's adequate title. However, to the Cuban poet this modernness was not only the "auratic" of new objects and inventions, or the panorama of great expositions or advertising, but the intention to reconnect modern life with freedom and liberation.

Martí's favorite motivation was to merge modern artistic innovation with direct and revolutionary political impact. Modern poets no longer can rest on the past, but must take its orientation from themselves, from their own contemporaneity. This mode of understanding is not fetishized fashion; but in order to carry on the project, self-reflection becomes essential. Martí's concept of modernity is grounded on the reflective relationship between subject and object, and on the communicative mediation of poetry. Nature is to be understood as the suppressed or excluded and outlawed parts of subjectivity, what Adorno and Horkheimer in *Dialectic of the Enlightenment* (1972:171) call the mimetic impulse which carries within it the promise of a "happiness without power."

But Martí's Man and Nature dialogization can also be understood as exercising a critical function in two sites of political tension: nature as the "great laboratory," as Marx puts it, and the individual as instrument of production. In other words, Martí suggests countering what Marxism defines as nature-as-commodity, and measuring the self against an economic totalizing system. In the *Grundrisse* Marx refers to soil and its utility in the following way: "The earth is the great laboratory, the arsenal which provides the means as well as the materials of work, and likewise the location, the basis, of the community" (in Lichtheim 1988:129). In *Capital*, Marx goes further, describing the labor process as "human action with the view to production of use-value," and appropriation of the natural world for human requirements. That is the "necessary condition for effecting exchange of matter between Man and Nature" (I:205).

Martí's prologue points in the same direction, since the aesthetic experience to him is an experience not only of form but of content; literature is a political performative. He suggests that aesthetic choices are made not in a vacuum but in a negative relation to other kinds of objects which could have been chosen. To strengthen this materialist position, another way in which we could theorize the relation between cultural capital and economic capital (Martí's Man and Nature) is, extrapolating from Bakhtin, the way in which the situational experience (Nature) organizes the experience of a Latin American identity. The analogy suggests the question of historical and individual agency as a construction open to the future. The call to nature Martí suggests is to be sovereign and not let oneself be subordinated (as colonial nature) to the condition of reduced labor, but to free both subjectivity and nature from bondage, or from the boundaries imposed by the colonial gaze/space.[4] What Martí projects in this prologue—and in his article "Our America"—is the notion of a cultural identity through innovation, to generate a cultural capital that belongs to the whole of society. It advocates a new culture of the self and of the social, constructed as a relation between primary and secondary nature. The human agent reappropriates the natural world as elaborated through the product of human work: what we now call cultural texts.

Martí's starting point, it should be noted, is that the self is constituted by its relation with nature (and others), and the constitution of self thus considered is not monological. This emphasis on the release of the self could be understood in a dialogical relationship with Marx's *Grundrisse,* in which the development of human control over the forces of nature—including one's own—is basic (see Anderson 1988:330–31; Brenkman 1987). This emphasis on otherness distances Martí from Schiller's aesthetic utopia, for example, which the Cuban socializes, since for him culture is not an end in itself, and the intensifying of feeling and reason is not disconnected from political action and social change. Furthermore, Martí advocates action within an enthymemic discourse (understood in the Bakhtin/Voloshinov conception of enthymeme) open to the future. The "unuttered" is in this case the yet-to-come humankind and nature and their material interchange; it also implies a reappropriation of the natural life from which the individual had been estranged through the social injustices and exploitation of colonialism. The constitution of the self's identity in this enthymemic discourse argues for a new dialogic relation with material-social practices, and a shared social experience through the medium of the sign. This re-accentuation of culture through poetry acts as an attempt to disenthrall the estrangement of the material world (nature), and also to secure a social identity through a relation to language.

Martí extends (and transcends) the romantic tradition in the epistemic discourse of modernism. He attempts to value freedom as a complex of material-social understanding. Thus, self-consciousness emerges from the awareness of outer nature, a distinction which advances a categorization of the domains of reality and sites of discourse: outer nature, inner nature, with the term *society* (the social) implicit as a third point in the responsive interaction of what Bakhtin calls the "created." These dimensions, which correspond to the objective, the subjective, or the changing dimensions of dialogicality marking modernity, are intuitively postulated by Martí in this prologue as indicative of the cultural deployment of the heteroglossia of the social world, which had been muffled—the possibility to stage the conflicts and complementarities of heteroglot cultures in the social semiotic. Dialogue becomes central for defining the constitution of self in relation to others.

Martí's concerns about the inner world connect with the ordinary feelings and experiences (his book of poems *Ismaelillo* establishes a dialogue with his son), to articulate them progressively to a more advanced modern form of social consciousness. He works with the diversity of the inner world to suggest the contradictory and restless activities that underlie the very nature of modern capitalist institutions. He comes to realize the diversity of social forces in a society, to understand that the inner self is socialized and can be drawn to social praxis. Lyrical poetry addresses the fears, the subjectivities, the family life, the cultural life in order to invite the reader to participate in the national life and the collective project. Martí ended his prologue with some points that well deserve to be reproduced here:

> One's personal life filled with doubt, alarmed, questioning, restless, and satanic; one's intimate life feverish, unstable, competitive, and clamorous—all this has become the principal factor, and with Nature, the only legitimate factor, in modern poetry. (1982:316)

Focusing on the inner structure (the inner discourse) of the collective, and through a liberated identity, he establishes a link between reality, the individual, and the social group. What Martí affirms as the new lyric theme is linked to renewal and is part of the current discursive political reflection. The process of the modernity he proposes originates in the desire for an emancipated self and a struggle against technologies of power which mutilate humankind and nature. Martí's foundational texts, in this regard, suggest that both consciousness and ideology are semiotic, realized in the form of inner speech, in the form of interaction with a collective, and in the mediated forms of creativity (writing). The internal dimension of inner speech exists so far as it is realized by the collective reflection of what it meant to identify with "Our America," at precisely that moment in history when new centers of power were emerging, endangering the project for autonomous modern collective identities. In this context of struggle in the face of North American imperialism, the internal organization of an American experience through language was central. The force and originality of Martí's perception is that he suggests the incorporation of all cultural voices (each individual nature, each psyche) to embody the cultural polyphony of being at once plural with many ethnic roots. The psychic nature of the new modern individual denotes a level of the new ethical consciousness inspired by a politics founded in and through a historical poetics.[5] Poetry appears as a form of knowledge, a way of organizing both individual and collective experience.

His program dialogues with Krausism (the most powerful and lasting Hispanic philosophical doctrine of the nineteenth century), and through Krause with Schelling's idea of a new mythology by which aesthetic intuition became the "highest act of reason" (quoted in Habermas 1990:89). Along the same line, Hegel's idea that poetry conducts humanity is introduced as an evaluation in Martí's dialogical discourse, imbued with precisely the new Latin American perspective. This dialogical angle is that of the legitimating subject position, which gives new semantic direction and meaning to the discourse of modernity. The implied model merely provided the material—what I have called a "creolization"—suggested in Martí's article on Casal, where he states that what began as an imitative quest was transformed by personal feeling and "creole wisdom." In Bakhtinian words, communities may share common languages, but each group employs the semiotic system to shape its own meaning. Political struggle also takes place in language, and culture is the site and event of social struggle.

If we rethink the deployment of European rhetorical idioms in terms of heteroglossia, then it could be said that the element of response is in hidden dialogicality, as this modernity is transferred from the European context to the new American enthymemic discourse. Bakhtin's concept of heteroglossia enables us to reintroduce politics and culture into the semiotic exchange; as situated utterances, changing from one social collective to another, the same idioms acquire new meanings and new points of view. Language is a space of confrontation of differently oriented social intonations. From the dialogical angle, words generate new meanings and social values beyond themselves; there is always a potential meaning disclosed in every new context. Meanings are not fixed, and their fluidity can be transformed, since there is not only class struggle in language (as indicated by Voloshinov/Bakhtin) but also, in our specific case, anti-colonial struggle. Martí's enthymemic discourse marks an altogether new relation, which will gradually be recognized by the collective of moderns. His is, so to speak, a first experience of participation in the concrete discourse of the community.

Interestingly enough, the modernist Martinian project makes explicit the openness and insistence on the present as a new beginning, but implicitly it is a deviation from the master discourse of naturalism in the metropolis. By 1881–82 the dominant discourses of naturalistic novels—Galdós's and Clarín's—articulated what was considered a "new" aesthetic discourse, as a form reflecting immediate human experience. However, it could be argued that as a cultural expression of liberalism, both writers disclose the dominant humanist notion of society as homogeneous and held in common by everyone. In contrast, the anti-colonial modernist discourse Martí proposes not only asserts the disputes over knowledges and makes it clear that words acquire new meanings according to the user, but also asserts that there was a general disidentification with the metropolis. The incorporation of French semiotic material into the modernist heteroglossia was in itself a position of struggle. The collectively intended social text is the elaboration of insurgency against cultural dependence; in Martí's words: "For France is a country where a hidden or confessed awareness of the general humiliation leads everyone" (1982: 243).

Poetry then becomes a source for the social integration of a centered subject set free from the estranged experience of both a dependent subjectivity and a dependent nature as a cognitive form of emancipation. Martí appeals to the constitution of a self liberated from colonial constraints of identity and representation. The modern poetics suggests that one's attitude toward the self is inseparably interwoven with one's attitude toward the collective and rises against "instrumental reason."

One last point: Martí's interior and exterior expression do not articulate the ironic voiced dilemma of the speaking subject. These spaces transpose the synthesized dialectic of interior and exterior to the very material of enunciation: it is not a consciousness of duality but rather a synthesis between the oppositional semes of the "unhappy consciousness." It suggests the identity of knowing and of ethical acting subjects. Martí owes this concept of poetics and modernity, developed in terms of a theory of liberation, to his critique of colonization and imperialism that set themselves inside the horizon of modernity. He tries to avoid the aporias of both a self-enclosed constitution of the self and an economically dependent subjectivity.

In the work of Martí we find one of the most radical attempts to create a form of "dialogical ethics" in 1882, which was not an isolated stand but part of a demand for a collective discourse activated between the Atlantic and the Pacific. What this modernist poetics demonstrates is that art was energized with the power of negation opposing the functional division of commodity and exploitation, and could stimulate an oppositional stand, that tropes and words had the potential of a critical and utopian content to establish a cultural and moral struggle (what we have been calling "organic hegemony"). But such historical poetics could not be detached from style, if "style" is understood as the reaccentuation of speech genres to redefine identity and constitute subjectivity.

The harmony between individual and society was to be found in the discrepancy with those modern ideals which had been instrumentalized by a complacent entrepreneurial bourgeois society and had lost their critical capacity. The poetics of the modern (later modernists) was directed against the "literary bourgeoisie" (a phrase Darío frequently used around this time), and against a traditional literature and dependent culture. This collective venture was a poetry neither realistic nor practical which—in Rodó's words—integrated false democrats of art. Confidently employing commercial language, in 1894 Manuel Gutiérrez Nájera disqualified the traditional and classical for their lack of "interbreeding" (read the heteroglossia of cultural *mestizaje*) and their refusal to profit from intellectual commerce (in Jiménez and de la Campa 1976:59). According to the Colombian José Asunción Silva (1895), at the dawn of the new age the *modernos* sang to the "eternal Psyche, in this distressing end" (ibid., 60).

However, modernism was a contested field and an ensemble of relations, and not an essentialist form of discourse in general. The necessary failure seems to appear in those who allowed themselves to slide into passive assimilation. While the critical moderns aimed at mobilizing the new states and the colonies through the possibility of liberation and construction of new social subjects, others yielded to the most subjective forms of expression. Action became not collective but the production of poetic idioms based in a spatialization of language, time, and memory, dislocating temporality, unifying both the sociopolitical heteroglossia and the diversity of social relations abstracted from the conflicts and engagements. By contrast, in others, the political fantasy challenged the imperialism of texts and the absolutes of politics, the idealist ontologies of forms, conceptual totalities, and atomistic facts, to bring together accumulated experiences so as to include the radical otherness of their social life. What is important to emphasize is that there was a constant process of redefinition.

In this respect, adapting the well-known distinction between Left Hegelians and Right Hegelians, I see that a division soon appeared between what could be called Right modernists and Left modernists. The crucial difference was between those to whom the present became a fictive fetishized object of neutral contemplation, and those for whom time consciousness was a perspective for reasoning, and from which to think through immediate social problems. Idioms, tropes, language were reproduced, remade with different political consequences and effects. This is the point where modernism becomes a contested discursive field: those for whom the complexity of social relations became a form of understanding the struggle involved, and those who yielded to the functional ideological conditioning, accepting the given roles, and passively reproducing rhetorical tropes into an imagined autonomy. Or, to reposition Kant's distinction of the three value spheres (cognitive, practico-moral, aesthetic), the opposition was between those modernists who made use of the aesthetic in the service of knowledge and collective struggle, and those who grounded the constitution of self in the dematerialized freedom that the aesthetic provided, thus etherealizing signs into a value-free sphere through a symbolic transformation that left collective social processes undamaged.

This cultural imagining, which was strengthened in the 1880s, could be linked to that heterogeneous collection of equality-within-difference by which Marx described commodity exchange. Modernism supposed the acceptance of diversity, a concern with situational circumstances (the Bakhtinian "event"), a skepticism about authority, a rejection of hierarchy, a refusal of the universal claims made by either European colonialism or North American imperialism, and the decision to find particular individual and collective solutions to different problems of values and ethics.

The new perceptions of time and space were connected to new views on the nature of consciousness. These essential motifs incorporated a vast heteroglossic and dialogical network to monitor the dialogical social imaginary, which presupposed discursive strategies of identification or estrangement of the familiar objective world. Speech genres are dialogized, open to contradictory relations, incorporating the carnival chronotope, as means for displaying otherness. The body enters texts in novel interrelations, to celebrate the world or to depict radical versions of the social. More or less, the modernist characteristics and strategies based on polymorphism and heteroregistrality would be the following:

- open, unfinalized works
- a heteroglossia incorporating different languages and cultures
- nondemarcation of speech genres
- artifice through precious-mannerist evocations

- superabundance of the ludic and the erotic as a transgressive critique of morality
- verbal reform against traditional rhetoric
- linguistic revolution that delights in parody and stylization
- the techniques of defamiliarization
- intertextual and interdiscursive virtuosity
- a wealth of social subtexts
- a critique of hegemonies and colonial domination

All of these strategies helped capture the complexity of the modern capitalist world, enriched poetic discourse, and provoked a new attitude toward reality. Experiments with structure and perspective abounded to thematize and allegorize problems of signification and interpretation. Used from different subject positions, they provided a problematics of the synthesis between the physical and the spiritual, and continuity between perception and cognition. The dialogical and heteroglossic were used to express the epistemological and aesthetic multileveled plurality of consciousness and their worlds: the interactive "voices" and their coexistences, the otherness of social life.

Since only the future constituted the particular horizon of integration and the present was directed toward that yet-unspoken and uncreated new world and new words, discourse was not blocked by monosemantic or monogeneric boundaries. Genre was relativized as a heuristic principle, making it possible to deconstruct immobile schemas, ready-made contents, and the stable. The variety of experiments with form tended to break the patterns that delimited the frontiers of prose and/or poetry in order to do away with conventions, making form transgeneric. From this constructive framework burst forth a plurality of styles and voices that mixed the comic and the serious, the trivial and the profound, the sublime and the vulgar, the cliché and the novel, the topical within the frame of a carnivalesque atmosphere. It was an inverted world that took pleasure in the exotic, in the eccentric, in the displacements of everyday life.

Aesthetic disrespect, the independence from norms, expressive dissonance, the incorporation of colloquial diction, social dialects, free verse, virtuosity of intertextuality and interdiscursivity, spontaneous associations (synesthesia), the sharp oxymorons, and the interpenetration of disciplines were transformed in order to overstep the authority of poetry and prose and to bring literature to other artistic spheres in intersemiotic relations. The distinctions between fictional and nonfictional writings opened, against fixed forms and hermetically separate enclaves of cultural production. Many of these strategies are still effective today; for example, the work of the Cubans José Lezama Lima and Alejo Carpentier, and the Mexican Octavio Paz, ideologically varied as they are, shape resistance. To a greater or lesser extent, the turn-of-the-century poets shared these sources as strategies to communicate the social integration of a liberated modernity.

Carnivalesque Structure

An archeological analysis would reveal sets of discursive practices indicating preoccupation with ambiguities subject to a variety of denominations. The reflections were in practice interpretations of bourgeois conceptions of production, and a version of unmasking the symbolic, and of the meaning of words in their relation to self-consciousness. The mask disclosed an important problem of principle, in a transposition of what Bakhtin calls the "carnival grotesque" into the subjective language of modernity (1968:36–38). It was a reaction against classicism, against cold rationalism, and, most important, against "official, formalistic, and logical authoritarianism." The didactic and utilitarian spirit of the Enlightenment and its narrow, artificial optimism were dethroned. It is since romanticism, Bakhtin adds, a private, individual carnival; the carnival spirit is transposed into a subjective philosophy by which the world becomes "an alien world." The mask hides, keeps secrets, deceives; it acquires a somber hue, the vacuum of the infinite interior. The heuristic force of such a symbol is the heterogeneous combination of reality, its irony.

Masks cannot be interpreted as single objects; they associate many meanings through a constellation of signifiers clustering around mask, death, the social. They help present to the eyes of the reader that all speakers are masked, unable to assert themselves. The concept requires that there is a reality behind what masks conceal. Emblematic masks were ways of seeing relations between the present and the past; they inscribed suspicion, but they were also related to myths, the way Lévy-Strauss has argued. Modernists not only linked the symbol of the mask to existence and connected it to myths, but it was also used to self-dramatize a lived experience. As a dialogic element, it played an important role in both the temporal and the spatial frames of reference of texts, and as such suggested different meanings for every speaker. Its conventional meanings change their function.

To Casal (Cuban translator of Baudelaire, Catulle Mendès, Maupassant) humans were "social clowns" (*cómicos sociales*); the gesture of unmasking them provided both diversion and repugnance (1890, in 1979 I:317). In another chronicle, "modern science" is that which "masks theories and exhumes procedures from other times" (1892, in 1979 I:109). Casal's critique of the entrepreneurial domineering form of a capitalist modernity in turn-of-the-century Cuba was conceptualized through the metaphors of masquerade and falsity, which he ironically defined as "the invasion of yanquism" (1890, in 1979 I:99), and North Americans, as "clowns," thus coinciding at his early age with the 1898 carnivalized portrayals of North Americans. His strategy was a social self-positioning to oppose the new market society through the semiotic production of moral principles, symbols, and ideals as the site of interpellation to mobilize a national identity.

José Asunción Silva provokes a critique of core themes, as he polemized with Nietzsche's deconstruction of church and state, and simultaneously disclaims as parodies of religion, art, science, and social relations the new commodity culture of the dawn of the century (in 1977). Hypocrisy, false morality, and utilitarian art were all demystified and unmasked as the new myths of modernity. The masks invite comparison with the present. More directly expressed, the Mexican Luis G. Urbina's "Masks and Masquerades" (1905; in 1971) opened a way to pursue the complex signs of the turn of the century. Urbina linked costume, mask, and carnival with the change and renovation which were inevitable in view of the irrevocable force of progress.[6] The masquerade—to put on the clown's hat, the *sansculotte* Phrygian cap, or the necromancer's pointed hat—was not a game, according to Urbina, but a necessity of nature (we must stress the polysemy of this term). Whether frivolous or serious, thoughtful, pessimistic, or unfortunate, dressed in outlandish trappings or pompous finery, humankind should recognize that the world is a stage and existence but a mask. The moral-symbol making was here linked to interiorized forms of cultural and social critique.

Urbina's carnival has a peculiarity which departs from the romantic's ceaseless transformations, since it is an idiom for progress. The distinct character of this carnival as ideologeme and the heteroglossic modeling of modernists becomes clear as we relate it to a few convergent themes expressed by the Mexican Amado Nervo (*Modernismo* [1907]). According to Urbina and Nervo, those who turn *inward* to listen to the innermost beating of the universe are in need of new words. To be reformed, to be transformed, to be changed is to allow oneself to be carried away by the spiritual and profound movement of an era that no longer believes in illusory naturalism or in dogmatic science, but in emancipation and independence from the new norms (87–90). For Martí, the world was already an "immense house of the masked" (vasta morada de enmascarados), and the poet's function was to "return men to themselves."

With ratios of intensity, and in a peculiar time and space, the chronotope of the mask is an axiological judgment to display otherness in different speech genres—from the journalistic chronicle, to short prose, to lyrical poems. If we follow Bakhtin's suggestions on the carnival, mask and masquerade draw attention to the grotesque body, and to the social roles determined and *given* by capitalist relations—what we would today call subject positions constructed by the realities of capitalism and imperialism. As idioms of dialogism, they point to particular confrontations, and offer themselves as parables, one could say, between relations of otherness.

The founders of Latin American modernism were readers not only of Schopenhauer but of Nietzsche (1844–1900) as well, and most (like Casal, Darío, and Martí) were also contemporaries of Verlaine, Mallarmé, and the symbolists, as confirmed by the chronicles of Casal, Gutiérrez Nájera, and Darío. What this intertextual re-accentuation, circulation, and transformation of "mask" represents here is the uncovering of the mechanisms of power after the wars of liberation. It stood for what could be called a "destruction of signs" in explicit irony and dialogical polemics with forms which were invested with myths, and the notably symbolic roles acted by life forms deformed and distorted by colonialism.

At times, the new dawn retrieved the disguise of an anarchistic aesthetic, and at other times of the carnivalesque "defamiliarization," which was understood as the search for the enigma, the mystery, the ideal through verbal reform. It was polyvalent symbol, choosing aesthetic categories to project questions of identity and social positions. The criticism within modernity was directed toward retention of the emancipation content; unmasking distortions, illusion, the superficial was the genuine ethical activity, since life itself is based on illusion, theatricality. According to Gianni Vattimo's (1974) lucid interpretation, if Nietzsche's critique is intended to liberate from the symbolic and to underscore the fact that conscience/language/subjectivity mask power relations, there the mask to these turn-of-the-century modernists could be both "defamiliarization" and a cultural critique. The Argentinian modernist-socialist Leopoldo Lugones (1874–1938), especially in *Sentimental Calendar* (Lunario sentimental, 1909), was superbly skilled in the seductiveness and complexity of "ostranenie" and the carnivalesque as privileged idioms. "Hymn to the Moon," "Evil Moon," and "Fireworks" combine melancholy with haunting, hallucinatory images that project the experience of exclusion, alienation, dispossession, "creolizing" all idioms in a speculative discourse determined by language games: they become a near-surrealist narrative.[7]

The carnivalesque can be both the public sphere to overcome the private appropriation of modern culture, and a revived spirit to regenerate the ethical and political totality by reversing old values and systems, old languages and rhetoric. Simultaneously, the carnivalesque relativizes the stable. This carnivalesque—and I paraphrase Bakhtin—proved remarkably productive as a means for capturing in art the developing relationships under capitalism, when "previous forms of life, moral principles and beliefs were turned into rotten cords' . . . and the unfinalized nature of man and human *thought* was being nakedly exposed" (*PDP* 167). In this sense, the carnivalesque is first the carnival of the oppressed which liberates from the symbolic, and second the nuance of crisis, of being on the threshold, to explore the internally unfinalized consciousness.

With Darío poetry, the carnival spirit paraded through the disguises of the classical tradition and motifs, from the Dionysian to the eighteenth-century carnivals; in his autobiographical figuration included in *Songs of Life and Hope*, dedicated to Nicaragua, the Argentine Republic, and Rodó:

> and very eighteenth-century; both old
> and very modern; bold, cosmopolite
> like Hugo daring, like Verlaine ambiguous,
> and thirsting for illusions infinite. (244)

Darío oriented his social imaginary to the external and the internal worlds: nature and an indecipherable maze of signs. Thus, he came to define himself as "a poor painter of Nature and Psyche," elaborating on the double impulse of the modern lyric described by Martí as the mastering and understanding of nature and the moral impulse to freedom. I will specifically address a way of presenting these two converging discourses that allows for a reading within a political framework of certain carnivalesque elements and anatropic inversions in Darío, but that also applies to other modernists.

If we start with the different series of carnivalized literature (the erotic series and, especially, the death series), we must go one step further toward a new reading of the performative force of the Pierrots, the clowns, Pulcinellos, harlequins, princesses, fairies, and aristocrats, all legendary representative masks of the Versaillesque carnival. One of Darío's first poems, "Carnival Song" (1896, included in *Profane Proses* [1901]), makes use of mythology, "creolizing" the European idioms. His point of departure is the overcodified cliché of the Dionysian frenzy, madness, and intoxication of the wild herd of Satyrs and Bacchants. Carnival is voluptuousness:

> and carry the swift breeze,
> sonorous, argentine, free,
> the victory of your laughter
> funambulesque. (191–92)

The extravagant and the masquerade (elements of the liberating carnivalesque also developed by the Spanish modern Valle-Inclán) set the tone of *Profane Proses,* a book inhabited by canonical masks, orchestrated through a code of lascivious ceremonies, copulations, eroticisms, libations, all ideologemes of the extensive demystifying universe of the aristocratic Versaillesque carnival. The profanations allow the reader to decode the message within the dislocation and redirection of the new canons, because the princess is sad, or because the "divine Marchioness Eulalia," dark heroine of "It Was a Cold Breeze" (Era un aire suave), is a mask whose laughter hides an enigmatic Psyche. Our Eulalia has an inner space, which is disarticulated in an inside and outside, semiotic signs of the "unhappy consciousness." In Darío's intertextual conditioning, both heroines have a different meaning, quite contrary to the more trivialized aristocratic heroines of fairy tales, newspaper serials of mass culture (or the culture industry) emptied of innovative force and critical content.

To elaborate further on the critical content of these carnivalesque chronotopes and ideologemes for the purposes of my argument, it is no coincidence that these masks also support the aesthetic utopia of the *commedia dell'arte,* with its stable disguises, whose real character the spectator recognizes because they are recorded in a canon of acts and actions. However, the cliché also allowed improvisations and liberties. Darío combines the stable identity of the mask with transgressions of the norm. It is a complex system of extratextual relations, a reception of the past that functions at various levels.

In the new modern correlation of the turn of the century, the meanings of the known symbolic worlds, already part of a topical repertoire, are redefined. The given cultural universe acquires new signification within the discursive formation of modernism. The historical past is revitalized in its dialogicality and operates in a double movement: backward (the common memory of the "given") and forward (the "created"). The past signified a dialogical point of view of the romantic opera carnivals (including the Wagnerian opera), whose mask concealed social classes; in the future, it would culminate in the Lugones *Lunario sentimental,* and in the expressionism of, for example, Schoenberg with his "Pierrot Lunaire" (1912), the series of songs in dialogue with Stefan George's poems. Picasso also provides a number of essential points within this multifaceted fantastic text of carnival.

Within the reading that I propose, Darío's carnivalesque poems of *Profane Proses* (as a selected modern example) could be read as humoristic and ironic parodies of the well-known code whose purpose is to generate deconstruction of or deviation from a stratified and normative world in the specific event of modernity. The oppositions and deviations grow; they are a consciously culti-vated architecture. It is worth noting that modernism assimilates from roman-ticism—the *Marriage of Figaro,* for example—the aesthetic utopia of political revolution. The rich or the poor could hide behind the mask, concealing social equality, a pillar of the French sansculottes and the utopian content of Hugo's *Hernani* and *Cromwell.* This universe of masks and carnival (of long tradition) was enriched with the spheres of the modern European arts (painting, music, decorative arts) that simultaneously incorporated, not without change, and broke with the theater masks of the English Restoration (1600–1700). The assimilation of the licentious, carnivalesque theater of the Restoration, in dia-logue with the French farce, is known to have validated a rebellion against English puritanism and morality.

The modernist carnivalesque was intertextually modeled on a series of con-ventions and traditions. The poet often used aristocratic disguises (Pulcinellos, Pierrots, princesses) as a way of subverting bourgeois morality and class society, with the intention of democratization. Valle-Inclán made ample use of this carnival atmosphere in his farces (Zavala 1990a) to expose the moral hypocrisy of the Spanish monarchy. Modernism postulates a deviation from norms, and a modern society captured in bourgeois ideals and instrumentalized along with them (I adapt from Habermas in another direction [1990:113]).

Finally, Darío's archetype "I, poor painter of nature" (yo, pobre pintor de la naturaleza) adopts the aristocratic mask as an idealized, though not nostalgic, opposition to a materialistic society—instrumental reason—obsessed with the capitalist and commodity culture. He disdains and ridicules entrepreneurial societies and the market economy, with euphoric cultural affirmations against North American geopolitical power. Darío's emancipatory cultural discourse relies on a game of cognitive relationships, on interchanges of individual masks or personae and subject positions: the Spaniards Azorín, Unamuno, and An-tonio Machado, the Italian Luigi Pirandello, and the Portuguese Fernando Pessoa articulated these spheres of multiplicity and plurality of dialogical voices, their inner speech and contradictions (see Zavala 1988a).

The canonical cultural codes of the past are subverted, the traditional and allegorical princesses are unhappy, and the marchionesses, such as Eulalia, are represented in a state of inauthenticity masking their true selves. The modern—or modernism—signifies in this semantic social field to democratize the world from the inside out, so that even the *metecos* are aristocrats, to paraphrase Darío, who ironically carnivalizes the Greek word *metekós* (foreigner or second-class citizen), projecting an upside-down world of the social, and an appropriation of a fixed hierarchical world. There is a constant association between the energies of transgredient liberty as a potential source of freedom. In the differentiation of the modern aesthetics I briefly described above, we see that the modernist poetics of negation represents a logics of validity and a violation practiced within the norm—what we will explore as "creolization" of signs as a writerly readerly practice.

Darío's poetics of negation establishes a game along a double plane of conduct, at war without remission against social puritanism or instrumentalized modernity. He dissolves the allegorical world of images into a reality which first gives meaning to the now-familiar horizon of emancipation:

> The present age is one of struggle:
> one is compelled, thus, to fight;
> it is impossible to rest amidst the noise heard;
> hesitation is too great;
> evil has grown too much;
> the ideal is worn out;
> God takes leave; this is terrible!
> It is impossible to stop that moral gangrene. (1885, in 1977:6)

The early poem—contemporaneous with Martí's cultural text—is grounded on a twofold dialogicality unfolded by the intonation of Martí's *Versos sencillos* (Simple Poems [1889]) and the polemic reference to Nietzsche and the death of God.

Among the possible readings merely outlined here, I propose that the classic motif of the Versaillesque-type carnival of masks and licentiousness, and of the topic of the fairy tale Sleeping Beauty (whose sexual symbolism has been disclosed by Bettelheim [1978]), reveals a displacement and a crisis-like inversion of the normative, stratified, archaic, falsely democratized life. Its axis is constructed according to canonical carnivalesque literature, codes or groups of codes that exist in the addressee's cultural memory. From the variety of expressions in this world of deconstruction of the traditional, with its specific role definitions, the reader receives structural signs from the modern version, whose reiteration and systemicity permit him/her to constitute a social reality in the light of its new historical significance over the erotic series of gallant festivals and Dionysian voluptuosities, the series of food and drink (both Epicurean and Dionysian), and the series of death. Death is evoked as "she," the enigma, the mystery, in Darío's lyrical representations. José Asunción Silva's demystifications and deritualized images and motifs, deconstructing the Oedipal by incest, have more than one point of intersection with Valle-Inclán's sacrilegious inversions through the interaction of irony, satire, and the parody of the liberating carnival spirit. This heteroglossic atmosphere is also the privileged realm of Leopoldo Lugones.

Indeed, we can observe that the carnivalesque's principal series are constructed in a complex nexus of textual strategies: artifice, overly codified lexicon, and clichés collide with romanticism's system of codes, as well as with the romantic claim for primacy of the mystified absolute subject. The verbal reform, and bold linguistic revolution, was necessary for capturing the multiple realities under modern capitalist societies, to work upon the diversity of social forces. These are complemented by a vast dialogical variety of discourses displayed in a variety of experimentation with the genre conventions, the intertextual and the interdiscursive. Such novelness makes ample use of vocabulary from other disciplines engendering a contemporary technically useful knowledge. Experiments with form and speech genres distinctively indicate the collective social and historical forces at work to explore inner speech and heteroglossia.

A close reading reveals that this modern historical poetics of negation dismantles the barriers of conventions and seems to free tradition through a virtuous game of assent and polemics with past norms and languages. In this way, the modernists pursue, beyond the axis of the *inside* and *outside* (or, alternatively, inner self and nature), an identification that merges two objective realities—modern decolonized states and an aesthetic utopia of emancipation— which until then had been independent realities. The poetic construct reunites the new anarchist ideals that had elevated this emancipated, unorthodox cultural text with an affirmative culture. In the 1880s, the group of individual nations conjoined in an association of cultures with common interests. Applied to the example with which we are concerned, Martí's concept of "Our America" is distinguished not only by its attitude regarding the future, but also by its opposition to the past, stating simultaneously negation and affirmation in order to construct a new society. His "naturalist images" suggest the anatropic perception of the cruel rites of colonization. This modern discourse was incorporated into the new institutions of constitutional governments, into the foundations of democratic will, and into the constitution of the self's identity as a liberated subject.

These initial cultural texts, which were constructed over the remains of a vast territory under the Spanish crown's empire, legitimized another world which does not appear to be either pre-Columbian or European or North American. Embedded in the cultural context along the epistemic dimensions is a self-conscious demythologization of antique motifs translated for another narrative. These marked changes not only in appearance, but also in function, to project and monitor a different dimension for the mythical (as for the past) that was no longer compatible with the new modern world. As a reflective cognitive discourse, it assimilated and transformed various systems of norms capable of conferring legitimacy on their own project, reorganizing them into a world-picture of the future. Thus the political philosophy of French republicanism and democracy, as well as of the first socialists, the economic and technological doctrines of the English and Anglo-Americans, the critique of Western thought, all were subjected to free discussion and re-evaluated and re-accentuated in order to determine which would serve as the best sources of legitimation.

Rather early in modernity, Latin Americans perceived the utopias painted by North American democratic modernization and technology through a critical optic, and as deceptive. Modernist poetics of negation disclosed what is known as the American myth and the American dream from the experiential horizon of an optics of displacement. This stance is captured in texts trying to demystify the illusions of democratic humanism; each trope would link expansionist power games with conflicts of collective social history.

But modernity in Latin America started with an optimistic relationship between technological development and democratic objectives. This legitimating narrative of a completely different Latin American identity assimilated the legacy of Occidental rationalism and culture to give shape to the new modern world. But these legitimizing discourses were acceptable only if acquired in a free and uncoerced consensus; decentering truths and worldviews as models of domination were unmasked. Negation of coercion and imposed values and truths were not merely a poetic negation but an explicit positive presentation of another world, a new world also created *by* and *in* language.

Prose and poetry (so thinly defined generically now) are energized with this knowledge and this utopian impulse. In *Songs of Life and Hope: The Swans and Other Poems* (Cantos de vida y esperanza, los cisnes y otros poemas), Darío interlaces the varying degrees of intensity of an implicit critique of capitalist culture as a metadiscourse that unmasks domination and the work ethos morality. He fuses dialogically the sacred and the profane, the secular and the religious in meaningful oppositions, invoking parallels with death and life, in a dance of concepts and a prodigious repertoire of poetic rhythms and forms. Language becomes more than a sign system. He exploits the semantic potential preserved in myths and tradition, activated by a driving force: life and death, virtue and sin, external and internal, inner self and nature, culture and nature are modernized and become the center and measure of actuality. The precise binarizations imply subject formation, and become an appropriate vehicle for dramatizing actuality, as a euphoric key of change. The predominance of actuality in the text goes hand in hand with the force of his enthymemic discourse of hope, synthesized in the chosen subject position of "Salutation of the Optimist," a masterpiece of metaphorical conceit:

> Illustrious most fertile races, blood of fecund Hispania,
> fraternal spirits, luminous souls, salve!
> Because the moment has arrived in which tongues of glory
> will sing new hymns. A vast rumor fills all boundaries;
> magic waves of life are suddenly being reborn;

> oblivion retrocedes, death retrocedes deceived;
> a new reign is announced. . . . (247)

It is as though the whole historical and cultural universe were giving to these Americas the word of acquiescence, and were testing hope and an open future. The poem invites readers as participants in the construction of the new nation, in a practice of writing which should be read in terms of the historical forces which bear on its production. All the possible conflicts between stasis and change are dialogized as an ongoing open event in that particular moment of history.

Neither tradition nor mythology is a drive for aesthetic transcendence to create a timeless, mystified ideal or a unified sensibility with the past, as in T. S. Eliot (see Norris 1988:119). Darío's originality consists in projecting and monitoring the modern subjectivity as a self-consciousness always haunted by otherness. Lyrical poetry reproduces the double truth of humankind and society through a triumph of form. His is a modern understanding of self. The subjective world, as he writes in his poem "Inner Realm" (1896), is decisive, since it accurately registers the internal struggle, the substitutions, the disputing elements, and the desire for harmony. In a Mallarméan synthesis, he associates the harmony of ideas with the harmony of words:

> the secret of rhythm and rule lies
> in uniting body and soul to the turning sphere,
> and loving Pan and Apollo in the lyre and the flute,
> be in the flute Pan, as Apollo in the lyre. (236)

Such equation of harmony and emancipation as self-understanding offers a way out of the aporia of a divided self, and brings out the perspective from which he projects modernity. The entire inner world acquires depth in the celebration of the dynamic. This poem suggests that language is not abstracted from reality, and that the cultural signs have a semantic value, since the discursive world is interwoven with a historical emergence conceptualized as a particular stage in the construction of self.

It is worth noting that Valle-Inclán, in *La Pipa de Kif* (1919), recovers the effective potential of the Rabelaisian comic of the grotesque and carnival's archaic representatives. The Galician modernist incorporates in this collection of poems much earlier compositions whose title reveals an articulated protest against the prevailing social authority. These poems disclose a high degree of carnivalization, even more ironic and parodic than what I proposed in regard to Darío's carnivalesque. It is not necessary, I believe, to insist on the obvious: the different contextual historical event, and the differences in critical perspectives that separate Valle from Darío. The former functions within the culture of laughter and within an encompassing, intersemiotic system of social, non-academic, and noninstitutionalized elements. Valle invokes the culture of folk humor through a heteroglossic atmosphere articulated in hyperbolic dismemberments of the body in their grotesque baseness. He also re-creates marginal character types and their countercultures. Although this parodical vein of grotesque laughter was not common in early modernist poetry, this carnivalesque signifying practice was present quite early, as an oppositional cultural practice against "yanquism," and can also be found in various bohemian expressions. In contrast, what can be found is a strong satiric vein, as in Silva's parodies of Darío's poetry.

It must finally be mentioned that Darío's modernist carnivalesque should be understood in the context of deritualization and demystification of what was called the entrepreneurial "bourgeois" naturalistic experience and the commonplaces of the old (*viejos*) by way of novel self-expression, within an intertextual rather than mimetic mode of reference. At the heart of this new anti-naturalistic poetic practice, nature—both interior and exterior—reunites apparently diverse but complementary themes. Points of contradiction operate in both cultural productions as competing ideologies. This modern experience of human nature as an acting force, inward and outward, serves both as a critique of institutions and as an exaltation of the life of the senses. There is a nexus between subjective and social experience; this heightening of life could be a vitalist polemic against the restrictions imposed by mercantile morality and morals. Vitalism frequently amounts to the emancipation of sexuality, implicitly directed against the institution of marriage and the family. This critique was set in motion not only by Nietzsche's dismantling of church and state, but most particularly during the First International, and was rather successful in fostering class interest, according to the anarchists.[8]

It is the question of the role played by carnivalization in the field of knowledge that we have been pursuing. The metaphor of the mask (or unmasking) monitors a questioning of the imaginary as recognition of the social existence and the selfhoods, as projections to alter conditions. The masquerade (*enmascaramiento*) discloses the crucial problems of individual/collective identities. Carnivalization becomes socially functional for its power to inspire laughter, or to rid the social community of fear, for its power to project a reorganization of social and political relations. It does not organize simply a difference in cognitive content but a specific combination of popular and official languages, of private and public forms of discourse which together organize the expressive possibilities on issues of cultural identity and cultural nationalism.

The asserted preference of carnival ideologemes suggests a re-accentuation of an unequally distributed cultural competence, not in mimetic passiveness and reproduction but as part of a "struggle for signs," to surpass the entrapment of the cultural limits imposed through colonization. It was initially historically operative (until around 1910); by that time the death of the swan was voiced by both Delmira Agustini and Enrique González Martínez, repositioning the myth within the field of cultural relations, and, thereby, in new re-accentuations within the broader social process. Taking into account the different political and ideological conjunctures (even Agustini's gendered reactivation) which the swan myth had entered during the course of his historical existence, Darío's given social role and function had lost effectivity in the broader social process.

If language is not understood outside the question of power, these modernist tropes—mythology, the decadent, and the mask idiom, among others—came to an end when the worldview they connoted and condensed lost its social and collective dimension.

Darío himself had emphasized the situatedness of his turn-of-the-century strategies in the well-known poem "I am the one / who only yesterday said / the blue verse and the profane song," included in *Songs of Life and Hope: The Swans and Other Poems.* The meaning of this collection of poems is constructed through the relation among the texts, for they have cultural value in view of the socio-historical contingency. Darío's modernist poetics also continues to exercise subjectivity through inner speech (the "Nocturnes"), alongside his enthymemic discourse of collective projections of America. Martí's own poems—*Free Verses* (1891)—also articulate this dual projection.[9] What modernist poetry is *not* is univocal, since enthymemic speculative discourse demands multiplicity of subject positions and of significations of a word in natural language, and this joy is at its height when significations are lexicalized in tropes which can be—like Darío's swan—ambiguous.

If in 1898 Darío historicized the political turning point through his swan allegory, he subsequently reworked an increasing textual complexity in *The Wandering Song* (El canto errante, 1907). This social debate was presented in a variety of arguments and themes: the multiform spectacle of nature, heroism, the past, human conquests, the image of the poet, fantasies, desires. He shows concern with the emergence of a national subject who can assume an empowered place on the stage of history. In keeping with change and social responsibility, Darío sought the historical to project solidarity, in a synthesis that embraces Latin America's own history from colonization to independence. In this book he included compositions dating from 1890, some dedicated to Christopher Columbus, to France, to Spain. His 1892 poem to Columbus is far from complacent:

> Unfortunate Admiral! Your poor America,
> your virgin and beautiful Indian of warm blood,
> the pearl of your dreams, is a hysteric
> of convulsive nerves and pallid brow. (308)

The unsettling vision of the present is an appeal specifically targeting a collective space of oppositionality aimed at transformation. However, no reader can miss that, indeed, this poem also represents a strong indication of a topical patriarchal Latin American phenotype, the "warm-blooded Indian" in many ways a symbol of Latin America itself. As a cross-cultural metaphor, it clearly denotes and conjoins the issues of sexism, and the nineteenth-century scientifically based topos of female neurosis. Nonetheless, this poem, as well as others in the book, further discloses that modernism was organically part of the anti-colonial struggle. In his extensive important prologue to this book, dedicated "To the New Poets of the Spains" (A los nuevos poetas de las Españas), it is clear that Darío's pan-Hispanism is the lived experience of a cultural-linguistic identity; he lives "with a love for Latin America and a passion for Spain." This assertion strengthens his political imaginary of an autonomous continent, ultimately free from North American oppressive closeness.

Optimism evaporates in the face of the overwhelming evidence: "Salutation to the Eagle" is a major composition projecting a political fantasy of collaboration between the two Americas: "Be welcomed, magic eagle of enormous and strong wings / to extend over the South your great continental shadow." The ambivalence of the metaphor is also an appeal for peace in 1906, and acquires meaning in dialogue with "Pax," a poem which preserves the sense of the collective memory of the turn of the century: "See the bitter example of torn Europe. . . . No: do not let hate shoot its arrow; / bring to the altars peace, honey and roses." Peace is the recognizable idiom.

Finally, in his pacifist tour through North America in 1914, he visualized the "great cosmopolis" as a space of social inequality, and the former idealized horizon of the urban landscape (he had previously shown enthusiasm for the great metropolises of Buenos Aires and Paris) vanished in view of a crisis of perception in the progressively inhuman and dehumanized modern world. His metaphoricalness was now directed to the grim realities of New York City, a metropolis with a dark side. Meanings made the alien landscape visible; through a huge orchestration of voices, Darío rearticulated images to direct the reader's perception toward concrete reality. In this undertaking he explored racism, the wealth of the few and the poverty of the many, the oppressive atmosphere, and the conflicts. Darío's poems anticipated the theme of racism, unfolding a social reality that would be re-accentuated years later by Federico García Lorca's *Poet in New York,* Rafael Alberti's *13 Bands and 48 Stars,* as well as Juan Ramón Jiménez's early *Diary of a Newlywed Poet* (Diario de un poeta recién casado, 1917) and the Puerto Rican Julia de Burgos. The spatial structure in Darío is described in unmistakable social oppositions of the alienating New York reality:

> and behind Fifth Avenue
> misery is dressed
> with pain, pain, pain! (469)

During this visit in 1914, just before his death, Darío also wrote poems of peace during wartime; while raising his voice against the horrors of a world war, he affirmed his anti-militarism, and sustained the ideal of a peaceful America—North and South—in "Pax": "Peace to vast America! Peace in the name of God!" (478). He now conceived a united role for the two Americas against the worldwide coalition of the First World War; his subject position here gave an objective voice to the dark fears of a global collusion. This transformation of subjectivity seems most probable within the new discourses about world pacifism. This unifying American discourse is the aftermath of a play of social forces, and produces a new position in the field of cultural relations.[10] The utopian element here is expressed through an alliance, a politics of inclusion, in the situationally defined new site of power, and the new relation of forces. This utopia discloses the embedded aporias of liberalism.

Within the social coordinates and organic ideological interpellations I have examined, the mask carries the dual potential to recuperate the natural state that existed prior to the acquisitions of "masks" through the falsification of life. As an epistemic trope, the mask also performs a double function: concealment and disclosure. But it is equivalent to the questioning sign of the swan and the blank page. As a metonymy for nature, the mask discloses and retranslates the swan's (poet's) question about the collective project. If modernism combines with the complexities of a historical narrative and the project for an autonomous form of modernity and modernization, it also assumes a social "I"—the writer's aim at an intersubjective experience to make visible the source of the self's double nature, a concrete space in the center of discourse, from which the world is problematized.[11]

The Hispanic turn of the century adopted this double system, organizing spatial structure into a topology of nature in an external and internal world inextricably woven into a whole. These oppositions did not have an exclusively rhetorical intention, nor were they just oppositional lexical entries. Both spaces projected socialized meanings, exposed to continuous historical contradictions and internal tensions. As an organic ideology, modernists perceived their internal space as one with the outside world, and not in a cumbersome exercise of isolation. At the thematic and semantic level, with greater or lesser efficacy, it is inseparable from specific historical events: 1898, the International, North American imperialism, and the First World War were inscriptions which dramatized representation and the represented self.

The fundamental distinction between "I" and "another" points against a monologic, finished-off category of the self. The "I" was a dialogic, open, and unfolding identity and subjectivity. The passage from one space to another required different subject positions as a process of cultural critique: an outside that was interiority itself in operation, a frontier of interrogation moving toward a contextually determined cartography. Within this interference and interaction, historical activity was inscribed in a dialogical nature that placed I/us exactly in opposition to you/them, which were at the same time sender/receiver. The dimension of this structure reveals the optics from which the questions were raised and their communicative efficacy. Dialogism here explains that the highly particular historical conditions at work gave these situated utterances a specific meaning, which would have been totally different had they been said in another place and time.

The nature of the dialogized, socialized "I" from which this discursive formation emerged should *not* be equated with the romantic lyric with its monostylistic structure (Paz simplistically defines Darío as a romantic in *Cuadrivio*). I want to highlight that difference against the background of this referential and socialized self of the modernists, who no longer relied on the likeness between lyrical perception and the claims for the primacy of an absolute and transcendental subject. This dialogized "I" refers to correlations between the historical event, the objective world, and the collective social coparticipant of the utterance. Utterances do not merely irradiate a closed dialogue in the closed system of subjectivity. As a form of dialogical utterance, modernism understood social and ethical values as the means by which the I/other-collective split articulates itself in an axiology. The "I" is both the sign and the direction of a tension between the poet and the social world: a social imagining hurled into an encounter with the external, with history.

Darío's poems of the swan series—as well as others in the same and subsequent books—are also articulated within a semantic socialized system different from that of the romantics, and from Baudelaire (see Zavala 1987). The self (lyrical "I") is oriented to the object, not only to the subjective inner experience. It does not exclude the possibility of equating the poetic experience with a concrete reality of the world as perceived by others, so well described by Martí. The pronouns are deictics charged with these intersubjective mutual relations; they are enunciative positions indicative of the values of the speaker. In a system grounded on such consciousness, the line "and so many millions of people will speak English?" discloses the dramatic question of the individual/collective who interrogates the sign of the swan. The writer's surpassing of the monostylistic boundaries of consciousness determined a new focus for the direction of the pronouns (*our* America, *us*) and for their social meanings. It led to the production of works in which the living event of the common cause with Hispanic values was expressed in different semantic keys in distinct stylistic tonalities. This call to a pan-Hispanism was intended to connect with the ordinary feelings and experiences of people, to connect their subjectivities, their cultural lives, and their linguistic identities with a unifying common project.

In its tonalities, the use of the lyrical "I" indicates how a discursive practice is individualized as a responsive interaction to reorganize experience, by virtue of a single system for its formation (cf. Foucault 1969; Reiss 1982). Such a construct refracts a complex representation of social reality, understood as an intersection of two spaces. The internal tensions and dilemmas of the constitution of self are expressed in a great orchestration of variants, among which the inside/outside is the privileged opposition when a socialized "I" attempts to transcribe the internal discourse of a yet-to-be-created new world. In Martí's words: "Neither literary originality nor political freedom can exist as long as there is no assurance of spiritual freedom" ("The Poem of Niagara," 1982:317).

IV

THE STRUGGLE FOR SIGNS

> In all of these approaches, the *point of view*
> contained within the word is subject to rein-
> terpretation, as is the modality of language
> and the very *relationship of language to the
> object* and *to the speaker*.
>
> —Bakhtin (1937–38)

> The word is in itself but a sign, or a combina-
> tion of signs. . . .
>
> —Darío (1907)

> It is assumed that American poetry is apt to
> sing only to the palm trees, to the great
> currents of water, or to the very high moun-
> tains; that the world of modern sensations is
> closed to it.
>
> —Carlos Díaz Dufoo (1895)

The Creolization of Signs

A century after the legitimating struggle against delusion and misconceptions, the tacit process of unmasking "mythologies" still remains unresolved. Writing and the problem of meaning were recurrent preoccupations among the modern(ists) as a means of approaching the real and its double-edged modern hermeneutics in their efforts to re-accentuate signs, against Eurocentric fixed and uni-accentual universals. Liberatory struggle was not reduced to economic and political battles, and modernists deployed language to redefine their own culture and selves. Given this position, the starting point was their own human experience, swarming with the most intense ruses of language turned around for their own cultural liberation. Instead of carrying these semiotic theories to their conclusion, we shall concentrate on the consequences they had for the cultural social imaginary of modernity. The particular aspect I want to readdress is that cultural production was a constituent part of the material production of social life (not an alienated realm), and that the struggle for signs thematized the material production of modern social life, not as an end in itself but because it embodied a valued form of human wealth and the new socially evolved needs. Art was a huge laboratory, as we have seen, and "a carnival of possibilities," to paraphrase Ernst Bloch's observation.

Martí's 1882 prologue and Darío's 1888 "creolization" (or Americanization) of modernism challenged, in a way, the valuation that opposed culture to necessity. Their arguments intuitively alluded to cultural development in terms of wealth, as well as to the potential of such values for developing modern societies.[1] Both epistemic discourses on modernity implicitly contrasted the new modern decolonized culture with colonization, through changing terminologies; however, they were the cornerstones of modernism. If Martí insisted on the interchange between nature and the construction of the self, both he and Darío pointed out that only by cooperation and mutual exchange would the new Latin American modernist culture develop.

To follow this line of argument regarding what is an enthymemic discourse which advocates new values by contesting the "given," it is necessary to begin by acknowledging the ambivalence of the sign, understood in the Bakhtinian context of ambivalence of the carnivalesque. The struggle for the sign provokes re-accentuations through symbolically mediated interactions of legitimation and contestation. What we see at work is the dialogical simultaneity of the poetics of negation with its intrinsic supplementarity against an economy of the symbolic—in other words, the Occam's razor principle that entities are not to be multiplied beyond necessity.

The Bakhtin circle's suggestion that the role of the artistic text is to stage the conflicts inherent in heteroglossia proves quite useful in examining the unceasing coincidences, coexistences, and competitions of languages and discourses. Voloshinov/Bakhtin address an important point on language as a primary semiotic system, and argue that class does not coincide with the sign community; thus, various classes may use the same language: "As a result, differently oriented accents intersect in every ideological sign" (*MPL* 82).

It is, therefore, conceivable that any sign can be "accented," or "re-accented," which is the Bakhtinian term used for appropriation. Consequently, every age "re-accentuates in its own way the works of its most immediate past," in "social and ideological re-accentuation" (*DI* 420–21). This frame strongly suggests an exploration of the process by which the differences in cultural preferences, or in context, became socially functional in Latin American modernity. There was a conflict in favor of the symbolic, in the sense that these modernists wanted their own symbolic system to be recognized to reshape not only its self-understanding but their cultures.[2] The new way of seeing was heralded and figured by many modernists in their reading and writing location.

If aesthetic experiences are an experience of not only form but content, the aesthetic choices are not made in a void; rather, they are in a negative relation to other kinds of objects which *could have been chosen*. The asserted modern preference for myths and mythologies—such as the swan myth, or Psyche—meant using an unequally distributed cultural competence to transcend the entrapment of the limits imposed by hundreds of years of colonization. Martí was quite definite on this issue as he revoiced Casal's Parisian idioms in 1893, stressing his "creole wisdom." In this sense, it could be said that the modernists demanded a strong critique of the social world, and not simply an inclination toward hedonistic values. This heteroglotic struggle for the sign was a major part of the effort to establish their right to speech, their own authority. This polemical revoicing is an element of avant-gardes in general, according to Tynianov; however, for Latin American modernists it was a fundamental means of projecting the construction of an "other" tradition, culture, even ordinary language, the total "liberty" Díaz Mirón had voiced since 1884 in a famous poem to the Russian czar Nicholas II.

My suggestion is thus that the modernists' gallicism was not only an alternative and the other of colonization but part of a wider complex of moral, aesthetic, and social attitudes, since Paris had long been a powerful symbol: the city of glamour, sophistication, elegance, and luxury, what Proudhon called the "center of luxury (luxuriousness) and light." This is the Paris Benjamin calls "capital of the nineteenth century," in which the feeling of life was conveyed by the new. The Paris of invention, technique, crowds, passers-by, advertising; "auratic" in a world of gross utilitarianism. The Paris which attracted Casal into allegorical meditations, but also the Paris of brotherhood and socialist upheaval. From this standpoint we have to accept Kramer (1988), who notes that from the 1840s the French city was thought of as the capital of the civilized world. This feeling was shared by the German radical Arnold Ruge, Karl Marx, and Heine, among others. Ruge called Paris "the cradle of new Europe," for the city was also a center of intellectual life and radical activity (Bakunin was there, for example), and a place where it was possible to evade Prussian censorship. To Adam Mickiewicz of Poland, Paris was a center of international brotherhood.

In this epochal framework and as a form of cultural organization, gallicism was not mimetic; the Latin American moderns' attachment to the aura of French signs was part of a wider move toward nationalization and cultural identity. Signs were "creolized," and the powerful revival of mythology by way of a "creolization" of myths and themes was an integral part of an interanimation of polyglossia. Consequently, there is a sort of doubling, by which those myths are seen from the outside, with another's eye, from the point of view of a potentially different language and style (I follow Bakhtin's lead [DI 60]). They do not remain the same in another situation; signs acquire other meanings through new inflections. Simultaneously, the text's polyglossia dramatizes the conflicts inherent in heteroglossia. The references are too numerous and familiar to need citing; however, the linguistic diversity, the different speech genres, the ample use of autochthonous words, of neologisms, of cultisms (Latin and Greek), words of French and English origin, words of African or indigenous origin, stand side by side as a constitutive feature of modernism and the modernness of international brotherhood.

At this point it should perhaps be observed that both prose and poetry evidence the variety of languages and cultures giving expression to the national spirit; in this way modernist discourse reveals its social diversity. From the topographical to the cultural, from the rich use of polyglossia through various languages, the texts reveal the reinforcement of heterology. In this respect I would like to address the inscription of Western mythology and of luxurious commodities as a "creolization" of the semiotic, and an aspect of the competing languages and social struggle. Signs become a space of confrontation, and the "struggle for the sign" reveals the intent to deploy language for self-identity and liberation. More specifically, I would like to suggest that many cultural modernist tropes and themes are "bounded verbal-ideological belief systems," generated in an interaction of languages and cultures experienced as indigenous. Since the sign—and I follow Bakhtin—is overlaid with the traces of its historical usages, it is not uni-accentual and endowed with an eternal or essential meaning; re-accentuated, the sign reveals and produces social positions. Signs are thus relational, existing with distinct contextual overtones, and not ersatz or degraded relations of imitation and reproduction.

Rubén Darío's *Blue* (Azul, 1888), published in Chile—which a century later, in 1989, Nicaraguan poet Ernesto Cardenal called "the beginning of a revolution which is still going on" (in *Nuevo Amanecer Cultural*, 30 July)—stands as a powerful heteroglotic cultural text of Latin American modernity. In seeking to overcome the cultural domination and one-sidedness of Spanish hegemony, it represents the celebration of an-otherness which was the common ground on the creative dynamism of the new validating perspectives. "Blue" was not just a color but a self-validating cultural space; as Gutiérrez Nájera wrote in the Mexican *Revista Azul* (Blue Journal, 1894–96), *azur* is not only Huguesque or Verlanesque but an "ideal of beauty."[3] With *Azul* one could say that a cultural heritage was created; in it the "new world" was reconstituted and then re-introduced into Europe. Darío opened new territories, and one could argue that if Mallarmé's "azur" had actually usurped Baudelaire, in the act of blocking out the successors, European moderns had inscribed the inevitability of their Darío's Latin American usurpation.[4]

Another highly controversial appropriation was the view of sexuality and its various sociograms of decadence, oriented toward a transformation from the hedonistic frivolity conventionally associated with "waste" into a critical exploration of cultural change. First and foremost, the idea of "decadence" was a socially constructed phenomenon, introduced into public consciousness by what we would now call media coverage; politicians and moralists presented it as an index of the breakdown of public morality and of the collapse of religion. It was a social sign which indexed the conflictual status of modernism, and the rejection was accomplished by way of essentialist and moralistic invocation.

The sociogram of decadence, so widespread in the 1890s (legitimized partly also by Darío's *Profane Proses and Other Poems* [1896–1901]), would need some clarification as part of what I have called "creolization" of myths and mythologies, or what Nájera called *mestizaje* or "crossbreeding," which was also an aspect of the anti-colonial cosmopolitanism. Since 1885 Nájera had been quite determined: "The writer travels, the writer is in intimate communication with all ancient civilizations and with the entire modern world" (qtd. in *Indice* 1968:37). Some attacked decadence on moral grounds, and deepened their hostility toward Darío and the "troop of *nuevos*" whose cultural imagining interpreted the new sensibility as a form of "freedom." While modernists— both in Europe and in the Americas—emphasized the progressive anti-bourgeois element in "decadence," the more established intelligentsia delegitimized on moral grounds "decadents" and bohemians. Díaz Dufoo, codirector of the Mexican *Revista Azul,* brought into sharper focus the actual circumstances: he saw decadence and neurosis as a cultural strength against scientificism and rational utility, and he also described it as the decline of modern civilization.

An examination of the work of Casal, Silva, Darío, and Lugones reveals a similar penchant for the same general features; there was a network of related generalizations between these Latin American modernists and their European peers. But in dialogical relation to other material signs, in the social semiotic "situated utterance," the same signs addressed different experiences. The redemptive and "affirmative character" in the Latin American re-accentuation was at heart an act of reclaiming a position of equality in the cultural field against colonial subjugation and a position of cultural dependence. The continuous references to a literature of "our own," or a liberated literature, indicate the discursive relation to power and self-legitimation which traversed the social body.

The dialogical relationship with the European symbolic capital was composed of "intertextual" (or of usurpation, if preferred) rather than mimetic modes of reference. It could even be argued that in the semioses of the modernist Latin American social text, cultural practice projected insurgencies and, simultaneously, ways of intervening in history in order not to remain "silenced." A case in point is the swan myth, to which I have often referred, as well as the Shakespearean Ariel/Caliban, privileged by Rodó, the sociogram of decadence or neurosis favored by Casal, and the erotic transgressions of Silva. *Revista Azul* and the other Mexican periodical, *Modern Journal* (Revista Moderna), disclosed the "creolization" of sociograms and ideologemes, born of the interaction of several cultures, which were experienced as indigenous: a *maroonization* in the Caribbean, and a *tequitqui,* or mixture of styles as discursive formation, in Mexico (adapting Moreno Villa's [1948] term).

This was also the power of *Revista de América,* a venture of Darío, Lugones, and Ricardo Jaimes Freyre in Argentina. These journals challenged the binary colonial division between New World/Old World, especially at the dawn of European (Spanish and French) "civilizing" domination. If colonialism separated races, geographical regions, nations, and cultures, the concern of the moderns was to do without classifications and hierarchies as to the geographical sites of cultural production and "refinement." What colonialism fragmented, modernists decentered in the semiotic struggle for signs. The modernist subject position was one of cultural affirmation. What this modern discourse displayed was the salutary effect of affirming language and signs as a potent symbol of collective identity, against a passive domestication and incorporation as a "colonized" language on a European social stage. Accents, intonations, contextual overtones suggest that in this situated utterance, modernists affirmed their own imaginative geography in an effort to put an end to the boundaries of concrete social exchanges. These signs voice the polemical word in monosemic understandings of language.

It is not surprising, then, that the new validating and situated perspectives of satanism, dandyism, esotericism, mysticism, and eroticism represented distinct social functions as practices to deal with or to mediate social contradictions. They all manifested different subject positions, since what modernity brought about was the general conception of heterology and plurality. The "voyeuristic eye" of the modern, which aestheticized every object, captured the icons of contending cultures (European, but particularly French) to introduce the heteroglotic world of the Americas. The postcolonial slipped from the metropolitan to the national. This cultural sphere of new mythologies included the by now well-known reappropriations of Greek and Latin sources, Nordic myths (e.g., in Jaimes Freyre), intertextual polemics against accepted meanings over myths (Lugones), the celebratory mythic reconciliation of opposites through the tropological dimensions of metaphors and art objects.

These tropologies could be reinterpreted in different forms, drawing from Bakhtin's language-oriented view of social practice, as an effort to understand how capitalism was increasingly able to reproduce itself without use of force. The Bakhtinian social-semiotic suggestions have the advantage of not limiting language and signs to dominant uni-accentual practices, and provide a way of readdressing cultural polyphony away from the passive context of Europeanization, delusion, misrecognition, and alienation. If language is not understood in a reductive Lacanian model, thereby structuring human desire in alienating and unexpected fashion but in the radically new set of problems suggested by Bakhtin, then cultural production is an arena of conflicting interests, and the imaginary a projection to alter conditions. In this context, a reference to Marx's "Asiatic mode of production" could further help clarify their collective capacity. Marx, in *Capital* (vol. III), was inclined to emphasize the progressive role of (Western) capitalism in disrupting Oriental stagnation, through a parallel method. It could be argued that this "Europeanization" was progressive, insofar as it helped to disrupt colonial stasis, on the one hand, and as a form of rejection of North American expansionist capitalism, on the other.

If the aesthetic utopia was a mediating access to the real, then those cultural interrelationships produced in advanced bourgeois capitalist societies became, among the Latin American modernists, anatropic inversions of the "naturalized" representations by which such societies attempted to conceal and deny the constructed development of their social norms and practices. A case in point is Martí's, Gutiérrez Nájera's, and Díaz Dufoo's stress on a nonparochial literature, on a rebellious acceptance of a subaltern perception, a resistance against the prescribed subject positions of colonization in order to reject the imposed boundaries of the "typical," of what became the Hollywood image (e.g., sombreros and tequila). On this view, the demystification was a critical practice launched from a conceptually grounded, decided position.

From a semiotic perspective, these moderns opened the way to our understanding of the discourses on wealth masking the languages of fashion: Julián del Casal's chronicles on the insulting extravagance of the colonial administrators, or his critique of "yanquismo" or utilitarianism. These exposures of the utilitarian had also found a powerful ally in Marx's *Capital* (vol. I), which discloses the monopoly of North American instrumental reason through what he called "Yankeedom." Both colonial and postcolonial modernists unsettled such attempts to stand outside such languages, not only as a reaction to the specific values and beliefs expressed within the dominant discourses, but also as an attempt to find a "third way." Through a deployment of this kind, the critique of modernity aimed at breaking down the terms in which Western European thought disguised itself as universalism, and thought to automatize instrumental reason in its new forms of technology, progress, and morality. What seems most deeply entrenched in these idioms is the encroachment of the new power and technology upon the postcolonial and still-colonial countries, as well as the desire of decolonized communities for an identity.

Let us take some other examples of modernist ethico-political redirecting of signs. The metaphor represented by neurosis as an illness[5] stands as a rearticulation of what Bakhtin calls the romantic grotesque theme of madness (1968:39), which makes the writer look at the world with different eyes—that is, "not dimmed by the 'normal,' " by commonplace ideas and judgments. This grotesque—according to Bakhtin—reveals the somber, tragic aspect of the individual isolation which was familiar to Renaissance folk culture thematized through "madness." Expanding on Bakhtin's romantic grotesque theme, it is possible to suggest at this stage of modernity, after the spreading of psychology through the naturalist novel and the renewed interest in psychiatric knowledges, that the theme of "madness" was transformed into the modern "neurosis"—a neurosis which was also interconnected with the figures of the phantoms of decadence, which haunted French intellectuals in 1814 and 1870, with the invasion of the Prussians (the barbarians) against the Commune. These were the figurations of Paul Bourget, Huysmans, and Verlaine, who wrote in *Langueur:* "Je suis l'Empire à la fin de la décadence, / Qui regarde passer les grands Barbars blancs" (I am the Empire at the end of decadence, / Who sees the fleeting of the big white Barbarians).

The dialogue as a rejoinder with an alien word that was already in the object (see *DI* 279) was the organizing principle of, for example, Díaz Dufoo's, Casal's, or Silva's neurosis or psychopathology theme, quite frequent in their poetry. Given this connection, and in lieu of the heteroglossia implicit in the modernist rearticulation, it was simultaneously linked to the sociogram of prostitution, common in nineteenth-century realist and naturalist discourse and, of course, among the bohemians. This sociogram has lately been analyzed as a "redemptive experience," in a significant foregrounding of Benjamin, who indicated a functional proximity of "woman" and "auratic." Accordingly, the prostituted body represents woman as the allegory of modernity (Rauch 1988), and as such, she is part of "the historical avant garde's program of aesthetic and historical criticism."[6]

Women, fashion, collectibles, *objets de vertu,* the luxurious and exotic articles (silk, gems, perfumes, Chinese *objets d'art*) which underlay Baudelaire's fetishism, for example, had under modernism/modernity an intrinsic value. The world of food and material objects occupied considerable space. We must be reminded of the important role of written and oral advertising and announcements (already present in Rabelais's oral *cris de Paris*), as well as the ample journalistic descriptions of shop windows decorated by way of juxtapositions of dissimilar objects whose character was thus temporarily suspended (on this see Moretti 1988:340).

If journals displayed luxurious objects in relation to production, street vendors still sang the wonders of tobacco or sherries and cognacs, making use of autochthonous music (on turn-of-the-century Puerto Rico, see Díaz 1987). Music became an instrument of urban commerce, and the ear became accustomed to associating sounds, instruments, and music with specific products. Tobacco wrappings and cigar labels, for example, became highly sophisticated *objets d'art,* according to some historians, because tobacco smoking was primarily a women's activity in the Caribbean, and to others because after Sir Walter Raleigh introduced tobacco to fashionable European society, gilt bands and colorful labels served as both advertising and identification to Victorian gentlemen and occasional Victorian gentlewomen.

As collectibles, objects were transformed into the unexpected, which endowed commodities with the auratic. The novelty and "strangeness" and the auratic dimension of luxury images can also be understood if we consider that the colonial society (and I am referring especially to Cuba now) was generations behind in the structure of industry and consumption. This modern world of commodities as a set of aesthetic suggestions was effective beyond literature, for it is also found in the paintings of the modern masters. In Cuba it occurs in the voluptuousness of the paintings of Guillermo Collazo (1850–1896), in the odalisques of José Arturo Morell, Antonio Sánchez Araujo, and Miguel Melero (all now in the National Museum in Havana). And most readers will be familiar with the Spanish modernist painter Julio Romero de Torres and the carnivals and harlequins of José Gutiérrez Solana, or with Gustave Moreau's work.

Everything related to material objects of beauty suited the tastes of consumers; this interaction created a symphony of modern life, in symbolically enlarged images of "houses of pleasure," a kind of libidinal "mythologization" and estrangement of the everyday world. These images were part of the great utopia of pleasure and beauty, and not a mere documentation of life in the realistic or naturalistic mimetic sense. There is a cry of the collector in the portrayal of these images, which are *ambivalent.* Their meaning is undecidable and indeterminate. They may show the other side at any moment—not the voluptuousness or luxuriousness of a fantasized everyday life, but the materialization of the world, its bodily substance. It is along these lines that Martí praised the beauty of modern life in the impressionistic French painting exhibition in New York.

Modern, in Hugo von Hoffmansthal's description in 1893, was the analysis of life and flight from life: "One practices anatomy of the inner life of one's mind, or one's dreams. . . . Modern is the dissection of a mood . . . almost somnambulistic to every revelation of beauty" (in Zavala 1990a). Valle-Inclán believed that modernism was best expressed through synesthesia: "The characteristic of all modern art, and particularly of literature, is the tendency to refine sensations and magnify them in number and intensity" (1902; in Zavala 1974). Casal and other Latin American modernists "creolized," reappropriated, this sense of beauty and its signs in the social semiotic "situated utterance."

To advance my analysis, I will combine Bakhtin's suggested contention of the sign in heteroglossia with a repositioning of Barthes's *Mythologies* (1957) and his semiological perspective on fashion. The modernist discourse I am examining can be understood as a challenge of the symbolic, and as the effect of unmasking the myths of the bourgeois monopolistic instrumental reason whose mythology was the "yanquism" of colonial Cuban society (needless to say, the same "yanquism" must have been evident in both Puerto Rico and the Dominican Republic), dismantled in many ways by modernist chronicles. The "neurosis" theme appeared as a reconceptualization of space itself, in the arena of struggle against the systematization of what Gramsci called "common sense." But "neurosis" was structured as figurative language, and constituted a composite of discourses which expressed a lack of confidence in the power of modern art, scientific advancements, utilitarianism, and logocentrism. Through the rhetorical trope of a contemporary illness, neurosis, the modernists voiced their doubts about the power of art to transform history.

It hardly needs to be demonstrated that these texts insist upon exteriority, symbolic exchanges, since they suggest and emphasize that what was circulating were disseminations of truths or realities as representations, signs to be reexamined at a deeper level; these "realities" included, for example, a fantasy of a luxurious house of pleasure, an Oriental odalisque, a Japanese object or painting, a princess, or a harlequin. (Modernism was gendered, as I have underlined.) The influence of European discourse on such topics and idioms had produced a cultural domination of the sign system accomplished through the modern lyric (particularly Baudelaire), which in turn reproduced in different forms the period of great colonial expansion into the Orient and Africa effected after the 1870s (see Hobsbawm 1987).

This worldliness of myths in Latin America stood as the inevitable "usurpation" of Europe, and a counterdiscourse to the doxographers of North American interventionism writing in the press. The point to be emphasized is that such myths acquired a sort of *structured* irony—modernist irony—of the principles of identity and contradiction. At bottom there is no specific "us" in those images, a modernist strategy which could be defined as "figural" (in Barthes's sense). The eye regrasps the interior scene of space as a consequence of the intimate estrangement from it through the theme of neurosis. It could also be read, this time drawing from Lacan (1977), when he analyzes the eye as organ of desire as well as perception; the eye is imprisoned by the essential qualities of the object, by the willingness to be taken in. As master of the object, the eye is caught in the frame.

The sociogram would suggest an exposure of the corrupt, of the vacuous colonial atmosphere, which is substantial in the prose of most modernists. Simultaneously, this unmasking of colonial life also served against the utilitarian instrumental strength of the North American way of life—what I prefer to call narrative—absorbing everything for its own use both intellectually and materially. The eye projects a totally reversed mythology in the ambiguity of irony, now called *modernist* irony. What these first modernists had in mind—as the legitimation of their own narrative project—was to reposit and reappropriate foreign cultures in order to defeat not only the materialism and mechanism of Anglo-American culture but also a classicist (and classical) Spanish realism turned sour after the wars of independence. The valorization had its own positive ideological project, if we place language at the heart of anti-colonialism. What mattered was not the myths themselves but their usefulness to reinterpret their own modern culture. Thus, like Casal, Gutiérrez Nájera, or Silva, anyone who mastered another culture (and/or language) was a modernist (spiritual) hero.

Such is the underlying motivation in the pages Martí wrote on Casal (1893) praising his elegance and "creole wisdom" (1982:243): "For France is a country where a hidden or confessed awareness of the general humiliation leads everyone as if intimidated or veiled." France serves as an alternative discourse in what Martí categorized as "a country without freedom." The etched crystal of Japanese delicacy, the color of absinthe and roses, the odalisques and serpentine were meant—at least in Martí's understanding—to function as Cellini's images, thus putting "Jupiter upon a saltcellar" (242). Fantasy "in a servile and disfigured nation" (to use his words) represents a form of struggle for the signs in this "situational utterance." The modernist appeal to include the web of contacts, the play of difference which weaves one culture into other, stood against the sameness and a restricted economy of Babel. What one encounters in the creolized sign is a politics of language which rests in both the power within language and the power behind language. The difference is invested with national identity, as subject positions are transmitted through texts and idioms, allowing the readers to identify themselves as members of a community implied by the books.[7]

The struggle for signs within this dialogical encounter is created through a tropological inversion—or anatropic perception—in order to undermine the reader's sense of the "real," thus to problematize a sense of recognition. Hispanic modernist poetics re-accentuates dissociation (distancing, irony, parody, estrangement) to undermine the dependence on colonial identity and mocks the respect for the historical continuity of the colonial bourgeois sense of reality based on fetishized goods. But simultaneously, the images of the Parisian cultural text are deflected into authoritative identity constructs; hence the stress on masks, irony, even parody to dissociate the readers from fixed stereotyped identities, and to disabuse them of the faith in absolute knowledge.

Modernist poetics unfolds the desecrated remains of cultural monuments, the theater of decadent Europe, at the same time that these crushed ideals serve as intermittent and ironic references to decadence and antiquity—what Martí called, in the case of Casal, "Jupiter upon a saltcellar," and what could be considered "the eating of the gods," drawing from Jan Kott in a different direction. Antiquity and mythology are dialogical figurative images employed to deny concrete readers the chance to recognize themselves in the topoi, and to undermine the sense of reality of colonial history. Identities are wholly provisional—in the neurosis and demystifications—and their perpetual change precludes any illusion of psychic continuity.

This whole didactic (and aesthetic utopian) process is neither difficult to understand nor difficult to explain. It could be described as the possibility of cultural texts to weaken the authoritarian dimension of language imposed by a colonial moralistic rhetoric; a way—as Martí captured all too well—to understand the situational utterance outside the bounds of power and the underlying conventions of ex-colonial and colonial social reality, at the dawn of Spanish imperialism and the rise of North American capitalist expansion in the Caribbean.

It is not surprising, then, that the first major works of Latin American modernity were Darío's *Blue* and the *Profane Proses* (together with Martí's prose and poetry, in the reception among Latin Americans themselves). Both texts shocked Spanish audiences, for not only did Darío make the "American" cultural space clear, but he also gave both Latin America and Europe their first substantial taste of the postcolonial modernist point of view. His language communicated an identity constituted not only by another use of the common tongue, but by a store of names, idioms, and memories of precolombian culture in a web of contacts, to figure a different identity. Neither the economy of the sign nor the economy of Babel was restricted; those texts were marked by heteroglossia, conceptualizing another form of social experience. For the first time, Latin America was revealed to Europe in a specific cultural text with its own particular dimension of language and civilization. The colonial experience of, say, the seventeenth century was different (i.e., Sor Juan Inés de la Cruz), since with this postcolonial modernity Latin America acquired a precise intellectual frontier which was no longer (or could be no longer) European.

The history of defeats of imperialist powers since the wars of independence helped dispute cultural authority, as many postcolonial national liberationists articulated identities not only in the means of production, but also in language. They speak from a place they considered their own in contemporary history, where a *différend* talks from its borders. We can say that modernism imagines a localizable, expressive, ethically proper space in which the dialogical cultures are not confined within the colonizers' myths. The repositioning of European "mythologies" was not a textual feature but the effect constituted by discourse on texts, and part of the larger ethico-political debate of anti-colonial nations. The moderns perceived, proclaimed, and invoked a creolized combination of European (not uniquely Spanish) and other cultural spheres, combining them with axiological value in the new dialogical interaction. They brought together their actualities, their spaces, and their ethico-political values into the hegemonic formation, reworking other cultural texts, and showing that the otherness of the colonial subject was precisely an-otherness. Such valorization indicated, however tentatively, the confidence that a culture can narrativize its legitimation. All speech genres grafted these discourses in interaction with subjective consciousness, creating the possibility of a new form of community. Only an optimistic belief in the responsiveness of the future (still so vulnerable) would defeat all forms of colonialism.

It was, in fact, a diversity of narratives against European figurations on cultural and national identities. If in orientalism, according to Said (1979), the influential idea was to construct the Orient as other while establishing coherent European national identities, by contrast, what these modernists had in mind was not a monolithic construction of Europe but the projection of another cultural sphere—the alternative I referred to in the previous chapter. It was not, so to speak, a discourse of power to create, incorporate, and control, but pluridirected discourses against power articulated within a heterogeneous and plurally inscribed discursive terrain. This cultural self-affirmation produced all the negative connotations preserved to the present.

While the "modern sensibility," the myths and mythologies were uni-accentual and endowed with a supracultural character as a European (French) cultural dominant mastery of the sign, this emerging cultural imagining strove to unfold such western European myths for their own liberation, as a shared territory of the utterance, also in ethnic polyphony. It was a way of thinking the present (modernity) otherwise. The way of organizing this intervention consisted in condensing the multiplicity of social accents of heteroglotic cultures. And as products of mestizaje (to use Gutiérrez Nájera's apt term), they represented the multitude of exiles and the polyphonic orchestration of cultural figures and references: from Jupiter upon a "saltcellar," to Momotombo, Tutecotzimi, or Daphne and the swan, to the Mexicanized Dionysus, and from the Castalian spring to the Niagara Falls.

The artistic polyphony of modernism embodied multiracial, pluricultural, and pluri-accented roots, crisscrossed with the intersecting boundary lines of other cultures and languages. Modernism was anything but monoglotic, passive in its relationship to other cultures. Modernist language orchestrated words of indigenous or African and European origins, interweaving with one another in distinctive patterns.[8] In colonial countries where Indian and black peoples had been victims of genocide and cultural domination, this polyphony was also a political statement: a decolonizing culture of resistance. The "struggle for signs" of utterances and myths invested with authority projected an imagining that was not to be subordinate to any authority based on the colonial territories, but to their own experience and life. There were no longer Frances, Spains, or Englands as distant authorities on the true Word (paraphrasing Said 1988 in another direction). It was a form of other-languagedness, travestying discourse, finally dissolving a unitary myth that perceived itself as a totality. Myths and mythologies were no longer the space of the sacred; they were "bounded" and thus voiced a utopian desire for cultural freedom.

As a historical chronotope, the modernist struggle for the sign established a relationship with the future; as a group of Mexican moderns wrote in a document in 1907: "Mummies, to your sepulchres! Open the way! we are going to the future" (in *Indice* 1968:25).

From their emergence, the modern Latin American cultures were what Bakhtin calls "bilingual," that is, a project conceived in not monoglotic but heteroglotic conditions. They functioned particularly against the background of Spanish; from the very first steps the Latin Americans viewed themselves (and their language) in the light of the Spanish word, through the eyes of the Spanish idiom, and theirs was always—as Bakhtin puts it—a word "with a sideways glance" (*DI* 61). This is what he defines as heteroglossia, which frees consciousness from the tyranny of its own language and its own myth of language. The interaction of this "cultural bilingualism" and even a polyglossia of language-cultures turned into what Bakhtin calls the "open Galilean world of many languages, mutually animating each other" (65). And since boundaries between "semi-stylized and semiparodic" discourse are always unstable, as he adds, it could be argued that the modernist needed only to emphasize the conventionality in stylized discourse for it to take the light overtone of parody or irony.

This struggle often took the form of carnivalized parody or of heteroglotic re-accentuations. What Martí called "creolization" could be read as the Bakhtinian word with the sideways glance. As an idiom, "creolization" lucidly suggests the dialogicality of the modern discursive formation against the Ptolemaic sealed-off world which understood the semiotic as uni-accentual and monoglotic. There are constant references to language use, reaffirming the vernacular (these comments abound in the Mexican *Revista Azul* and in Darío, among others) against the confining Castilian grammatical rules. The vernaculars put up an ideological fight; anyone familiar with the prejudices against Black English and the question of language for postcolonialism will be sensitive to this linguistic struggle. Darío's *Azul*, for example, was mockingly abused in the Spanish press for its grammatical "irregularities"; and it is a known fact that the authoritative voice of the novelist Clarín was raised against the Nicaraguan poet for his ignorance of "Spanish grammar."

As a whole, the modernist struggle for the sign was multigeneric, multistyled, multilingual, reflecting in its fullness the heteroglossia and plurality of voices of multiple cultures, peoples, and epochs. Texts reinforced heterochrony and heterology in mixtures of prose and poetry, of everyday living speech and highly elitist cultism, multiplicity of rhymes and meter, figural language coming from cultural texts which might be using the same language—Spanish—but were accentuated with different intonations, idioms, myths, from Tierra del Fuego to

Santo Domingo. It was, to paraphrase Bakhtin (*DI* 60), a mirror of constantly evolving heteroglossia, in which any direct word, and especially that of the dominant discourse(s), was more or less bounded, typical and characteristic of an era, aging, dying, ripe for change and renewal. The modernist's speech genres liberated the object from the power of language; they destroyed the homogenizing power of myth over language; they freed culture from colonialism, and from the walls that had imprisoned a cultural imagining open to the future, in a polyglot literary consciousness.

In this sense, as a project, it was also a modern decolonized hermeneutics, what Paul Ricoeur calls "hermeneutics with a double edge and a double function." First, in its struggle to creolize the signs, it was a struggle against idols, and therefore somewhat destructive; but simultaneously, it produced a critique of ideologies, and a critique of escape into other worlds to safeguard authority, and brought about a struggle against fables as well as a rejection of bland moralities. It was a hermeneutics aimed at disalienation and demystification; modernists make vivid to us the genealogical histories and long use of the "decadent," the "pervert," the gallicized modernist as some people's weapon against others, and the coercive power of the "modernist" or "modernism" as a negative differentiation.

Dionysus and Eros

Closely connected with modernist hermeneutics was the intent to decolonize culture and rid modernity of the North American utilitarian and marketplace functionality which was afflicting both postcolonial and colonial societies, and could easily be transformed into a new colonialist dependency. New imaginary positions were projected against a new bourgeoisie directly identified with North American capitalism; Casal's journalist chronicles in colonial Cuba are an example. Discourse evokes a space wherein ethical values and critiques could neutralize (if not abolish) forms of mimetic reproduction, empowering collective traditions as forms for generating negative associations against a dangerous complacency.

The oppositional stand against capitalist society was connoted through concrete framings of the North American capitalist ethos in the forms of direct or half-hidden and completely hidden varying degrees of alienation or assimilation of another's quoted word. The role of the other's word was part of the drive toward identity, and the boundary lines between someone else's speech and their own were quite flexible. These boundaries moved from the construction of texts as mosaics out of the texts of others, to the double entendre of irony and parody. This hermeneutics shed light on the character of the literary enterprise, and it helped to emphasize some thematic traces of Nietzsche as an important subtext woven throughout modernism in the exorcism of the angelic impulses—although, in general, the adherence to the existing system of good and evil is evidence of an admitted belief in (Catholic) God. What was demystified was what Nietzsche called "the lie of the moral world order" (*The Antichrist* 26). Tracing Nietzsche through this modern literature would reveal the differences of certain tropes, and the "creative misreadings."[9] On the surface, what I am examining is the atmosphere of the Dionysiac—both as a trope and in its carnivalization (as we have already seen).

However different the styles or the speech genres, the modernists obsessively retell a story of intending to rewrite the signs from the margins, and in every respect Dionysus and Eros are linked with duplicity, with the enigma of fatality, what Nietzsche called the *Doppelgänger* (*EH* 255), or being at the same time the decadent from the old world and the beginning of a new one. Retranslated, it was also the "Enigma," and often a liberation from the spirit of gravity and seriousness as well; the Dionysian joy appears also in the form of lightheartedness, gaiety, as in Darío's *Profane Proses and Other Poems,* for example. The semantic concentration on concealment, on masks, so related to the carnivalesque, in which the person disappears and finds his or her *Doppelgänger,* is not only the "other" personality but also the "other" of language. This mask of language—what Voloshinov/Bakhtin called the "unofficial consciousness, or the underground"—brings forth internal speech. It indicates the ambivalence, but it simultaneously denies identity and embraces alterity.[10] Such Dionysian powers of regeneration were thought to be capable of exploiting the nihilistic indifference of the modern age, and this is (following Habermas 1990) what differentiates them from the romantics, who wanted to rejuvenate modern society.

The whole thematic spectrum of the sociogram of sexuality, for example, indicates a fictive projection of moral worlds and the obscurantism of the old systems of perception, the blind struggle for existence, a relentless competition, deceitful repression. It is, so to speak, a treading on the edge of a new morality, one which is not yet formed. The questions at issue were connected with instrumental reason, which was shaping an entire universe of discourse and culture; however, the Dionysian was also meant to undermine the stability of domination through subjectivity, which since Herbert Marcuse's *Eros and Civilization* (1951) one can associate with the utopian horizon.[11]

The semantic energies which Benjamin located in auratic art were considered autonomous, since in still-nondeveloped bourgeois societies, autonomy and use could be reconciled; in fact, some were postcolonial, others still colonial, so they conjoined as a culture of resistance. If desire is social, here it was defined by what it excluded, which was thrown into the symbolic circulation, in an inclusion of sexuality in social life through provocative signs.

Sexuality referred to a localized domain of erotic practices surrounded by clear-cut prohibitions, and the dominant moral discourse on sexuality referred to these practices as abnormalities or perversions. What the modernist captured was a society in which sexuality spoke through fashion, social life, nightlife in cabarets, the emergent media, visual arts, and other forms of discourse, in an open and manifest way throughout social life. Modernists expressed a textual sexuality no longer private and hidden or repressed, tending to encourage rather than limit sexual activity. It was posed as what we could call today a *social construct,* as the product and effect of dominant discourses. As a modern project, it was also part of the dominant goal for liberated labor as a form of desire and satisfaction. It projected, theoretically, a symbolic exchange, since for religion in traditional societies, sexuality is worldly and evil, and for bourgeois morality, it is a private activity. However, most modernists experienced the erotic dimension as the knowledge of that which transcends life and yet is unattainable. Like "neurosis," eroticism is structured as a figural composite of discourses which express lack of confidence in the intersubjective and in logocentrism. Through the rhetorical trope of sexuality, the modernist voiced doubts in transcendence or the metaphysical.

Cultural anthropology has disclosed that the body is mediated and socialized, and that its individual representation has been used as a universal metaphor for the social body. That is precisely the powerful argument which arises from the Bakhtinian chronotope of the carnivalesque. Modernists were, so to speak, sexual liberationists championing the freedom of desire from its social constraints, however masculinist and misogynist most texts are. Urbanism, cosmopolitanism, the allurement of objects, the "neurosis" trope, the confusion between time and space—in Benjamin's sense (1977)—were all semiotic phantasmagorias of representations, aesthetic commodities, hieroglyphs of the present. As an allegory of the present they operated as the dynamism of European conventions in another socially produced category to generate cultural capital, inviting an intellectual (and emotional-volitive) political reappropriation. The meanings were not given in each individual text but were constructed in the dialogy between texts, in which and by which the texts were capable of exercising a critical function.

But eroticism, or the erotic, as life force was not the most original venture of the modernist revolution. It was essential in the formulation of a particular kind of space and nature (the one Martí so clearly described in 1882), and in all its willful incoherence, it did embody a revolutionary potential in its stimulation to consciousness and within the general understanding of a heteroglot cultural modernity.

The identification of these modernisms with a European (and Anglo-American) modernism in what was supposed to be an institutionalized commerce with art would suggest, again, a false universal. Nor could it be compared with the ambiguous status of art in metropolitan bourgeois society, since modernisms form shifting configurations of symbolic practices whose political validation changes with each context and situation. As situated utterances, modernisms cannot be treated as unitary languages, but as complex crisscrossings of ideological contestation. In the Latin American modernity I have been discussing, there did not seem to be a voiced skepticism or doubt that poetic language can be a medium for discussing norms, values, or even anti-colonial resistance.

The link between colonialism and language is part of the program for self-determination and identity. In fact, the convergence between capitalism and the printed word set the stage for the modern nation (as Anderson [1983] has argued). Poetic language was the medium to project the possibility of new forms of imagined collectivities; it was, so to speak, a poetry of the present. The insistence on the present—its actuality, as I have suggested throughout—was not only a new beginning but also the inheritance of the past, which simultaneously expressed a denial of cultural hegemonies which tended to make parochial the colonial past cultures and also the very present. The struggle for the sign was also aimed at returning the historical subject (or human agent) to its temporality, since it necessarily set differences into play. In fact, it punctuated the hope for the breakdown of cultural imperialism, and the process was conceived negatively. This discursive development had cognitive consequences as it instantiated the ethico-political debate. The appropriation I have suggested is best described by Ricoeur: "Appropriation is the process by which the revelation of new modes of being . . . *gives* the subject new capacities for knowing himself" (1980:192).[12]

Connected to a legitimating discourse, Latin American modernism was not a textual feature but a contested space. If, as *Marxism and the Philosophy of Language* states, manifestations of ideological creativity cannot be entirely segregated from the elements of speech, within each "situated utterance" modernist practice was but "the positions of various subjects, expressed in a word" (*PDP* 151). The problem this social semiotic theory suggests is one not only of varieties of modernism, but of how texts are connected to voices of resistance, and to imaginaries which question practices of subordination exercised by dominant privileged categories, and the view that any dominant discourse univocally appropriates all dissenting positions. By beginning to account for resistance in the set of turn-of-the-century social relations, these modernists put forward a dialogics of cultures open to the future. They marked both difference and otherness as multiplicity, and a cultural production generated by a plurality of writing and reading positions determined by a confrontation with antagonistic articulatory practices which represented the negation of the subjectivity of the collective.

As a cultural practice, it initiated a questioning of how races, cultures, and groups are subordinated. But it also enables us to understand the dialogicality of upheavals and polemical productivity, which relativizes meaning, giving signs new contents while retaining old meanings. In the wealth of its speech genres, this "situated" modernism was inseparable from social and ideological struggle. In the variety of its parodic form, the ambivalence of the carnivalesque I have been pursuing is then the conjoining of two sign systems, in which the hidden internal of discourse with "the sideways glance" constituted a symbolic rebellion of oppositional cultures. The stylizing established a distance which created the ambiguity, and by this very act it produced a relativized re-accentuation of the fantastic, of phantasmagoria, and the mystical symbolism and the macabre naturalism, with the pathological (e.g., neurosis) states of the soul. These elements, if we follow Bakhtin, had more structural than thematic significance and often appeared as explorations of language and writing. Within the "situated utterance," these signs acted as cultural idioms with redeeming content.

Analyzed in this direction, the gallicized tropes and the Parisian fantasized world of half-imagined pleasures were neither mimetic reproductions (as monolithic notions of discourse would enunciate) nor forms of ideological alienation (as abstract models of semiotics would imply). Bakhtin's semiotic view of social practice helps bring forth the political struggle deployed by language, and suggests how segments experience or live signs diversely, and shape their own meanings staging the conflicts of languages and discourses. In this context, the signs we have pursued became evident as systematized projections to unsettle the cultural, material, and intellectual relations within a history of a heretofore unchallenged Spanish dominance. Furthermore, through this modernity, Latin America was revealed to Europe in the autonomous materiality of its cultural texts, in its intonations and civilizations. Likewise, in this struggle for the sign, Latin America acquired a definite intellectual and historical dimension with which to contest the ideological myths of an enlightened administration with its "civilizing" missions. As such, these texts were capable of exercising a critical function.

The creolization I have suggested oriented language and power, bringing the discursive dimension to collective identity. Reformulated in this dialogical interrelation, the modernist poetics of negation was directed against centered and centralizing histories and cultures, exploring forces of heterogeneity, polemic, fragmentation, and difference to project a decolonized and national culture. The clash between self-validation and contestation of colonial cultural capital is the "inner speech" of the generic forms themselves. Furthermore, they refract relevant conflicts of interpretation against the inner wall of colonial cultural traditions which restrict the scope of every experience. Viewed against this background of contesting signs, Díaz Dufoo's epigraph at the beginning of this chapter can be understood as an objective assessment.

The struggle for the sign I have outlined suggests that if literature as a practice acts upon language and enters into a dialogical relation with language practices, those heteroglotic relations shape the social relations of the "situated utterance." And within the new situational context, they separate from those previous contexts to validate themselves, since the sign is in itself social and, as such, contending. The deeper understanding of this decolonizing process in the struggle for the sign could be stated as follows:

> A living human being cannot be turned into the voiceless object of some second-hand, finalizing cognitive process. . . . In a free act of self-consciousness and discourse, [there is] something that does not submit to an externalizing second-hand definition. (*PDP* 49)

Such movement (which Todorov called *exotopy* [1984]) indicates that the signs as constructs also enter a polemic against cultural privileges.

V

THE DIALOGICAL CULTURAL SIGNS

> The barbarians, France! The barbarians, dear Lutece!
>
> —Darío (1893)

> If there is politics in these songs, it is because it is universal. . . . Tomorrow we may be yanquis (and it is most probable); in any case, my protest remains written on the wings of the immaculate swans, as illustrious as Jupiter.
>
> —Darío, *Songs of Life and Hope* (1905)

The Idea of Difference

Modernism could be distinguished by its plurality, separation, and distinction, a change from the unity imposed by the foundations of colonialism(s). Its struggle was both a refusal (often heroic) to remain enclosed in imposed identities and an affirmation of a nonreducible difference. It should be remembered, however, that while modernists were united by this affirmation of difference in their questioning of power and domination, that difference did not count in the same way. Their common hegemonic position cannot be limited to the oppositional term of a poetics of negation—negation understood in its dialogicality, and not in the poststructuralist avant-gardist materialization of heterogeneous subject positions; rather, this commitment was traversed by the assertion of national identity as resistance and emancipation.[1] Their poetics of negation was both a counterdiscourse and a practical and symbolic resistance to imperialism and colonialism.

Culture was part of the site of the problem moderns signified through references to the subject. They were elaborating a cultural practice connected at this juncture to emotional loyalties, to moral sentiments and knowledges. It was a symbolic identification worked out within language and idioms, by the accentuations of shared terms projecting the self as sign.

This self-identity was woven from a multiplicity of heteroglossic speech subject positions, irreducible to any univocal principle. The textual release of difference excludes reductive readings, and the preliminary reflections on the word *modernism* exclude the possibility that it may have some clear and monologic signification. When Darío used it for the first time in 1888, it denoted a style which disrupted the solidity and stability of received meanings, and by 1899 social circumstances made him expand the definition:

> The social modern soil is a breeze that comes from the outside and enters the window. . . . For better or for worse, because of our cosmopolitanism, and, let's say it, because of the audacity we have preserved, American thought has been able to reach a transformation, which has produced among a lot of weed, fine gold, and the way is open. (In Zavala, ed. 1989:13)

In his prologue to *Profane Proses and Other Poems* (1896–1901), modernism is polemically described as the "collective work of the new ones in America" whose work is still vain, since many have not yet realized what the new anarchist art is all about. Yet, what will become the family of concepts is there. In 1907, in his extensive "dilucidations" to *The Wandering Song*, he definitively calls it a "movement of liberty." In his words, "It [modernism] is not, as some academics and journalists suspect, the transference of a rhetoric. . . . No. It is, above all, a question of ideas" (1907; in Zavala, ed. 1989:57).

The same word emerged attached to different connotations, different emotional and affective values. It had both a vague descriptive meaning and a rich emotive meaning subject to constant redefinition. Its persuasive force, however, was meant to designate a genealogical restoration of the past, as well as a deconstruction of colonial and imperialistic dependence—deconstruction understood here as a practice in relation to dominance. Since the modernists placed great emphasis on the relationship established by language (therefore by form) between speaking subjects, in this sense, modernism is at once an analysis, a critique, and an "event" of individual and collective subjects directed to a "third" toward the responsiveness of the future. It is not only an *alternate* culture but a historical *alternative* writing its own cartography of liberation, and rewriting itself.

Cuba, Puerto Rico, and the Philippines in 1898 constitute the "event"—in the Bakhtinian sense—of the coincidence of location and time of what is now part of a history of anti-colonial resistance, even though in Puerto Rico that emancipatory narrative has been deferred. But after 1898, nothing was ever the same, and the "event" was inscribed by the dialogical interrogation open to the future, as its hidden agenda. The dialogical here entails three dimensions: an overview of texts, a description of texts, and a function within texts (Zavala 1989a). In its modern inscription, it is a perspective from which to think through a concrete, immediate social and historical problem; as a spatial metaphor, it provides an adequate understanding of the speaker's situation which will inform a practice. As a model of responsive communication, it enters the past, but it does not suggest repetition, as each new attempt at understanding creates a new "given," and a response in the "created."

In evoking specific modernist themes and the common reference system in turn-of-the-century cultural discourse from a Bakhtinian approach, we have underlined the latent utopias, and signaled the social and political interanimation. The modernist dialogizes ready-made materials in anti-imperialist fantasies, and often, by appropriating existing discourses, through anatropic inversions, deploys the force of the dominant against domination. The strength of parody and carnivalization rises to the surface in different signs and in a wealth of intonations at the juncture of the cultural polyphony against the American invasion. Idioms take on accent and ethnicity as some words are carriers of the deep currents of culture. What Bakhtin calls the "differentiated unit of the epoch's entire culture," its dialogism operates within all cultural production and incarnates in specific idioms that constitute the symbolic rebellion. From the festive to the parodical grotesque, signs promote a critical relation.

In this juncture, Valle-Inclán was concerned with the "yankees" in 1895, an idiom associated with the new organization of power spread throughout society. The idiom became part of the "common sense" of the age, and spontaneous conception against North Americans, and was used often with parodical intention by most modernists. Silva, for example, in his novel *After-dinner Conversation* (De Sobremesa, published in 1928 but written around 1896), depicts North Americans as "athletic and blood-colored yankis" who infect the air with Virginia cigarette smoke and kill themselves with whiskey. American pragmatism was also seen as a menace to nature, while others, as we have seen, ridiculed and parodied the "good for business" expansionism.

Darío takes over the symbolic center of social life in an actualization (creolization) of ancient myths to modify the represented plane in the swan series—totally embedded with this "event." The series *Los Cisnes* uncovers an orchestration of denotative texts which actualize their meaning by the sign of the swan, with its dialogical construction of an initial apostrophe, and a prosopopeic closure, thus giving face to the mythical bird. By a compact network of formal analogies and semantic similarities, the swan interweaves a variety of thematic constructs. Through memory mechanisms, Darío organizes his emotional world and encodes the swan with a chain of correspondences and associations. The mythological bird is symbol of the poetic voice, of inspiration, of the forces of history, and it also becomes (in the last poem of the series, no. IV) an allegory of writing. The affinities with Baudelaire, Mallarmé, and Yeats only actualize the differences. The overcoded and monumentalized myth acquires a new semantic series of diverse meaning, which portrays the social function of the lyrical experience.

Darío splits the sign/swan into two phases in the first poem of *Songs of Life and Hope,* as an overture of the situated event, which takes shape in a specific historical discourse, and a socialized form of collective communication, therefore inseparable from the social purview and the social audience. Darío's swan poem leads to an allegory of history; the poetic closure is a figurative dialogue between the two swans, giving hope in the midst of chaos:

> And a Black swan said: "Night preludes day."
> And a White one: "Aurora is immortal! Aurora
> is immortal!" Oh lands of sun and harmony,
> Pandora's box still holds Hope! (263)

The reader will recognize an ideological opposition in the two swans in a network of intertextual patterns: from antiquity (Horace's Black Swan, the Platonic Swan/Poet) to the poet's present. The textual production attempts to produce a fictionalized event with an apostrophic dramatization. Darío's modernist worldview gave rise to a speech genre which favored the selection of hypothetical constructions expressing uncertainty and provisionality in the semantic field; the dialogical response is still open (see my detailed analysis in Zavala 1987:131–46).

The poem's modernist textual production is revealed through the medium of a dynamic signifier which dialogically clearly points, in the imaginary plane, to a specific identification with the defeated (Spain, Cuba, Puerto Rico), at the same time that it provokes an estrangement from the invader. Darío projects a liberatory message, as he clearly promotes a collective overthrow, and invites his audience to transform history. The problem which the concrete social speaker—the lyrical voice—faces in his/her social imaginary is to elaborate on the artistic and political potential of the social imagining. Darío answers the challenge in terms of a collective ethico-political possible future construction of social life. In redirecting the sign of the swan, he calls upon a realization of history outside the imperialist frame. History is not derealized or made ethereal; it could be said that the emancipatory narrative triumphs, as he reconciles subjectivity, solidarity, and autonomy.

In Darío the textual praxis of the speaking subject is at the level of the symbolic (in the overcodified swan motif), transformed in the metaphor, its displacement, and the metonymy/condensation. The ideological interpellation is made through the process Laclau describes as "condensed connotation"; the internal logic is that of simultaneous identification and estrangement in the subjective/collective imaginary, a concrete syntax of history particularly sensitive to the double ideological representation of the imaginary in the collective and in the psyche. Both merge and energize each other within the general logics of the dialogical social imaginary, within the systems of reproduction and representation and their interchanges. This is not a vague, nebulous zone of the social but its concrete form: the symbolic assassination of the invaders, which articulates historically the social formation of modernism.

Across a dialogical threshold, the swan is the symbol of modernism, the "other" of Caliban, much like the allegory of Rodó's *Ariel*. The passages of Darío's poem just quoted cross the dialogical borderline between negation and affirmation; the sign of the swan is the reposition of the symbol and the proposition of its truth. The symbol is not only creolized but internalized and collectivized, whereas the myth of Psyche in other poems becomes the sign of signification. The birdlike form of the sign mirrors parabolically the forms of classical beauty and allegory of the future which, like the Sphinx, speaks in hieroglyphs, and as such is polysemic and enigmatic. Darío dramatizes this epoch by putting the symbol into a new position concerning the future deciphering and answering of the enigma: thus the sign becomes the sign of answerability.

The architecture of the poem is the material and the form of answerability, by which its parts are conceptually joined, through an act of perception, opening questions of epistemology, ethics, and aesthetics. The poem materializes the problem of what Bakhtin calls "great time," in which every meaning will have its "festival" (SG 170, AA 1990). The dialogue and the meanings of the past are renewed; the past individual meaning stored in the underground reservoir of the symbolic is re-accentuated by the public/collective meaning manifest in discourse. The enigma invokes the symbolic resistance of the creative imagination.

The poem (and the whole series of swan poems) reconstructs the fabric of the semiotic in potential semantic energy; history is not conceived here as passive but as an activity, an "event," for Darío articulates an ethics of responsibility. These are the dimensions of his reactualized Psyche myth as well, also charged with difference and answerability. Both myths were re-created in his modernist discourse to grasp the changing scenario in its contingency. Bakhtin's emphasis on the unfinalized against a normalizing stasis suggests that what is created "always has some relation to value." "What is given," he adds, "is completely transformed in the created" (SG 120). The multiplicity of chronotopes found in the single re-accentuation of mythology helps us illustrate how time, space, and value are inseparable. In fact, these swan poems raise the question of how much a sign can change and still look like the same thing. It exemplifies once more, in a way, what Barthes calls a writerly reading.

The Event: Shared Opinions of Difference

> [A] democratic yanquism, atheist of all ideal
> . . . invades the world.
>
> —Paul Groussac (1898)

We have seen that around the last decade of the nineteenth century, the communicative role of literature and its systems of meaning were promoting a disclosure of relations of force, and thus were intertwined with a political emancipatory struggle. Modernity emerged as the organizing notion or coherent vision linking different discourses and challenging conventional ways of characterizing selfhood, as well as provided a critique of false wholeness. These intersecting discourses were "productively activated" (in T. Bennett's term [1983]) by concrete readers who drew from the subterranean dimension to re-create their own utopia. As a hegemonic form of discourse, modernism shared with the political avant-garde a terrain of ethico-political values on subjectivity, identity, and self. Darío's pluridirected reactivated mythologies—not only the swan but also Psyche, the centaurs, the minotaur—demand a high degree of critique of the social world, and they all disclose not only instrumental reason but imperialism in the form of territorial invasion. However, as we have under-lined, his judgment was fundamentally moral and operative through the cultural and linguistic codes of a common symbolic geography.

Modernist projection of an emancipatory identity was firmly grounded on a pervasive anti-yanquism, in utopian constructions projecting the "third way" I have suggested: neither North American nor passive Europeanism. These en-thymemic projections had been dominant in the 1880s; however, Darío's swan series and Rodó's *Ariel* (1900) can also be identified with another stance of the modernist project and its aporias.[2] Rodó's "pedagogical fiction" (González Echevarría 1985) *Ariel,* framed around the institutional pedagogical and rhe-torical structures, discloses the indeterminate and unstable paradoxical dou-bling of some modernists. This text potentiates the economy of duplicity, and could be better understood by the *mise en abîme* of representation known to deconstruction. This becomes apparent in the book's structure, which mirrors itself; the receding mirrors of the introduction reflect the last paragraphs of the spaced last chapters where the same introduction reappears. Therefore, the reflecting representation folds back upon itself by reproducing itself in circular correspondence, thus tautologically including itself, and translating itself into its own totality.

The structure is directing an inverted duplicity of difference (as understood in Derrida's "Living On: Border Lines"), and represents tropologically what Marx calls "commodity exchange." The appeal to heterogeneity and otherness—thematized by the opposition Ariel/Caliban—becomes a duplicating model of a spiritual humanistic dimension which would later be undermined by its vio-lence. At the turn of the century this spiritual humanistic dimension, often invoked by modernists, had not yet been weakened; the opposition to instru-mental reason and to the violence of authoritarian technology and modern North American imperialism was disputed through the impetus of humanist claims.

The text is a dialogical meditation on meanings and values set off against subordination; Rodó's classroom panopticon can be placed in a general theory that concerns the relationship between knowledge and power. What Foucault calls "the tyranny of vision" is, in a way, represented here as a technology of the individual in the internalization of power, through the rise of empirical sciences (new pedagogy). This organization of power spreads throughout society associ-ated with the faculty of vision (also visionary), and is materialized in the text through the institutions within which the text was produced. Rodó's text

identifies the discursive condition for the emergence of collective action, articulating a democratic transformation of social relations in a field crisscrossed
with amalgamated struggles and conflictuality.

In a revealing letter written in 1897 to Venezuelan Rufino Blanco-Fombona,
Rodó writes:

> I will always profess the *Americanist* theme that I wrote once and you liked so
> much; but we differ in that your Americanism seems to me rather belligerent, a
> little intolerant; and I try to reconcile the love of our America with that of the old
> nations to which I look with a filial sentiment. (My translation; in Rodó
> 1967:78)

This is precisely the enthymemic potential of *Ariel*.

The basic underlining of the text is a "paragram" (in the sense given to this
term by Kristeva [1969:140]), by which the author continually reflects on his/
her own scriptural praxis. The paragram emphasizes the idea that language is
doubly constituted. Rodó's paragrammatic text displays an ideological fantasy
founded on the privileged status of "European." The pedagogical paragrammatic fiction incorporates an emergent modernist discourse into a figurative
system to expose the limits of scientific and theoretical instrumental reason
(North America) and offer an alternate discourse based on "classical Western
culture" against the rationalization of labor.

Rodó's *Ariel* is inscribed with technology and resists those totalizing systems
which dominate nature; its dialogical polemic is against authoritarian conceptions of technology and an instrumentalist thought empowered as utilitarian
metaphysics. Nature—spiritual/material (Ariel, Psyche/Caliban)—is a trope to
indicate the impossibility of choosing between a totalizing reason and the
referential abyss of the material world. The trope also works in allegories; as
nature became utilitarian after scientific technologies undermined its utopian
significance, it negatively redoubled and displaced its difference. As a trope,
nature has no specific extratextual referent; it stands as sign of an aporetic event
between two referential poles.

Literary discourse is the arena and battleground for social hegemonic control
of meaning in the symbolic exchange. Modernist "literariness" (referred to by
Yurkievich 1976; Foster 1983) is an ideological sign which indicates both the
intention to create a national language and a mediation which redirects the
reception of individual texts, thus reappropriating the core concepts and
propositions in a hegemonic understanding which could support the constitution of the subject in its Latin American identity. The legitimation of a cultural
language is also projected onto the dimension of the unification of symbolic
exchange of goods which accompanies the fusion of economy, cultural production, and circulation (on this see Bourdieu 1982). The "third way" of the
modernist project takes, after 1898, a specific internal reference system in order
to activate productively the Christian and Latin past to reveal the material
interests of the North. In the economic exchange, the social imaginary redirects

a symbolic negation of hegemony and domination. As a performative, it productively engages the present for a future effect. All the core concepts of modernity conjoin, and mutually define and modify each other, and sustain a historically modernizing ideology. It is articulated into an organic ideology, historically effective as it hopes to construct a configuration of differences into a unity. It is a contingent and open-ended text indicating the pluralization of modern cultural identities.

This revitalized collective memory is submitted to allegorical seductive power as a critique opposing instrumentalization. Metaphors, metonymies, anthropomorphisms are poetically and rhetorically redirected to expose and contest instrumental reason in the self-image of North American imperialism. It is a version of deconstructionist thinking, by which science and logic are denied epistemological privilege and are understood as self-deluding forms of discourse on account of their totalizing truth claims. Rhetoric and innovative language—the allegorical—are polemical tools to unmask the instrumental mastery of modern techniques of domination of the self behind the facade of universality.

I would like to go back to the line of thought that links a modernist negative poetics and dialogicality in discursive practice through openness, diversity, and generic indeterminacies as counterdiscourse of symbolic resistance. Through such negation we will recapture the aesthetic critique of modernity. The generic indeterminacy and unstable boundaries of *Ariel*—well recognized by critics from different positions—which recently have been linked to the Socratic dialogue (González Echevarría 1985), deserve further attention. We shall return to Bakhtin's suggestions on carnivalized literature (*PDP* 1984), and to how the "carnival sense of the world" and its joyful relativity weaken the one-sided rhetorical seriousness, rationality, singular meaning, and dogmatism. This carnival sense of the world in (Hispanic) modernism has transforming power (107–108), and the characteristics suggested as radical changes in the time and value zone are:

- the living present is the starting point from which to understand, evaluate, and shape reality
- heroes of myth and historical figures of the past are deliberately and emphatically contemporized
- heroes of the past speak in a zone of familiar contact with the open-ended present
- the genres do not rely on the legendary and do not sanctify themselves through it; they rely on "experience" and on free invention
- a deliberately multistyled and heterovoiced utterance is developed; single-styled discourse is rejected

Inserted genres, retold dialogues, parodies, reinterpreted citations, a mixture of prosaic and poetic forms of speech, authorial—personal—masks serve to create a double-voiced discourse. Bakhtin's suggestions will provide an attempt to articulate the Menippean lineage of *Ariel*. Of definitive significance has been the written tradition, Bakhtin stresses—the Socratic dialogue and the chronotope of the Menippean satire (in *PDP*). Rodó undertakes the oral Socratic stage, which, as a memoir genre, consists of reminiscences of actual conversations and transcriptions of remembered conversations framed by a brief story; he also retains the method of dialogically revealing the truth and the external form framed by a story. The dialogical means of a search for truth is counterposed by a monologism which pretends to possess a ready-made truth, and the naive self-confidence it indicates. Truth is not individual but is born among people collectively searching for it: the "young" pupils who listen to Prospero's multivoiced dialogicality, through the basic devices of *syncrisis* and *anacrisis,* oppose polemically "the aspiration of the United States to a hegemony of contemporary civilization" (Rodó 1967:201), with the "Arielization" (his neologism) of the future.

In this complex text, Kantian ideas on beauty and the transcendental subject (probably through Schiller), as well as Schiller's aesthetic utopia criticizing the "system of egoism" of bourgeois society (the utilitarian materialism of the North to Rodó), are the supporting double voice of the textual. Its dialogical structure indicates that there is an explicit and implicit juxtaposition of various points of view on nature, culture, aesthetics which the mastery of anacrisis meant to expose, as the falseness of preconceived opinions.

In Rodó's *Ariel* the network of voices is the purely ideological event of seeking and testing truth, and Prospero is equivalent to the Socratic *ideologist* (*PDP* 111) standing on the threshold to test an idea. It also combines the Menippean freedom of plot and its invention and use of the fantastic devoted to the ideational and philosophic end (114–15). In this sense, the classical allegory privileged by Shakespeare (already a deconstructivist trope to the French Argentinian Paul Groussac and to Darío) is used by Rodó as a means of provoking and challenging truth: it engages in a dialogue with the Menippean content, which is a series of adventures of an idea or a truth in the world.

The North American intervention in the Caribbean is the "tempest" which dramatizes the new/modern usurpation of power of the savage and the deformed "slave" of instrumental reason. It draws from Shakespeare in its spatially delimited usage, in a location of its own. The Menippean chronotope is combined with a specific evaluation, as judged from a particular point of view. In fact, the text is structured in heterochrony which brings together, as simultaneous and inseparable, an ethico-political value. From a late-twentieth-century perspective, his set of oppositions—Ariel/Caliban—has been found ill defined because Rodó accepts them uncritically.

If, in general, the Menippean chronotope combines the free fantastic, the symbolic, and even the mystical-religious element (and also slum naturalism, which is absent in Rodó), the turn-of-the-century modernist organized these voices to posit the ultimate question about Latin America's destiny. The implied threefold character in *Ariel*—Olympus and the nether gross world—allows the confidence of a critical philosophy of history. Just as the materialistic, utilitarian spirit becomes autonomous within the sphere of North American society, so does the speculative spirit in the realm of the mind (the ideal). Ariel exposes enlightened subjects to a twofold compulsion: nature and moral freedom. Ariel's "spirit of reason" calls for the need of unification other than the merely positivistic and authoritarian fixed by relations of force.

He will invoke an array of genealogies—Renan, Carlyle, Martí, Shakespeare, Schiller, Spencer (in a negative way)—to posit a radically new set of problems: those concerning culture as an arena in which conflicting interests are represented and fought for. However, Rodó's discourse is a condensation of all humanistic logocentric drifts toward origins and self-present truth, invoking a higher reality of essences; the concept of truth as *aletheia,* or inward unveiling. It is, if we follow Derrida's deconstruction of Plato in "The Double Session," the unique authority of Socrates' teaching, whose word enables this truth to take hold in the minds of his genuine disciples. *Ariel* instruction has a range of lessons to impart on writing (and I follow *Dissemination* [1981] on this point): the authority of the book, the decidability of truth, and the equation of truth with a genuine *mimesis.*

One can recognize the allegorized Americanization of the spirit of modernity and its ethical totality, inspired by a poetically grounded democracy. The program recalls Kant's ideas about aesthetics, as incorporated by Schiller, Schelling, and Hegel, in particular about an "aesthetic education of mankind" (paraphrasing Schiller's text of 1794). If subjectivism is the spirit of modernity, confirmed by the vivid experience of crisis, Rodó projects the reconciling power of art. Art is, in his social imaginary, a form of communication which could bring harmony in society. In Schiller's words, "Only the communication of the Beautiful unites society" (in Habermas 1990:49). Like Schiller's implied dialogical voice, Rodó aims at mutual understanding and the inclusion of art in life. Rodó carries on his critique of reason from reason's own perspective, in the projection—by way of the Ariel allegory—of a comprehensive reason (in the Kantian sense). Ariel, he writes, is the immortal protagonist, "since with his presence he inspired the weak efforts of rationality to the prehistoric man" (Rodó 1967:248).

Rodó's rhetoric projects symbolical/cultural acts of power against the ethos of capitalism. He enacts a form of cultural criticism encouraging European epistemology against North American pragmatists. *Ariel* is also a speech genre of cultural prophecy against materialist arguments, which, however adversarial, indicates minimal active opposition to American capitalist society. His could be defined as expressions of a transcendental culture (pan-Hispanism), measured against the totalizing instrumental reason of North America. Tropes spiritualize in symbolic flights of moral analogy, hoping in the future as utopian horizon.

In this "event" aesthetics is not independent of epistemology. Rodó's magisterial rhetoric in *Ariel* makes organic use of the classical trivium—logic, grammar, and rhetoric—in plays of indeterminacies, firmly establishing that philosophical activities were on the side of "fiction" (and poetry) against the doxic, thus accentuating that art could oppose its answerable truth. The pedagogical dialogization, along the line of carnivalized literature, monitors the multileveledness of the objective social world, where opposing camps (two opposing points of view on democracy and technology) were the modern condition of society. The text's dialogical "answerability" is in the "third position," open to the future—as his dedication to the American youth suggests—and not in any one textual voice. Neither Prospero (the "magician") nor the reflexive disciple Enjolras gives an answer, for this answer can be reached only in interaction with the cultural and speech community. This "third" is also a participant, since no single element is structured toward a nonparticipating "third." The unfinalized nature of the text is the firm background open to the ultimate dialogicality (*PDP* 18).

It could also be argued that Rodó's text (as well as most modernist texts) clearly indicates the split between what was considered literature and non-literature, since it was a society where literature was a question of social category openly denoting a privileged access to reading and writing. Such class and ethnic privileges are evident in the net of intertextual voices from the classics, the moderns, philosophy, other languages (followed closely by Brotherston). In the context of what Balibar and Laporte (1974) have done on the functioning of literary texts within the French educational system in the nineteenth century, Rodó's *Ariel* could be understood in the context of development of a uniform national language, and restricted use, both indicating aspects of class struggle. Of course, Rodó's values are infused with projects possible to the oligarchy's faith in an ever-open future. His grand narrative of moral knowledge as liberation was an invocation to moral grandeur within the reliance of a democratic humanism of universal values. He also reorganized that heritage, actively working upon and transforming critical concepts in the process of his anti-imperialist concerns.

Other Allegories of Difference

> No, I cannot, I will not be on the side of those buffaloes with silver teeth. They are my enemies. . . .
>
> —Darío (1898)

The opposition Ariel/Caliban implicitly or explicitly represents the dialogical cultural sign of the polemic against North America. Paul Groussac was quite literal in a memorable speech rendered on 2 May 1898 (in Rodó 1967:197), where he resorted to carnivalesque metaphors of a dismembered body to describe "the monstrous collective organism" which had invaded the geographical space from the Pole to the tropics. Such invasion, he continued, had been under way since the wars of secession and the brutal invasion of the West. The "ill formed and Calibanesque" body of yankee spirit was looked upon with terror and distrust by the old world, which feared this arch-new (*novisima*) civilization pretending to supplant ours (197).

Darío monitored a parallel carnivalized representation of Caliban in a polemical article which was sustained by an array of metaphors and tropes to expose North American interventionism. It was first published in *El Tiempo* (Buenos Aires, 20 May 1898) under the title "The Triumph of Caliban," and was reproduced in a shorter version in *Don Quijote* (a Madrid radical leftist magazine) as "The Yanquis" (5 Nov. 1898). The polemical opposition of civilization/barbarians (also voiced in France against the Prussian army) is the subtext bracketing all questions of moral and political dissent deeply involved with a national destiny. Darío's rejection is the enthymemic plenum of modernist political representation since the 1880s. He could not, he writes, be on their side; they are our enemies: "They are the haters of Latin blood, they are the Barbarians. Every noble heart quivers this way, every honorable man who still conserves milk from the wolf protests this way" (in Zavala, ed. 1989:161; my translation).

The whole essay is a condensed and passionate meditation on simultaneously naturalistic, irreverent, and symbolic details, which touches on the carnival spirit. Darío's speech is internally dialogized and impregnated with polemic. The historical significance of such texts is that ideology was not merely parodied and inverted but revealed, distanced from within, as the bodily imagery serves as a means of inverting the menace of a social, moral, and political order which could devour the narrative of emancipation. The American invasion put in jeopardy the organic unity of the Americas, and, in effect, the narrative of national identity and liberation, and the common cultural values. In this juncture, Darío triggered the entire massive ideological repertoire in both Latin America and Spanish history, superpositioning nation (the "Latin" Americas) over all other differences.

The essay in fact begins directly with a polemic with the historical event and its contemporary public. He enters into argument with all his contemporaries. Such is the dialogized and equivocal verbal style and tone, so typical of the carnivalized Menippea. The entire carnivalized description of the "yanquis" (also "yankees") is markedly familiar and desecrating, built upon implicit oxymoronic combinations to debase and bring down to earth the might of the invader. The essay abounds with the symbolic system of the carnival and of a crude naturalism that includes even an anatropic inversion of cultural signs. Everything—culture, people, and ideas—is pushed to its boundaries and turned over to its opposite, taken to the extreme, to its limit: Emerson is an imitator of Carlyle, Whitman a democratic prophet at the service of Uncle Sam, and Poe, the "poor drunken swan," died in a country where he will never be understood. What Darío is now contesting is that the function of art in North America (with the exception of Poe) is to further social development in an instrumental sense: that art was put to the service of imperialism. He intuitively brings forward the argument of the ideological functions of symbolic forms, now a point of controversy among Anglo-American scholars.

This carnivalized spirit, which relativizes all that is externally stable, is grounded on a heuristic principle making it possible to discover the new. With its pathos of change and renewal, its dialogicality points to a future. In Darío's words:

> From Mexico to Tierra del Fuego there is an immense continent where the old seed is fecundated and prepares the vital sap, the future greatness of our race: from Europe, from the universe we receive a cosmopolitan breeze which will help invigorate our own jungle. But from the North, tentacles of railways, arms of steel, absorbing mouths are set out. Those poor republics of Central America will not have to fight against buccaneer Walker, but with the channeling *yankees* of Nicaragua. . . . (165)

Darío's effective essay combines all the signs of power that North America had inflicted upon its neighbors throughout the nineteenth century: it refers simultaneously to the different invasions of Nicaragua (in 1855 headed by the North American "buccaneer" William Walker, who named himself president of the country), the construction of the interoceanic channel started by Cornelius Vanderbilt, as well as the 1846 invasion which forced the annexation of Mexican territory in Baja California, New Mexico, and Arizona in 1848. Biblical and at the same time derogatory metaphors in their highest carnivalized form are evoked against the autocratic and potential violence of the menacing neighbor. The text concludes with an articulate and rigorous attempt to optimize various forms of knowledge—epistemological, ethical, and aesthetic: "I who have been a believer in free Cuba, even if it were to accompany in its dream so many dreamers and in its heroism so many martyrs, am a friend of Spain." However, he adds, the Spain he defends is not that of the fanatic, or the pedantic, or the unhappy pompous pedant who disdains the America he does not know. The Spain he defends is called "Chivalry, Ideal, Nobility; it's called Cervantes, Quevedo, Góngora, Gracián, Velázquez; it's called the Cid, Loyola, Isabel; it's called Daughter of Rome, Sister of France, Mother of America" (166).

I have quoted extensively from this essay to indicate how carnivalized literature and the carnivalistic, muffled laughter remain, as in the Socratic dialogue, in the structure of the image, in the method to develop the dialogue (on this, *PDP* 164–65). The carnival sense here is hostile to any sort of conclusion, and the historical event is relativized in the heuristic principle of the participating responsive "third." The text even reveals the exceptionally acute contradictions of Hispanic modernism and its ideological duality, as well as the shared belief in language's (and art's) power to transform history. It is based on a mimetic conception of the word and exemplified in the anatropic inversion of Emerson as an imitator of Carlyle and Whitman as a prophet of violent (imperialistic) democracy, since to Martí and Darío himself, both had been paragons of modernist claims to aesthetic utopia. What the inverted image indicates is modernism's belief in the referential power of language. And lastly, the shared belief that texts and an ethics of reading were vital in the constitution of self suggests a reading formation (in T. Bennett's [1983] concept) of the modernists:

an ethics of a culturally determined reading which dynamizes and mobilizes texts in a relation constructed by the text users on the basis of different social practices. It suggests the Barthian writerly reading, by which the reader/writer makes the assignment of meaning in the context of another culture (another universe of meanings).

This carnivalized text, as well as Rodó's Socratic carnivalization, contains a voiced polemics with both socio-economic and "racial" (understood as cultural) overtones. In the nineteenth century, according to Guillaumin's pertinent clarification (1980:45), social amalgams became groups of individuals, "individuals linked together by their natural character." Therefore, the term "racial" came to be part of a naturalist conception of social groups—the "idea that social groups were races or natural amalgams"—and came to be applied to human groups of a certain size, and to involve the idea of somatic cohesion, and the notion that such groupings were naturally constituted (46).

The anti-imperialist conception which emerged was associated with a major theme of "Latin" versus Anglo-Saxon reformulations, energized since the French defeat in 1870 which destroyed the image of a pacific and pacifist Germany (the Germany of the Niebelungs and Richard Wagner). In corollary, the defeat of the Italians at Adua in 1896 and of Spain in 1898 by the North Americans raised a question of power-knowledge relations. The "Latin race" (which encompassed both Rome and Greece) issued the interrogation of the historical conditions of a potential for the decadence of "Latin" cultures. As a first step, the Spaniards remapped their relationship with France, which had been precarious after the wars of independence (Lovett 1972), and then the conflict came to implicate a confrontation between all the European Mediterranean countries and northern Europe. The new profile was built around a pan-Latinism, which reached its peak in 1898 (see Litvak 1975, now in 1990). The Spanish defeat in 1898 became the focus to entertain the claims of the role of the Latin world in modernity.

D'Annunzio made a global appeal in 1898 against the "Barbarian invasion" (qtd. in Litvak). The function of "race" as a universal problem here was a debate over who upheld reason, in a seemingly neutral conception of nations' roles which can be disputed. However, it meant a disqualification of instrumental reason and capitalism through a system of power and its principal agents. Instrumental reason and domination were identified as a constituent feature not so much of Western civilization but of northern Europe and Anglo-Saxon control of nature and culture, and the apparent invincibility of North American power.

Evidence of the above-mentioned solidarity is the maximalization of the differences. In Darío's essay (as well as in Rodó's text, among others) dialogicality is productive as a means to capture the developing relationships under modernity, at a time when the previous forms of life turned ambivalent and the unfinalized nature of historical and political thought was exposed. The parodic references deny the readers a chance to recognize themselves in the negative images and undermine their sense of the reality of history. Darío dissociates the reader from the figures (buffaloes, Calibans), whose identities are wholly provisional, and whose perpetual changes preclude any illusion of continuity. Here, the North American invader is subject to the allegorical mastery of carnivalized language, in a taxonomic frenzy obsessed with the heterological. Language is used here to organize another world in its alterity, to project an all-encompassing ordering of knowledge with no resemblance to the negative cultural identities expressed in the recognizable negative symbolic language of differences, organized as political constructions of emancipation mediated by a fictive control of representational (denotative) language.

In the intense struggle against authoritative knowledge as a possible source of future identity constructs, parody and dissociation are meant to debilitate a sense of univocal truth, of a subject which presumes to know. Hence the insistence on "race" in its polysemy, *ratio,* as the creative idea of the universe, the hegemonic unity of humanity (on this see Spitzer 1948) which since Buffon was meant as types of humankind in anthropology, and used as forms of violence since the Conquest. The taxonomical model—here implicitly invoked—was based on binary oppositions of race/nation, savage/civilized; but by metalepsis, the rationalistic eighteenth-century classical binary opposition nature/culture, which denied the possibility of social organization to the state of nature, is here altered. Modernity, technology, scientific knowledges are ascribed to the savage, language, ethics, and morality to the racial difference of the civilized. The word *race* discloses the suspect implicit aporia of the tendency to elevate nation before class through the copious use of the national allegory. But simultaneously, this allegory asserted the difference between different historical projects of modernity: the North American and the Latin American.[3]

In this sense both Darío's and Rodó's essays could be considered "genealogical"; they disclose the buffoonery of history through parodic doubles (Puerto Rican modernists continued this practice well into 1917, as we shall see). Carnivalesque is not just the other, but includes the other within itself. The carnivalesque is then a specific kind of doubling where each is in turn simultaneously subject and addressee of discourse. The dialogicality of the carnival suggests that both signifier and signified, or represented and representer, are included; they are irrevocably double. Dialogicality also indicates in both texts how language may fail to achieve its wished-for effects and unfold its intrinsic aporias on race and culture, since they ground heterogeneity in "spiritual" difference. A critical rereading in this direction discloses that in a drive for aesthetic transcendence, there was a tendency to mystify the ideal or tradition in a sort of unified sensibility. However, the monitored social imaginary is directed toward a concrete symbolic resistance and victory, and oriented to a symbolic negation of hierarchies, thus rooting its function in the constitution of an emancipated subject. The social imaginary does not work here as a misconception and remoteness from truth; its link with the unconscious activates a dynamic differential of ideological images of liberation open to the future.

Cultural signs here concur with the emergence of both the modern "Hispanic" subject and the construction of a discursive subject that assumes a newly empowered position on the stage of history. These modernist discursive practices visibly rely on the unconscious—the subterranean political underground—thereby structuring liberating desire in the constitution of self.

The political tradition of opposition I have briefly reconstructed in its master concepts and categories argues for subject positions straddling multiple realities—Spanish American and Latin (from the Latin world), in their multiple ethnicities—which were frequently conscious and perspectival productions of meaning in unspoken and spoken interrogations.[4] What is interesting is that in the advocation of strong hermeneutics, these modernists stand against the globalism which would subsume the local in the synchronic. They also would seem to suggest that the realms of politics (the two politics defined by Hegel, Althusser, Bloch) are dependent upon each other, and both position a moral choice in the linguistic self-concept of national liberation.[5] They regulate the brutality of the emergent and developing economic-multinational networks and lay the foundations for a differentiated, heterogeneous criticism through a cumulative politics of metaphors to constitute such a critical perspective. Ideology operates through the category of a heteroglossic subject, and both these dialogical texts in their openness suggest that truth is responsibility and finalization, that it is not an individual decision, since cultural processes are linked to social relations.[6] As utterances, they polemize with the cultural power of the alien words.

VI

CULTURAL SPHERES AND RESISTANCE

> Let's say it with the consecrated word, anar-
> chism in art, the basis of what constitutes
> modern or modernist evolution.
>
> —Darío, *Contemporary Spain* (1901)

> Oh sea of the free, welcome me!
> Oh land of slaves, Goodbye!
>
> —Manuel González Prada (1908)

Social Acts of Insurgency

If we return to the cultural space in which the complex and evolving ideologeme of modern/modernity/modernism emerged against the background of the International and the growth of labor movements, both symbolic and political resistance are context-bound, or "situated." The utopian element of the modernist literary production (the aesthetic utopia) is balanced by the foregrounding of consensus in dissent against instrumental reason and against the violence of both capitalism and imperialism with their authoritarian and oppressive technics of exploitation. The idea of modernity as a democratic use of technology, which had been the picture of social progress drawn in the master discourse of the nineteenth-century liberals' industrial revolution(s), soon came to represent the impoverishment and underdevelopment of the labor class.

Marx, who had voiced his advocacy of technology and modernization as the point where the "mobilization and revolutionizing of life-conditions" had experienced the greatest acceleration since the Communist Manifesto (1848), soon developed a critique of capitalism and the imaginary relations (ideology) of misrecognition and misconception which mirrored reflections created (well noted by Habermas [1990:60–61]). Mikhail Bakunin was no less critical: he analyzed modern times as corrupted by the struggle for power and money. While he criticized the capitalist age, he simultaneously projected his vision of the new anarchist society as a world without inequalities and tyranny. Bakunin and the Bakuninists (like Proudhon before him) projected images of creative destruction against the organization of modern industrial life by which human-kind was a made slave of machines and cut off from a dignified human life—what was called the utopic "Ideal."

In this critical argumentative monitoring of the imaginary and the symbolic, I wish to emphasize that the claim of being modern is the unifying ideologeme, in its variations of either a critical deconstructive perspective toward modernity or a noncritical acceptance. Modernism is both a form of social organization (modernity) and a term of epochal diagnosis of the localized crises of the fundamental problems of technology and industrialization, of aesthetic experi-ence and commodification. As such its critique had the goal of uncovering stagnation through mobilization, of changing the compulsion to repetition (the "commodity of fetishism"), mediated by the unmasking of signs. Modernism, in all its semantic meanings, gave consistency to a project to decolonize life from technology; all the threads of opposition began to fuse into a strong movement for cultural identity. Without an anatropic inversion of signs, the apparent positive and democratic changes in life conditions masked the illusions that concealed a truly revolutionary movement.

At this juncture, an alliance emerges in the critical space between the political avant-garde and the cultural avant-garde, what we have been addressing as both a dialogical perception and an organic bloc, a hegemony which calls together different positions: modernists, symbolists, anarchists, socialists, the Spanish "generation of '98."[1] I will use the terms *modernist* and *avant-garde* syn-onymously as a collective intended social act of insurgency which lasted from around the 1890s until approximately 1910. This critical cultural avant-garde corresponded to Baudelaire's (in Benjamin's reading) founding area, which now associated itself especially with the anarchists. Anarchism is the space of conjunction of modernity and revolution; indeed, at this historical juncture the alliance was profoundly revolutionary, very specifically in those geographic areas where the forms of dynastic *ancien régime* persisted (Mayer 1982), and Spain and Latin America were two of them.

Ever since the introduction of Bakuninism in Spain (with the 1868 revolution which dethroned Isabelle II), the downfall of the old order had been the meeting ground of republicans, Bakuninists, federalists, and socialists. The common adversary which joined these socio-political forces was the contested space of a democratic technology and modernity. Revolution gave the image of hope, and anarchism in particular, the prospect of an imminent overthrow of the old order. What emerged was a rather Jacobinic view of the coming of European revolution (and by extension of revolution) as the hostility toward capitalism deepened among the working-class groups.

Traditional societies embodied no positive factors, and the element of per-sonal freedom and revolution as unfolding humankind's dormant powers be-came dominant, together with the populist ideas of Russian refugees in Europe. The last years of the 1880s were particularly active, with Prince Peter Kropotkin leading the anarchist-communists, and new "apostles of the idea" carrying propagandistic campaigns after the International came out of hiding (a clandestine International) in Spain in 1881; the activity was also widespread in Latin American societies, and immigration played a major role, especially since many Italian immigrants were or had been anarchists.

The utopian energies of the cultural modernity served as criterion for the hegemonic alliance, for expressive subjectivity was crucial to both, and there emerged a sort of cult of immediacy and ideas on the subject's anarchism of the soul (from Oscar Wilde to Leo Tolstoy). The explanation for this alliance with anarchism—to a greater extent than with socialism—at the turn of the century is complex and in need of further analysis. However, one could argue, as a working hypothesis, that the less moralistic attitude toward art, sexuality, and moral institutions (church, state) created a common ground, at the same time that it provided the major differences upheld by Marx and Engels and Bakunin during the First International concerning the bohemians. While the first two disregarded the revolutionary role of what they called the "lumpen proletariat," Bakunin believed in the revolutionary force of the outlaws, the brigands, and the outcasts, and laid great stress upon liberty. At the same time, he analyzed modern capitalist states as a form of tyranny.

The strength of his beliefs was not so much against the inequalities of wealth as in the exercise of authority, which perverted: "all submission to authority humiliates," he wrote (see Brenan 1978:133). The idea of justice and revolution was based on economic collectivism, political anarchism, and religious atheism: "It is atheist in religion and anarchist in politics; anarchist in the sense that it considers power as a very passing necessity; atheist in that it recognizes no religion, because it recognizes them all" (in 1978:149). Modern life was artificial to Bakunin, and human needs and desires took precedence over economic laws; for the same reason, he had high hopes for the revolutionary potential of the "proletarian intelligentsia," the *déclassés,* to carry out propaganda. All in all, it should also be stressed that both factions of the International departed from the notion that intellectuals can form a revolutionary vanguard.

The critical role of intellectuals, which lasted throughout the nineteenth century, took a definitive change around the Dreyfus affair (1893) during the Third Republic, when the word *intellectual* was coined (see Charle 1990). The important anti-Semitic trial, which organized the radical intellectuals, inevitably became a model, which was again used in other epochal experiences, the trials and torture of Andalusian anarchists in 1892 and the Montjuich tortures and trials of 1895–96 in Barcelona, in which a group of leading anarchists— Anselmo Lorenzo, Federico Urales, F. Tárrida del Mármol, Teresa Claramunt— were jailed and tried for execution, and then exiled (Pérez de la Dehesa 1970). Police brutality, as reported by Tárrida del Mármol, provoked the reaction of the European left; drastic state repression was used against anarchists and the nature of anarchist terrorism against the symbols of what they believed was a "corrupt bourgeois life" (e.g., *Liceo* and the Corpus Christi procession bombings). If there was a consensus against police brutality in the Montjuich trials, the same model of solidarity among the European left was again a catalyst in the Catalan educator Francisco Ferrer's trial and execution in 1909 for anarchy.[2]

As a collectivity, both the "intellectual" (the organic intellectual, to go back to Gramsci) and the "intellectual proletariat" (in Bakunin's distinction, used by social scientist Ernesto Bark) joined with the political avant-garde at the turn of the century (see Zavala 1977, 1988a, 1990a). The role of the intellectual in politics, as well as the relationship between cultural vanguards and revolution, was crucial until World War II, as the famous debate over aesthetics and politics of the 1930s between Adorno, Benjamin, Bloch, Brecht, and Lukács indicates.[3] In the 1890s, a period of anarchist terrorism, the severity, meanness, and self-righteousness, as well as the artificial form, of bourgeois society were the target of both anarchists (now also called "libertarians," a word invented by Sébastien Faure in 1898 to evade censorship for his journal *Revue Blanche*) and artists. They both disapproved morally of the complacent, dull, and repressive bourgeoisie, and also of the results of industrial life; the anti-industrialization was part of the major concern with oppression, and a return to the Middle Ages represented, at least to Bakunin and Kropotkin, a return to collectivization, not a nostalgia for the past.

The historically differentiated term *avant-garde,* first coined by Fourierist Gabriel-Desiré Laverdant, was also the strategic title of a Bakuninist newspaper in 1876 (after Bakunin's death), when Paul Brousse started a libertarian publication in Switzerland under that name, with important contributions from Peter Kropotkin (Woodcock and Avakumovic 1971). The newspaper soon became an organ of the French federation of the International, and was simultaneously a way to prevent centralized Marxist control over the whole European (and Western) socialist movement. At this time, Kropotkin not only was one of the leading libertarian figures, but he was concerned with developing an *anti-metaphysical and anti-dialectic* philosophy of a free society. This last point of metaphysical deconstruction is worth pursuing, together with Bakunin's strong anti-metaphysical positioning, which made him develop an anti-Cartesian and anti-Russonian critique in ways which announced deconstruction.[4]

Around the 1890s, anarchist ideas on revolt became a distinctive concept on the contemporary scene in general, and were reproduced by the mass media as a means of repression, as in the Montjuich prison trials and the repression of Andalusian anarchists in 1892, when a peasant army headed by Fermín Salvochea invaded Jerez de la Frontera, a region stricken by famine and unemployment. The repression against anarchists, which had been publicized throughout Europe during 1883–84 because of the Black Hand Trials, revealed police torture and a network of repression. Judges, police (Guardia Civil), and religious institutions all convened in the practice of repression on both social and moral grounds. In Spain alone, between 1892 and 1893 more than 20,000 people were arrested (preventive arrest) in connection with anarchist trials.

According to Maîtron (1975), around 100,000 people were influenced by anarchism in France, while in Spain it is believed that around 1884 there were at least 30,000 (most of them from Andalusia); even if both figures were highly exaggerated, the strong emphasis on utopia, dignity, happiness, integrity, change, anti-authoritarianism, and anti-centralization of the libertarians provided overhasty hopes of a fusion with the artists' experience of loss of identity and marginalization. It also provided libidinal release for many writers, like the idea of "la bombe esthétique" of the symbolists united around *Le Chat Noir* and other periodicals.

Expansion of the movement can be dated to 1881, when anarchists broke definitively with the "authoritarian" socialists (a Marxist faction of the International).[5] The period of terrorism took place during the 1890s. This atmosphere was created as a response to "propaganda by deed," which led to some anarchist terrorism (such as Ravachol 1893, the assassination of Sadi Carnot in France in 1894, of the Spanish politician Antonio Cánovas 1897, and of King Umberto of Italy in 1900). The concern among anarchists with art, literature, and education in the constitution of emancipatory and revolutionary subjectivities is well known. By 1880, not only were there many affiliates to the libertarian movement in Spain, but proletarian freethinking schools (such as Ferrer's) abounded, as did publications (newspapers, poetry, short stories, novels). Anarchists also encouraged popular music, and there emerged a cultural production of interrelated cultural universes between the literate and nonliterate, in forms of popular music (tangos, for example), intensely dialogic.

The optimism of the workers' utopian "ideals" also was manifested in the emergence of the First International in Latin America, particularly in (but not limited to) Argentina, Mexico, Peru, Uruguay, Venezuela, and the Caribbean (Cuba, Puerto Rico). The openness of the horizon was formulated as the projection of a truly socialist society in which power, production, and culture would be democratic and heteroglotic. Culture was understood as the force generating material conditions for such a possibility in the immediate future.

This hegemonic alliance was of collective importance and functioned across more than one rubric, all conjoined mainly around the anarchists, who voiced more openly (and ironically) their critique of the bourgeoisie. The main anarchist periodicals were *Anarchy* (Madrid, 1882–85, 1890–95), *The Social Journal* (La Revista Social; Madrid, 1881–84), *The Producer* (El Productor; Barcelona, 1887–93), and *The White Journal* (La Revista Blanca; 1898–1905). But the capitals all had their own journals, which during repressions and censorship became culturalist publications (Lida 1972; Litvak 1990); they even changed their names, as we have seen, to evade police prosecution.

Such publications usually included work by well-established writers from the so-called Generation of 1898 (Benavente, Unamuno, Valle-Inclán, Corominas, Pio Baroja, Azorín), by renowned bohemians (Alejandro Sawa), and by social scientists (such as Ernesto Bark). This polemical production of heterogeneities and alternatives, whose energy arises from an ethical revolt against the violence of modern capitalism, was part of the experience of most modernist writers. Even Juan Ramón Jiménez (Zavala 1974) responded to these beliefs and shared experiences, and wrote two poems drawing attention to urban modern violence on the theme of poverty which were published in an anarchist newspaper.

The condition of incredibility toward the Enlightenment's metanarrative of capitalism and industrialization technics is questioned by this cultural modernity whose adventure is the political emancipation of humankind. In this endeavor, the organic alliance of moderns, in all its differences, is now con-joined against exploitation and political rhetoric, and simultaneously invali-dates the universal metalanguage of technology (science, instrumental reason) of the triumphalist bourgeois liberalism. An infinite field of possibilities is opened, traversed by a multiplicity of heteroglossic languages, in which each subject position is engaged at a different pragmatic post, and in which a legitimation of a different modernity is immanent. Sawa, a close friend of Darío's, published *Literary Anarchy* (La Anarquía Literaria, 1905), which was but one of many publications dealing with the avant-garde, modernism, moder-nity, emancipation (see Zavala 1974, ed. 1977, 1990a), in the direction from which French symbolists and English (Bernard Shaw, Ford Madox, Joseph Conrad) or Italian modernists approached anarchism as a reference point of a free intersubjectivity: what the early D'Annunzio called "o rinnovarsi o mor-ire." This was the cultural space of the subversive expression of forces.

In the last decades of the nineteenth century, particularly after the Commune of 1871, there was a systematic agreement between the "intellectual" and the social movements as heterogeneous fields of subversion. The basic line postu-lated at that time was a historico-philosophical distantiation from the reification of the sovereignty of instrumental reason—to free subjectivity from coercion. Enthymemic writings, such as Kropotkin's *An Appeal to the Young* (1880), to the workers, to women, and to the young, were frequent, as was messianic rhetoric of a revolutionary extremism appealing to a vague social revolution of the *exaltado* Jacobinic tradition. Kropotkin's brief pamphlet was widely re-printed, was translated into fourteen European languages, and appeared in the United States and South America. Was Rodó acquainted with this moving exhortation to youth?

This was the cultural space of the last decades of the nineteenth century, in which social discourses (forms, speech genres) were changing the structures of the concrete forms in which they were manifested. In light of Bakhtin's writings, which replaced a radically new set of problems concerning culture as the social arena in which conflicting interests of different classes were represented and fought for, *modernism* was the magic word in the topography of the modern cosmopolis. As an ideologeme it represented an anti-hegemonic discursive formation expressing an optimism to overthrow the oppressive social struc-tures, and escape capitalist relations as both individuals and collective. What became decisive in this juncture was not only that human labor was turned into commodities (already a point of reference since the 1880s, as we have seen), but that the logic of capitalism traversed increasingly numerous spheres and social relations: culture, education, family, sex, religion.

But even apart from the fact that ideologemes are constantly rehistoricized, the space of modernism was contested through numerous struggles and dif-ferent subject positions, each with its own heterogeneous claims, critical strat-egies, and contradictions. The perspective was multiple, with different points of observation, variously contested, supported, and subverted. Many times the claims of the moderns overlapped, and enunciated the structuring themes of various concurring discourses emerging at different moments. Thus understood, what we have been addressing as modernism is distinctly heterogeneous at different cultural, national, and historical moments. However, it was in the context of the reorganization which took place after the 1890s that a series of changes occurred, and the new hegemonic formation was articulated.

In the economy of symbolic exchange, the explicit reference to an object reveals its contrary; therefore, the specific word *modern,* later *modernismo,* as the word circulated in France thanks to the Goncourt (Greenburg, in Watson 1984), reveals the material interest of the user. As a "situated utterance" it could be used in defense and support of the authority and legitimation of domination, or, on the contrary, it could express the symbolic negation of hierarchies. Both meanings are simultaneous and depend on the user to communicate one or the other. Those who, like F. Rossi Landi (1961, 1965), M. Pêcheux (1975), and P. Bourdieu (1982), have studied the symbolic interaction of language, insist that the performative force of words lies in the institutional condition of their use. In symbolic exchange, the user of language authorizes or unauthorizes meanings. In such a space, *modern*(ity) became the representation of the democratic myth, and an integral part of social discourse (in the sense given to it by Escarpit [1970]) and of the variety of doxical positions, of its speech genres, its topics, and its tropes. Each contending social and speech community constructs a different relation with this specific discourse, on the basis of the different social practices.

In the social heteroglossia, the diversity of meanings is ascribed to precisely such a word against the reified majority opinion of the moral discourse of tradition. In the midst of all these simultaneous discourses at the turn of the century, the intervoiced meaning produced around this operative concept is stimulated by what Adorno and Horkheimer called the "mimetic impulse of promise." As an enterprise, modernism was the social myth, as well as the aesthetic utopia of the future.

Modern Cosmopolis

> It is the ferocious capitalists who have for a heart a dollar bill. . . . Owners of houses, owners of land, would be owners of air and sun.
>
> —González Prada (1907)

One of the utopias of the future was modern cities in illusory constructions which could be traced back to the Greco-Hellenic world and the seven marvels of the ancients. The urbanism of "invisible cities" (borrowing Calvino's title) runs through the modern world (it is central to Rabelais's modernity, according to Bakhtin) and became a particular theoretical inquiry in the nineteenth century, with the first socialists and the romantics. It is quite well known that the opium eater fantasized about modern cities, in urbanistic revelries of the future, while Charles Fourier dreamt falansteries and Auguste Comte believed his modern jail or panopticon would solve the problem of crime and punishment in the modern states.

William Morris, who had been redesigning the world, worried more acutely about the rationale behind modern architecture, and his architectural imaginary was a motif to the Pre-Raphaelites, while John Ruskin's anti-industrial ideas on beauty and nature warning of a future apocalypse were widely publicized. Morris's conversion to socialism after 1876, at the time of the so-called Eastern Question, is present in his popularized utopia *News from Nowhere*, where he seriously fantasizes about a return to the natural life of the Middle Ages (a point he shares with Kropotkin, from another perspective).

A no less important nucleus of modernity was *urbanism*, which had been posited as correlative with organizing modernization since the Argentinian Sarmiento's *Facundo* (1845), and critically experienced in Paris by Baudelaire's perception of the mobilized, concentrated, metropolitan lifeworld, so thoroughly investigated by Walter Benjamin. It was also the capital city of "luxury and light" to Proudhon, who worried about modern *pornocracy* in the 1870s, suggested a "moral and sane" life for the laborer, and energetically expressed that domesticity was women's natural life: "the sphere that nature has assigned to them" (1875:385). But it is well known that a veil of modesty and chastity fell over Baudelaire's poetry and Flaubert's novel, and that after the experience of the Commune, moral compression was a sign of the intensity of forces at work.

The experiential sphere of the great capitals' urban space seemed a way of organizing power and change in its socio-symbolical dimension (Foster 1983; Sarlo 1988). The "teichoscopic" (view from the wall or top) optics created social and sexual, even ethnic, boundaries of the space of modernity, in the metaphor of a map and labyrinths, which made power visible. These socio-cultural boundaries reveal what anthropologist Edward T. Hall (1959, 1966) calls "proxemics," or the way in which space defines culture.[6] What became pressing were the forms of capitalist occupation of social space, and the changes economic growth made in general urbanization. The workers resented their transfer to the urban peripheries, and the new forms of subordination created within the heart of the new modern societies.

Discourses linking cosmopolitanism and modernity were frequent with the avant-garde; some critically disclosed the shockingly modern Eiffel Tower as a galvanizing symbol of commercialization and the haunting image of a new order. Casal from Cuba, Darío from Buenos Aires, and Sawa and Bark as well as anarchists from Barcelona would point to the unsolved problems of wealth from different subject positions, denouncing some architectural constructions as boundaries of triumphant bourgeois liberal life (the Liceo theater, for example), built for the Universal [*sic*] Exposition in Barcelona in 1888, which was followed by the Paris Exposition of 1889. This space points to the triumphant industrial and technological imaginary which emerged earlier in the century.

Other urban spaces—cafés, taverns, and cabarets were a unique phenomenon at the center of the upheaval in the arts after the famous Chat Noir (1881) in Montmartre and Barcelona's Quatre Gats (1890)—tended to be subversive both socially and artistically (see Segel 1987). Chansonniers and cabaret performers provided not only entertainment but also performative songs of cynical or satirical criticism. This space of oppositions, particularly dear to the bohemians, seemed to be the fusion of high and trivial culture and was believed to have a transforming, illuminating, and liberating way into life forms reified by capitalism, at least in Benjamin's notion of "profane illuminations." To other critics (Salaün 1990), public spectacles (cuplés, in particular) were deformed and distorted by consumerism. Hence the multiplicity of demands, social relations, their antagonisms, struggles; language refracts the complexities and heteroglotic mixture of social life through polyphonic discourse, parodic carnivalization, polemically colored texts. While the socially marginalized—the poor worker, the immigrant, the lumpen—try often to take over the symbolic center of social life in their own social spaces, through the discourse with a sideways glance of popular music. A complex and rich language, popular music no less refracted these positions for the struggle against inequalities and the claiming of rights.

In the range and variability of writing, as a constantly contested space, *modernism* came to be equated by its users with an activity of critical perception and cultural heteroglossia. That is the meaning projected by such anarchists as Anselmo Lorenzo (founding figure of Spanish anarchism) and the Catalan anarchist Federico Urales, as well as the editors of the journal *Don Quijote* (Zavala 1990a). Around 1898 the identifications between modernism and anarchism became stronger against an instrumentalized society, and the concept received its fullest and richest formulation as it was associated with the signifying practices of the nuevos, modernos, jóvenes, bohemians. These groups promoted, at least on a symbolic plane, a redistribution of social roles, and critical relation to all official discourses, whether literary, political, or ecclesiastical, at times with lucid carnivalesque connotations.

In this sense, modernism operates at the points of contradiction between competing ideologies and oppositional cultural practices, which were constantly redefined and articulated. Leopoldo Alas (Clarín) parodied Darío's endecasyllables—a polemic the Uruguayan poet responded to in 1894—and by this he also ridiculed modernists on their attire, morals, and even semiotic disposition of the words on the page—what was parodied as "graphomania"; likewise, other anti-modernists accused them of moral decadence and homosexuality. The degree of resistance toward modernists (and bohemians) from Spanish writers was often tinged with organicist notions of national culture and temperament. These held the idea that intellectual and aesthetic values were rooted in the soil of a native tradition that preserved itself by maintaining a resistance to exotic imported ideas. Many concluded that modernism was nothing more than an exercise in shallow ingenuity, a product of the *épater le bourgeois,* thought as indigenous to French intellectual life.

Modernists became stereotyped as frivolous, or arrogant with chic postures to shock and affront traditional values. There was a polemic atmosphere from 1885 until at least 1910 (see Litvak 1990). Unamuno, for example, rejected on moral grounds what he understood as frivolities; the redefinitions and rearticulations shifted constantly. In other cases, the framed critical narratives of some moderns, such as Alejandro Sawa or Felipe Trigo, were unsurprisingly judged "pornographic" by the established literary critics. Far from offering a simulacrum of an erotic world where sex was available at all times, both novelists used sexual themes and employed sexual imagery for social and ideological functions. Essentially, the particular position of the moderns was governed by a negativity to make real headway toward the social and economic transformation of society, and confronting the social through language, as a form of social instrument.

By the 1890s the unifying tendency between modernism and anarchism grew stronger; the new aesthetics was frequently defined as "anarchist aesthetics," "literary anarchism," "Platonic anarchism," "socialist aesthetics" (e.g., Casal in Cuba). Thus, at the end of the nineteenth century there emerged a new signifying economy, denoting a challenge, which also accentuated provocative dispositions of words. It would seem that the theory of an "anarchist aesthetics" was popularized by Henri Cornuty, a Frenchman who also provided the fertile grounds for decadence in Spain (Zavala, ed. 1977:30). In a short period of time, "literary anarchism" became the alternative definition for modern poetics; in Spain, young José Martínez Ruiz called himself a "literary anarchist" by 1893. Many followed. All these modern theories also advocated an ethics of cosmopolitanism, as well as a whole problematic addressing the issue of the hegemonic rationalism of modern society. It prompted reflection about the link between the instrumentalized social hegemony and the constitution of individual psychic structure. In general, the identification with both notions was used to disclaim separate spheres for art and politics.

At this juncture, and more specifically during his trip to Spain in 1899, Darío began to present this component of identity in his *Contemporary Spain* (1901), drawing from a cosmopolitanism of the imagination to explore the political exigencies of modern societies. Anarchism, and an anarchist aesthetics, had become the truly viable ethic to other writers in Latin America: Manuel González Prada (1848–1918), an anarchist himself, the Argentinian Almafuerte (Pedro Bonifacio Palacios, 1854–1917), Leopoldo Lugones, or Uruguayan modernists such as the dramatist Florencio Sánchez (1875–1910), Armando Vasseur (b. 1878), and Angel Falco (b. 1885).[7] The adoption of this socio-artistic approach was also the potential of his alliance with Valle-Inclán and Juan Ramón Jiménez (who published *Songs of Life and Hope*) and his collaboration with Sawa. Anarchism provided an analytic insight into the basis of art itself, and the driving energy constitutive of modern life. In this historical event, as an avant-garde, many modernists were identified with the various forms and patterns of anarchism—what Darío had given in 1896 as a modern formula as he hailed the young Lugones as "a socialist poet."

This challenge was seen to induce a confrontation between the stasis of bourgeois order and the pulverization of the old social structure. The work of González Prada and Lugones at this time came to exemplify an artistic practice inseparable from an anarchist social formation. Both wrote vigorous poems uniting the "modern" concept of literature with anarchism: Lugones's *March of Flags* (Marcha de las banderas) closes with a determined effective visual representation of the red flag: "Oh red flag which guides the Aurore; / painful purple of the tragic west: Hosanna!" Indeed, as the mark of a network of social energies, his poetry comes to illustrate the semiotic dimension of the signifying process, evoking language as a challenge to authority.

González Prada engaged in an open ideological confrontation, transposing its force through rhythm and shattering the syntactic linearity through free verse. The revolutionary force of poetic language was linked here with social revolution as a practice, introducing into poetry the production of the new. He dreamt with a poetry "free from the rude carcass of rhyme" (in "Dreamt Rhythm" [1901]). His is a semiotic practice which pluralizes and condenses through rhythm ossified forms. González Prada's conception of the ethical function of art was not separate from a progressive ideology; he actively participated with anarchist groups in Lima, while he served as a representative of an avant-garde socio-historical practice, and was translated by Italian anarchists.

There is an omnipresent involvement against capitalism, and an optimism toward the future. An open system, founded on a truly egalitarian society, deepened the fight against capitalist and industrializing bourgeois states. Looked at within a broader perspective, we see that the consequent emphasis on and credulity toward "ideals" and collective celebration were a commitment to change, urging a striving for a certain equilibrium in the social and the experience of individuals. A Peruvian proletarian wrote eloquent lines in 1900 in favor of the "Proletarian Ideal" in the midst of this "century of progress." The "Ideal," shared by both anarchists and modernists, included freedom, leisure, vitality—what Kropotkin had called "strength in action."

The idiom "ideal" in that social horizon fused into a strong cultural-political affirmation, in meaningful opposition to the lack of "ideals" of the utilitarian, oppressive capitalist society. It became a joyful affirmation of change. "Ideal," "dream," and "promised paradise," as well as "socialist gospel," were open-ended processes that promised emancipation from want. Modernists focused many of their discontents on these idioms, but "ideal"—often used by Darío, for example—also meant a critique of the quality of life under a regime of standardized utilitarianism and gross consumption. The "ideal" was lived as a utopian desire, although in different ways, yet in solidarity.

Pedro Emilio Coll of Venezuela developed his major themes under the umbrella of the modern cosmopolis (also a main concern of Sawa). Coll published a variety of articles in *Cosmópolis* (1894–95), a Caracan journal advancing modernist ideas on modernization, and a series of short stories (*The Castle of Elsinor* [1901]) devoted to the vast repertoire of libertarian ideas (see González

Stephan 1988). In this context, it is important to stress that he was among the first to recognize, as early as 1897 in an article published in *Mercure de France,* that the Cuban experience—specifically Martí—helped constitute modernism. He wrote: "The first symptoms of the Cuban insurrection have coincided with an intellectual and artistic movement common to all of Latin America" (in Zavala 1975, 1988a).

Furthermore, he explained, the insurrection had a double meaning: in the Antilles it was a struggle for national liberation, while in other Latin American countries which had already gained their political independence, the rebellion expressed itself as a literary revolt against the precepts and traditions imposed by Spain—an imperial Spain, he went on, whose banners once floated over the broken feathers of the Indians. The new literary movement, which Coll names *americanismo* or *criollismo,* was thus the manifestation of Latin American spirit and its self-realization in art.

Martí represented the "living symbol of our state of mind." Martí was, he continued, the indefatigable lover of Cuban freedom and the delicate poet who proclaimed aesthetic liberation, free from the yoke of dictionaries and grammars. He advocated a literary language which could break away from old rhetorical formulas. In the *Mercure de France,* Coll wrote that by doing so, Martí instilled in his prose the profound tremor of Latin American rivers and wrote verses as radiant as the "lonely star of his flag." He continued:

> Yes, Latin America is an immense social laboratory: our cities will give asylum to all political refugees in the approaching social war. Our virgin lands will embrace the European proletariat under the murmuring leaves where the ancient parroquete repeats with nostalgia the forgotten language of the Indians. (In Zavala 1975, 1988a:90)

Coll's perception is that the Spanish-American War helped give coherence to the movement, and bridged the Latin American and Spanish developments clustered around the same experiences: the sinking of the *Maine,* which inflamed American opinion, as well as Admiral Dewey's attack on the Philippines, the Treaty of Paris which signed away Cuba, Puerto Rico, and the Philippines, and the 1902 crisis in Panama. This movement toward self-constitution and identity on the threshold of modernity was embodied in the antagonistic contents of the European moderns; it was *not* a particularity of the New World's modernism but a common ground of the cultural space.

Coll's attitude as an anarchist and modernist was motivated by a profound concern with urbanization, poverty, and inequality. At the beginning of the century his critique was directed against "industrialization, civilization" (1901:123) in a use of the term which suggests a deconstruction of its positive content. A similar angle of vision can be found in the Venezuelan modernist Miguel Eduardo Pardo's novel *A Whole Country* (Todo un pueblo), published by the editors of an important journal, *Literary Life* (1899), whose tropological dimension is the representation of an alternate social system, based on positive science (see González Stephan 1983). Such is the emphasis of Sawa's novel *Everyone's Mistress* (La mujer de todo el mundo; 1885), which was enthusiastically reviewed in the anarchist press (Zavala, ed. 1977).

Cosmopolitanism and urbanization played an important part for the new critics of modernity as a symptom of differing discourses in their rejection of a parochial, regional, holistic nationalism, and the desire to revolutionize social space. The route of modernist architecture in Catalonia, which reached its height in 1900 with the decorative spirit of asymmetry, as well as the bricolage between decorative arts, glass, and ceramics (see Litvak 1990), was an expression of scientific optimism. This modernist spirit was also promoted and constructed in the Balearic islands, especially Sóller, Lluc, and Palma de Mallorca (Murray and Seguí Aznar 1989). The modern alternative of the city as an aesthetic discourse in its sculpted monumentalism was balanced with the struggle against the totalizing impulse to subordinate and assimilate the dominant entrepreneurial control under the dissident subcultures. This defined the view of the city as cultural text, by contesting voices and heterogeneous universes interrogating the semantic and symbolic density of the social world.

However, the "extravagances" of bourgeois urbanization were particularly stressed by the working-class movements; in Barcelona, anarchist workers expressed that they were denied access to a dignified life, and that modern civic constructions made inequalities more evident, since large segments of the work force were denied access to the much-propagandized joys of bourgeois consumption. The surge of women into low-paying jobs was accompanied by an equally vigorous feminist anarchist movement; the important strike by textile workers in 1883 indicated the awesome poverty and exploitation in the midst of growing affluence.

The reaction toward industrialization took many forms (Cano Ballesta 1981); however, one can conclude that much of the so-called alienation from modern urban life was due to the impoverishment of life. It needs to be emphasized that when modernists referred to the "social situation," they meant the condition of the industrial working class and the lack of satisfaction of basic human needs. Some, such as Coll in Venezuela and Sawa in Madrid, disclosed the poverty of the tenement sections, infant mortality, prostitution, the overflow of unemployed immigrants. Others, including Ernesto Bark and the group of social scientists, as well as the labor movements (the well-known socialist *Informes*), revealed the gap between bourgeois triumphalism and poverty; in 1900 Madrid had the highest mortality rate in western Europe.

Bourgeois optimism was caricatured, while others made visible the multiplicities of unequal social spaces and exploitation; these moderns were extremely attentive to the signs of prosperity and declension, and inscribed with polemics the emerging chronicle of journalism. New modern periodicals and newspapers supplied a forum for the contending voices in the scriptural culture.

The city expressed polar aspects of one and the same problem of separation.[8] Around 1893, Darío voiced a concern about the new technics of architecture as he parodied the apotheosis of steel in great urban areas:

> The yankee is proud with his Brooklyn Bridge? Paris allows the monstrous Eiffel
> Tower to humiliate with its black skeleton the Gothic jewel, the great H of Notre
> Dame. How right is the writer who affirmed that the Eiffel Tower is the bell
> tower of a temple consecrated to the cult of gold, whose mass should be said by
> the American pope Jay Gould, who would raise in his hands, at the ring of the
> electric bells, the host of the check. (In 1953 IV:613)

To this must be added that he clearly saw the discontents of a modernization
process that promised progress and emancipation from want, but which delivered oppression and various forms of capitalist domination in return for meager
gains. In 1903 he wrote a soliloquy of the poor, strongly stressing the excluded
minorities:

> He [*sic*] speaks in his own way of the cruelty of contemporary life for the
> disinherited, and points to something more horrible: on the side of the crushing
> mammoths of capital, the crushers from the scientific juggernaut, those who
> have taken away from the poor past consolations, those who have left them
> without God and hope and in return have given them nothing. (In Zavala, ed.
> 1989)

Darío's perception clearly points to the the destruction of local cultures and
beliefs.

Through countercultural critiques and practices, anarchist modernists aimed
to offer a corrective to the pattern of social strident extremes in an aesthetic
response deconstructing the adulatory mystique of the traditionals and con-
servatives (the *old*). The aesthetic ideology was believed to be a potent force to
demystify and disclose the veiled conservative implications of language and
politics. At each stage, they asked questions on science, social sciences, economics, medicine, anthropology, what Foucault calls the discourses of the
science of wealth in *The Order of Things* (1973). In fact, the titles of various
journals and publications directly allude to these questionings, such as *Social
Science* (Ciencia Social), a Spanish anarchist journal directed by Anselmo
Lorenzo in 1895.

This new epistemic critique can be found in a number of short-lived periodicals—there were at least fifteen known, such as *Don Quijote* (Madrid,
1892–1903), *Literary Life* (1899), *New Life* (Vida Nueva; Madrid, 1898–
1900), *New Journal* (Revista Nueva; Madrid, 1899), *Spanish Soul* (Alma
Española; Madrid, 1903–1904), *Helios* (Madrid, 1904–1905), *Prometeo* (Pro-
metheus; Madrid, 1908–1912). Special mention should be made of the anarchist journals *Free Humanity* (Humanidad Libre; 1902), published in Valencia
by women anarchists, and *Free Conscience* (Conciencia Libre; 1902), edited in
Cordoba by Belén Sárraga, Amalia Carvia, and Soledad Arenales. Both were
devoted to anti-clericalism and feminism, projecting a social imaginary of an
egalitarian utopia also based on gender equality. Still other journals, such as
that of Bark's *Germinal* group (Madrid, 1897–99), may be regarded as an
archeology of the human sciences and their new configuration of repressive

knowledges in the modern age. Their task was to reappropriate and reconstruct those sciences in a liberating reinversion in their obsession with urban poverty (see Bark's *Social Statistics* [Estadística Social], n.d.).

The major fictions, poetry, essays, and journalistic writing voiced the unwelcomed truths of capitalism, colonial oppression, and police brutality through parodies, attentive journalism, and hyperbolic writing, exposing lucidly the talismanic virtue of money and wealth and the stock market, as well as the moralizing of classical culture pumped into schools and universities. The monopolism of learning was understood as an extension of the authoritarian state, and was a major point against centralized authority, the religious veneration of the past, and the belief in the continual progress of mankind.

There was a rejection of the sugary version of the bohemians (such as Murger's) for a portrayal of the starving underbelly modernist bohemian of the turn-of-the-century great cosmopolis. The solutions ranged from sentimentality, to lucid unmaskings, to the extreme radical emotional individualism of the right to be left alone (Vallès was read enthusiastically). In most of these publications, the concerted cultural space includes both Spanish and Latin American modernists, as well as translations and collaborations of French symbolists and "decadents," Vallès, Kropotkin, and Marx, among so many others.

Drawing connections from this cultural space, the modernists' position was to disclose the mechanisms of power which were accompanied by the production of effective instruments for the formation and accumulation of knowledge (I follow Foucault). The methods of observation of the social sciences, of techniques of registration, such as statistics, procedures of investigation and research, apparatuses of control through juridical and medical prescriptions, and a political theory of power, merged with a network of domination and coercion—the new type of power which Foucault describes as the "fundamental instrument in the constitution of industrial capitalism and of the type of society that is its accompaniment" (in 1980:105).

Of particular relevance in this context is the polemical reception of Max Nordau's *Degeneration* (1892, translated in 1902), which outlined a medical analysis of turn-of-the-century writers, drawing from political technologies of the body, in particular psychiatry and psychopathology. The Hungarian-born journalist and practicing physician enjoyed a renowned reputation from 1883 until the beginning of World War I, particularly for this book, which provoked replies from Bernard Shaw, Italian physicians, French philosophers, and some Hispanic modernists, while he became the rallying symbol for many moderns who were concerned with Spanish political and cultural "decadence" and believed science was the key to the future.

Degeneration is a polemic with the modern modes of art and literature (mainly impressionism and expressionism), as well as with the younger generation's search for identity. Nordau's cornerstone was a belief in ordered progress based on the potential of natural sciences; supported by such knowledge, humanity would be able to develop, since science and progress go together (see

Morse, intro. to 1968 edition). The absence of such a formulation—physical laws which apply to man as much as to nature itself—led him to place many writers among the degenerates, and made him believe in applying to contemporary artists the tests by which the Italian Cesare Lombroso habitually judged criminals: "psychiatric research to literary criticism," in Lombroso's definition (1894).

Nordau's elaborations on the formulas and qualities necessary for human progress and to shape the future—among them the power of will and the discipline of hard work—were the attributes of the bourgeois, in his internalization of instrumental reason which would sweep out false transcendentalism. If instrumental reason were ruptured, it would lead to excess, since human solidarity was based on the unity of living matter with a scientifically determined universe. His equality, however, did not mean equality of functions (xxi).

In the much-criticized liberal view, he equated modernity with progress through order, will, and rationality, and thus he condemned all "mystics," "ego-maniacs," and those who rely upon their imagination rather than observations.[9] His taxonomy included Zola, Rodin, Nietzsche, Verlaine, and Ibsen. Nordau combined his belief in science and human progress with an organic view of natural evolution and his ideas on psychology, inspired by Lombroso (*Genio e Follio,* 1863) and his catalogue of criminals, which advocated the death penalty, and the French psychiatrist B. A. Morel, who had popularized the word *degeneration* (xxiii). Lombroso, who had also written scientifically against anarchists (*Gli anarchi,* 1894), became the privileged subtext of *Degeneration.*

Both Nordau's and Lombroso's technologies of the body were directed to "discipline and punishment," whereby beings were transformed into subjects and objects of knowledge for the human sciences (on this point see Foucault's *The Birth of the Clinic* and *Madness and Civilization*). A liberal reformer confident of salvation through evolution, science, and reason, Nordau developed a thesis against the anarchists of modern art. The analyses prompted a reply from Darío, while Sawa made his own independent contribution by popularizing the French symbolists and decadents in Spanish periodicals (thus implicitly defying Nordau); Darío polemized dialogically with Nordau in *The Estranged Ones* (Los raros, 1905) by reversing the taxonomy of the gallery of horrors and defending Wilde and Verlaine, among his illustrious heroes. In his words:

> Needless to say Max Nordau's ideas on art reveal an extremely singular and utilitarian aesthetics. The steel car and science have destroyed, according to him, religious ideals. . . . Today, in the sphere of humanity, after the passage of the scientific monster, trees bloom full of flowers of faith. Neither can art be destroyed. The divine half-mad, "necessary for progress," will always live in their celestial asylum consoling the earth from its barrenness and hardness with a harmonious rain of splendors and a magnificent richness of dreams and hopes. ("Max Nordau," in Zavala, ed. 1989:120)

The nonconformist contribution of these modernists to culture came from the short-lived periodicals, journals, and brochures, what Malcolm Bradbury calls "the shock troops of modernism" (1976), through which the modern aesthetics, as well as the critique of instrumental reason, came to be known to the public. Equally significant were a second-hand Nietzscheanism, or the Oscar Wilde brand of socialism, and most certainly his stand against bourgeois morality (known in Spain through translations since 1892), or anarchism, or Zolaism, or Schopenhauer, if not the sublimities of decadentism to give sense to the growing awareness and denunciation of the industrial bourgeoisie.

Let us remember that Baudelaire had already assessed himself the most fundamental of questions of what to do with the spirit in a material age which did not recognize its existence (Gilman 1979 on decadence). If anarchists and socialists offered hospitality, so did the moderns, by joining forces to sponsor innovation in a dialogical pluralism of dissent against the uncritical concept of progress. For them the constitutive forces of social life were science and a continuum of capitalist wealth, a time in which European predominance was uncontested, and both European culture and technological achievements seemed the natural goal.

As an ideologeme with differing meanings to each user, modernism is an integral part of such economic and political concentration in a world with electricity, railroads, steamships, cheap daily newspapers, compulsory education, and new mass movements. It is also the expression of the impact of and the changes in industrial organization based on increased mechanization and a stepped-up pace of work, which affected not only the public but what Tannenbaum (1977) called the private sphere of life, and provided a challenge to the general values of society. Societies draw the line between public and private affairs rather differently (Moore 1985); questions were also raised about rights against political interference, among many others. Some, such as Nordau, adhered to the lucrative side, while others, including Sawa, lucidly posited revolution as the only challenge in 1885: "Oh, European continent, old Europe, old damned Europe!; the time of great justices and great vengeance is near. . . . A new era is coming" (in Zavala, ed. 1977:44).

It is not surprising, then, that the Krausist philosopher U. González Serrano, in an essay published in *Germinal* (11 June 1897), in blunt opposition to an indifferent and pitiless naturalism, argues that anarchism projects "a pietist neo-mysticism such as Tolstoy's"; disputing those who believe that science conceives only the mechanical, and that wealth is its only divinity, he firmly asserts that anarchism strengthens "a doctrine of abnegation and love to the poor." Furthermore, he maintains that at least anarchism succeeds in showing the deficiencies of previous theories. His assessment connects cultural value spheres with interest positions and the subsequent conflict between them. Therefore, González Serrano, in his own way, is actually speaking from the site of what I have referred to as the heterogeneity of social discourses comprising the ideologeme of *anarchism;* he exemplifies a voice in the polemic with and a counterdiscourse against social contradictions, by adopting differing attitudes toward specific cultural value spheres.

The Critical Rationale

In his *Autobiography of My Books* (1913), Darío wrote that he had brought to Spain the principles of "intellectual freedom and artistic personalism" which had been the basis of the new life in Latin America's thought and art (147). In Spain and France, however, he came in contact with anarchism in its modernist blend; and this "literary anarchism," that is, the embeddedment of anarchism in social discourse, corresponded to the eruption of heterogeneity in the midst of a homogenized world of everyday experience which had been normalized through bourgeois morality and instrumental reason. The critique of such rationality and scientificism—already unmasked by Nietzsche from another perspective—offered an aperture to the outlawed, which will be provided by the hospitable ground of literary magazines adopting a critical attitude. Both anarchism and modernism project a different value-space which simultaneously, in its dialogicality, penetrates the same institutional domains, in allied cognitive, ethical, and aesthetic orientations of antagonistic nature against the resulting image of society as an iron cage.

The polemic around Nordau was an essential test for the contending cultural spaces. The result was a split between those who aligned cultural discourse as part of a critique of instrumental reason, and those for whom art was the ally of science, rationality, evolution, progress, morality, and the general welfare understood in terms of instrumental reason. While some were strongly against Nordau, others (quite specifically the *Germinal* group) brought the theme of national regeneration into agreement with Nordau's commitment to a systematic revolt with art as programmatic for social progress. The aim was to address rationally and positively the questions of reform and regeneration. The contending groups had diverse, and in many cases opposing, optics: while Nordau feared the literary anarchists, they, Darío included, in turn antagonized "medical literature" and "scientific criticism." Darío even made it evident in *Los Raros* that, once the diagnosis of art as a disease gained acceptance, the estrangement from those ideas which were part of the sickness would follow. While some hoped to bolster bourgeois morality and order, others were committed to the salvation of an aesthetics that would free humankind from instrumental reason.

These perceptions are also apparent in two periodicals which provided an integration of moderns in Paris: *Heraldo de París* (1900–1904) and *Nuevo Mercurio* (1907), published in Paris by Gómez Carrillo as a bond between Spanish-speaking intellectuals; Nordau contributed an article on modernism in Spain and in Latin America (March 1907). Also instrumental was *Le Mercure de France* (1890–1965), founded by Alfred Vallette to succeed *La Pléiade*

(1886; 1889–90), the most important symbolist periodical, which inaugurated in 1898 a special section on Latin America. Leopoldo Lugones, who had been a correspondent for *La Nación* in Paris, also published *Revue Sudaméricaine*.

The *Heraldo de París,* directed by Puerto Rican–born Luis Bonafoux, is recognized as an anarchist journal with contributions from Errico Malatesta, Tárrida del Mármol, and Ricardo Mella (key figures in Italian, Spanish, and Latin American anarchism), as well as from Alfredo Calderón, Darío, Unamuno, Azorín, Juan Ramón Jiménez, and Rosario Acuña (among others). This newspaper was in contact with the well-known French *Revue Blanche* (1891–97; 1898–1903), directed by Alexandre Natanson, one of the principal anarchist publications, to which Darío sent articles, as well as Mallarmé, Verlaine, Proust, Gide, Strindberg, and the Hispanics José María de Heredia and F. Tárrida del Mármol (both Cuban-born, like Marx's son-in-law, Pierre Lafargue).

The prestigious *Mercure de France* inaugurated a special section on Latin American news, with articles from the Venezuelan Coll and the Guatemalan Gómez Carrillo (Zavala 1975, 1988a), a friend of Nordau's and one of the chroniclers of what could be called the transitoriness and reproducibility of modernity. His vignettes and collages ranged from boxing to modern dance (he was an admirer of Isadora Duncan), from jewels to fashions; he was also an enthusiastic second-hand vulgarizer of literature and art, pioneering reproductions and the illusory apparatus of fetishisms. This general descriptive framework leads us to conceive a whole new series of social relations, which call into question forms of subordination, and also the meaningful alliances which occurred at the level of social relations and new hegemonic formations, consolidated, to some extent, through the dominant modes of cultural diffusion.

Journalism and literature frequently combined in a concurring exercise of information, political analysis, criticism, and book reviews. The increased role of the popular classes in cultural life drew heavily on writers; Marx was also at this juncture a modernist writer, a newspaper chronicler, like Martí and Darío. Darío's intention in his bricolages on art, literature, and politics was also part of that social formation which brought together artists and audiences with a clear mark of their social identities.

The politics of these chronicles is important, since they help define the symbolic order and explore cultural practices in a space which makes explicit the ethical content of the modernist narrative. Darío's articles make clear the new version of the modern project: articles on socialism and socialists (he wrote on Marx), on anarchists and anarchism, on political affairs, against militarism, against exploitation and capitalism in its modern form of technology and industrialization, linking—as in the libertarian orbit of Bakunin—the economic tyranny of the modern capitalist world (see the recent anthologies published by the minister of culture in Sandinista Nicaragua [1983, 1984]).[10]

On that same critical basis, Sawa wrote a series of articles on anarchism, while at the same time depicting social and sexual inequalities, as he mocked the operations of *castellanismo* and colonialism, and the logic by which such fiction was constructed.[11] Sawa's perspectives and views are multiple—chronicles, a posthumous prose collage (*Illuminations in the Shadow*), fiction—and the different points of observation fragment and multiply events and situations. He privileges multiplicity, contrast, and dissent while staging Spanish culture as a means of commenting on institutions and moral high ground practices. In direct inversion of Eurocentrism and a universalism, "civilization" becomes for Sawa (and other modernists) a cloak for greed and destruction. Texts have a negative and a positive ideological project.

Against the barbarism of modern life, many texts tend to fortify, even monumentalize, anarchists, to disclose the horror and hypocritical game of power. The sociogram of the "anarchist" or the "anarchist saint" became the favorite of many modern writers (Turgenev, Dostoevsky, Tolstoy, Conrad, Blasco Ibañez, Valle-Inclán, Unamuno) based on images of Bakunin, Nechaev, Kropotkin, or the Gaditan Fermín Salvochea, who was frequently portrayed in Spanish novels as a "lay saint." While nihilism, in Nietzsche's diagnosis, was the malady of European culture, anarchism became a polyvalent metaphor for extreme individualism, and also the will to a constitution of self to conform with scientific modernity; and in the Russian version of "Neither God nor State," a revolt against the monopoly exerted by the instrumentalization of liberal bourgeois society, and the geopolitical hegemony of the church.

Around the opposing views on technology and science which Nordau's book disclosed, there were not only competing aesthetic discourses—that of the modernist literary anarchy or a scientific realism aimed at glorifying progress— but also a differing polemic over rationality: on the one hand, those positivists, social scientists, and regenerationists who displayed a lineal and continuous optimism about the idea of progress through order, will, and rationality, and on the other, those whose critical attitude toward the modern age meant a disbelief in the stability and progress of modern society sustained by technological growth in production. The followers of Nordau defended both the claims to the exclusive validity of technological science and the relative autonomy of civil society (order), while the others attempted to recover what Nietzsche called the Dionysian powers of regeneration through a modern art that could awaken the utopian possibilities of freedom. Art could be conceived as aesthetic education to restore nature and ethical community to the overly rational, subjective individual or modern society.

As with a wide variety of other experiences, the presence of the supernatural also brought about the archaic experience of the occult, mysticism, the exotic Orientalism(s), the chaos of human nature, perhaps in the dynamic direction of Schlegel's "new mythology" or Hölderlin's resurrection of the Dionysian myth, conceived not as an aestheticization of rational ideas but as a return to archaic sources of social integration (cf. Ingram 1988:86). The heightening of subjectivity beyond the objective boundaries of reason—from decadent sociograms, to satanism, to dandyism, to primitive Christianity, to esotericism, or "mythologies"—with the distinct social function which we have analyzed, acted as a mechanism for dealing with or mediating social contradictions (in the pertinent

Lévi-Straussian distinction). These idioms are present in Valle, as well as in other modernists; the critique of the artificiality of modern life had induced Bakunin to defend an anarchism based on feudal community life, while Kropotkin also found precedents for his social theories in the village communities of the Middle Ages, and even in the Greek cities. I agree with Brenan (1978), who perceptively underlines that there is in anarchism a strong element of reaction against industrialization, without renouncing the advantages of modern industrial processes, but there was a hope for the freer human life of the Middle Ages, for example, to preserve a sort of mysterious sense of collective memory. These are constants in most Hispanic modernists.

If this industrialized and technological utilitarian society hoped to construct individual subjects through the collective activities, practices, beliefs, and values of instrumental reason, the inversion projected through the social imaginary blurred such images by not reconciling the individual with the social position assigned by the capitalist distribution of wealth, fashion, and "good taste." From a semiological perspective, these moderns opened the way to our understanding of the discourses on wealth masking the languages of fashion, and often made attempts to stand outside such languages. The picture in some ways follows the direction which Martí had suggested since the 1880s, and which Darío had developed in an endless flow of parodic metaphors against imperialism and industrial underdevelopment, while uncovering an underlying capitalism, conventions, and tyrannies, and announcing the "good news of socialism" (in 1984). This dual focus is the repoliticized Darío that Carlos Fonseca, leader of the Sandinista Popular Revolution in 1974, restored (in 1984). It would seem that Darío's collective story still compels.

In addition to the conflicting models of cosmopolitanism, periodicals, and books, art functioned as signs. Through this deployment, the metaphysical illusion of science, progress, and morality was undermined. The superman left its symbols in modernity; anarchism (both literary and as a labor movement toward utopia) helped to disclose the growing artificiality and moral vigilantism of bourgeois life, the fictive manipulation of news and information in a reaction against aggression and against the corrupt struggle for power and money. The strife was toward more liberty and more leisure, since dignity and freedom had been dehumanized by factory life and state and police violence. But this modern art carried at the same time the social utopia and the alienation of history (paraphrasing Barthes's *Writing Degree Zero* [1967]); the unmasking of mythologies through anatropic inversion represented—in the dialogical social imaginary—both ideological criticism and semiological dismantling by challenging the symbolic and power itself.

VII

PENINSULAR MODERNS AND THE SHATTERED MIRROR

> In America we had this movement [modernism] before Castilian Spain, for very clear reasons.
>
> —Darío (1901)

> Poets, painters, orators, writers, musicians, your task is to show what art can do for the triumph of Justice.
>
> —E. Picard (1897)

Anarchists, Socialists, and the Modern Sign

As we have seen, in Spain at the turn of the century there was a hegemonic bloc constituted by different positions, anarchists, socialists, bohemians, and "organic intellectuals." New cultural forms called into question relations of subordination in a variety of often conflicting ways, from an egalitarian imaginary to new democratic alternatives. In these circumstances, it is important to emphasize that modernity was the articulating force, subject to a constant process of redefinition. Modernism was, like any socio-cultural identity, a floating signifier, and thus open-ended, denoted and connoted in different ways throughout the hegemonic alliance. It is here that we connect again with Bakhtin's ideas on meaning as social values; in his words: "The *point of view* contained within the word is subject to reinterpretation, as is the modality of language and the very *relationship of language to the object* and *to the speaker*" (DI 237).

At this particular point modernism—in the forms we have pursued—has a potential meaning to connect the inner or individual to the shared experience of the social, in the dialogic structure of consciousness. The particularity of the situatedness was fundamental, and underwent actualization into outer expression in the context of an active, shared participation within a dialogical unit. This fundamental problem of cognition was mediated through modernist language, with all its accentuations and re-accentuations. The project of language and the project of selfhood, which had drawn together Latin American modernists in the shared experience to monitor a new form of community, also created in Spain the possibility to set a stage for a modern nation. The simultaneity of these dialogues was merely an instance of the larger polyphony of social and discursive forces which, at the given time of the North American invason, set the conditions to shape a larger dialogism. Its distinctiveness was the particular combination of different discourses into a whole we have called the language of modernism, understood from the point of view of a historical poetics.

In Spain, the period 1896–1907 saw the formation of a common cultural republican-socialist alliance as a result of the repression caused by the Montjuich trials of anarchists Anselmo Lorenzo, Teresa Claramunt, F. Tárrida del Mármol, Federico Urales, José Llunas, and the young Catalan intellectual Pedro Corominas (among others), to which we must also add the defeat in Cuba and the electoral fiascos of the left political parties. The unpopular, disastrous Cuban War (1896–98) produced a strong anti-militarist feeling in the country; at least 200,000 Spaniards died, and the nation converted to pacifism. This strong stand became evident in 1909 in an uprising in Barcelona against calling up the military reserves for service in Africa. Working-class and intellectual reactions took different forms.[1] Anti-militarism and anti-imperialism became a matter of public commentary. The common project of this cultural alliance was a modernization of the country through democratic industrialization; however deep the hostility to capitalism, the dominant tone was the stress on a genuine labor movement with democratic aims.

The new enthymeme took the shape of an unuttered social and aesthetic utopia. In the discursive episteme of this conjuncture, the consensus was to subvert culture, to shatter the mirror of historical repetition and cultural reproduction. A new language became the medium to infiltrate the symbolic target of cultural production itself, and to allegorize the social utopia and class struggle by way of an exchange on truth and freedom affirming negativity as the shattered mirror of society. So the aesthetic attitude signified freedom, at the same time that the theoreticians of anarchist and socialist aesthetics demanded sensual and utilitarian gratification. Their aim was to project a vision of active spectators and readers, and not a passive consumer stupefied by a bourgeois cultural commodity. Rather, they thought that subordinated groups could subvert ideology by deliberately identifying with or distancing from bourgeois values.

I would like to address this practice from the perspective of both Bakhtinian carnivalization and difference as the social grounds of discursive heterogeneity. As a responsive communality, the moderns linked the conjunctural "event" to a dissension against political rhetoric, cultural difference, and the mirage of identity projected by the instrumental reason of bourgeois interests, in light of the violence and repression instigated by the state.

Anarchist and socialist publications, together with leftist critical journals and periodicals, embraced the projected new potential for growth and human development, and evidenced the material conditions of the end of the empire in the Peninsula. Such was the purpose of the anarchist journal *Revista Blanca* (White Review, 1898–1905), with editions between six and eight thousand, initiated by the leading Catalan anarchists Juan Montseny and Teresa Mañé, better known by the pseudonyms Federico Urales and Soledad Gustavo respectively. This important journal, which came out at a time in which censorship had been tightened (the Law of 1896 against anarchist propaganda), included the critical organic intellectuals of what later came to be known as the construct Generation of 1898 (among them Azorín and Unamuno) and published a literary supplement, *Land and Liberty* (Tierra y Libertad), directed mainly by Gustavo, which stressed the revolutionary character of negativity, sharpening struggle and antagonism, and "mirroring" the density of the social and ideological hegemony of traditional collective representations.[2]

Its first issue provided a specific new discourse which made possible the dynamic modernity that became dominant. As Urales writes: "We are satisfied with our work. We were right and feel the satisfaction produced by the thinking and knowing minds who have aspirations, the spirits who seek new sentiments and new ideas" (15 July 1898). Anarchists, such as Urales, and socialists, such as Pedro Iglesias, were mobilizing workers toward anti-capitalist struggles, since many modes of life were threatened by the emergent industrial order. After the Montjuich trials, Urales was exiled in London and Paris, where he worked with Tárrida del Mármol, well known to French intellectuals, and contributor to the journal *Revue Blanche* on Latin American questions.

The collapse of the social order following the Cuban War, as well as the radicalization of workers, produced a whole new set of circumstances, and an organic crisis which reduced the hegemonic capacity of the monarchy and its government. As Spanish imperial hegemony disintegrated completely under Alphonse XIII and the conservative regenerationists, the government's power was weakened; anxiety among the dominant classes prompted the government to adopt a strong repressive stand against radical political parties and terrorism. A surge of pessimism among intellectuals coexisted with a more critical attitude: "All is broken down in this wretched country: no government, no electors, no parties, no navy, no army. All is ruin, decadence," wrote R. Macias Picavea in 1899 (in Carr 1982:524).

While the traditionally so-called regenerationists were defining "Spanishness" and reworking "heroic" medieval sagas (el Cid) into the popular memory, praising the quixotic ventures, Spanish "honor," heroicism, and humanitarianism, the interpolitical rivalries intensified, and workers' movements defied hegemonies in conjunction with the younger generation of modern/modernist intellectuals. However, the quixotic spirit became a symbol to play off the moral superiority of the decaying Spanish empire against the crude materialist aims of the encroaching North Americans. The discursive space was overdetermined by this set of circumstances, and both "radicals" and "reactionaries" were defending a type of identity under threat. This same evaluation was present in Latin American modernists, as we have seen, who also re-accentuated a set of common categories peculiar to a joint culture system: from the Cid to Don Quixote.

Within a contradictory interpretive frame, the same ideologeme is operative in Unamuno's *Life of Don Quixote and Sancho* (1905), in Darío's poems "Our Lord Don Quixote" and "Things of the Cid," in Ortega, Azorín, and Urales (among others), who accentuate this moral superiority through ideological interpellations projecting spiritual values (see Zavala 1989c). The quixotic ideologeme works in the social imaginary with the ideology of "heroicity" as a counterimage, in much the same way Velázquez's *La rendición de Breda* became the cultural text of the "heroic imperialism" of the disillusioned Castile of Philip IV; the social auditory would identify with the portrayal of the supposed "nobility and grandeur" by which the Spanish accepted capitulation (see Zavala 1989c).

However, it is possible to detect primordially two dimensions in the discursive field through, on the one hand, the opaque pessimism of those whose aim was to reconstruct and mobilize tradition, and, on the other, the potential optimism established by the alliance between republican-socialists and the modern intellectuals (similar to the alliance we have suggested for Latin American societies). In Urales's words: "In the present historical moment a transformation in the spirit is emerging, one that sooner or later will modify social relations" (*Revista Blanca,* 1 July 1898). The date 1898 was both the real event and the symbolic moment which triggered latent anxieties made more intense because of the North American victory: it seemed that the epochal dominance of the Spanish "race" was drawing to a close.[3] The *Revista Blanca,* as well as the Partido Socialista Obrero's (now PSOE) journal *The Socialist* (Madrid, 1886–1925), directed by the founding father of socialism, Pablo Iglesias, defended (with Catalan republican federalists) the independence of the colonies together with a socialist identity against the radical inconsistency of bourgeois hegemony.

The organic intellectuals also joined the socialist publications (including Clarín), since different subject positions became at that juncture the site of antagonism. The common denominator of all this contesting "unity" within plurality was the defense of a certain identity against the hegemonic signifier. The modernity which was definitively emerging was the confrontation between traditional culture and innovation—a democratization of technology and progress or the reinforcement of an authoritarian state. This year marked the critical passage of a worn-out system of domination, and the alliances between different groups and social forces to achieve positions of leadership; the alliances pointed to winning support and consent among intellectuals and sectors of the dominated classes themselves.

Hegemony at this crucial moment also marked the emergence of what is now called "cultural identity," and what Raymond Williams called "a structure of feeling" (in another context). Modernism rose against conformism, and adopted different forms of discourse. Although a somewhat vague notion of culture, what I have been addressing as modernism seemed to give consistency to a project to decolonize life from instrumental reason and industrial capitalism, as well as provided a common substrate in the fundamental problem of expressing new forms of cognition and understanding, mediated through language. It included a variety of discourse, ranging from the inclusion of the popular in culture (Valle-Inclán), to the slippages of Unamuno's voices, to the plural selves of Azorín's pseudonyms, to the heteronyms of Antonio Machado or Pessoa. They all reveal plurality, contradictory positions, the decentered subject.

It is at the level of the social that we can begin to see how interconnected these contingencies of lived experience were. The disintegration of the empire led to a critical questioning of modernization: some gave in to conventional re-accentuations of inherited forms of national subjectivities, mythologies of imperial Spain, while others questioned the past and opposed the need to reconstruct and mobilize it. What was highlighted was a zone of deconstructive positivity to articulate democratic tasks and a socialist leadership. The speculative operation was practical and discursive in the contingency of the historical event, to constitute a new way of seeing and undermining traditionalist forms of representation which became militantly "populist" among organic intellectuals. The point of interest is that modernist aesthetics compelled new ways of seeing; in Urales's words: "If to love art for art's sake is beautiful, to love art for *progress* is even more so" (*Revista Blanca*, 1 Mar. 1899).

This first modernist phase (with all its denominations) broke with the past—all its contradictions included—while others intended to reinvent or re-accentuate Spanishness. Traditionalists, together with a strong and militant Catholicism, believed that the pure and unadulterated Spanish Castilian traditions could be recalled from the past and projected to the future. The general strike in Barcelona in 1902, the wave of anarchist strikes in Andalusia (1903–1905), the Tragic Week of 1909 which resulted in the execution of Ferrer, all led to the conservative government of Antonio Maura, whose traditionalism could be synthesized in his famous political program: "We are ourselves. We have no need for any other symbol: that is our ensign" (qtd. in Brenan 1978:32). Years later, much like the paradox of English modernity (examined by Colls and Dodd, eds. 1986), the two visions appeared simultaneously: a regeneration of the past and a break with it. Therefore, among the forerunners of Spanish (and Hispanic) modernism(s) were the anarchist and socialist journals and periodicals, the reception of Zola, Ibsen, Hauptmann, Björnson, Ruskin, William Morris, Grave, Malatesta, Nietzsche, through whose discursive mediation the critical perception of Spanish society was reasserted.[4]

It could be claimed, then, that *representation* became the social arena of the contending signs. The mirror metaphor was used as a cognitive anatropic perception of social reality, by which the social auditory was incorporated into the literary event. Turn-of-the-century anarchists and bohemians inscribed identifications in a history of similarities, contiguities, and correspondences with the social context, as social oxymorons in literary texts, with contiguous negative and positive evaluations. The binary oppositions bourgeois/proletarian, exploitation/equality, salary/capital, rich/poor, lack/opulence, war/peace, justice/oppression are the preferred tropes and ideologemes to project class struggle. A particular set of idioms and semes—country, motherland, bourgeois, worker, family, religion, art—produce and redistribute meanings with a semantic function of expressing either identity and recognition, or otherness and distortion.[5]

In these conditions of chiasmata and fissures, cultural texts are clearly a reflection on the similarities or equivalences of the referential surface which are the foundation of utterances, in social hierarchies and changes of meaning. The whole undertaking is carried over into an epistemological theory of reflection. Foucault's words in his introduction to *The Order of Things* (1970) are relevant: "The history of the order imposed on things would be the history of the Same—of that which, for a given culture, is both dispersed and related, therefore to be distinguished by kinds and to be collected together into identities" (xxiv).

Anarchism and socialism, as well as "decadent modernism" and "literary anarchists," became part of the history of the other (and *anotherness*), like madness; the "other" was both interior and foreign, and one which the authorized signifiers hoped to exclude and shut away, to exorcise the interior danger. Among so many other discourses from religion, medicine, and the social sciences, Max Nordau's and Cesare Lombroso's taxonomies help to legitimize the exclusions. In contrast, Bakunin and Kropotkin, who were widely translated and read, could be included with Marx among what Ricoeur calls the masters of suspicion, who provided theoretical grounds to demythologize social oppression.

The cognitive anatropic metaphor of the "mirror" will be privileged and reaccentuated at this time to invite inversions, and used as a model of an organized semantic and social universe. The epistemic break of this cognitive metaphor seems to call into question the existence of a preestablished and hierarchical cultural network of semantic fields and social universes. As an anatropic inversion, the mirror metaphor could be said to be an open-ended metaphor of the threshold of social transformation. Mirrors—concave to Valle—could enlarge, reduce, distort, invert, but most certainly were channels of social critique. The interlocutors could either identify themselves with what they saw, or use the virtual images to break the mirror reproducing a prefabricated reality, in order to move toward real social relations. The sense of rage against the degradation of the quality of life under industrialization and capitalism is simultaneously uttered with the potential of self-realization; awareness of alienation and disalienation as a moral possibility is the grounding logic of this anatropic inversion to monitor appearances and "realities." This was the point of their insistence on the social; literature is intended to break through dead habits of behavior to a restored perception of the actual world. This problem is not alien to Marxism, and is pivotal in the canonic definitions of ideology (including Althusser's). It also has methodological importance in Lukács's reflection theory and the Marxist canonical theory of realism.

At the turn of the century, representatives from a host of graphic and scriptural universes (caricaturists, bohemians, modernists) made wide use of demystifying languages in an attempt to project cognitive processes in order to subject ethical and political norms to a performative discourse which would project specular images. These texts aimed at making visible the spectacle of duplicity through an ironic canvas, which would then be decomposed and recomposed according to a critical law to monitor the apparent sobriety and morality of political and religious institutions, as well as the (dis)honor which hid behind the mask of truth and national mythologies. The mirrors of anarchists and socialists were intended to restore social visibility by bringing forth the invisibilities of the state's and monarchy's degradations. The performance of the texts consists of bringing out these invisibilities, in stable superimpositions of signs; the mirror image provides the metathesis of social life in redefinitions of the individual, the collective, and culture.

The anarchist cultural project is based in the following logics:

1. The aim is to produce open-ended texts, unfinalized in the present to transgress all closure through heterogeneity and the force of signification.

2. The ethical function is structured through a poetics of negation that implies simultaneously a negation of bourgeois art for art's sake.

3. The semiotic production is made to serve a poetics of the beautiful as enthusiasm (which Lyotard's [1984] contemporary aesthetics on the sublime would seem to illuminate), and to project an expenditure of energy involving the reader or spectator in the experience.

4. As a social phenomenon, the "new," "modern" art favored the social egalitarian tendencies and aspirations of contemporary society; artistic production is the means for a revolutionary modernity.

5. Art was an extension of vitality, including desire and the sexual, against artificiality and deceit.

6. Art was an expression of the quest for a truly egalitarian society, liberty, and rebellion (not only of revolutionary ideals).

7. Art should be "realistic"; that is, new meanings may be created through a close relation to "reality," but it should be real (natural), authentic, and *scientific*.

8. Modern art should monitor the inequalities of bourgeois society, including gendered inequalities (such as the specific project of Teresa Claramunt's theater and articles in *The Combat*, and Soledad Gustavo's writing).

9. Since art is labor and thus production, it should be liberated from its dependency on the economic laws which transform it into a commodity article (what Adorno calls the cultural industry); therefore, there is a rejection of the

institutionalization of art in museums, galleries, and the book's commercial industry, while they will promote inexpensive or free publications, and also reposition and re-accentuate the serial (feuilleton) with a liberatory message in their newspapers.

10. Art is fundamentally a collective endeavor and should be popular (in the meaning Brecht gives to the word *popular*, which is not to be confused with popularity).

11. The literary artist is the spokesperson for the outcasts of society.[6]

This is the anarchist and socialist poetics of negation, of open-ended discourses and a philosophy of the beautiful which provides the referential dimensions of texts in novels, short stories, poetry, theater, and graphical material. Sometimes they will experiment with the blanks in the page, as in the figural displacements which haunted Mallarmé. Social problems are privileged, if monitored from an anatropic perception. Open-ended "realism" is the most dynamic common cultural feature, and the writer is understood as an *ideaist* (*ideísta*) or "ideologist" (the same word Bakhtin used to explain Socratic carnivalization, and later Dostoevsky). Anarchists might disagree with the political ideology of a given artist, but if "reality" (understood as exploitation and inequality) were projected, it would compensate. This point is clear in the *Revista Blanca*'s analysis of Ibsen:

> His dramas are primarily ideaists (*ideístas*) and by being ideological they are necessarily revolutionary. . . . A new ideal is needed, the ideal of all modern thinkers and writers, the conquest of a new society, which liberates man [*sic*] from injustice, misery, ignorance, and tyranny. (*RB* 15 Nov. 1898)

According to *The Socialist* in 1887, art is considered "the mirror of society," but a mirror which should reflect other customs and morals, since theater portrays only human "caricatures." This is the mirror to be shattered in order to monitor the invisible realities of social life and the imposed social identities. In the *Revista Social* (1884) an author lamented that (commercial) theater was still dwelling in traditional themes of conjugal honor or patriotism. The ana-tropic image would question which honor and whose country—in other words, from which social hierarchy both honor and dignity are inscribed.

In 1894, Salvador Canals, another anarchist, wrote in *El Proscenio* a chroni-cle about anarchist theater, employing the metaphor of a face/mirror (reality/appearance), strongly stating that as long as Madrid's reality was represented by the sexual abuses of the rich (*señoritos*) and the vices of the procurers and pimps, no one could protest: "What we have to change is reality, and then its reflections will change."[7] Bourgeois morality was particularly repugnant to anarchists, who aimed at a moral upheaval in abjuring religion, vice, and alcoholism, and adopted a strong feeling of disapproval against bourgeois philistinism and self-righteousness. Another anarchist, R. Costa, was quite eloquent as to the didactic and truth-value sphere of anarchist aesthetic utopia:

"To decide to fight is what is convenient. One should not leave the field open to those who exploit the sentiments of simple folk" (*Revista Blanca*, 15 Dec. 1898).

Abstracted from the historical event of a practical political context, these commentaries could be confused with an Enlightenment morality indifferent to the truth-value of the First International, if we are not attentive to their situatedness of revolutionary projections. They are addressed against a realistic antispecular theater, which reveals not life but its simulacra—in Marx's words in the often-quoted *Eighteenth Brumaire* (1852), fraudulent at work, the play of mirrors of reproduction and repetition. What these cultural texts suggest is an invitation to unfold social contradictions by dislocating and demystifying the present and inducing a new discursive relation to reality. This is both Brecht's and Valle-Inclán's program.

Federico Urales wrote in the *Revista Blanca* in 1902 that the new art should reflect "an exceptional reality, with high meaning, beautiful, harmonious." And, he went on, "the artist should establish a moral relation between the two realities which divide life, and take sides for the beautiful, inspired, optimistic and good-hearted, and its superior intellectual state" (15 Oct. 1902:235).

Even expressed in nineteenth-century rhetoric, the anatropic metaphor of the mirror and its two realities is recognizable. Art is associated with taking distance, a connection which seems to open more effectively the social imaginary, where the interplay of otherness and same occurs. It is an appeal to the community made a priori, and the idea of beauty is situated in freedom and a feeling shared between artist and audience, which echoes Kant's ideas on the beautiful and the sublime. If enthusiasm is the extreme mode of the sublime (following Lyotard 1984), of anticipation of something that "remains to be determined," Urales in simple terms suggests this event, this occurrence, this "want."

Kropotkin's ideas on the function of art in *Ideals and Realities in Russian Literature* (1905) and William Morris's *Art under Plutocracy* concur with that open-ended project. Their point was not to reproduce bourgeois artistic practice but to create a new one; the task of literature was to provide questions, and to bring out the emotive underground of the audience. For anarchist and socialist moderns, the imaginary interchange is grasped in terms of the anatropic visions I have suggested, in order to defetishize objects and reality, and to liberate humankind from the static correspondences of mythologies. In the mirror metaphor they looked for a shocking confrontation in which the present could be reread in light of past myths and mystifications; this allowed the present to reinterpret itself through the past and into the future. Such is the enthymemic force of this discourse; it was left to allegory to penetrate the web of social distortions and exhaust its misrecognitions in order to forge, from its shattered mirror, a new reality.

It should not surprise us that the anarchist Urales wrote in his journal in 1898 that art should embellish life, and although he was clear in distinguishing beauty from bourgeois decadence, he was definite about contributing to the creation of a "modern art"; if there is modernity, there is modern art. Therefore,

> I declare that if by modernism you understand the staging of our passions, our miseries, and our problems, I am a *modernist*. . . . We are not modernists because we chose to be so, but because our souls are not satisfied with present artistic entertainment. Our tastes must obey an evolution in taste, and not the whim of the writer or the extravagances of the neurotic. (15 Oct. 1898)

This text finally works with the spatial and temporal form of modernism as a core concept of modern life. In Urales's re-accentuation, a whole repertoire of values and propositions mutually define and modify one another. At the level of the associative meaning, this text brings together an understanding of modernism as peculiar to a specific projection of language. Modernism is here opposed to a bourgeois culture system. Anarchists preferred naturalness to artificiality and "literatism," in Unamuno's word (*Revista Blanca,* 1 July 1898), an idiom close to what the formalists called "literariness." Underlying this conception was the assumption that there was no fundamental discrepancy between literature and life, that the language of literature and everyday language were not cut off from each other. This principle highlights the dialogical assumption that "natural" language, as well as "natural" beauty, was in fact aesthetic.

Urales addressed two aspects which are worth underlining: his modern conception of the evolution of taste (explored more recently by Galpano de la Volpe and Pierre Bourdieu from different perspectives, for example) and his emphatic negation of Nordau's taxonomy on the moderns. It parallels, from a different subject position, Darío's deconstruction in *Los Raros.*

Anarchists and socialists aim at inscribing a difference in the anatropic carnival atmosphere of the positive celebration of utopia; they monitor a rupture with hegemony in an art of the future. The *Revista Blanca* directly addresses a modernism capable of making the notions of modernity and revolution converge; in fact, modernism, modernity, and modernization are the open possibilities they project as vital experiences of the aesthetic utopia. So the aesthetic attitude signifies freedom from economic necessity, as well as sensual and utilitarian gratification.

The theories compel readers to either distance from or identify with subordination, and to subvert ideology by a deliberate selection and reinterpretation. They contest commercial entertainment as projecting false images and stupefying audiences into a passive acceptance of bourgeois melodramas. Culture was defined in terms of resistance to the forces of domination, to appeal to solidarity, to an egalitarian imaginary, to concert a shared social goal. In this sense, Valle-Inclán—modernist, "populist," experimenting with distance, identification, and popular culture speaking from the margin—synthesized the awareness of the double play of ideology and language games, and re-accentuated the parodic, dialogic, and carnivalesque strategies of modernism as a critical practice, and anti-imperialism as a political fantasy.

Valle-Inclán and the Shattered Mirror

> We reserve our mockery for that which is
> similar to us.
>
> —Valle-Inclán, *The Horns of Don Friolera*
> (1925)

No one could exemplify more aptly all the idioms, ideologemes, and vernaculars of modern/modernism/modernity than the Galician Ramón María del Valle-Inclán (1866–1936), whose denotative force transforms the allegorical signifier into the shattered fragments of Spanish social life. Novelist, dramatist, poet, short-story writer, essayist, and chronicler, he displays the richness of heteroglossia, the ambiguities of the carnivalesque, with the complex bodily carnality of the carnival, in a scandalous atomization of material fragments of reality which are transformed into meaningful constellations. The triumph of Valle-Inclán's texts lies in the subtle imbrication of the dialogical and the carnivalesque. His texts englobe the multiplicity of languages, dialects, vernaculars which both reveal and produce social and gendered positions. He strove for a multiaccented world, to stage the conflicts and contradictions of Spanish society, sharing, in a way, the pan-Hispanism of many Latin American moderns.[8]

Since my emphasis on the textuality of knowledge requires an expansion of the concept of text, I will limit myself to underlining the shifting system of relations in Valle's writing, within the intertextual and institutional networks. My analysis will focus on the multiplicity and simultaneities of constructions of textuality which are reinscribed in his texts, both diachronically and synchronically, to constitute its meanings in the function of its multiple historicities. I will examine the process of intertextual and interdiscursive inscriptions through which Valle's texts have been constituted as modernist social texts, and limit myself to his experiments with structure and perspective, which I consider more important. I propose the following synthesis of his historical poetics:

1. Valle-Inclán chooses not to demarcate language; therefore, he overcomes this textual convention through modernism. He expels the illusion of a homogeneous textuality or a univocal speech genre by renouncing the static enclosures of traditional genres. He opens them up, inscribing difference. His texts incorporate mass media, popular discourses, intersemiotic codes, sociological and historical material, letters, advertisements, and inscriptions of his own texts, often in self-parody. Frequently the same historical or fictive character is rewritten-with-difference through either persuading intonations or ironic perspectives.

He diminishes the authority and location of the speaking voice, in an interplay of subject positions, revealing the multiplicity of particular subjectivities borne by the same individual. Thus neither representations nor voices are self-enclosed or indifferent to one another: he often projects dialogically people, ideas, things—what Salper (1988) has correctly seen as recurring characters, but which can be extended also to dialogues, idioms. For example, the Marquis of Bradomin is privileged, but so is representation of the anarchists Bakunin, Nechaev, Fermín Salvochea, and Darío; subjects in history and subjects in texts exchange positions. Every perception intersects with another, and they are drawn into dialogue, to provoke new questions, to argue or reinforce meaning.

2. Valle dispenses with ontologically grounded differentiations between language varieties and puts all discourse on a par through plurality and multiplicity of styles and voices, to shatter the illusion of unity; the rigorously encoded writing opens the scope of imaginative play through mixtures of the comic and the serious, the sublime and the vulgar, of what Bakhtin calls *joyful relativity*. They stylize and/or parody canonical texts through direct or indirect quotation and paraphrasing.

3. Bilingual or polyglot texts appear often, inscribing heterology, heteroglossia, and polyglossia. Motifs and functions from the idyllic, the chivalric romance, and the folkloric chronotopes are ironic and parodical, mercilessly critical, and presented as bounded texts, often as fragments of a formerly unified world. His texts belong simultaneously to two or more generic forms, to activate the metaphorical and metonymical, to subvert every transcendental signifier.

4. Texts are mirrors of heteroglossia, where direct words—especially from the dominant discourses of the monarchy, the church, the state—are presented as bounded, dying utterances, ripe for change and renewal. I have in mind here particularly (but not exclusively) the heterological texts Valle named "farce" (the first one dates to 1913) and "esperpento" after 1920, where he articulates huge heterologies of parodically refracted words and voices from literary tradition and historical traditions.

These structural devices of representation signal the destruction of epic and tragedy, since the world is upside down. Valle delves into misalliances, profanities, eccentricities, laughter, licentiousness so as to abolish hierarchies and degrade high images by trivializing their representation through the grotesque, instituting a tradition rich in verbal play, equivalent to that of James Joyce, Thomas Mann, and Brecht, for instance. Valle's linguistic awareness liberates the interlocutor from the power of homogenized language, trying to free consciousness from the power of authority and the conventional words (rhetoric) which have imprisoned it. Valle explores the limits, the absurd side of the totality of politics and society (around the First Carlist War in 1834, and more specifically from 1868).

His is, from the beginning, a word "with a sideways glance"; this is an important feature of his practice from 1894–95, when he started publishing in journals and periodicals. Varying degrees of transgression are interwoven in the short stories, in the ironic autobiography and memoirs of the patrician Carlist Marqués de Bradomín (consisting of four short novels titled *Sonatas* [1902–1905]), on religious cults and family clans in Carlist Galicia (a series titled Barbarian Comedies). In all these texts self-consciousness organizes itself around the particularized memory of the national ideal represented by ancestors or a clan (Bradomín, Montenegro) *deprived* of a future.

The critical progression moves from a re-accentuation of modernist irony and humor (especially but not exclusively in the *Sonatas*) to an expanding parody growing in width and depth toward the historical inversion of the folkloric chronotope in farces and esperpentos, which reconstruct and reanimate the series of the Rabelaisian carnivalization.[9] Valle polemically opposes the new picture of Spanish society; the ideological body of the state (monarchy, church, militaries, politicians, canonized texts) is perceived mainly under the sign of decay, of crude and dirty physical licentiousness. Valle's semantic somatics of the dismembered body is portrayed in a variety of aspects: clownish and cynical characters, the fantastic, grotesque allegorizations, grotesque exaggeration to liberate from dogmatism, completeness, and limitation.

The heuristic force of Valle's farces and esperpentos intends to rid people of social and political fear; they are ambivalent, meant to show the "other side." Valle re-accentuates a modernization or contemporization of laughter by means of the atmosphere of the fair, in the combinations of abuse-praise, in the comparative and superlative atmosphere of the entire system of popular festive images, or colorful and dynamic prologues with their strings of billingsgate abuses. Every text is full of allusions to contemporary events in hyperbolic terms. His whole literary corpus acquires coherence in the interior of a system of communication and interaction. The carnivalized chronotope (as described by Bakhtin) and all its seven series have their logic and their dominant features. All intersect one another, since normally more than one is found in a text or a series of texts.

Valle materializes Spanish society, showing its other side, while the mirror metaphor allows him to create and re-create illusions and representations and varying social relations through repetitions, reproductions, ironic repositioning, and polemic dialogism to place his interlocutor in crisis. The specular metaphor is a *continuum* (to use Benjamin's well-known term), and systematically it dis-reflects or distorts: it elongates, cuts, enlarges, magnifies, disfigures, makes characters grow taller or smaller, fatter or thinner, in different directions and degrees. His preferred target is authority, and frequently the same character will be refracted in opposing mirrors. Valle makes contiguous what is normally not associated, and he distances in estrangements what is normally contiguous, destroying the familiar, and creating new matrices of language and thought (cf. Bakhtin, *DI* 237). He slips off and out of the boundaries of the "given," framed, or historically finished representations, to "strip, as it were, the object of the false verbal and ideological husk that encloses it," in Bakhtin's suggestive description of carnival.

Valle's literary carnivalization of modern society and his uncovering of social contradictions can be better understood if framed in two broad spheres: his first texts (from 1894 up to around 1912) can be placed in the sexual series and death series—*Sonatas, Comedias bárbaras*, the Carlist War trilogy. His mirror is *concave*, thus elongating the figures as a Renaissance painter or El Greco does. The human body is portrayed in a variety of different aspects: first comes the stylization, then (around 1912–14) follows the cynical (in the farces), which concludes in the fantastic and grotesque allegorizations of the esperpentos and a trilogy of novels called *The Iberian Bullring* (El Ruedo Ibérico). The mirror is now *convex* and Goyaesque; bodies are dismembered and represented in their coarse anatomical aspects. All the series interpenetrate one another; in Valle's carnivalization there is a cohesive homology between the body, dreams, linguistic structure, and social subversion.

Carnivalization becomes enriched and dominant, and Valle provides a key to the important hierarchies of codes in a book of poetry eloquently called *Kif's Pipe* (La pipa de Kif, 1919) to allude to the phantasmatic of dream-worlds and social opiates. All the carnivalesque series of the Rabelaisian chronotope join in a funambulesque dance of sex and death, profanities, eccentricities, parodies, laughter, dismemberment, drunkenness, violent and "unnatural" copulation, defecation. This carnival dance is not meant as a disruption of etiquette, but as a symbolic rebellion where behavior becomes anti-behavior, gestures are deritualized and demystified and stripped of social hierarchies; the body is fragmented into grotesque postures and degraded images. The face, the mouth, the nose, sexual and erotic parts are looked at through a magnifying glass or minimized and fragmented into disconnected parts. This carnivalesque atmosphere is not to be confused with an ersatz festivity, since Valle capitalizes on projecting rebellion against finalized world-views and systems.

Spain becomes a *bullring*, a *bullfight*, a *carnival*, a *circus*, a *stage*, a *scaffold*, a *wooden target*, inhabited simultaneously by Lilliputians and Gullivers, dwarfs and giants, carnival monsters, King Kongs. Images mutually parody themselves. Texts form a system of deforming mirrors; they are the arena of parodic doubles which makes caricatures, ridicules and deforms heroes, authorities, ideologies, objects. A national hero is seen as an assassin or a tyrant; Valle's anatropic eye turns Spanish imperialism upside down by showing the other side of the conquest. For example, General Juan Prim, the hero of the Spanish 1868 Revolution which dethroned the Bourbon queen Isabella II, is called a "slave owner" (*negrero*), thus re-accentuating his negative role as a colonial administrator in Puerto Rico, and is projected as an image in a deck of cards. For the same reason, the Spanish embassy and the representatives of the Spanish bourgeoisie in Mexico are portrayed as tyrants or obscene figures in *Tirano Banderas* (1926), a novel which may well be considered the inception of the genre of the tyrant in Latin American literature. Valle also projects a negative dialectics of the Cuban War in *Carnival Tuesday* (Martes de Carnaval; in Spanish there is a polysemy in *Martes*, which refers both to the day of the week and to the god of war, Mars) as an all-encompassing anti-militarist, anti-imperialist critique. But the military (from real heroes to literary heroes) participates in a negative projection of the monarchy, the nobility, and its triumphant war, which in the farces is ridiculed and degraded: the queen is animalized to magnify her sexual lust as an insatiable nymphomaniac; the king grows smaller and smaller and resembles a domesticated lap dog.

Valle characterizes two dimensions of art as the imagined and the perceived. In the words of Maese Lotario in the Italian farce *The [Woman] in Love with the King* (La enamorada del Rey, 1920): "In art there are two roads: one is architecture and allusion, logarithms of literature; the other, realities as the world shows them, in this way they say Velázquez painted his masterpiece." This farce, on the other hand, explores the role popular culture plays in libidinal fantasies, since the woman character has fallen in love with the monarch, through the libidinal fantasies projected in popular (mass) literature. It is a bold experiment in the libidinal economy of popular culture.

Valle's farces unmask national historical and cultural mythologies through a parade of carnival signs, re-accentuating (like the earlier Latin American modernists) the *commedia dell'arte* in a critical way. Therefore Pulcinellas, Pulcinellos, Pierrots, Pantalone, il Dottore, Columbine, Arlechin, as well as the tradition of Greek mythology, promenade though these farces in a dethroning of signs, an "eating of the gods." The reader should be reminded of Latin American modernists' struggle for the sign, and Darío's re-accentuation of princesses and carnival types. In his extraordinary *Lights of Bohemia* (Luces de bohemia, 1920), Valle further explains the second way as "classic heroes who are taking a walk on the Callejón de Gato"; the set of mirrors in this small alley in Madrid (which still exists) projects grotesque deformations in "perfect mathematics." The idiom Callejón de Gato explodes in meanings: it is an alley as well as a cul-de-sac, and in tauromachy, it is the space between the barricade of the bullring and the first row of seats. It seems to suggest that as an aesthetics, it is a mirror which both reflects and shatters the Iberian bullring.

The position of the observer is fundamental in this dialogical world. In Max Estrella's words, that is "the only way to represent Spanish reality," since Spain, he thinks, is a deformity of European history. It is important to stress that the particular angle of refraction comes from the outsideness of Estrella, a literary representation of the bohemian Alejandro Sawa (a close friend of Valle's and Darío's). His dialogical word is articulated as a version of axiology, in the act of perception of this modern Odysseus, blind as Oedipus, strolling down the labyrinth of Madrid's dark streets, which remind the reader of Joyce's *Ulysses;* both are contemporaneous, and serve to remind us that these were the preoccupations of a whole generation. This esperpento brings together in time and space Max Sawa, Darío, Bradomín, and other important figures of bohemian life, and together with *The Horns of Friolera* it emphasizes the nature of tragedy in modern life, the control of historical determinates over human lives, the power of time and history over the artistic work; Valle's mirror is bound to refract and reflect what it negates.

The esperpento suggests simultaneous registration, dialogicality; it is a poetics of the modern world. Valle-Inclán incorporates the heterovocality of modern life, in multiple interdiscursive networks and interrelated cultural universes, in familiar contact with popular culture, and all the social series. The whole spectrum of social discourse enters his texts; he interanimates both literary and non-literary discourses. Valle understood what Bakhtin formulates as literature: "An inseparable part of culture and it cannot be understood outside the total context of the entire culture of a given epoch" (*SG* 2). Dialogism operates within all cultural production. In Brecht's words: "Literature cannot be forbidden to employ skills newly acquired by contemporary man, such as the capacity for simultaneous registration, bold abstraction, or swift combination" (1979:57).

The past is in Valle's historical materialism the subject of deconstruction. Valle intends to break the *present* away from its reified historical continuity and repetition—repetition understood as a history drained of substance, but away from the fetishistic cult of tradition, of old truth-values, or romantic idealization and excavation of the past and the spiritualization of scroungers and parasites. It is the degradation of a capitalist society, still repeating (feudal) social relations; in the contingency of the First World War and the Russian and Mexican revolutions, bohemians and modernists, together with aristocrats, all lost their *aura,* and were turning into a degraded version, generating commodities. In this sense, there are several ways in which Benjamin's thesis on history, the aureatic, and his *Trauerspiel* would help illuminate Valle's practice.[10]

What we are trying to comprehend in seeking to define Valle's modern/modernist projection of the contradictions in Spanish society can also be explained by Bakhtin's "dialogical imagination," which highly depends on polyphonic orchestration. The inception of the diversity of languages, with their distancings, refractions, reserves, and parodies, is intended to denounce and destroy repetitive historical patterns. His deeply rooted carnivalization is connected with fundamental realities to strip bare all false and ideological preconceptions that had distorted and kept separate historical truths or myth-making mechanisms. Valle-Inclán masters double-voicedness, and the system of duplicity simultaneously revealing and concealing his intended meanings. He also shows a proverbial capacity for the infiltration of popular discourse into the individual's fantasy life, in a prodigious interfacing between the popular and the libidinal (what Lyotard calls "libidinal economy").

His farces and esperpentos are somehow close to—but not quite—the postmodern parody; he does not claim to speak from a position outside the parodied, and his "repetition with critical distance [allows] ironic signaling of difference at the very heart of similarity" (in Hutcheon's [1985] definition of postmodern parody). I said close, but not quite, since neither modernism nor postmodernism is a textual feature; Valle's purpose is to reconnect with popular liberatory forces. His ambiguities, parodies, and carnivalization are grounded in historical materiality to monitor a dialogical social imaginary of subversion through anatropic perceptions in ways that offer promise.

Through his poetics of negation and allegory, he projects what the court, the monarchs, the church, institutions, politicians, artistic production are *not;* the mechanisms of satire and parody deploy an authority of dignity.[11] He aims at the symbolic assassination of authority and power by shattering the mirror of reproduction and repetition of commodity fetishism, establishing a dichotomy between appearance and concealed reality, and the loss of aura. In his own words:

> Life . . . is always fatally the same. What changes are the characters. . . . Formerly, Destiny carried dignity and pain on its shoulders. . . . Today, it's the same

Destiny, the same fatality, the same grandiosity, the same pain. But mankind who carries them is different. . . . That is its source of contrast, the disproportion, the ridicule. (1930, in Dougherty 1983:192)

Unamuno and the Dialogical Imagination

> I will be author, actor and public.
>
> —Unamuno, *Solitude* (1921)

Beneath the contradictory and open-ended nature of the work of Basque-born Miguel de Unamuno (1864–1936) lies the felicitous embodiment of the dialogical imagination. Contributor to both *Revista Blanca* and *The Socialist* (among other workers' periodicals), he was anti-imperialist and anti-military, both in his philosophical discourse and in the variety of genres he produced in his fifty years of writing. Of polymathic intelligence, he practiced a vast variety of modern discourses, in a prodigious interplay of subject positions. His texts make demands of the reader's erudition and powers of analogy, while completeness is always relative. His love for variation, diversity, perspectives in dealing with the same questions, made him aware of the internal unfinalizability of his thoughts.

Taken together, Unamuno's texts pose problems around a theory of subjectivity, including a wide variety of reflections on epistemology, ethics, ontology, culture, and history. The radical specificity of the individual, the uniqueness of being, allowed him to provide his theory of the subject. The point in Unamuno is the inclusive I/you, the simultaneity that makes him treat both concepts together, an essential conception of self he shares with Bakhtin. Unamuno's obsession after the early twentieth century was the inclusive also/and, this/that.

Unamuno's semiotic practice unfolds a displacement from the metaphysical to the dialogical in a creative construction of self, which reveals a subject constitution whose knowledge is never already given or fixed. His unfinalized texts, of which *Mist* (Niebla, 1914) could be considered a privileged example, are open-ended and present an aura which contains no possibility of definite truth. Unamuno's voices enter and reenter his characters' visions and become material for his own personal voice. Paraphrasing Bakhtin's analysis of Dostoevsky, whenever the question "Who am I?" is posed, the only possible answer is "Who is he/she?" or "Who are you?" Unamuno's enthymemic voice intensely and constantly addresses itself, another, and a "third."[12] In his own words, in the (post)modern *How to Make a Novel* (Como se hace una novela, 1925–27): "I do not want to refer, my reader, only to my I, but to your you, to our I's [yos]. That we and the I's are not the same" (*Obras completas,* X:910). In this novel— and Unamuno often chose aesthetic categories to discuss philosophy—he reminds the reader that proper names are also signs, and names (as well as identities) present specific problems when regarded as signs, and not as fixed entities.

Unamuno's reconceptualization of the person's creative construction of self is made visible in his conception of style and writing. Writing is the creative appropriation of another's voice, and the creative unfolding of the self. *How to Make a Novel* is a complex multidirected dialogue with himself, with the reader, history, his own fictive characters, in an open-ended interchange between writing and interpretation. In his words: "Let's return once more to Jugo de la Raza's novel, to the novel of his reading of the novel, to the novel of the reader, the reader-actor, the reader to whom reading means to live what is read" (875). The whole text is a "Japanese lacquered box," he says, commentaries on commentaries on commentaries. In fact, it is a complex ontological commentary on interpretation, writing, language, and history. His passion as a philologist (he was a scholar of classical Greek in Salamanca) overwhelms readers with an interpretive process, semantic possibilities, allusions, in a plurality of contexts which destabilize fixed meanings. Unamuno interchanges subject positions—as philologist, poet, philosopher, translator, journalist, novelist, dramatist, essayist, scholar, Basque, Spaniard, family man, republican, heterodox—and it is the nature of this differential and contradictory positioning which supports his multivoicedness.

Unamuno's "artistic thinking of humankind" (to use Bakhtin's words) speaks directly in a polyphonic creative thinking extending beyond the bounds of any traditional genre, including poetry and the novel. Unamuno produces what Bakhtin would call a sort of "zero degree" of dialogue in the tripartite dimension of language, in which the third (superaddressee) is not part of the dialogue but the one whose responsive understanding is presumed, either in some metaphysical distance or in historical time. This "third" is ideally true responsive understanding (*SG* 126). Any informed reader can recognize Unamuno's responsible inquisitions on selfhood, the subject, language as communication, representation, history as open-ended questions in dialogue with his multiple subject positions and his co-authors and co-readers in the future. Unamuno creates a heterological universe of exotopies without privileged signifiers, a universe of simultaneities of others and *an*others.

His "death of the author" after *Niebla* (1914) manifests the crisis of the word and its symbolic efficacy, a crisis of language which extends to a critique of those mechanisms which tightly secure a univocal hermeneutics. This "death of the author" emerges as the textualization of the seepages across boundaries of self, and the entities which emerge in the multiplicity of encounters between authoring and voicing, the creative appropriation of another. This metaphor anticipates many postmodern epistemic metaphors, but it should not be confused with the normative poststructuralist libertarian celebratory inventive reading, or with the contemporary idea that an author cannot instrument his/her discourse. His position is close to the Bakhtinian struggle for the sign, which constitutes not only metaphoricity but the construction of self, as we have seen with the Latin American moderns.

Understanding of the crisis of language is indicative of a crisis of its performativity and is accompanied by a critique of the social world, and of the unified subject. If the subject is constructed by language (an insight which brings Unamuno close to Bakhtin but should not be confused with Lacan), and contrary to the Cartesian subject it is not a given entity, the memorable encounter between the fictive character Augusto Pérez and the narrator Miguel de Unamuno in Salamanca textualizes the explosion of the aporia, the *mise en abîme* of the subject.[13] The novel unwinds the decentered subject of knowledge; Unamuno removes the subject from the center of consciousness, and hence knowledge becomes a false problem. While he also textualizes the decentered subject as a project in *How to Make a Novel,* in this earlier novel he materializes language (writing) as an epistemic metaphor for the encounter of the different evaluative utterances which constitute subjectivity. The novel is rich in insights into a politics of signification.

In the 1907 manuscript of *Niebla,* the disciplined Aristotelian agent disappears. There is a way in which John Barth's parallel ideas on "Literature of Exhaustion" (1967) would seem to illuminate Unamuno. When Barth writes that the idea of the death of the author condemns the idea of the artist as "politically reactionary," it is not difficult to paraphrase it in Unamuno's terms, as the process of liquidating the hegemony of the signifier, which is in this sense a subject without a signified. The fictions and ontologies of the social which Unamuno unmasks are like the famous Scheherazade of the *Thousand and One Nights* so dear to Borges and Calvino: Scheherazade tells Sharhyrar a story (so aptly studied by Todorov). The Salmantinian study is transformed into a Chinese box (or is it Japanese?) in a topological structure of infinite and impenetrable reality: the study of the forked paths.

Unamuno's strong belief in language as communication in simultaneities, which he recurrently redefines throughout his work, is also textualized in what Calvino (1986) would call "levels of reality" through metacommentaries, metaliterary and metatheatrical processes which disclose the *mise en abîme* of specular discourses. The ideological sign in Unamuno emerged with modernity, and in the crisis of modernity he acquired consciousness of a series of conflicts on the social subject, language, and history. To paraphrase his own words: the subject and the psyche are a social product, and truth is a collective responsibility.

Modernity in Unamuno is made apparent in the fact that for him text production is both an instrument of reflection and an expressive means, whose narrative "knowledge" intends to raise social and historical questions. *About Casticism* (En torno al casticismo, 1895) is not the only text in which Unamuno thematizes historical problems, but it is probably the first to question the archeology of its origins. The five essays it contains interrogate the internal organization of the historical national formations and historical identities, through teleological principles: nation, historical caste, the essence of the Castilian. What is particularly relevant (and modern) in the text is the temporality of the problems analyzed: Unamuno questions the *present,* since he is concerned with actuality.

The references to actuality as a specific historical situation—both in this text and in his "historical" novel *Peace in War* (Paz en la guerra, 1897)—make possible a philosophical delegitimation and deconstruction. What is important is that his reflections are grounded in the *present:* the addresser is both the subject and the actor of the historical drama; he problematizes his own discursive actuality. The textualized "us" deploys a cultural and historical collective characterized by its actuality. This questioning of the actuality and the *present* of which the subject of the utterance is a part are visible signs of modernity (clearly analyzed by Foucault). What distinguishes Unamuno's discursive practice is the temporality/actuality of his questions and the complexity of the varying subject positions of his utterance.

This modernity in Unamuno is expressed by three epistemological metaphors which correspond to three modalities: the use of the sign as a destroyer of reality, which is opposed to symbol and myths—reminiscence or recognition; the use of language from varying subject positions (or enunciative subject positions), which is opposed to the unity of the subject as a given entity; and the progressive use of dialogism which opposes the dialectical suppression of the "other" and a division between "contemplation" and "agony" (lo contemplativo y lo agónico), semes meaning inactivity and praxis, since *agony* is used in its etymological sense of "struggle."

Unamuno's dialogical universe is structured in such a way that there is a coexistence and interaction of diversity and plurality in spatial simultaneities, and not in stages of the development of consciousness. This self-reflexivity and internal dialogism of the subject are grounded in an epistemic world of interchanges and communication. Unamuno explores a distinctive modernist discursive practice and a variety of subject positions to open a wide range of ideological interpellations. His heretical and hetero-doxical discourse becomes a masterful exercise against hegemony on many fronts within a range of social contradictions and movements. It is intended as a struggle against received values and against the tacit complacency of organized order and power. If power is multidimensional, Unamuno's discourse comes from the multiple subject positions to undermine and disclose power, in a reciprocal interplay between centers of authority and practices. Unamuno is a modern in his critique of the traditional scavengers of the past, and of an inhuman (or dehumanized) modernization and instrumental reason and rationality.

Both are the target of *The Tragic Sense of Life* (1912) and *The Agony of Christianism* (1926), among multiple essays and meditations. The "tragic sense" is a polemical meditation against scientificism, the instrumental reason of the Enlightenment, the drive for progress, metaphysics, to which he opposes Don Quixote's impulse toward "becoming." Unamuno's critique of metaphysics and his linking of philosophical and philological discourse prefigured the poststructuralist critique of metaphysics, the unified subject, and the master plot of the Enlightenment, reasserting simultaneously the material body: the man [*sic*] of flesh and bone, against epiphenomena and metaphysicized subjectivities, not without internalizing contradictions by appealing to truths above interest groups. However, his insistence on truth as open-ended and an active project of *becoming* can be understood in the light of Bakhtin's dialogics.

Unamuno's dialogical social imaginary is monitored by way of six ample (and complementary) themes, which are inscribed in his discourse as ways of social evaluation: (1) deconstruction and demystification of the state; (2) anti-colonialist, anti-imperialist, and anti-military ideology; (3) a theory of a socio-democratic political organization of society; (4) decanonization of traditional ideas and traditional socio-discursive formations; (5) a critique of the moral-value and truth-value domain; (6) a polemic against rhetoric and the tropology of the past (representations, images, technologies, idioms, languages). He aims not only at transforming the text of history but at projecting new collective memories, a political underground open to the future.

His subject position is interrogative, and an analysis of his speech utterances would demonstrate elaborate techniques of systematic reactivation of signs, a re-accentuation of irony (the so-called modern irony), and the crisis of fixed meanings. They are all indicators, lucid and sagacious markers, to project "suspicion" and disbelief in the interlocutor, who must cooperate in filling in gaps and blanks and must reassess contradictory utterances. Unamuno's texts are intensely dialogized in what Bakhtin calls a "living addressivity" toward one's own self and toward the other, in an orchestration of self-reflexive voices projected in multiple and simultaneous spirals and supplements, or displacements.

I started by recalling three epistemic metaphors: the first was his use of the sign as a principle of modernity.[14] However, signs here are selected by Unamuno from the collective semiotic expressions, and not from a dissocialized language. The symbolic world offers taxonomies, assures salvation and the access to mystery. Against this closed semiotic world, Unamuno produces a universe of signs, of confusions, or nebulae, of reversible signs on difference and identity. In constant displacement, signs—such as the mirror—are multiplied and repeated infinitely. The mirror helps the seepage across boundaries; it is the passage of the proliferation of elements which contributes to yet other forms of opacities where referents are inverted as an exercise of the critical faculty. The mirror is always reconstituted: a symbol, a fiction, an appearance, an image of the self, a simulacrum. "Everything is a mirror" (Todo es espejo), says the character of the mystery play *The Other* (1926–32). The mirror is laden with multiplicity; it may undistort by showing many angles of a personality simultaneously, or many perspectives on the same problem. It becomes a trap for the gaze, what Lyotard calls "the death of representation." However, the mirror does not reflect imaginary relations (master/slave, real/false); it becomes a site of interacting evaluations in the heterogeneity of life's situations: *The Other* reveals how I and the Other are situated in a given moment, exchanging places and evaluations. It could be said that this text acutely dramatizes what Bakhtin wrote on the inner and outer body in "Author and Character in Aesthetic Activity" (*AA* 1990), and in his final notes on the Dostoevsky book (1984).

Signs are displaced, deployed on vertical and horizontal axes circulating his textual production, interchanging functions—similar to but not the same as the Borgean *Aleph* or accepting the de Manian "receding mirror" according to which as tropology itself it unceasingly unwinds the authority of discourse. Unamuno's mirror has an axiological position to experience the self as another, to stand outside, not to become a double of the self, but outside one's own life, and to perceive the self as an other among others. The mirror includes yet another mirror: the mirrors themselves become specular; thus their ability to represent the world is reduced. Unamuno's mirror undermines belief in external reality. This necessity and impossibility overlaps the subject, discourse, culture, the world. They are all ciphered semiotic universes; looking at oneself in the mirror represents the act of getting into the mirror (like Alice in Wonderland), of traversing subject positions in their absolute irreversibility. The sign is not fixed, or timeless, or transcendental. This movement is not reduced to generating signs but to becoming a sign: the subject is its own language, or is constructed by language.

The hermeneutic mirror-sign in Unamuno discloses a disbelief in mimetic representation, and in the specular/reproductive as cognitive model, what Rodolph Gasché calls "the tain of the mirror" (1986).[15] If philosophical tradition has been conceptualized in terms of an optical operation, self-consciousness designates the reproductive action of the mirror, and at the same time the specularity of the mirror itself, a process which induces the mirror to mirror itself (1986:17). For Gadamer (1975), even if the specular image lacks a self, it is an appearance as a result of the perception of the self's gaze as an image. Specular vision is identified with dialectical thought, because it establishes a difference between subject and image and it unifies them, as a result of identity and non-identity.

In Unamuno the specular epistemic metaphor slips into "anotherness" (*otredad*), and does not merely mean psychological or psychic alterity (*alterité*), but signifies "another" subjectivity. He thus anticipates a critique of a reductive psychoanalytic semiotics, which brings him close to Bakhtin. By transforming the mirror into a social sign, he avoids an idealist theory of identity. The text's articulations within the contradictions inherent to the modern capitalist world are fundamental to explain how his particular gaze was constituted. Like Bakhtin, Unamuno recognized the self as a sign.

Unamuno's mirror does not reflect the anamorphosis which manifests distortion or disorientation—e.g., anarchist and socialist recognition, Valle's concave or convex mirrors—nor does he produce a schizoid fracture between the eye and the gaze, what Merleau-Ponty calls *the madness of seeing* (la folie du voir; see Buci-Gluckmann 1986). Unamuno's mirror resists the Christian panoptic—God as a totalizing gaze (look). His sign raises suspicion against solipsistic theories of identity. "Everything is a mirror," because the subject is multiple, with multiple subject positions—the notorious different "I's" of his heuristic hermeneutics. The mirror concretizes appearances, simulacra; to see oneself within the self signifies to Unamuno an exterior which excludes the whole (not the totality). The mirror only offers material for objectifying oneself, to place oneself outside: the individual is in front of the mirror but not inside it, Bakhtin reminds us (1986, 1989). Dialogical dialogue in Unamuno also has these properties: dialogue as responsiveness, as knowledge which responds to an anti-hegemonic conception of language. If the word is open-ended, there can be no hegemonic signifiers. Unamuno's contending voices were present in the actual reality of his time, beyond (as Bakhtin would put it) his narrow ideological aspirations.

The crisis of authorship in Unamuno is part of the crisis of the character and the monological text. The development of Unamuno's specular theory is linked to an anti-coercive conception of language and against an authoritarian organization of both subject and textuality. What he proclaims is not only the "death of the author" but the incorporation of the "hero's" (character's) subject positions. All resist conclusiveness and finalization; all resist the privilege of the definitive last word. In his dialogical universe, we are not only actors, *an*others, but we also author ourselves. His unfinalized *How to Make a Novel* is an indication of this perception: the intimate connection between the project of language and the project of the self, the self as a task to be created and re-created, the self as authorship. Narratives are embedded and framed in various series of possibilities, from different optics, shaping the ideological, conceptual system of culture instead of the coherent "realist" finalized historical master plot of Spanish society.

This, I would suggest, is the marked rewriting-of-difference of Unamuno's representation of the protagonists/antagonists (his preferred opposition): they come close and distance themselves, they are part and whole, "I" and "you"; they collide and polemize with one another without ever depriviledging the other, without triumph and apotheosis. They are, in this sense, what Bakhtin calls the "catastrophe" (*PDP* 289) which reveals the incapability of resolution under earthly conditions. Unamuno suspends meaning and sense, as his utterances insistingly assert that there is always the possibility of saying something else, because nothing is fixed or homogeneous, because semantic positions collide with their points of view on the world, and utterances respond both to others and to the others embedded in the self. His textual production is the materialization of humankind under conditions of class society carried to the extreme in this turn-of-the-century capitalism, which—if we follow Bakhtin—inscribed the dialogical.

The semantic positions I have briefly outlined are embedded in his "heroes"; the semantic architecture corresponds to confession, biography, autobiography, the lyrical "I," which refer to diverse phases of "otherness" (or anotherness). The biographical and autobiographical are particularly relevant since there is no defining frontier between the two. This is the semantic substance of *Paz en la guerra,* for example, whose historic-philosophic hermeneutic exegesis can be found in *En torno al casticismo, Life of Don Quixote and Sancho,* and *The Tragic Sense of Life* (1912). In the semantic layer, the truth-values which organize the hero's life are first of all a desire for glory, which indicates the urge to be recognized inside the cultural humanity of his/her national history. Personality in Unamuno's philosophy is the process by which the integral person unfolds in the future, in the dialogicality of the ultimate whole, not a semantic future but a historical future. Love is the second moment of truth-value: the desire of wholeness through responsive understanding, the vision and constitution of the subject in another's conscience.

This second moment is expressed through metaphors of different kinds of love, primordially physical and spiritual in various correspondences. Physicality is central, and even his unorthodox religious interpretations are grounded on the materiality of Christ, a fact which makes him reject a religion based on abstractions. Finally, there is the valuative fabulation (or fictive narration) of an unconcluded or inconclusive life; Unamuno organizes infinite open-ended fictions, and the viewer (reader, coauthor, interlocutor) plays an equivalent active role. His dialogical universe invites participation. His autobiographical biography of Don Quixote (*Life of Don Quixote and Sancho*) is a narrative which gives no firm support for monology (not even Cervantes's) but is structured to make dialogical oppositions inescapable. Unamuno creates elaborate fictions in essays, poems, narrations—called monodialogues, conversations—and, like Rousseau, gets caught in what Derrida called "the supplement of the duplicity of writing," since Unamuno's world is never monostylistic, monochordal, or monological, but is a scene of multiplied writings and readings. In this way, the superaddressee withholds the responsive understanding.

I have been referring to various constitutive modalities of Unamuno's modernity/modernism, and I had suggested a parallel with Foucault's notions on discourse, the (Nietzschean) archeology of Foucault's discursive formation, and Unamuno's infrahistory (*intra-historia*) in *En torno al casticismo*.[16] Both are connected to the philosophical and historical problem of memory (collective or individual); from Plato to Hegel the *Erinnerung* is obsessed with memory. Nietzsche proposes forgetfulness as a precondition of the present in his *Genealogy of Morals* (1887); the past does not sustain the present since the future is becoming, and this fluidity creates for Nietzsche the moral of resentment. Therefore, what I wish to establish now in my reading of *En torno al casticismo* is a dialogue between "genealogy," "moral," "infrahistory," and "casticismo."

Genealogical research comprises not only origins but something begun in the past which continues in the present, something which is always present. Indeed, genealogy exposes moral prejudices, discloses and demystifies cultural production. Modernity would be that essentially illusory dimension of the present which is affirmed through negations of the past and tradition, since the present has a myth as origin. I am not concerned with the trope of the genealogical intellectual, but with Foucault's hermeneutics, linking genealogy and modernity with texts which avoid reifying "scientific" discourse.

Unamuno's infrahistory projects suspicion into the past, onto national myths and mythologies, as he deconstructs the mythems of the Castilian historical uses of a hegemonic signifier. The five essays that make up *En torno al casticismo* (all published first in the journal *Modern Spain*) reorganize a critique of hegemony, reactivating the struggle for the future and the potential for a demystification at a moment of crisis. His demystification of knowledge demonstrates that despite the transcendental intentions of Castile, as a myth it has operated in the past on the basis of several motives: war, the Inquisition, linguistic homogeneity. The titles are self-evident: *Eternal Tradition; Historical Caste; Castilian Spirit; From Mysticism to Humanism; On the Present Confusion in Spain.* The agony will be the result of his struggles against a hegemonic metaphysics, an authoritative theology, and a culture which denies or conceals the differences.

Infrahistory could be defined in present-day vocabulary as a countertradition set against the seductive claims to privilege and to authority. Infrahistory is the silent underground of unspectacular lives, the bedrock over which the cataclysms of history are played out. What Unamuno intends is to liberate the historico-political underground (what he calls tradition) from the past, by projecting new memories to demythologize the metaphysical and anthropological model of collective memories. He seems to intend the rearticulation of the stagnant *habitus* which is, according to Bourdieu (1977), that socio-cultural phenomenon which reactivates and potentiates the rich deposits of collective memory. *En torno* is grounded on three dimensions—the experienced past (*casticismo*), the perceived present, and the imagined future. The relations between them are the dramatic tension of present history. Casticism is the habitus, that historically durable generative principle which produces practices, which in turn tend to reproduce casticism again and again. The circularity of casticism as a mirror of reproduction is obvious. This Unamunian theorization, though not in itself complete, is closer to Marx's more sociologically and economically oriented analysis of the "mirror of production." Both Unamuno and Marx speak as modernists, from their situatedness in capitalism.

As a modern intellectual, Unamuno conducted genealogical research to disclose what made the national identity what it was, and how new subject positions could be found. He destabilized the myth of the historical caste of imperial(ist) Spain with a truth which had suffused the state by endless repetition. Infrahistory is not an alternative history which runs inthe underground, a social history of the exploited, but a tradition to be liberated by its liquidation, to reconstruct a past through an anatropic inversion. It is not far from Benjamin's idea of history as a continuum and the practice of a present that turns the past upside down, or "the past upon its axis," in Eagleton's words (1985:51). Neither was he distanced from the modernist Italian Benedetto Croce, whose philosophy Gramsci repositioned and radicalized; the point is worth pursuing. Furthermore, the habitus Unamuno is disclosing to project an open-ended future could also be related to Rodó's *Ariel*, from whom human dignity could be achieved only in the future: "We must work in benefit of the future," he wrote.

Unamuno's modern text at the turn of the century manages to project a dialogical social imaginary against the mythologies of the foundational hegemonic subjectivity which grounds the genealogy of the Castilian and the castizo: it postulates that memory is the bottom line of resentment (a term he would not use until 1936, before his death). Paraphrasing Foucault on Nietzsche, I would say that the aim of Unamuno's critical modernity was not to discover the roots of national identity but to commit himself to its dissipation.

Anarchists and socialists, Valle-Inclán and Unamuno argued for a cultural critique which they all thematized frequently through the epistemic metaphor of the "shattered mirror," by way of enthymemic discourses challenging the present, its hierarchical valuations, and projecting, locating, even struggling against the sites of social antagonism and subordination. The complex identity of the forces in struggle was then submitted to constant shifts, which called for constant redefinition, for changing subject positions in order to address the whole range of social contradictions and movements. Their modernity took place in a specific moment in which the division of political space and the old mythologies had exhausted their productive strength in negativity and the opaqueness of the social, thus problematizing modernity in a reflective attempt to think through the liberating mediation of aesthetic utopias, history, and society. It was an invitation to conceive together the promise of a future; their experimental imagining projected questionings and testings of heretofore un-disputed claims which, going beyond the contemporary contradictions, would bring effective changes: "Today is still always," in modernist Antonio Ma-chado's perception.

VIII

HETEROLOGY AND POPULAR CULTURE IN MODERNITY

> Blacks came from Spain to Cuba, and with them in their drums and guitars [*vihuelas*] came an already mulatto music from Andalusia.
>
> —Fernando Ortiz (1965)

> There is something evident: primitive dances brought from the Peninsula will acquire a new physiognomy in America, as they come in contact with the black and the mestizo.
>
> —Alejo Carpentier (1972)

The Modern/Modernist Tango

The modernity I have been reconstructing inscribes plurality and dialogicality in national cultures, at the same time that it attempts to inscribe a narrativity of the self while raising questions on language. If on the one hand modernism is determined by the capitalist world market, it also discloses the social conditions of forced modernization on the other, and the intersection of the cultural field of the popular (and even populism) in some other cases. The strength of popular cultures emerges as a link between the popular classes, the modes of production, and social life. Therefore, the relationship with immigration, social advancement, clothing, and literacy, as well as the changing use of public spaces, is important.

In this context, dancing and singing—activities highly open to change—became an important part of social and sexual life. It is significant to note that particularly in this period, they were not directly mediated by the monologic elite culture, which privileged European dances such as the minuet and the mazurka while also (at least in Mexico) enjoying, beginning in the 1880s, the scandalous cancan of the burlesque. Dancing and singing were a celebration not only of solidarity, unity, pleasure, and recreation but also of courtship, and by the 1880s, according to historical accounts and newspaper chronicles, there emerged a rapid popularization of new dancing styles: those which in France were called "real acts of prostitution . . . aphrodisiac dances" ("comme de véritables actes de prostitution . . . des danses aphrodisiaques," in Marrus 1977:153). The atmosphere of cafés and public dancing brought about the revolution of couples dancing, which the Straussian waltz had started among upper-class Europe, with its egalitarian kind of sexual contact (153). If the chronology of this music and song is uncertain, what seems to be clear is that these popular expressions reveal how ordinary Latin American moderns lived their everyday lives in a world where their own cultural norms prevailed, and also how the full integration into modernization destroyed local cultures.

If we go back to Bakhtin's suggestions on the dialogical, the modern space irreducibly gives voice to a diversity of discursive types, or heterology in Todorov's (1984:56) translation. That is, the heteroglossia or diversity of languages includes a heterophony or diversity of individual voices in the social horizon. In this heterology "every word gives off the scent of a profession, a genre, a party, a particular work, a particular man, a generation, an era, a day, an hour" (*DI* 106).

I have already suggested a creolization of the sign within modernist discourse; popular songs transfer into the symbolic exchange not only creolization but a cultural maroonization.[1] Both modernist cultures—"high" modernism and popular culture modernism—reveal the network of exchanges between the New Worlds and Europe, since a rhythm or a genre of song or dance immigrates to the new territories and is there transformed, and in turn is returned to its source re-accentuated, and comes back to be reappropriated and reclaimed. Tangos and boleros were brought with the Spanish colonizers, mixed in with the heterological cultures of the Africans, then returned to Europe, there condensed, decomposed, recomposed, and retranslated. The phenomenon of "transculturation," in Fernando Ortiz's apt term (1940), is well known to social historians and particularly important to Braudel (1949, in 1953).

Against the constrained rules of the elites in some areas, and the colonizers in others, this social diversity becomes an uttered element in popular culture. These popular discourses also frame a sort of common language within heterology, in reality reinforcing it. I suggest that as in the Bakhtinian novelistic genre, in these modern times the flourishing of popular culture is connected with the recomposition of ideological systems, and with the reinforcement of heterology both within the literary dialect and outside it (cf. *DI* 182). A distinctive social dialogue occurs in modernist popular culture, in which working-class and elite utterances, as well as European idioms, African, and aboriginal (in some places), transmigrate in flows of dialogical relations. Popular music reveals the profound polyphony of cultures, and the force of the multiplicity of social accents. This could explain some well-known and documented facts: that the English country dance migrated to France at the end of the seventeenth century, and from there to America in the eighteenth, giving rise to its polemical counterpart, the Cuban *contradanza,* in the nineteenth, which, transformed into the *habanera,* remigrated to Europe and returned to the Platine area, and is at least, if not the mother, the cousin of the tango. Music and songs refract social diversity, both linguistic and individual. They offer in fact a small-scale model of the changes we find in the macrocosm of socio-economic life itself.

The lyrics in popular music bring prominence to the complex and differentiated working-class voice in an anti-authoritarian tone within the dominant communicative space. The Caribbean bolero and the Platine Argentinian and Uruguayan tango revoice, as a contested space, (high) modernist practice into popular music. In the heteroglotic space, there is a seepage across social boundaries, since discourse is never fixed or sutured. Both forms givab04e voice to the popular civic cultures; as such, they could be called the idioms of the vernacular cultural identities of different geographical areas.[2] In fact, in general, both popular expressions offer cognitive mappings of Latin America.

The emergence of this music stands as so many different moments in the history of modernism and the events from which new contradictions spring. In this context, it becomes possible to link together in a single figure what are believed to be two incommensurable realities, two independent systems of signs: popular and elite cultures. Huyssen's (1986) treatment of these cultural phenomena makes it clear that the modern was bifurcated into two distinct sets of aesthetic practices, "high modernism" and the "historical avant-garde." While the former is experimental but politically unengaged, Huyssen argues, and becomes inaccessible and not easily appropriated, the historical avant-garde has a hidden dialectic with mass culture. My view represents a departure from such a logic, based on Bakhtin's theories of dialogism. In what refers to the specifics of Hispanic culture, such a distinction between "high" modernism and the historical avant-garde fails to define the space of the modernism(s) I am reconstructing.[3]

Following one of the central arguments of the Bakhtinian cultural critique, I propose a rather different hypothesis, namely, that there was a complex network of affiliations and institutional contexts within which the intellectual work was produced, debated, and consumed. In the specific Hispanic context, modernism had been from the start in dialogue with the working-class movements—anarchists and socialists—at the turn of the century, and there was a reciprocal dialectical relationship between the two social groups and cultural forms as active forces of history. However, the working class cannot be reduced to passive consumers colonized by modernists, but must be recognized instead as active agents who re-accentuated the ideological and political significance of modernity. Community and solidarity acted in consonance with modernist practice to underscore a democratization of cultural capital. The interdiscursive relations among and between modernists and popular-cultural texts constituted the heteroglossic and heterological component of the postcolonial (and colonial) cultures.

The heterophony of popular music at the turn of the century significantly expanded the scope of the aesthetic production of modernism, which cannot be ascribed only to the emergence of the bohemia; the social framework of modernism itself must also be taken into account. The cabarets, which were the center of urban life, helped to institutionalize the connection between bohemia and modernism; here one can find a kind of intellectual coalition which formed codes of opposition. Cabarets came to constitute the boundary of taste formation, at the same time that they designated a bohemian-modernist intellectual style (illustrated by Sawa in Spain). A number of forms of contestation and disrespect for entrenched cultural norms appeared in cosmopolitan Latin American cities. The Platine area (Buenos Aires and Montevideo) became the modern space conditioning proletarian leisure life and the socially frustrated goals consolidating a heteroglossic space from a wide spectrum of sources to re-accentuate the Andalusian tango, the habanera, and the neo-African space of the *candombe* around 1880.

The tango itself is one of the best examples of heterology and transculturation I am proposing. On closer scrutiny, this rich and intricate weave of signs from Europe, Africa, and the Caribbean was cross-fertilized in an associative interplay energizing the Latin American tango. During the 1880s, in simultaneity with the first references to modernism (Darío's *Azul*) and the Cuban *danzón,* the first tangos were sung in an interplay of voices, of positioned utterances, and dialogically interrelated speech practices, each marked by its own intonation, meaning, and values. In this polyphony, it should not be surprising that tangos and boleros interanimate modernist poems (among them Amado Nervo, and some of Darío's *Prosas profanas* [1896]), dialogizing the exuberant and "aristocratic" idioms. This modern popular music englobes all these languages and idioms; modernism was, after all, a "structure of feeling," adapting Raymond Williams's apt term.

It seems that the first documented references to the tango date to 1866, linked directly to black representations in light comedy in theaters (Barreiro 1989). Originally the idiom *tango* signified in Cuba "any gathering of black *bozales* [nonassimilated slaves] to dance to the rhythm of their drums and other instruments" (Pérez Fernández 1986:69). The modernist tango emerged as a product of transculturation between African rhythms and the multiethnicity of "New World" cultures. Instrumentation at first consisted mainly of the guitar (brought from Spain and Portugal by the slaves), and later the bandoneon. Both instruments give subjective expression to the emotions involved, bringing them closer to make them coincide with the lyrical subject. To be sure, the bolero was highlighted by the isolated qualities of the instruments themselves, the guitar and later (in the 1920s) the piano.

The turn-of-the-century tango originated in suburban brothels and working-class dance halls (*peringudines*) and incorporated in its discourse the growing pursuit of cultural *(an)otherness* of the heterogeneous social groups marginalized by the development of the capitalist system of production. In many cases, these songs expressed resistance to the disappearance or destruction of the artisanal identities and the social, cultural, and political ways of life which disappeared with them. The different idioms incorporated into the rhythm and texts of the tango are a recognition of the heterogeneity of identities and their voices. Its emergence disclosed the presence of Afro-Cuban music, especially in the combination of the habanera with the Afro-Uruguayan candombe (81–83). It emerged as a mixture of cultures and languages also including the *milonga,* originally the song of the traveling country singer (*payador*), which gradually acquired a choreography in its urban setting. However, it is important to stress that many of the *payadores* in the Platine area were black; this distinct popular character became a sociogram in one of Argentina's gauchesco literary classics, *Martín Fierro* (1872) by José Hernández. It would seem that the first tangos were also called milongas. The tango is an embodiment of social differences and suggests a more open articulation of the erotic, of pleasure and labor, often employing a compactly intertextual network between high modernism as a shared territory to orchestrate social voices, and what Bakhtin calls "grotesque realism." This type of realism externalizes basically a carnal, sensual material which shares with the modernists the impulse toward libidinal rebellion.

Furthermore, the first tangos expressed a contempt for the middle classes (a practice we have identified as especially anarchist) in specific gestures and poses, through "cuts" and lascivious movements and transgressive language, which contrasted with the polka, mazurka, or waltz danced by the elites. With time, these stood for foreign imports, in contrast to the tango, which by 1903 was understood as properly national—creole or Argentinian—incorporating a rich variety of themes: from melodramatic love stories, to delicate lyrics on idealized love relationships, to social struggle. The tango was written to be sung to specific audiences, as a direct expression of feelings. As musical practice it is justified by the social tableau itself, and the physical movements which come to be seen as accompaniment. It solicits the listener/spectator toward sheer emotionalism, broken by silences and repetitions.

The heteroglotic atmosphere of the first tangos incorporated the argot— *lunfardo*—of the working class and the vernacular of the districts and slums, a vernacular which interested modernists greatly, as can be seen in Darío's article of 1894 in *The Reason* (Uruguay) connecting the lunfardo to Rabelaisian "jarbonnogs." Songs have an organizational point of view, each tango being treated as an objectification of and distantiation from bourgeois life. The lyrics of the tango contained, to a significant degree, the colloquial, the metastatic, the polyglossia of the immigrant mixture of languages. Furthermore, the language was marked by a wide range of hyperbolic and metaphorical euphemisms for sexual organs. Themes included the daily life of the streets, the homeless, and the unemployed, the distress of the poor, as well as the discourse of the urban outlaw (what in Paris around the 1890s were called *apache* songs; see Rudorff 1973:79). The songs were typically realistic and even naturalistic, voicing the laments of homeless immigrants, with popular jargon and the argot of the streets, similar to the lyrics of the songs which could be heard at the Chat Noir in Paris.

"Taita" (The Bully), written by Silverio Menco and composed by Alfredo

Gobbi, is representative of this atmosphere of carnivalized realism. From two million inhabitants in 1870, Buenos Aires jumped to four in 1895; by 1887, six out of every seven men were European immigrants (Barreiro 1985, 1989). The new picaresque rogue and the outlaw animated the powerful and vigorous songs of thieves, prostitutes, and streetwalking plebeian Romeos. Tangos offered the "other side," the *anotherness* of the gaucho or the poor immigrant within the social heterogeneity of the urban capital. This tango is considered among the earliest:

> I am the bully in Barracas
> with greased hair
> and well-ironed shirt
> when I want to show off.
> If attacked I defend myself
> with my long knife
> and leave anyone
> like sausage meat.

> Soy el taita de Barracas
> de aceitada melenita
> y camisa planchadita
> cuando me quiero lucir.
> Si me topan me defiendo
> con mi larga fariñera
> y me lo dejo a cualquiera
> como carne de embutir. (In Barreiro 1985:148)

It could be argued that the tango originated as a semiotic text of behavior, as a white parodying of black dancing; in the words of a nineteenth-century specialist: "The milonga is danced only by the urban *compadritos*,[4] who created this dance as a parody of the black" (1883, in Barreiro 1989:12). The first tangos also gave expression to the material life of the immigrant, and to the life of the imΩ overished gaucho, the tragic life of the prostitute; for example, in "Dame la lata" (Give Me the Chip), "lata" is the tin object a man gave a prostitute, to be exchanged for money, which she handed to her pimp or the owner of the brothel. Many tangos conclude in tragedy, or the hero ends up in prison, or in perpetual wandering. "The Steel Thrust" (El fierrazo), another tango, directly alludes to the sexual act.

Other lyrics make various references to female organs (e.g., "concha" [shell]), or to women immigrants called "parrots" (*loras*) because of their supposedly unintelligible language. Women were a commodity to a predominantly male population, as both sexual objects and economic possessions. But the parody of ethnicity and Babel is not exclusively focused on women, for the *cocoliche*—used to mean broken Spanish spoken by Italians, and by extension applied to other immigrant national groups—is often the butt of ridicule as the nonassimilated foreigner. Incidentally, the tango was first mainly a male dance (obviously no indication of homosexuality), a sort of test of virility and power; gradually it became a forbidden couples dance, performed only in low quarters (Barreiro 1989).

The orality of the tango is evident in the complex semiotization of gestures, body, words, emotions. Directly denied a cultural platform, since immigrants were debarred from access to these resources—especially education—its lyrics express orally and bodily the texture of proletarian life, almost as performance. There was a deliberate primitivism, favoring an elemental response from the listener/spectator. Originating in the parodying milonga, it first played an essential role in the dance halls of the marketplace, and traveled throughout the lower-class milieu: its quarters, streets, ill-famed houses, gambling places where the *niño bien* (high-class "playboy") met the *compadrito* or the prostitute. The thematic variety includes sexuality, humor, parody, tavern brawls, economic problems, discrimination, jail and anti-police coercion, and social inequalities of all sorts. Anarchist themes are also common as part of the utopia of social justice, a point we will develop further.

The early tango challenged the symbolic constitution of society and its image of social authority and domination. It was, however, a totally male-dominated or gendered discursive formation, as the above summary makes clear, and for the first time (as in North America) the industrial West threatened to destroy and incorporate all other geographies, as Buenos Aires became what Ezequiel Martínez Estrada called in 1940 the "head of Goliath." This was the process of subsumption of cultural diversity of huge urban areas, with their pockets of poverty promoting heterogeneity, decentralization, and small-scale spaces resulting from economic expansion and cultural contact situations. The development of urbanization and popular music were very closely related. The popular element represented a re-accentuation of spontaneity, and also provided insights into the polyethnicity of the area, with groups from all parts of northern and eastern Europe (anarchist newspapers were also published in Italian and French), including Turkey.

The heteroglossic integrated cultural idioms into a meaningful perspective. The actors were driven by the larger cultural totality, and explored the dialogism between culture and the individual's agency, choices, and strategies in its familiar scenario. There was a dialogue with a cultural other, and a re-accentuation and reactivation of political and national identities and meanings. The (an)otherness reentered social discourse with localized cultural themes and icons: defiance, bonding among men, images of fighting animals (cocks), masculinity, violence, honor and dignity, kinship, love. The narratives illustrated how the gaucho and the Indian (together with the immigrants) became proletarian in the urban areas, fleeing from new rural laws and police order, from the advancing technology of railways, electricity, the barbed-wire fence.

The early tango verbalized the narratives of the proletarian compadrito, who survived in the urban milieu in a hidden, closed way of life, through semiotic practices of social behavior which revealed peripheral rituals.[5] Clothes, language, and behavior show nonassimilated forms of life of the layer of modernized culture imposed on the thick stratum of proletarian society, in the insistence on a public behavior of defiance. Speech forms related to sexuality were liberated from norms, hierarchies, and prohibitions; they became a special argot in the tango and created a special collectivity initiated in an open and liberated atmosphere. Note the forms of behavior implied in the following tango portraying a "court of miracles," written by "El Negro" Cele (Celedonio Flores), entitled "Splashing Mud":

> Beggars, delinquents, boozers,
> a real killer, once in a while
> the social hangover of a hundred nations,
> poverty and dirt vegetating.

> Fabriqueras, malandras, curdelones,
> un matón de verdad, de cuando en cuando
> la resaca social de cien naciones,
> la miseria y la mugre vegetando.
>
> ("Chapaleando barro," in Barreiro 1989:17)

The signifying elements are composed of three sequential parts: the gesture, the act, and the tango as a "behavioral text" (to adapt Lotman [1985:109]), in polemic with the elitist culture of the modern bourgeois. It was originally played as a dance with an eminently sexual choreography, in which the three signifying elements worked simultaneously. According to a vivid description by a contemporary, the dancing style made explicit its sexuality: "The tango is an old-fashioned dance: the only difference is that formerly it was danced lying down, and now it is danced standing up" (in Zubillaga 1986:17). This tongue-in-cheek definition polemically coincides with that of the Cardinal Archbishop of Paris, who proscribed modern dancing, while the anarchist journal *Le Peuple* called the tango, the fox-trot, and the shimmy around the 1920s "a sort of precocious and dangerous virginal defloration" (Marrus 1977:141).

However, social behavior is not the only element, for the social polemic also includes the reappropriation of signs, such as the modernist delicacies about women: "Venus" reveals the intertextual bond with high modernist culture. "El Negro" Cele confirmed this "struggle for the sign" as he affirmed that his tango "Margot" (a classic in Carlos Gardel's voice) was written in polemic with Nervo and Darío (Romano 1973). As part of the changing moral codes in modern Europe, if by 1890 everyone was dancing the Brazilian *maxixe,* by 1910 the tango was popular because of its measured crossing and flexing steps and the dramatic pauses in the center of the glide (Marrus 1977:155). By the twenties, the tango had left its early privileged popular space. Intersemiotized by the bourgeois and the elite cultures as it was exported to Paris, it often became a nostalgic discourse; however, many of the well-known tangos come from this time—"The Cumparsita" among them. Carlos Gardel, who helped internationalize the music, is famous for some extraordinary tangos, such as the philosophical "Gira, Gira," or "My Sad Night" (Mi noche triste). "Griseta" and "Madam Yvonne" still make visible the modernist atmosphere and idioms. "Griseta"—lyrics by José González Castillo and music by Enrique Delfino—

tells the story of a French prostitute re-accentuated by the vocabulary of the modernists and symbolists; the picture that emerges is also reminiscent of Fellini's Gelsomina:

> She was a mixture of Museta and Mimi
> with caresses from Rudolph and Schaunard,
> she was the flower of Paris
> that a dream of romance brought to the city slum.
> And in the frenzy of cabarets
> to the sound of some low-life tango
> she held an illusion:
> she dreamt with Des Grieux
> and hoped to be Manon.

> Mezcla rara de Museta y de Mimí
> con caricias de Rodolfo y de Schaunard,
> era la flor de París
> que un sueño de novela trajo al arrabal.
> Y en el loco divagar del cabaret,
> al arrullo de algún tango compadrón,
> alentaba una ilusión:
> soñaba con Des Grieux,
> quería ser Manon. (Barreiro 1989:82)

Bohemian Parisian modernism is the driving force in this song of the suburbs. Tangos were thematized later as metaphorical nostalgic reconstructions of the past, frequently in Borges's poetry, for example.

If modernism, as I have suggested, transgresses the monologic and the uni-accentual, the popular music of this period (in the light of Bakhtinian catego-ries) displays alterity in marginal—even peripheral—practices which shatter, at least on the symbolic level, oppressive hierarchies, consequently redistributing social roles and giving voice to the heteroglossia inherent in society, including the Africanization of Latin American cultures through inflected musical idioms that migrated.

The Modernist Bolero

Social diversity and heterology define the cultural voice of the Cuban danzón and the bolero as well, which also emerged around the 1880s (the first docu-mented danzón dates to 1879, and the first bolero to around 1885). The name bolero comes from the Spanish Andalusian music which inspired the modernist Ravel, but it was *maroonized* (so to speak) in Cuba. The circularity, or round-ness (*boleado*), of this Andalusian dance found its way into the title of the Americanized version. The origin of the danzón was similar to that of the tango, in that it meant the breach of a norm of established speech, which the bourgeois disapproved, and within the full range of both cultural texts as modernist imaginings, they disclosed alternative cultural tastes, oppositional practices, and rituals of resistance in the modern social formation. The danzón was created by the mulatto working-class musician Miguel Failde in Matanzas, and during the 1895 war it was used as a parodying carnivalization of the Spanish colonizer. The first one documented was called "The Heights of Simpson" (Las Alturas del Simpson). Interestingly enough, as a dance, it is a parodical travesty of the minuet, which was the favorite among the elite Cuban society of colonialists and landowners (see Orovio 1981; Fernández Valadez 1984). Other expressions were the *tango congo* (related to the rumba), of which one of the earliest is "Mamá Inés," associated with the coffee laborers (see Urfé 1977:219), which was also the subtext of the contradanza, the habanera, and the first danzones of Failde, as well as the *afro son,* the milonga, the tango, and the blues (222). They all assimilated the rhythm of the tango congo.

Within the structure that Failde gave the danzón, José Urfé included the stylistic and rhythmic format of the *son oriental,* which accentuates the carnival atmosphere of the music. It capitalizes on the festive, and reveals the polyphony of cultures. In contrast to the rich carnivalesque perception of the humorous *son,*[6] and the Cuban tango congo, the bolero addresses a world of amorous prelude and erotic seduction, without being obscene, in a prodigious intertextual network with modernist love fantasies. It offers fictive corporality instead of abstraction, and the result is the simultaneous provisionality and timelessness of the experience.

The bolero, related to the habanera and the danzón, was mostly urban, and originated in Santiago de Cuba. Most historians agree that the first bolero was written by José "Pepe" Sánchez (1856–1920); however, there were innumerable troubadours before Alberto Villalón and Sindo Garay introduced it to the Havana public (see Alén 1990). The percussion rhythm and its binary musical structure reveal a composite of classical music, and its African subtext. The bolero rhythm has more than one point of contact with blues and jazz. The blues probably developed after the Civil War, and the guitar was most commonly associated with it (Ferris 1979). Some historians suggest that the bolero emerged around 1898. It is known that when the North Americans invaded Cuba, among the soldiers of that army was William Christopher Handy, one of the forefathers of the blues. Boleros were frequently named *bolero blues;* the voiced experience of the lyrics suggests that as narratives the bolero and the blues are related.

Whether in the 1880s or in 1898 (its exact date of emergence is uncertain), the bolero created a fruitful dialogue with what was called the "romantic song," and thus it embodies a network of intertextual relations with the love poetry of Western culture through the modernists.[7] This creative re-accentuation was directly enriched in Mexico, an active agent of Caribbean popular culture, after the habanera "The Dove" (La paloma) was popularized in 1866 by the singer Conchita Méndez: "When I left Havana / so help me God" (Cuando salí de la Habana / ¡válgame Dios!). At the turn of the century habaneras shared popularity with *danzas,* mazurkas, and waltzes (Garrido 1981), which were normally played in public places and cafés until the phonograph arrived in 1897.

Therefore, before the creative use of modernist idioms in the bolero, there was a widespread dialogue between popular music and the so-called highbrow culture. The nineteenth-century danzas incorporated romantic love poetry, and the now-popular poems of Spain's canonical romantic Gustavo Adolfo Bécquer, among others, were heard throughout *alamedas* and on Sundays were played by local bands on the main square. In Puerto Rico, Juan Morel Campos, the principal composer of danzas, who set to music many lyrical lieds written by Bécquer, also wrote danzas around 1891 to advertise sherries and cognacs. The use of music to advertise luxurious consumer goods (alcohol, tobacco) was not uncommon.

By 1901, what is called the "romantic song" appeared; it became a sort of trade for Yucatec musicians. In 1920 the Salón Mexico introduced the danzón; a Mexican version of "Martí Should Not Have Died" became "Benito Juárez." Finally, in 1925, from Yucatan came what is known in Mexico as the first song with "bolero rhythm," called "She": "She, whom I would have loved so / the one who cast a musical spell on my soul, / tenderly asks me to forget her, / to forget her without hate or tears" (Garrido 1981:57). From this point on, the bolero rhythm crossed the borders of the signifying chains of elite poetic language. Significantly, bolero composers dissolve the hierarchies of value assigned to poetry by the academic elites and their canons—e.g., what is a "good" or a "bad" poem—for they adapt and find inspiration without following the prescribed preference of a group; their selection is motivated by an openness to the exuberant variety of cultural elements available.

This cultural polyphony embodied a mixture of the literary and nonliterary artistic traditions, in a dialogue between tradition and popular speech. The semantic treasures of modernist poetry were soon put into music in Mexico, Cuba, Venezuela, and Puerto Rico: Gutiérrez Nájera, Amado Nervo, Juan de Dios Peza. One of the most popular boleros—"Little Black Angels" (Angelitos negros), often performed by women (the Mexican Toña la Negra, the Puerto Rican Ruth Fernández, and the Cuban Olga Guillot)—is a musical re-accentuation of a poem written by Venezuelan poet Andrés Eloy Blanco. In Cuba, many modernist poems were set to bolero rhythm by the composer Barbarito Diez; of great popularity were the renditions of the two "decadent" sonnets "Kleptomaniac" (Cléptomana) and "Abandoned to Her Grief" (Abandonada a su dolor) by the modernist poet Agustín Costa. Another popular combination was Eusebio Delfín and poet Pedro Mata, while composer Graciano Gómez put to music a well-known sonnet of Chilean writer Pedro Silena (born in 1893):

> This old wound hurts beyond measure
> exhausts my soul, from a long dream . . .
> for not being like everyone else
> I go about defending, romantically,
> this old wound which hurts beyond measure.
>
> Esta vieja herida que me duele tanto
> me fatiga el alma de un largo ensoñar. . .

> por no ser lo mismo que toda la gente
> yo voy defendiendo, románticamente,
> esta vieja herida que me duele tanto.

Since Werther, men *do* die of love . . .

More recently, Venezuelan composer Armando Rojas Guardia re-accentuated the colloquial lyric expression of the classics in "I Who Knew about the Old Wound" (Yo que supe de la vieja herida, 1985), a narrative about contemporary urban life: "I who knew about the old wound / whose blood raptures the dart / the silent stubbornness of the arrow wound" (see Suardiaz 1990).

Composers popularize highly sophisticated poetry, sung by female and male vocalists (María Grever was rather popular in the early 1920s), and Latin Americans dream, dance, and flirt and seduce to the idioms of Venuses, princesses, swans, and the conceit metaphors of elite poetry, as well as to the fantasies of male erotica. Beautifully constructed tensions, which often adhere to the rules of the courtly love, discreet poems, veiled or smuggled messages, everything migrates to the bolero. It was created with the "common language" of colloquial lyricism. Reproduced, repeated, it still survives as one of the most vital examples of modern popular culture.

All the possible emotional nuances of lyric love poetry (from the closed or intentionally obscure medieval *trobar clus,* through Petrarch and Baudelaire) constitute the semantic underground from which the bolero draws its words to articulate desire (Zavala 1989c, 1991c). The poetic designation is at the boundaries of all its available cultural referents. The semantic capacities of the given word emerge from the potentiality of the singer. The bolero is generically neutral, yet the live semantic energy acquires definiteness under the influence of the intonation and the voice of the interpreter, who can give a *gendered* coloring to the text. The bolero is sexually ambivalent, to the degree to which it mediates between lyrics and voice and listener. It remains a privileged medium for the expression of emotions and demands that the lyrical subject stand as the vehicle for individual emotions. The singing guitar (like the singing bandoneon in the tango) has symbolic value as the embodiment of subjective excitement. Both are influenced by the changing social functions of their performers as well. The bolero is dialogical; the emotional (and erotic) potential is always in the future—hope in love, hope that wounds will heal, hope that s/he will return—and its suggestive power is highly dependent on love pacts (very similar to the seductive pacts of the classical Don Juan or Doña Juana) in which seduction is not essentially gendered. What the bolero indicates is that as a cultural voice it was not indifferent to other discourses, and the elitist love language and the popular mutually reflect one another, even if on the surface the elitist ignores or excludes the other social groups with which it is in relation.

It should be noted that both the tango and the bolero, so fundamentally different, break down the conventional opposition between the lyrical and the ironic. It is in the articulation of different modes of language, of different registers, that these texts are generated. Both create new speech genres, halfway between love poetry and popular song. The tango, a sort of realist/naturalist discourse, often shows the reverse side of modernity, through the proletarian jobless life, with its new, tragic heroes embodied in the prostitute and the tough compadrito at the turn of the century, before it reached the dance floor of the bourgeois, traveled to Paris, and returned to Buenos Aires. The 1920s bolero, specifically with the Mexican Agustín Lara, incorporated the sociogram of the prostitute (*mujer de la calle*), giving some boleros a touch of unconventional "decadence" of male erotic fantasies; elements of depraved virginity, women as creatures of cruel moods and passions, the typical Messalina, even "vampires of incarnate degradation" ("Señora tentación" [Lady Temptation], for example) were frequent.

At the same time in metropolitan Spain, the popular *cuplé* (from the French *couplet*) was popularized in the modern(ist) café concert, inaugurating—like the tango and the bolero—an urban popular music, which also spread nationally (see Salaün 1990). From the distance of a century, one could say that the cuplé became hegemonic in Spanish popular culture in the same way that the tango did in the Platine area and the bolero in the Caribbean and Mexico. There was a dialogue among these discourses: cuplés and *chotis* (sung in musicals and cabarets) used the rhythms of the tango (the Andalusian tango), habaneras, waltzes. The themes varied from singing to the automobile to the lives of French courtesans. The *zarzuela* "The Great Courtesans" (Las grandes cortesanas, 1902) is reminiscent of Platine tangos, while the waltz "The Saleswoman of Kisses" (1908) was the central song of an operetta called *The Republic of Love*. By 1919 favorite topics were the Moroccan war and the Russian Revolution—"The Lockout" was quite popular; it tells the story of a girl who is carrying on an affair with a syndicalist, as references are made to communist leaders and sympathizers, with a refrain which says:

> Two pictures of Pestaña
> he has on the wall:
> he has subscribed to *New Spain*
> and says Gorky and Soviet.
> "We will soon be Communists,"
> he says around the block,
> and from everything I earn
> I must give him half.
>
> Dos retratos de Pestaña
> puestos tiene en la pared:
> se ha suscrito a *Nueva España*
> y dice Gorky y soviet.
> —Vamos pronto al comunismo—,
> proclama en la vecindad,
> y de todo lo que gano
> he de darle la mitad. (Salaün 1990:282)

The *género chico* and the zarzuela predominated in the theaters of Madrid and Barcelona with singers from various parts of the world (both Europe and

America) in what was called, using a carnivalesque neologism, the *sicalipsis* or pornographic wave around 1915. In the competing languages and discourses of entertainment, the interlocutors projected in the shows tended to foreground sexuality and city pleasures, even sexual freedom (as in most cosmopolitan nightlife in the rest of Europe). Popular cultures here were connected to popular (and popularized) pleasures, which actively opposed moral vigilantism and puritanical fortresses, as well as state intervention and censorship, which had been intermittent after the Bourbon Restoration of 1874, which ended in 1898, and a practice of conservative ministers or military (Maura from 1907 to 1909, Canalejas, and the dictatorship of Miguel Primo de Rivera in 1923; Valle-Inclán's favorite target, they were particularly notorious).

The cabarets' repertoires varied from imported rhythms to the flamenco shows (by 1919 Madrid had heard its first all-black jazz band).[8] The *varietés* and music halls combined the vernacular cuplé with sentimental love songs, very much like the selections by the well-known Eugénie Buffet and Yvette Guilbert, famous chansonniers of the Moulin Rouge in Paris around 1890 (see Rudorff 1973; Segel 1987). In Spain, the turn of the century brought a wave of women *cupletistas* who used the adjective *the beautiful* before their names: la Bella Angeles, la Bella Chelita, la Bella Diana, la Bella Otero. Raquel Meyer was popular along with Pastora Imperio, and the cuplé singer María Conesa, who became famous in Mexico for cutting the mustache of a revolutionary general! The risqué of the cupletista was at its best in *The White Pussy Cat* (1905).

The pleasure capitals were the site of triumphant bourgeois liberalism, with its bold and daring songs, gestures, clothing, autobiographical accounts in haunting invocations punctuated by a guitar in Argentina or Cuba or Mexico. Dazzling explosions of sentiment in the bolero conditioned a Caribbean, Central American, and Mexican cultural signifying, with its complex network of heteroglossic voices combining the European, the African, the Afro-American with the Latin American—the cultural polyphony of New World countries. These songs gave utterance to different cultural voices—muffled, suppressed, or evident—from the Spanish, the Afro-American, the Indian, the Jewish, the Italian. Both modernist popular musics staged the conflicts, the complementarities, the hopes and fears and dreams of heteroglot cultures. Each of them was the product of what Gutiérrez Nájera called mestizaje: the polyphonic orchestration of references, of subject positions, the composite interweaving of European signs, that in this kind of cultural inversion were no longer Europeanized, because when they were transplanted, their function had already changed. Once transferred, they took another value.

If the blues are the vernacular expression in North America, according to Baker (1984), the tango is the vernacular of the Platine area (and South America), and the bolero that of the Caribbean region. Both semiotic systems are inscribed with the changes of modernization, the demographic deployments, and the expressiveness of the immigrants, or the mestizos recording their own tribulations and fantasizing about love or erotic relations. They are inscribed with alternative cultural tastes, oppositional practices, even rituals of resistance (the tango particularly). They also represent the active re-accentuation of the elite in the popular, the dialogue between the two cultures, instead of a passive consumerism and reproduction.

The tango's narrative (at least in its origin) constitutes the first voiced manifestations of the gaucho, or the immigrants' trans-Atlantic tragic disruption from their social homogeneity, the loss of the way of life of the native village, and perseverance in a social behavior which signals a loss of the self. The tango tells of the sentimental (at times even violent) sense of loss, the misfortunes of poverty and squalor, or the utopia of freedom. The tango is inscribed with the economic, the conflicting heterogeneous ethics, the ensemble of social practices whose modes of life were threatened, or those who were marginalized and pauperized by the emergent industrial order. These tangos are overlaid with the contextual overtones of symbolic overthrow of oppressive social structures. Each narrative explores a concrete relationship of humor, anger, fear, libidinal excess; the voice (normally male) dominating the narrative is ironical, or parodical, or defiant, in order to mark the weight of the account. Both the bolero and the tango represent popular versions of cultural nationalism and the politics of knowledge in emerging nations and industrialized societies, and not a domestication of idioms or languages.

The Cuban-originated bolero, whose link with the blues I have underlined, is a narrative embodying the social heteroglossia and subject repositioning of traditional elite lyrical love poetry. The "given"—the palimpsest of high modernist vocabulary, myths, images—in the discursive pattern suggests a grounding for desirable modes of sexual relationships in an image of vast pleasures coding an eternity of utopian Gardens of Eden of amorous bliss, through re-accentuations from an emotional standpoint, creating new perspectives, new imagery, new metaphors and idioms. Its music and lyrics stand as signs for the pleasure; the subliminal role of the guitar or piano is a means of guiding subjective fantasies and emotions. What the interlocutor introjects through fantasizing desire frequently becomes the gendered identity of the image, since the gender of the "you" in the bolero is often purposely ambiguous and androgynous, an inscribed difference, or at least not clearly defined or aquatic.

Possibly the most influential Latin American popular music, until the very recent *lambada,* the tango and the bolero reveal the different mechanisms whereby societies express sexual and social drives, and overlook interdictions, prohibitions, and taboos. They allow us to understand how such experiences came to be constructed in the emergent national identities, the knowledge(s) that caused individuals to recognize themselves as subjects of sexuality (I follow Foucault's lead in *The History of Sexuality*). Social and individual behavior, which are part of the rise of modern knowledges, are linked in these discourses to social practices, and through them, the individual experiences the self as subject of desire. The interlocutor, and the "listener" (the third), is subjected to both a recognition and a construction of itself as subject of pleasure, in intersections between mimesis of passion and desire.

Both discourses play the game of truth and the game of desire simultaneously in invitations to enforce moral codes or in compulsions to transgressions. Consequently, they indicate the mode by which individuals situate themselves in relation to moral codes of sexual conduct, marriage, erotics. In fact, they are carriers of various discourses that converge to produce modes of male and female sexual behavior, and are central elements for understanding gender constructs throughout the region (in other cases, ethnic constructs). The self-affirmation is also linked to gendered roles, through the theme of male virility and mastery (particularly in the tango). Many boleros, by extension, project that moderation is male, and passive abandonment to pleasure is female—although the situation may be reversed: one of the classics, "Bésame mucho" (1941), was written by a sixteen-year-old Mexican, Consuelo Velázquez, who gives voice to women's flood of unconscious material. Many women have composed boleros in Cuba, Puerto Rico, and Mexico. In fact, the bolero is one of the privileged performative texts of women, as both musicians and singers.

Words provoke excited reveries or carefully phrased anxieties; what is implied is that in the construction of the subject of desire, males know how to use and govern sexual pleasure. Precisely what both modernist popular discourses suggest is a relation between knowledge, sexual desire, and the question of values in heteroglossic societies. Both vernacular idioms underwrite the modern ideological tropes that constituted the period's genealogy of morals and the discontents of civilization (read also technologies) in the dramatic intensity of promises of a future, as the modernity of the new century broke free from the imprint of the past.

The tango and the bolero are *transcultural* idioms suggesting the heteroglossic and polyphonic cultural identity of the national hegemonies. They are emotional narratives of turn-of-the-century open-ended conditions of possibility in a still-noninstitutionalized cultural and social discourse of modernity, which are dialogically combined with narrative (autobiographical) experiences of the displaced gaucho and immigrant, and the narrative of love of the heteroglotic societies of Cuba and Mexico (the areas where there was more African presence). Both cultural idioms privilege the psychic dimension as it comes to be heterogeneously inscribed in the cultural texts, and can also be recognized as national agents of culture. If the theories that suggest the mixture of Spanish and African as the origins of the bolero are correct, it is interesting to stress that it emerged (like the danzón) as a postslavery expression of the new social and cultural cohesion around the master narrative of decolonization. If the danzón visibly projects the caricature of the oppressor (so does the Puerto Rican carnivalized *plena,* or the Afro-Puerto Rican *bomba*), the self inscribed in the bolero is that of the cultural cohesion which independence and national identity projected.

The modern period (from the 1880s to around the First World War) also saw the expansion of cultural territories. And in the major discursive shift at the end of the last century, in which the dialogical range of forceful Latin American national identities was produced, both discourses became part of a new civic national culture. They can also be regarded as part of the uneven cultural development of urban "Argentinianness" or "Caribbeanness" or "Mexicanness" (with Agustín Lara in the 1920s), that is, the lived relations of peoples—immigrants, expatriates, settlers, mulatto working class—and their significant impact on the domestic cultures.[9] Both discourses provided the rhythms which would come to dominate modern city life and constitute the bricolages of culture, which was a feature of the urban experience of modernity. These civic cultures were cognitively pursued in the negritude literatures of the Caribbean (the second generation of modernists), which includes Cuban Nicolás Guillén, Puerto Rican Luis Palés Matos, Martinican Aimé Césaire, Jacques Roumain, Jacques Stéphen Alexis, as well as the national cartographies of the civic poetry of Pablo Neruda, César Vallejo, and Puerto Rican Julia de Burgos and the bricolages of Argentinianness of Borges. All of these emerged as the narrative of turn-of-the-century modernity ran into a dead end—after the olympic swan's neck was bent ("Tuércele el cuello al cisne") in Mexican Enrique González Martínez's 1910 sonnet.

Popular Discourse and Revolutionary Ideology

Since the 1880s anarchism had become the strongest proletarian form of association in both the Old World and the New World, and with it there arose a considerable attempt to popularize anarchist principles. Broadsheets and songs, as well as popular literature (short stories, novels, poetry), became widely used as ways to attract more recruits. The intersection of culture, technology, economics, and revolutionary ideology became an important site of political struggle, and art (literary discourse) an important way to organize social relations. Culture became an agency for social regulation, in the same manner that modernists expressed sympathy toward socialist ideas (specifically anarchism); in their demythologization of the complacent middle-class society, anarchists not only developed newspapers, schools, community music choirs, and theater to create signs that could promote universal alliance, but they also used the signs and idioms provided by the high elitist culture.

The semantic field also opened toward the new modern popular culture itself; consequently there was a different treatment of narrative structure, a response to the demand of a different audience of communication, and an audience subject to a different economy of symbols. Modern music became a form of integration into the utopian modernity. Instead of symbolic remedies for misery, these songs became agents for potentiating critical analysis and to project a social imaginary of utopia. It should be stressed that anarchist federations were rather strong in what is called the "formative period" of anarchism in the Platine area (periodicals go back to the 1880s; see *Report* [1973]) and in Peru, where anarchist newspapers developed at the turn of the century (see Espino Reluce 1984).

Social upheaval and revolutionary change are inscribed in anarchist songs, as part of the modernist idea that art could play an important part in shaping a new and better world. Consequently, as an alternative to commercialized art (principally theater), the anarchists had been struggling against the culture industry to use art to denounce social and political contradictions of the capitalist systems. Art provided a commitment for liberation, through a set of strategies which were fundamentally based on a symbolic exchange which could be understood and re-accentuated in different cultural spaces. Music was a privileged medium to make a popular appeal to simplified complex political theories and socio-economic analyses, in much the same way the Latin American Nueva Canción accomplishes this at present (see the pertinent analysis of Reyes Matta 1988). These songs function as utopian social projections, giving voice to a rupture with the state and dominant discourses, as well as denouncing abuses and social inequality.

In the first part of the twentieth century, revolutionary songbooks began to appear. The mode of publication was not new. Since early in the nineteenth century democrats, republicans, and socialists had made wide use of popular forms of publishing, and a proletarian alternative culture focused on the discriminating system of bourgeois canons. If industrialization led to destruction of local cultures, socialists and anarchists worked against the exclusionary culture capital of the bourgeoisie by creating cultural centers, through which a socialist cultural identity would be developed. Denied access to schools, cultural centers, and culture itself, large segments of the working class were drawn to this alternative culture, which provided a vehicle for a truly democratic dialogue.

What is particularly interesting at this point is the anarchists' extensive use of modern songs—habaneras, tangos, milongas, *ajiras, jotas,* waltzes. Popular rhythms provided a mnemotechnic mechanism to learn and understand the meaning of the highly developed economic and political rationale of the social theories. Anarchists and socialists re-accentuated and reappropriated not only music but also biblical and religious language to project their transformation of society. Both sacred and profane, biblical and religious language provided a permanent tension and unfixed coordinates which redefined produced spaces of practice within new social activities for the plethora of utopian plans for the socialized *Acracia.*

Music helped to draw from the political underground, at the same time that this political underground absorbed the inflow of new information. Both European and creole rhythms were exchanged in the construction of these political and cultural identities—the Marsellaise was popular and entirely compatible with new re-accentuations. Also, the popular rhythms of the time were favored—from tango, to camel-trot, to *yaraví,* or *pasillo,* or polka. Collections of music (like the commercial *cancioneros* or almanacs) were first published in the press, and then in anthologies published by syndicates. These publications appear to have been an alternative to the commercial cancioneros which were frequent around the 1920s, as records, movies, and the radio provided more access. It is at this point that we encounter the opposite reaction as an alternative, which may be summed up as the search for a proletarian cultural identity. The prologue to a collection entitled *The Rebellious Lyre* (La lira rebelde), published in Lima in 1922, said: "These songs will carry to our spirits the echo of pain which will give impulse to our energy to fight to live like free men [*sic*]. . . . They express the freedom we proletarians desire" (in Espino Relucé 1984:38).

One such collection appeared in Buenos Aires, *The Revolutionary Songbook: A Collection of Hymns and Libertarian Songs in Spanish and Italian* (Librería La Escuela Moderna, n.d.), which includes songs from different epochs. Cuban music and Platine tango combine to form a discourse on social revolution, projecting desires of social change. The guajira "My Desires" (Mis deseos) is representative:

> I work for my redemption
> and to live without scroungers
> who vilely (hideously) exploit
> the workers.
> Politics and religion
> disappear from the world
> and into the darkest abyss
> violently fall,
> Pope, King, and President
> with all their filthy escort. (P. 4)

> Deseo mi redención
> y vivir sin *vividores*
> que con los trabajadores
> hacen vil explotación.
> Política y religión
> desaparezcan del mundo
> y al abismo más profundo
> caigan violentamente,
> Papa, Rey y Presidente
> con todo el cortejo inmundo.

Another tango is called "War to the Bourgeoisie," an habanera "Damn the Bourgeoisie," a milonga from the Libertarian Payador "Social Milongas." This last one presents an important twist, by contesting the image of aggression and violence normally constructed by the media and crime-control agencies to connect social anxieties in the population with crime. Since authorities legitimated through those images a more coercive state role, the anarchists vigorously projected a positive image against state-controlled antagonism:

> Loving audience who listens
> to the anarchist payador,
> don't turn a blind eye
> with a certain expression of horror;
> that if when I tell you who we are

happiness comes to your face
in the name of Anarchy,
I welcome you with love. (P. 9)

Grato auditorio que escuchas
al payador anarquista,
no hagas a un lado la vista
con cierta expresión de horror;
que si al decirte quien somos
vuelve a tu faz la alegría
en nombre de la Anarquía
te saludo con amor.

The payador goes on to define their ideal of justice, egalitarianism, liberty, a unified proletarian front, and in the political carnivalesque atmosphere blames governments and laws for wars, inequality, and poverty.

The same pamphlet includes a political carmagnole written by William Morris and a collection of Italian songs on the same themes, based on Tuscan songs or the popular "Funiculi Funicula," as well as a hymn to May First (in Spanish), inspired by an aria from Verdi's opera *Nabuco*. The Peruvians included songs by the Italian anarchist Ana Negri, as well as songs written by proletarian women from the ranks.

The Peruvian collections—with texts from 1900–1926 and from various sources—are practically identical: there is a "Communist Marsellaise," a waltz titled "New Songs" (music by Jorge Chávez), the polka "The Working Woman," a hymn to the strike of the "14th of September" with music from the Spanish *paso-doble* "El relicario," and a song called "A Desperate Man" with music from the yaraví (Paraguay?) "Black Flowers" (Flores negras), a title common to romantic songs and boleros.[10] Another one with the same source music was called "Red Flowers:"

Red as the stonemason's hammer
        are my songs:
and amidst shouts of anger
        from the rebellious,
while the masters bellow
        their imprecations,
vibrate like clarions
        my red songs.

Rojas como cucardas
        son mis canciones:
y entre gritos de ira
        de los rebeldes,
mientras rugen los amos
        sus maldiciones,
vibren como clarines
        mis cantos rojos. (Espino Relucé 1984:110)

Most of these carnivalized popular songs project triumph in the social imaginary against the largely repetitive history of proletarian defeat. Like the Bakhtinian notion of popular political carnival, these songs unleash images in a liberatory semiosis, submitting to ridicule both transcendental and state signifiers, through relativism, grotesque realism, parody, satire, employing all the representative genres of creative memory, those popular genres which would guarantee uninterrupted continuity. Bourgeois values are ridiculed and questioned and displaced into opposites, while libertarian values are reanimated and rearticulated in a deconstruction (at times blasphemous) of authoritarian signifiers.

The solemnity of authority is turned upside down, codes are read differently, and messages clearly render an inverted image of the libertarian self. What emerges is the social utopia, in an open-ended discourse to the future. The symbolic assassination of the oppressor releases the potential for the utopia of the future. These anarchist texts express the "unuttered" in enthymemic discourses trying to foretell the future, preparing a place in the dialogue of the present, in Bakhtin's words, a "yet unuttered response in an already unfolded dialogue" (*DI* 90).

The images—which could be related to Brecht's estrangement effect or Valle-Inclán's esperpento, but certainly to political carnivalization—follow the modernist poetics of negation and the new speech genres of heterology I mentioned earlier: they are both reconstructive and deconstructive, producing dialogical projections which provoke positive representations in the interlocutor, against the negative images of the authoritarian signifiers. The Libertarian Payador projects not only an alternative culture but another social system, while others, such as "Damn the Bourgeoisie," encourage oppositional practices through the full range of imaginative acts of symbolic assassination. Both simultaneous images provoke proletarian solidarity and comradeship. The two drives support each other, and interlock in the same sign; utterances here have a "sideways glance," giving the potential other meaning. Happiness and vitality echo through the popular song rhythms of milongas and habaneras to evoke festivity and pleasure and revoke solemnity and authority: pleasure and happiness are what anarchism would inaugurate. These songs are constructed by cultural and social inversions, and the function of the music helps to project that life is a continuous striving for happiness, and that life, pleasure, and love form a unity.

Anarchism's doctrine of love (which took intense ethical reflections in Tolstoy's mysticism) is expounded here in the emotional vernacular of the higher truth of social revolution. Libertarian truth is presented in solidarity, incarnated in social revolution through collective work, alongside other consciousnesses.

Latin American modernist popular music is part of the cultural polyphony and ethnic mestizaje, in its variations of creolized and maroonized heterology of modernity—clearly, the new situation of exchanges provided under the new modes of production which, in the Platine area, and in the whole of the huge urban concentrations of the modern cities, the emergent capitalist bourgeois

society brought about. In these radically new situations, polyglossia and heteroglossia provide the energy for creative mixtures uniting the complexity of
differences in a vernacular national identity. The heteroglotic part of the vocal
emerges in continual seepages and negotiations, in multiple encounters with the
literary through different subject positions. Within the behavioral situation of
the popular, modernism is re-accentuated through an amplification of its heterogeneity, in relation to its politics of signification. Heterology becomes part of
the vernacular, determines it, and acts as dialogical background of the social
heteroglossia, which orchestrates the meaning; heterology prevails in this creative and familiar contact with the high literary sphere to such an extent that it
becomes the exotopy of modernity.

IX

OTHER MODERNIST OPEN-ENDED BEGINNINGS

> Then, forgetting future generations and not
> thinking beyond anything, they dream that the
> apple tree would give tasty fruit in Havana and
> the palm juicy coconuts in Washington, as if
> under mortal climates both trees were not
> condemned to die.
>
> —Ramón Emeterio Betances, 1892

Colonial Puerto Rican Moderns

The Antillean island of Puerto Rico was not marginal in this cultural polyphony of the turn of the century. It shared with Cuba first an anti-colonial stand against Spanish rule in search of emancipation, and then an active concern with North American expansionist power games. Anti-yanquism had pervaded cultural discourse on the island since Eugenio María de Hostos, Julio J. Henna, and Betances's struggle (the last two formed the Puerto Rican section of the Cuban Revolutionary Party) and projected a dialogical social imaginary of national independence, with the alliance of both Cubans and Spanish republicans. The difference between "us" and "them" became clear with the First Republic in 1873; however, these "first moderns" devoted their activities to the political sense of freedom as well as to their valuation of culture.

The political dimension of their cultural texts unfolds from the coercive conflicts with colonial censorship (see Zavala 1977; Zavala and Rodríguez, eds. 1980). On the island, the question of domination and power cannot be separated from language and culture. The colonial desire for an identity is obviously connected to nationalism; in both literature and politics this anti-colonial drive centered around language. For the Puerto Rican to speak or write in the colonizers' tongue (English) calls forth a problem of identity in the material sense, since a choice of language is a choice of identity. This dilemma and struggle persists to the present.

On this smaller Antillean island, the metropolitan colonial fears of another war similar to the Cuban brought about a Charter of Autonomy, which came too late. In July 1898, United States armed forces disembarked in Guánica, quite possibly the same place where Columbus landed in 1493, bringing the first neocolonialism to the Antilles (and to Latin America). On October 16, 1898, Puerto Rico passed into the hands of the United States, whose expansionist aims had long been fixed in the Antilles and had struck a responsive chord among plantation owners and landowners who had been asking Washington for help (Cuba's situation was similar). They trusted their partner in the north to support them in their struggle against the usurious practices of Spanish commission agents and against the colonial government.

Let us recall that there is a historical relationship between slavery and capitalism, since slavery bondage had long been part of the world economy (see Mintz 1985). Slave plantations had been transforming exotic luxuries (tobacco and sugar) into "proletarian necessities" in Europe since the eighteenth century. By the middle of the century it was said that the poorest English took sugar in their tea.

Slave labor was part of the larger Atlantic commerce, and Caribbean sugar plantations linked Pennsylvania farmers and New England fishermen with iron manufacturers in Birmingham and textile workers in Nantes (see Davis 1987). In the nineteenth century, both Cuban and Puerto Rican colonists were highly dependent on African labor (in Puerto Rico slavery ended in 1873), and North American interest was heightened by the fear of British and French intervention, especially British because of the dread of English global domination. By the 1890s this process of capitalist economy and imperialist growth was the controlling model for both Caribbean islands. Betances's warnings had been in vain when he wrote, like Martí before, that only independence would "be able to save us from the American minotaur" (in Zavala and Rodríguez, eds. 1980:20).

The exact extent of Puerto Rican anti-imperial struggle in 1898 is still under discussion; according to some historians, the North American invasion favored the sugar-cane landowners who hoped for open markets, since from the end of the eighteenth century the United States had been the principal buyer of sugar on the island. Therefore, after 1898 not only did the sugar-cane owners accept annexation, but this alternative was also popular among the Creoles and laborers (see a summary in Náter Vázquez 1988–89).

The aspect that set off Puerto Rican modernism from Cuban will remain an essential motif; a line was drawn between the two islands whose political fate had been linked until 1898. It was an imaginary of independence that articulated both modernities in their struggle against Spanish colonialism and the anguish over the "minotaur." Since the 1860s the organic intellectuals of both islands had joined together in a common endeavor against North American expansionism. But the common history of the two Antillean islands bifurcated in 1898; the transition was a passage from what became an independent nation-state in one (by 1959 a socialist revolution), and a commonwealth after 1952 in the other. Yet, broken, but carrying within itself the fragmentary of colonization, the Puerto Rican social imaginary was nourished extensively from the cultural repertoire in ways that sharpened the outlines of ideas and figures, to which ideological myths were put into service.

To those concerned with modernism in the form of neocolonialism in the Antilles, it is important to identify the oppositions used to organize the anti-colonial discursive field, the politics of style behind writing, the asymmetrical antagonisms behind the figural, the reverse discourses, the polymorphous exploits of tropes to exercise critical power. The claim of language is to be measured here in two dimensions: the horizontal axis which reclaims the past in the memory of the language users, and the vertical dimension which opens up the present. This play strengthens the stability of cultural assignments of values to the positions along each axis. An axiological element supports signification, and the positionality of the subject. The already spoken and already written triggers the imaginary to rewrite the same narrative, with different images, portraits, expressions, idiolects. The impossibility of not looking back at what the past has wrought shows the modern to think beyond the contemporary scheme and ring changes.

The emphasis in choice is conceived as a resistance to the power of the past and the present. The past is, in a way, repository of all one could desire; the modern writer emphasizes choice, dissuades of the siren's song and the music of the centaurs' flutes, to persuade beyond bewilderment, to show the contradiction, the acceptance of which is tragedy. Texts invite the questions and introduce ways of looking at oneself, a point from which to view the castration. In order to decenter the world of the colony, to change the place from which that world is viewed, modern colonial and neocolonial writers introduce a new place from which to look at themselves. The Dionysian frenzy of the carnivalesque and the castrating power which subtly possesses are the options; mimesis gives way to semiosis to destabilize the received, to assume a culture and to think against the bland acceptance, and deliberately to raise questions on identity and language. This describes the conception of the task since modernity.

Drawing from the background of a culturally decolonizing modernism, I should like to recover the critical-utopian social imaginary of Puerto Rican modernists, trying to avoid the reductionism which identifies the unmasking of instrumental reason and the imperialistic technologies of power with either a nostalgic anti-modernization or a nostalgic return to a Spanish colonial past. However ambiguous this unmasking was (specifically among Puerto Rican moderns), a cultural formulation of the relation between a complete deprivation of self and the realization to constitute a subject was asserted.

In the early twentieth century, the voices of national identity confidently and defiantly proclaimed a radically nonimperialistic norm of human interaction. The anti-colonial narrative at the turn of the century was the proffered projection of a modern woman poet—Lola Rodríguez de Tió—who also lived and published in Cuba, and had a solid reputation among her modernist peers (Casal's last article, in 1893, was a review of one of her books). She wrote a hymn-poem of the island, "The Borinqueña," which strings events, actions, and passions celebrating the utopia of liberation and freedom. The poem speaks through and by virtue of the æsthetic utopia of an ideological fantasy of an emancipatory imagination: "Wake up, Borincans, it is time to fight." In 1868 she urged the colonized to insurrection and to revolutionary impulse against Spain, even when the definition colonizer/colonized was conceived under the old epistemic system. But such a process of resistance was initiated early on the island, in the struggles since 1868 against the old empire.

In my recuperative reading, the modernist aesthetic utopia in Puerto Rico redefined issues, remapped frontiers of knowledge, and was best experienced in both prose and poetry by José de Diego (1866–1918). A lawyer who had studied in Spain, de Diego vigorously contributed to anarchist newspapers in the 1880s and early 1890s. Luis Lloréns Torres (1876–1944) also put forward a critical modernist poetics, while formal tendencies were disseminated through the main periodicals: *White Journal* (Revista Blanca, 1896–1902), *The Carnival* (El Carnaval, 1899–1912), and later *Journal of the Antilles* (Revista de las Antilles, 1913–18); they all published prose and poetry by Darío and other modernists.[1] These journals played an important role in the development of strategies of resistance. The disparaging thrust of nationalist discourses came to a stop after 1898 with the North American invasion, which, according to many witnesses and documents, helped aggrandize self-confidence among the invading military. As is to be expected, there was little cultural activity on the island as the army took over all functions, and one general triumphantly affirmed that within a year everyone would speak English. In 1903, one of the intellectuals commented in a private letter: "By what strange coincidence after the American regime has there been a visible intellectual decline in literary culture on the island?" (qtd. in Hernández Aquino 1968:31).

A periodization of Puerto Rican modernity/modernism would include as its peak the fifteen years between 1903 and 1918, which represent the culmination of Puerto Rico's annexation through the Foraker Law—drafted to give Puerto Ricans citizenship, granted mainly because of the need for soldiers during the First World War. During this first period under North American colonization, the heightened hostility was emphasized by way of a cultural imagining which drew on the intimate connection between the project of language and the project of a national self. It is important from the outset to understand that in this imaginary the potential source of freedom was ineluctably associated with language as a modeling system for anti-colonial social and ethical values. The position of anti-colonial struggle was projected through positive images of the Antilles as a cultural and historical totality. These combined with forms of semiotic creolization and carnivalized parodies of North Americans. Literary projections aimed at reinforcing an anti-colonial self, and a defense of language as basis of national identity. This antipathy toward the new colonizers was nourished through a re-accentuation of Spanishness, which here, as a "situated utterance," helped fortify national identity against total subjugation. Moral and cultural superiority were played off against the crude materialist aims of the new theories of conquest.

If anything defines Puerto Rican modernism, it is this cultural imagining and the gradually deepened hostility to the various forms of rule. The aesthetic utopia stood for the unfolding of the dormant anti-colonial powers through negative images touching on caricature and parody. In this context, de Diego's poem "Aleluyas" is particularly relevant: "Gentlemen from the North marvelous and fecund / the center is also part of the globe" (my translation; see Hernández Aquino anthology [1967:18]). His most powerful modernist utopia can be found in his cartography of the islands, his decisive anti-colonialist stand, and his humoresque (carnivalized) portrayal of North Americans before the Foraker Law. Both the conceptual and the fictive creative disruption are oriented toward a cognitive literary production through the condensation of fictions, metaphors, analogies, scenarios, possible worlds that tend to stress the "Spanish" origins of the island.

In *Pomarrosas* (1904), the poet laments the "strong hand of the colossus" as he emphasizes that the events on the island will be the joint fate of all "our unfortunate Latin America [América latina], if a powerful federalist movement does not save her in the future." In a poem titled "The Setting Sun," he condenses all the emotional rhythms in a fabric of colors which constitute the denoted opposition between the two Americas. The forces of freedom depend on the labor of displacement:

> The Latin sun will die in America,
> crepuscular light from the pole will come;
> dark eyes will die of cold
> and the melancholic blue will come. (My translation; in de Diego 1966:xv)

In 1916 de Diego found himself reconstituting the Antillean Union and writing a set of articles and poems defending the teaching of Spanish in schools, and the sense of identity through language. His "Hymn to America," "The Bilingual World," and "Mother Waters" all project an open-ended discourse on future liberation for the Antilles. This modernity can also be defined by the fact that a utopia of language as power is conceived, and a displacement of language to project a new subject. De Diego's stand weakened by the 1910s, yet he epitomizes that moment of protest and dialogical polemical move against neo-colonialism. His writing reveals an inexhaustible range of signifying practices to make a political case against colonization.

Lloréns is no less polemic in his construction of a decolonized subject and decimates imperialism in "To Franklin D. Roosevelt" and "Mare Nostrum"; here he engages the cultural past as part of its concrete struggle against the present for the future. Each of these poems is a concrete struggle opening possibilities between the cultural imagining of the poet and the responsiveness of the future:

> Mare Nostrum, sea that harangues,
> with versicles pregnant with future,
> your islands
> and the lands that amorous surround you; . . .

Sea that still feels colonial pain,
and choleric, hurls epithets of lightning and thunder
when you see raised in your islands
exotic flags proclaiming
that you are not our sea. (In Ortiz 1977:63–64)

"Song of the Antilles" is a cartography of the islands which exalts a unified history in an intertextual virtuosity of classical names and battles.[2] The poet enjoys the imaginary liberty by projecting oppositions and conflicts. The arrangement or disposition of the long poem is a rewriting of an already written past, thus bringing about a mutation of reality. Lloréns suggests the dual necessity that the Antilles be regarded at the same time from the viewpoints of language, the body, and history.

The future is the indispensable dimension of the poetic dialogical imaginary projecting a space of resistance; what defines this enthymemic dialogue is the responsiveness of the poet's audience. Far from reifying the forms of freedom and destroying the utopia of liberation, Lloréns demands a future that imperialism hinders and blocks in the present, while parodying annexationists through his neologism *pitiyanquis* (petit yanquis), an estranged metaphor reminiscent of turn-of-the-century anti-yanquism.

Both de Diego's and Lloréns's cultural texts are heteroglossic and invite a critical hermeneutics, against the passively consuming worlds and voices presented by history. The reader must somehow have in mind the projected values in order to be able to perceive the polemic against the received doctrines, the doxae of colonization. These modernist texts provoke questions of identity, rewrite genealogies, and textualize the geographical body, the materiality of the world, to see what revisions can be made and what paths traced out of familiar topoi. This perspective delineates and centers a world; the texts introduce a way of looking, even of defining one of the characteristics of modernism, its historicism, which insists on the necessity of inheriting. The enthymemic in the poems is an invitation to think together the resistance to any reductive system. The project was to testify to the situation of the island as "the only nation in Latin America subjected to the yanqui flag" (*Revista de las Antillas* 1913:51).

Similar situated awarenesses can be found in Luis Palés Matos (1898–1959) and Julia de Burgos (1914–58). In "Mulato Antille" Palés encloses the gendered idiom of national identity as much as the symbolic representation of the male gaze caught and framed by desire. "Festive Song to Be Wept" (Canción festiva para ser llorada) is a powerful geographical mapping of Caribbean colonialism; one by one he names the islands—Haiti, Guadeloupe, Martinique, Cuba, Puerto Rico, Saint Kitts—mocking and unmasking the signs of colonialism as idioms and signs of fragmentation. More than the Bakhtinian carnivalesque, what Palés Matos discloses tangibly corresponds to Freud's uncanny and castration, *das unheimlich,* or Lacan's "fragmented body" (*corps morcelé*). This fantasy has a structural relationship to the alienating identity in

Lacan; in Palés Matos the *disjecta membra* call upon colonization as a whole. Poetic imagery here has a broad social sweep and helps produce a map of the colonized Caribbean and a cogent political message.

The castrated bodies and limbs of the islands gesturally perform a macabre dance staged in the foreground of a mastered geography visually enumerated to the last detail, whose uncannier representation is Puerto Rico itself: "Cuba—black and happy-go-lucky / Haití—voodoo and pumpkin head—/ Puerto Rico—hodgepodge." The symbolic significance of this poem is the act of looking at the castrated bodies, the spectacle of the severed selves, mutilated and dismembered by colonial oppression and epistemic violence. The carnivalesque is absent here, for this is not a symbolic festive song but the lament of fragmentation and castrated identities.

In *Tun tún de pasa y grifería* (1937), Palós Matos models heteroglossia, but also the seepages between boundaries of festive carnivalization and the castration of the uncanny. The mirror is emptied of optical content (I return to Lacan) and produces *mirages* rather than sensory images. The mirror is turned into a spectacle (the specular into the spectacular). In the poet's mirror world, nothing changes to its opposite and back again; it is not the world of the reversal of the carnival, but the mirror of the uncanny representations of castration and mutilation. What is enacted in such poems is the transformations which have been fixed in the bodies split into fetish objects. The remapping of the Antilles for Lloréns and Palés Matos is revealed in the form of bodies split into pieces, with language divided within itself by all the oppositions and differences it must convey.

This is not the place to do full justice to Julia de Burgos, who reveals in her poetry a project of self-definition as a Puerto Rican, as a woman, and as poet (see Díaz-Diocaretz 1990). She internalizes the alienations and splits of her society, the loss of connection, the falsity of gendered roles, and the ethnic prejudices. What her poetry often uncovers are the multidirected oppressions of many colonial women, caught between patriarchy (also ethnic in her case) and imperialist ideology. Her subjectivity is constructed within multiple social relationships and repositioned as the product of different class, ethnic, and cultural specificities. Her poem "To Julia de Burgos" locates the traces and sites of these oppressions: "They say I am your enemy / because I give your inmost self to the world in verse. / They lie, Julia de Burgos. They lie, Julia de Burgos. / The voice that sounds in my poems is not your voice: it is my voice" (in Flores and Flores, eds. 1986). This poem testifies to the *unsilenced* subaltern woman (employing Gayatri Spivak's use of the Gramscian concept) through ironical twists between submissiveness and defiance. The poem's closure is a deliberate defiant dismantling of these constructions:

> While the multitudes race about frantically,
> leaving behind ashes from burnt-out injustices,
> and while with the torch of the seven virtues

the multitudes pursue the seven sins,
against you, and against everything unjust and inhuman,
I shall go into their midst with the torch in my hands.

(Flores and Flores, eds. 1986:81)

The Puerto Rican poet uncovers the black masks behind white identities, the denied and despised black or mulatto identities, installing a divided subject denied the right to subjectivity. She experiments to reposition the woman and colonial bodies with respect to language, to identity, and to time. With Lloréns and Palés she begins the serious game of remapping and the practice of charting new sets of beliefs and values. Make-up and masks indicate precisely the limitations in a vast network of intersecting and horizontal lines; silent, visible, or invisible, the masks are there, they are part of the bodies. The description of these topographies leads either to the atopia of the nowhere, or the utopia of freedom. Her texts stage the body and figure desire of such places defined by the subject's gaze: "I am a runaway Rocinante / sniffing at horizons for the justice of God." Taken together, Palés Matos and Julia de Burgos (in a triad with Cuba's Nicolás Guillén) provide an intense dramatization of anti-colonial subjectivity and liberatory struggle. They are the cartographers of the Antilles joined by the other voices in the multilanguagedness fragmentation of the Caribbean (see Arnold's [1981] excellent analysis of Césaire's modernism).

In Puerto Rico, the social imaginary and fantasy evoke the colonial condition, in shifting to politics of race/sexuality and the complexity of the psychic projection in the colonial relationship. This imaginary may be nationalist (as in Enrique Laguerre's novels), socialist (as in Juan Antonio Corretejer's poetry), or pro-independence (as with René Marqués), but they all share this position as a productive space. In all of these texts (since the 1880s), Puerto Rican identity is projected as that imaginary point where the stories of subjectivity meet the narratives of history, of a culture.[3] The appeal to language as basis of national identity is still strong in Puerto Rican literature, even when neocolonialism means living under multinational capitalism, and even postindustrial oppression.

Modernity is expressed in Puerto Rico as emancipatory voices and a program to explore the past and the differences, based on "(an)otherness" of language and culture; the Spanish language is the instrument of national identity and the "cultural underground" of resistance.[4] The resistance to imperialism was compensated by a revalued power of tradition (the Spanish past) to stabilize a difference, and by cultural production as the means to achieve and maintain subjective freedom. These are precisely the aporias inscribed in Puerto Rican modernist discourse, and the failure of that historical conjuncture which created a new terrain on which a new type of colonization was formed.

The organic ideology (what Gramsci called organic or historically effective) of this modernism constructed a unity out of difference in the fragmentary and contradictory nature of "common sense," which spoke to people's experience out of the deep social crisis of the colonial past. The organic crisis of dependence in the open-ended hegemony was finally articulated into a set of strategic alliances in the 1930s, and by 1952, under a new form of colonization through a commonwealth; the social imaginary of anti-colonial struggle is still a commitment to the project of independence, an open-ended project of critical thought against the closed discourse to hegemonize the intellectual world. This question arises also in the literature of contemporary Newyoricans, where language is also embedded with their own political anti-colonial evaluation.

The work of Puerto Rican modernists seems to me to be marked by a painful distress and an attempt toward a psychic wholeness or unity which the historical situation always threatens to shatter. A vision of a world of fragments (for instance, Palés Matos and Julia de Burgos) recurs, either in the poets themselves or in the readers' minds. There is a feeling of damaged existence, of a maimed present, and of fragmented selves as psychic impairment caused by neo-colonialism.

As a historical poetics of negation, modernism takes many forms in Puerto Rico—it may have the frenzy of the carnival to unmask oppression, the fragmentation of a castrated body and an alienated identity, or the sobriety of Mnemosyne as part of the liberating impulse, as a completion of the thoughts of emancipation of the past. Carnivalization, parody, the grotesque representations of the "yanquis" and "pitiyanquis," the word with a sideways glance give access to the utopian of liberation, while the dialogical is oriented precisely toward an actively responsive understanding. Writing does not expect passive understanding, but a creative response.

We are reminded of Marx's well-known letter to Arnold Ruge (1843): "It will turn out that it is not a question of any conceptual rupture between past and future, but rather of the completion of the thoughts of the past." For the notion of memory for neocolonialist cultures is a nostalgia for the past only superficially; projections of the unfinalized future are displaced, often dressed as nostalgia, against a present which cloaks an inauthentic future. Memory serves almost to justify an anticipatory phenomenon.

There is, at times, even a defiant nostalgia as a political motivation, a nostalgia for the wholeness and conscious of itself, product of a dissatisfaction with a present on the ground, not of a past but of a future plenitude.

Gendered Modernities: The Corridor of Women's Voices

> I was in your cage, little man,
> little man who gives me a cage.
>
> —Alfonsina Storni

Modernness is also the time/space of the powerful emergence of hidden, semi-hidden, and diffused women's voices. At that precise point one begins to hear voices in languages and styles, as means of realized expression of women's "unuttered" voices. The corridor of women's voices (to gender one of Bakhtin's favorite metaphors) augments the polyphony of modernity, and gendered dialogic boundaries intersect the entire field of modern life through "enthymemic utterances" (to use Díaz-Diocaretz's concept [1989a]) which release new signifying practices.

It is no secret that women writers were on the margins in the spatial projection of the polyphony of modernities at the turn of the century. Modernness and modernization inherently exemplify the actual advances in feminism(s) within the broader set of historical and political processes. If modernism is, as I have been suggesting, a capitalist social formation which cannot be analyzed outside an anti-imperialist struggle in Latin America and outside an anti-capitalist exploitation in the metropolis, it can logically be assumed that implicit in this mode of action were women's emancipation and an emerging construction of the female subject. The broadening of the system of domination into a wider social anti-hegemonic struggle, in the context I have been arguing, assumed ethical, moral, intellectual, and cultural, as well as economic, dimensions. The emergence of a modern construction of the female subject includes these spheres, which brought about the unity of economic, political, and cultural-ethical aims.

Another dynamic force in Latin American modernity was women's cultural practices as an activity to reposition the powerful discourses of modernity. In line with the modernist aesthetic of renovation of knowledges, most important journals include poetry or translations from the English or French written by women, short stories, poems. Among the salient names were Adela Zamudio (Bolivia), Esther Lucila Vázquez, Juana Borrero, Mercedes Matamoros, María Villar Buceta (Cuba), Laura Méndez de Cuenca, María Enriqueta Camarillo, Gertrudis Tenorio Zavala "Hortensia" (Mexico), Peruvian novelist Clorinda Matto de Turner (1854–1909), and Puerto Rican novelists Carmela Eulate Sanjurjo, who wrote a naturalist text, *The Doll* (1895), and Ana Roqué (*Light and Shadow*), as well as anarchist writer Luisa Capetillo (1880–1922).

The domain opened up within each modern society came to provide a fertile ground to other writers, who could be called the "second generation": Alfonsina Storni (1892–1938, Argentina), Gabriela Mistral (1889–1957, Chile), Dulce María Loynaz (Cuba), María Eugenia Vaz Ferreira (1875–1905), Delmira Agustini (1886–1914), and Juana de Ibarborou (1895–1979, Uruguay).[5]

Writing in an occupied territory meant, as we know now, breaking mirrors: it meant rewriting the well-known images of the *speculum ecclesiae,* with the types and anti-types of highly conventional roles encapsulated in traditions. "Modern women" were not submissive objects of representation but liberated their own newly defined bodies. If modernity was a a construction of self, implicitly it was also a definition of the body and sexual desire, both being culturally defined. Modernism facilitated a movement in style that was already expressing itself. The individual striving for beauty and style—two aspects which were part of the modernist attitude—re-accentuated a fresh articulation of the image of the self. The virtuous and the fallen—idioms of the male erotica—were given bold strokes through the changing patterns in dress, marriage, education.

In the 1880s and 1890s these changes came to be known as the "woman's question." Newspapers and journals had been instrumental as a means of expression for women since at least the late eighteenth century; during the nineteenth century they were a vehicle for Puerto Ricans Lola Rodríguez de Tío and the anarchist Luisa Capetillo. In our century, for example, Gabriela Mistral was an assiduous chronicler, and before her there were many women among the anarchist and socialist moderns. A case in point is Clorinda Matto de Turner, writing in Peru, whose *indigenista* novel *Ave sin nido* (1889) about Indian exploitation in the area created a scandal and caused her exile. The novelist was a collaborator with González Prada on anarchist causes, as well as a firm believer in social and racial integration. Heteroglossia and polyphony point in many women writers to the dialogical angle to give voice to a "created" cultural space. Some gave voice to the ethnic polyphony (Avellaneda in Cuba, Turner in Peru, Capetillo in Puerto Rico, Mistral in Chile, Castellanos in Mexico), deploying different cultural voices. Social accents condensed gendered idioms with force and audacity to stage the conflicts and complementarities of their struggle.

It is significant that since the turn of the century some women modernists were consciously elaborating and repositioning language and discourse. Poetry, letters, and diary writing, which used to reflect the previous forms of hegemonic private literary practices, no longer constitute the main and sole activity to verbalize women's ideas, as more and more women begin to intervene in the cultural struggle to transform hegemonies. There had been, of course, the romantics, such as Gertrudis Gómez de Avellaneda, and the utopian socialists, projecting the social imaginaries of egalitarian utopias.

This newly culturally defined body is the idiom of Zamudio, who authored the daring poem called "To Be Born Male" (Nacer hombre), which defies patriarchal authority at the same time that it favors women who are victimized by men. She expresses the liberal desire for equality with men, an idea we also find in María Enriqueta Camarillo, who published her first poems under the pseudonym Ivan Maszowski, obviously usurping male authority. She reclaims everyday themes and interiors concerning the woman's world, through idyllic portrayals of family life. Quite different is the aesthetic energy of Cuban child-poet Juana Borrero (1878–1896), who internalizes the signs and idioms of the hypersensitive, nihilistic, and mystic sensualism of decadent modernist themes. She was highly esteemed by Casal, and she, Vaz Ferreira, and Storni make up a triad of poets regarded as "eccentric" by their male contemporaries.

In practice, within these two generations, the modernist repertoire of the women poets includes a fervent national identity (Rodríguez de Tió), the historical, a cartography of the country (Mistral), and the erotic dimension, producing allegories of male cruelty and female vulnerability. Their texts suggest the common experience of reading material culture within certain conventional borders, at the same time that—specifically the second moment—they produce defiant demythologizations of tropes and rhetoric. One such unmasking is the swan motif, which in Agustini acquires a definite erotic component, or the demythologizations of Storni, later shared by the Mexican Rosario Castellanos and the Puerto Rican Julia de Burgos.[6] Storni, Agustini, Ibarborou, and Loynaz reclaim the right to self-representation (I follow Díaz-Diocaretz 1990), while recoding and reterritorializing themes and lexical material, potentializing a "woman's register." The struggle for the sign is gendered against the "modality" (Díaz-Diocaretz's word) of the practice of writing and patriarchal subject matters.

I am tempted to say that women writers' modernist discourse moves from an epistemological problematic toward an ontological dominant.[7] The epistemological questions of "knowing" are shifted to "modes of being," and both are sought persistently even by the same poet. The preoccupation with ontological questions leads, in practice, to a disbelief in the referential function of symbolic systems, which include both myths and social norms, with a spatio-temporal imagination displaying a sense of the future and of new frontiers for the self.

Yet, the rights to narrative knowledge bring out the central aporia of these modernist women poets: they sought as individuals to oppose autonomously the authoritarianism of the social order, but the only way in which this was done was through the internalization of patriarchal authority. Vaz Ferreira, Mistral, Ibarborou, and Agustini pose the dilemma well; the difficulty arises in the ambivalent function of the erotic, and in the gender construct of images of women and related stereotypes—the extreme "feminization" of the internalized woman's role which will even cause Mistral, for example, to intensify the maternal image, and both Agustini and Ibarborou to focus on the erotic. Piaget's (1965) suggestions in this context are illuminating: he maintains that the "struggle with the father" can never produce autonomy, but only compliance with the law, motivated by fearful submissiveness. Piaget seeks to show that true autonomy can be learned only in reciprocal interaction between peers, or else there is no autonomy but submissiveness.

Women modernist poets of the first epoch were particularly drawn to "familial poetry," which indeed is one of the many discourses of modernity, as exemplified also by male poets such as Martí, Juan de Dios Peza (Mexico), and José Santos Chocano (Peru), and it had previously been a privileged set of themes of José de Campoamor (Spain), greatly admired by the earlier modernists. Such poetry manifestly condemns society as a lower order in an unfulfilled, incomplete mode of existence. However, modernism is essentially concerned with female representation, which was, needless to say, a constant resulting from male fantasies in texts, photographs, paintings; the ideologeme of female representation is definitively modified in women's writing. From the two generations of women, the first (e.g., Puerto Rican Rodríguez Tió, who was a prolific writer) is determined by their concern for a national problematics. The Yucatec "Hortensia," who contributed to the important journal *Violets of Anahuac* (Violetas de Anahuac), was engaged in a feminist struggle and created a feminist society in the 1870s (Civeira Taboada 1978:30–31), while Borrero delved into the nihilistic, within the polemizing modern perspective of the gallicized ideologeme I have previously described.

The second moment of modernists is more determined by both a national remapping (Mistral) and an exploration of the subject in its inception of an identity and a refusal of the subjected (and gendered) limitations imposed. Women writers are an integral part of the general rhetorical enterprise of Latin American modernism, and amply illustrate that the sharpest and subtler point of subversion is inseparable from the sexual. Stated in other terms, the urgent question was an unmasking of the symbolic contract, for they no longer wished to be excluded from language; therefore, they relativized modernity's critique of the notions of truth and values in society. This was a critical stand which marks a tone of distance from the critique of the moderns, generating a gendered modernism. The problem is one not of varieties of modernism but of articulating and constructing gendered experiences through language.

Mistral took up the modernist historical task of a dialogical social imaginary in her articles, chronicles, and prose poems. In her first collaborations in 1904, written in local periodicals of the Elqui Valley, Mistral used the pseudonyms Alguien (Someone), Soledad (Loneliness or Solitude), and Alma (Soul), and she also signed with her own name, Lucila Godoy y Alcaya. By 1912–18, she had published not only in her own country but also in modernist journals in Paris, such as *Elegancias* (Elegance), which was directed by Darío. At that time she began to use the pen name Gabriela Mistral.[8] Her wide variety of interests responded to the reconstitution of the idea of unity—America—which had been the organizing nonessentialist, multiaccentual project of modernity since the 1880s. Mistral's theoretical gains were made through the recognition of difference achieved by the great insights of the turn-of-the-century modernists, by re-accentuating Latin American heterology and heteroglossia in her "messages" (*recados*) to "America," which she wrote for *The Mercury* (El Mercurio) of Santiago de Chile and other Latin American newspapers for many years. The quality of these texts is expressed in a semiformal speech genre (similar to Emily Dickinson's brief notes to her neighbors), and the multiple perspectives of the recados disrupt any impression of univocity or fixity. The plurality of discourses contained in the project of turn-of-the-century modernism is materialized in a "Message [to America] about the Jews":

> Beware of not seeing this clearly: Jewish persecution, especially in overcultured countries, is only an aspect of European hatred of the Asiatic. . . . We are not going to follow this satanic adventure. There is on the coast of our continent more Asian blood than we know, and the American mestizo who is ignorant of this has everything to learn about his/her intimate geology. (16 June 1935, qtd. in Arrigoitia 1989:296)

Gabriela's work is directly descended from the enthymemic prose of modernists such as Rodó, and she also puts strong emphasis on heterology and heteroglossia, as well as on the mixed component of Latin American identities. Her tone is often biblical, and she was totally devoted to a new definition of the human subject, in the specificity of the individual. In this (and in other ways), Mistral was concerned with fundamental questions of epistemology, ethics, and, indeed, social values. Thus, in her representations of Americanism and the establishment of cultural identity in the projection of community, her texts challenge the univocal and uni-accented, privileging the multiplicity of cultures and ethnicities of the Latin American geography and space.

Of particular importance at this juncture of heteroglossia and contending signs are the new modern women (not to call them feminists) who emerged in Spain around the 1870s and 1880s from republican and working-class groups. The many newspaper and journal articles which appeared in the Spanish press referring to the "woman question" and to "feminism" clearly indicate the critical passage and the consolidation of alliances between different sectors and social forces in the process of construction and the victory of popular consent for women's emancipation and women's role in social emancipation. This spectrum ranged widely from the activities of liberal women, who followed Stuart Mill's positivist ideas in *The Subjection of Women* (1869), to the anarchists who championed free love against marital oppression, and who favored feminists in general, although voicing a critique of their reformism and suffragism.

The international role played by the modernists Clara Zetkin and Rose of Luxembourg after 1892–96 in the Second International is well known, as is Alexandra Kollontai, who directly defined the "new woman" of female liberation in a series of books from 1909 to 1913 published under the title *The New Morality*. The basic element in her modernist vision of the future was the position of independent women (which Luisa Capetillo had also advocated), those who "call to the temples of science and art" to Kollontai. Finally, the anarchist activities of Vera Figner, Vera Zasulich, Praskoia Ivanovskaia, Olga Liubotovich, and Elizaveta Kokalsskaia—the five women against the czar—between 1860 and 1880 were well known; these anarchist women were heralded as "saints," "Moscow Amazons," "Valkyries"; such a representation was also constructed around Louise Michel during the French Commune of 1871.

Together with working-class modernists, there was also a group of women concerned with modernity and the multidirected exploitation of women through the institutions of church, state, and family. These modernists analyzed the effects of industrialization, or the strong hegemonic discourses of religion and marriage, labor, prostitution, divorce. These had been the idioms of Emilia Pardo Bazán, of Concepción Arenal, of the freethinker Rosario Acuña, who contributed to anarchist journals and periodicals directed by Luis Bonafoux.[9] All these women were chroniclers formulating alternatives and utopias, subverting the imposed system of coercive constraints from different subject and class positions (both Acuña and Pardo Bazán were aristocrats).

It could be argued that "the woman's question" became an ideologeme with contesting meanings in the symbolic, from Catholic reformism and political conservatism to working-class arguments (see the anthology by Nash [1983]). Clearly, this type of thinking about women was the property of right and left alike, and full-blown treatises on the subject appeared, which varied from the typical female hysteria to the no less topical "angel of the house," as ideological mystifications on every level. Both are historical tropes of modern life and modernness, causes in a way of the development of capitalism. The two extremes—the "housewife" and the "prostitute"—have far more in common with each other as ideograms and sociograms, in which forms of consciousness are materialized. The sociogram of the woman takes absolute extremes: from the "angel in the house" to the "anarchist angel." No wonder that a Catholic conservatist in 1882 exhorted modern women to honor Christ through the independence they could acquire in holy matrimony: "And all these, my ladies, you owe, not to sciences, or to literature, or the arts, or culture, or modern progress; but to Jesus Christ, who liberated your souls from the slavery of sin" (qtd. in Nash 1983:92).

Such thinking is marked by the will to repress and control. In contrast, literary anarchists such as Sawa and Felipe Trigo wrote extensively in favor of feminism, disclosing the oppression and economic exploitation underlying prostitution. An example is Trigo's articles published in *The Socialist* in 1888–89, of which the one on prostitution led to a civil process against Pablo Iglesias, the director of the journal (Caudet 1982). Sawa wrote an article about Louise Michel which was a moving homage: "She is someone who preached against evil, according to her sense of goodness"; the "anarchist angel" Michel became an inspiration for many writers, among them Victor Hugo in 1871, when she was condemned to prison, Verlaine in 1886, when she returned from New Caledonia, and also Henry Bauer and Laurent Teilhade, all from the Parisian symbolist (literary anarchist) group (see Zavala, ed. 1977).

Catalan anarchist modernists Soledad Gustavo and Teresa Claramunt (1888–1931) and Communist leader Dolores Ibarruri, "La Pasionaria" (1895–1989), remembered for her phrase "They shall not pass," definitively asserted their conflicting critique of capitalism, instrumental reason, and modernity. At the turn of the century, the modernist critique of capitalism was also the practice of Belén Sárraga, Soledad Arenales, and Amalia Carvia, who were all engaged not only in the anarchist movement but also in its publications, among them the ones I have already mentioned: *La Conciencia Libre* (Córdoba, 1902) and *La Humanidad Libre. Diario Feminista* (Valencia, 1902), as well as *The Modern Woman* (La mujer moderna, Manresa, 1904). Most of these women, such as Soledad Gustavo, Arenales, Carvia, and Sárraga, were schoolteachers (like "the anarchist angel"), and were deeply involved in a social imaginary of liberation. Teresa Claramunt was particularly active; she was in and out of prison for more than forty-five years (Iturbe 1974), thus suggesting the evident parallel with Louise Michel. She participated in the campaigns for the independence of the colonies in 1896–98, in the Montjuich trials, and in the Francisco Ferrer execution, while simultaneously launching a valuable cultural practice through a theater of proletarian character, and through her books and chronicles. Thanks to the intensive efforts of these modernist women, a new style of engaged intellectual was established which became central in the interwar years and after World War II (the Pasionaria, for example). Their politically committed art took over the ethical stand of the modernist movement and a critique of dominating rationality.[10]

Exhortative articles to youth and enthymemic discourses on capitalist exploitation and bourgeois violence are the direct social referencing of their discourse. The editorial of *Humanidad Libre,* for example, incited an experimental imaginary of concerted efforts: "We come to collaborate in the great cause which will secure the triumph of our redemption" (I:1902). The journal announced contributions from Teresa Claramunt, Soledad Gustavo, María Caro, María Losada, and Ana Mazzoni, as well as from Louise Michel and Emma Goldman. Along this same line, Claramunt wrote *Woman: Considerations on Her State* in dialogue with Flora Tristan's well-known *L'Union ouvrière,* published by working-class publishers the Future of the Laborer in 1905.

Soledad Gustavo's articles in the *Revista Blanca* are of major interest, since she employed, like Urales, the idea of an aesthetic utopia based on the social: "Art must turn social, better yet revolutionary, since revolution is latent in our society," she wrote in 1898 (*RB* 15 July). The second series of the anarchist journal, in 1923, proceeded with more caution in the alliance with the organic intellectuals, whose peak was, as I have suggested, between the 1890s and 1905. Federica Montseny definitively defended what she called a "moral vanguard" against the literary vanguard in 1929, while she projected in her novels and short stories a revolutionary human emancipation.

Interestingly enough, Montseny revitalized turn-of-the-century modernist idioms and themes; among them was a recognition and re-accentuation of Isadora Duncan as the ideal of the modern woman and artist. In her words: "Isadora Duncan's *Ma vie* has transported me to a superior world of pure art and new morality" (*RB* 15 Aug. 1929). However, there were historical moments of tension in the alliance; the antagonism between working-class movements and modernists became crucial as modernist artists became established; social identities were contested and redefined constantly. During the period of the Second Republic and the Civil War, the modernist project was reestablished, and one can perceive the importance of the anti-fascist struggle which conjoined the members of the Generation of 1898 and younger intellectuals. The important congresses for the defense of culture in 1935 and 1937 helped reconstitute a broad strategic anti-fascist front to win popular consent, which also attracted Latin American writers: Paz, Neruda, Vallejo, and Mistral, among many others.

It is important to recognize the significance of women—which I have barely underlined—in the modernist aesthetic utopia. If, for the first time in history, artistic, cultural, and political revolt became dialogically concerted at the turn of the century against capitalist exploitation in the form of imperialism or instrumental reason, capitalism also brought together, totalized, so to speak, human labor. In the universal pretensions of modernity, disclosed early by modernists Marx and Nietzsche from different positions, capitalism succeeded in providing a foundation not only for the cosmopolitanism and the transnationalism of commerce but also for equality of the sexes as workers in factories, for example. Capitalist societies are also concerned with the conversion of both men and women to active work. However, this particular historical moment opened up the field for feminist politics. One can then perceive the importance of a woman's liberatory imaginary forcefully engendering the modernist narrative, and reacting against the imaginary significations and the symbolism linked to overdetermined sexual and social roles in society.

There can be little doubt as to the breadth of change that occurred in the structures of feeling at the turn of the century, as it was unambiguously represented in visual arts (I am thinking of Mary Cassat and her extreme opposite Frida Kahlo), women as performers (Isadora Duncan), as singers of both canonical and popular music (I referred to French Eugènie Buffet and Yvette Guilbert in Paris), and most certainly the modernist bolero and tango singers— Pastora Imperio, Spanish modernist singer and dancer, who interpreted Falla's *El amor brujo*; and Spanish cuplé and *tonadilla* singer Raquel Meller (1888– 1962), who was active from 1907 and became a prominent name among women artists in Paris, as well as a champion of the modernists, who transformed her into a "popular muse."[11]

Since modern societies are closely implicated in processes of reproduction and transformation of social relations, it is expected that projects to transform society and to constitute the self, as well as anti-colonial discourses, were produced by women modernists to change the habitus through the experienced and the imagined. If there was a consistency with the Hispanic modernist impulse to create a radical break with the past, at that critical time it became possible to launch an engendered modernist narrative whose project was carried out by women cartographers of liberation, who have been greatly overlooked or ignored and who deserve closer analysis. Modernness was not only a contested space but a contested narrative of emancipation.

Women moderns' cultural texts indicate strategic possibilities of delegitimizing an existing discourse, which would again sustain a totality. The double necessity of their critique lies in reconceptualizing (regendering) modernist inquiries into subjectivity, self, identity, society. The reader of the woman modernist must somehow have in mind the values of the modern text to be able to hear how their texts speak against them. Their dismantling suggests a significant cultural modification of the utopian impulse of modernist emancipatory narrative. Women modernists implicitly reproblematize modernism, whose concept of the individual was gendered; what emerges is a regendered modernity as they remap the web of meanings to articulate discursive space, or "connote and condense" (in Laclau's terms) the ideas of modernism.

(IN) CONCLUSION

DECOLONIZATION AND SOCIAL IDENTITIES

Modernness and the rustle and ruse of the new language govern several different kinds of objects as negations and fulfillments. Both clearly correspond to what we have called a project, a historical narrative. Although the term *modernism* has often been used as a somewhat vague notion of culture in the countless retellings to which it has been subject, apparently modernist discourse gave consistency to a project designed to decolonize life from instrumental reason and industrial capitalism. Hegemony at this crucial moment points to the emergence of national and cultural identities, and also to a set of alliances to win support and consent among intellectuals and in sectors of the dominated class itself. Martí's and Darío's emerge as but two examples and moments of the moderns—such as modernist Karl Marx, or modernist Friedrich Nietzsche, or modernist Mikhail Bakunin, or modernist Alexandra Kollontai, or modernist Teresa Claramunt—who produced prophetic, enthymemic discourses against expansionist capitalism from different subject and even gendered positions.

Like Marx, these turn-of-the-century Latin American modernists used the chronicle to disclose "yanquism," to unmask the utilitarianism of "good for business," the "splendid little wars," the "manifest destiny," the debasement of human life under the sign of Moloch, the numbness of daily urban life to suffering. This flight took many forms, from the harnessing of metaphorical power from the social sciences (the naturalist entropism of decadence and degeneration, for instance), to the catastrophes which haunt human imagination, and the mapping of desire.

These phenomena were intensely familiar to moderns, embodied in allegorical images or symbols as materialized daguerreotypes of meanings. The exquisite was interwoven with gross naturalistic slices of life (for instance Casal, Silva, Sawa), and idioms and literary material led a double-voiced life, integrated into the whole of utopian collective unity.

The moderns also experienced a sense of international solidarity with the rapid explosion of industrialization. It was in the spirit of such brotherhood that Marx and Bakunin joined the workers to create the International and the Latin American moderns projected the dialogical unity of "Our America." What all

194

these moderns had in common, from different spaces, spheres, and subject positions, was indeed a reaction to the use of new technics, and that reaction contributed to the confrontation between traditional culture and innovation. They also shared a common cultural enterprise to disrupt from within the solidity and stability of received meanings, of other cultures' constructions of the real, including that of language.

At such a moment in history, the artistic impulse itself was related to the wholeness of the political and the social. The arguments remind us of Schiller's ultimate solution that "it is through beauty that we arrive at freedom." Words were double-voiced and signaled passages from the predominantly aesthetic to the historical and political. The fantasy-loaded rustle of modernist language—swans, minotaurs, centaurs—helped redefine a family of concepts: subject, self, speaker, nation, independence, liberation, future. This re-actualized modernist language was used to remap new social, political, and cultural frontiers. Above all else, these idioms, within their crisscrossing chains of signifiers, intersected at a specific moment to assign and transmit values and projects of the future. They are not in a pantheon of models; they are our storied past, and in a sense, they are engraved in our memories. They draw the figure of what could be called an unfulfilled future, in the figures of swans, gods, Mnemosyne which tend perceptibly toward the hope for the future to find their completion.

Modernity designates those national and cultural identity-forming ideas connected with the evolution of the contemporary capitalist world. In this way, as a modernizing ideology it partook of both nineteenth-century liberalism(s) and socialism(s). The tension between conservative and progressive tendencies is at the core of the social. I thus include in this modernism and modernity both the critical discourses and the legitimators of tradition, or progress, as well as the individuals who, like the cabaret singer, were an integral part of modern life. From this standpoint I think modernism is better understood within an analysis of hegemony as organic wholes, lest we are blind to the wholeness of the social. What constitutes the organizing principle of modernism is formed by a plurality of discourses dispersed through the plurality of practices in each society, concerning cultural identity, national identity, the workforce, morality, crime, women, human nature, and science. In the Latin American context, the reaction to these technics took the specific form of anti-imperialist discourse in the embattled Caribbean and Central America. What I want to stress is that modernism can be understood only as part of the logics of capitalism, and as part of the discontent with a modernization process which promised development, emancipation, or the utopian myth of democratic technology.

The sense of international solidarity, the hegemonic alliances among intellectuals and the dominated classes themselves, all in search of new definitions of self, and in constructing new subjects and subjectivities, also account for the vigorous articulation between popular and elite idioms. My position is that there was a fruitful exchange between popular and elite cultures, as can be seen in the sophisticated idioms of the tango, the bolero, and anarchist socialist-utopian songs. The rigid division between "high" and "low" culture, which tends to separate cultural spheres in a sort of neo-Hegelianism with its separate and distinct spheres of ideology, seems to me inadequate, most specifically in this modern period. It is not possible to deal with this problem comprehensively, but it is feasible to establish the interaction I have suggested, based on the integration between Gramsci and Bakhtin and the central issue of a modernist discourse whose direct address is toward popular consent.

Looking back from the present at this modernist narrative, at a time in which this "great narrative" is being reexamined, the aporias embedded are made more evident—aporias, however, which are more historical than textual. Having emerged, as I suggested, around the 1880s in the Caribbean and Central America as an alternative discourse against instrumental reason and undemocratic technologies, modernism gained strength in 1898 with the Anglo-Spanish struggle over the Caribbean, when North America invaded Cuba and Spain lost its last colonies to the United States. It was, however, one of the intellectual achievements of the nineteenth century; as a cultural text, it was unique in its close relationship with the anti-imperialist movements of the time.

Indeed, the reason for viewing modernism dialogically becomes apparent; as such it can be conceived not only as the master code of the enlightened modernity's historical journey to reason. To the contrary, the modernist texts we have analyzed show, however tentatively, anatropic inversions of universalism, and the correspondence into values as pragmatic views absorbed by capitalism as the hegemonic force. In this sense, the modernisms we have explored indicate an attempt to protect areas of culture from instrumental reason. Turn-of-the-century modernism becomes framed within colonialism and new forms of imperialism, which became to many an evident mask of greed and destruction, while a sense of cosmpolitanism united many nations.

A dialogical analysis helps rework modernist discourse as critiques of modernity; genres of discourse were re-accentuated to disentangle them from the lures of instrumental reason and project creative constructions of self and social reality in dialogic relation to others. The dialogical-polemical interaction, both simultaneous and contiguous, of self-affirmation through heteroglossia, projected a creative conception of self, collectivity, and reality in relation to others. With "situated utterances," modernists set out to change the world, as well as to interpret it, through enthymemic discourses which were intended to have a practical effect by helping to build anti-colonial, anti-imperialist consciousness and national and cultural identities. Modernism was heralded as an anticolonial discourse by Antilleans (primarily the Cuban Martí) and the Nicaraguan Darío. Rodó understood the dilemma quite well, as he wrote in *Ariel* in 1895:

> Everyone who consecrates him/herself to propagate and defend, in contemporary America, a disinterested ideal of the spirit—art, science, morals, religious sincerity, politics of ideas—must educate his will to the perseverant cult of the future. . . . Won't you see the America we dream. . . . At least think about her. . . . (1967: 245)

The meaning of this "open" society Rodó speaks about often embodied the economic individualism which was transformed into capitalist societies, and was also the contested space of the more radical modernists and has been, therefore, continuously expanded. However, it is clear that modernism had different connotations and could be combined in different ways. At the juncture of 1898 it was reworked in combination with anti-imperialist struggle.

If modern life became, according to some critics, suffused with the ephemeral and the contingent (a generalization I oppose), modernity entered these other countries, with another completely different sign. To begin with, they opposed the fragmentation imposed by colonialism and strove to consolidate an understanding in terms of a dialogical whole of cultures and interests; if the transitoriness makes it difficult to preserve historical continuity (Berman's [1983] and Schorske's [1980] theses), in this case the historical continuity which was being opposed was that of the forms of colonialism imposed since 1492. A project to liberate human beings from colonization, "modernity" gained strength in the Caribbean following Haiti's example, and then early in the nineteenth century, in a simultaneous impulse during the Cadix Courts of 1808–10 with the Spanish emancipatory struggle against the Napoleonic invasion.

On this view, modernist cultural practice is of crucial importance in providing the starting point for a comprehensive analysis of anti-capitalist struggle— such as the one the modernists themselves were unable to complete—affecting the capacity of colonialism to survive and of socialism (even social democracies) to come into existence as a new form of society. The controversies over the interpretation of modernism(s) as alienated, conservative, at best liberal, which are continually reanimated by cultural changes, seem under present circumstances particularly favorable for an attempt to understand its heuristic strength and its continuous ideological interpellation for freedom, and the new society of liberated individuals. At the same time, many of the modernist conceptions have been absorbed into the general intellectual and political underground of Latin American (and Hispanic) developments in the late twentieth century.

Their emphasis on national liberation, on cultural identity and diversity, has proved to be of great importance in contemporary national or ethnic consciousness, and in the form of the national liberation movements which still engage many modern societies. It is sufficient to say that this narrative followed in some cases the course that had been anticipated—I refer specifically first to the initial impulse of the Mexican Revolution, and then to the Cuban and the Nicaraguan revolutions. As a cultural text, the modernist social imaginary of an opposition against oppressive capitalism and the different forms of colonialism, and its aspiration for a new society, is still constitutive as an imaginative vision of societies of the future. Generally perceived as positivistic, technocentric, and rationalistic, the North of the Americas was identified then as an expansionist power with a work ethos of capitalism, believer in nonhumane progress, as creating a utilitarian and democratic myth, and by way of contrast, these modernists privileged heterogeneity and difference, re-accentuation and "creolization" and "maroonization" as liberative forces in the redefinition of cultural discourses. The heteroglotic struggle for the sign constituted not only style but subjectivity itself.

All these threads fuse into modernism, whose critique of modernity embodied the utopia for the unfolding of dormant powers and new potentialities of growth and human development, even in its accentuation to play off the moral superiority of the Hispanic against the crude materialist aims of the encroaching instrumental reason of the North. The power of their accomplishment in restoring a suppressed history, as well as raising the construction of self to the level of national emancipation, or drawing cartographies of anti-colonialism, or exposing the burdens of colonial affliction, is neither peripheral nor marginal but a central issue of the social and cultural landscape.

As cultural texts, ambiguities and contradictions are best expressed through simultaneity, complementarity, openness, which textually unfolds in various forms; it is evident in Unamuno in his very (post)modern attempt to give various, mutually exclusive endings to his texts, as exemplified in *Niebla;* it is illustrated in the ways writers inscribe otherness and anotherness, and in the intense distrust of all universals or totalizing discourses, even of the self. What all these examples have in common is a rejection of universals and globalizations, when such metanarratives purportedly led to colonization—in the case of the Latin Americans—and to the illusion of the grandiose metaphysical claims of the Castilian myths and mythologies for the Spanish moderns I have mentioned.

Extensions and re-accentuations of Unamuno's inquiries can be found in Borges's famous "The Garden of Forking Paths," and he is present in the most distant relationships from Borges to Mallea. In other cases, poetic language expresses a reversibility between outward and inward, celebrating the earth (nature to them) and shaking metaphysics, moving away from the ontological to come nearer to the very essence of the material world. This is the underlying thought in the celebration of earth and humble things—which Martí advocated in 1882—and the process by which the certainties of subjectivity are undermined in Darío's poetry, for example. Later, this nonmetaphysical, nonontological approach to earth takes a turning point with Pablo Neruda's *Elemental Odes* or *Alturas de Machu Pichu,* and in Gabriela Mistral's poetry, while the uncertainties of the subject are embedded in César Vallejo's, Octavio Paz's, and Rosario Castellanos's poetry. Likewise, the great cartographers of national identity in the Hispanic Caribbean—Nicolás Guillén, Luis Palés Matos, Julia de Burgos—confronted and dealt with the overwhelming sense of fragmentation of colonial selfhood. Such cartography is also the strength of Ernesto Cardenal, Lezama Lima, Alejo Carpentier, women poets from Nicaragua and Salvador, younger generations of narrators and poets in Cuba and Puerto Rico, and Newyoricans and Chicanos who are taking possession of their past in a range of inventive fantasies, where the carnival and the dialogical play a major role. It is present also in the Hispanic *salsa.*

In 1863 Baudelaire wrote that modernity was the transient, the fleeting, the contingent, and the other half of art was the eternal and the immutable, through the central concern with an experience of time, space, and causality; confronted with the same overwhelming sense, these turn-of-the-century modernists worked the paradoxical unity of disunity, to "make solid what could melt into air," in a metalepsis of Berman's (1983) term. While to be modern in European terms meant to be part of a universe in which, according to Marx, "all that is solid melts into the air," the emphasis of what is normally called high culture introduced in Latin America a whirl of innovation to a dialogical understanding of the whole. The rustle of language pursued the knowledge of self, unfolding new ways of seeing in relations between the present and the past through a constellation of signifiers clustering around identity questions and language, linked to social emancipation. This way of looking at what the past had wrought put a responsibility upon their heirs. In this sense, turn-of-the-century modernness was obviously far vaster and more all-embracing than a style or a way of writing. The signs connected visions of cities with the original African or Indian homes, in patterns that also connected the crisscrossing chain of islands of the Antilles with the South of America, and with the isles of Greece.

In my anatropic inversion, of course, I do not claim that this dialogical event ironed out differences or contradictions in any simple way. If one reads the texts by these modernists of the 1880s or in 1898, one is led to expect a revolutionary epochal historical development emerging. And indeed events offered considerable evidence that such a development was occurring. These modernists were part of the utopian imaginary strengthened in Spain and Latin America since the 1880s, and played a central role in the libertarian anti-colonial struggle, as they were in touch with the avant-garde of the post-colonial and the still-colonial Latin American countries. At the very forefront was a growing dislike for capitalism in its crudest and sharpest form of exploitation.

While the bohemians and the organic intellectuals, such as Unamuno and Valle, and the anarchist and socialist movements were facing the problem of industrialization, the Latin American moderns were carrying forth a liberatory struggle for social and cultural emancipation. The Russian Revolution of 1917 and the Mexican Revolution are the crystallization of this perspective of history. After that, there was a new historical conjuncture, in which different forces came together to create new terrains. As a dialogical polyphony, Latin Americans were again drawn together in 1936 to stand united against the Franquist coup which put an end to the Second Spanish Republic. Neruda's and Vallejo's books of poems defending the "Republic of Workers" echo the dialogical sign of Darío's swans in 1898.

Whether or not this narrative was doomed from the start because so much value was placed on cultural opposition, and whether it can still inspire twenty-first-century thought and action, are crucial questions. There are those, like the Sandinistas and the Castrist Cubans, who continue to support this project from different subject positions. There are others who voice a certain pessimism under contemporary social and economic conditions. And there are still others, such as the Puerto Ricans, who continue their struggle for colonial emancipation, often based on a linkage with a Hispanic national identity forged in the Caribbean at the turn of the twentieth century. It has been crucial, however, to maintain the narrative of liberation. In other cases, as deceptive myths and ideologies, they no longer have any currency. Worse still: they became naive narratives, easy alibis of spiritual transcendence.

What, then, remains of commitment? Instead of a universe of seepages and significations, we can try to construct a world more solid and immediate. Imagine texts unimpoverished by the constraints of passive imitation, consuming voices, and worlds neatly presented by culture. Think now of texts which instigate new ways of looking and seeing, and which give us access to perspectives on the self and the social, and the plural and the collective. Texts which make the reader think against received theories. Texts which aim at rewriting the self, and raise questions about how to think the colonial and postcolonial subject, and project doubts about traditional conceptions of meanings. This experimental imagining on the social was, I think, the conception of this turn-of-the-century critical modernness. If the intent to ring changes to the past was the perspective which delineated these ways of looking, the unfolding of the narrative in time is yet to come. The manifest content of many cultural texts is still carried out in their openness, in the latency of the ultimate meanings, in the light of the future which they embodied.

NOTES

Introduction

1. I extrapolate from the Critical Theory's term of instrumental reason, while the other one is ascribed to Weber. It should be evident that I agree with those critics who identify modernism and capitalism, as well as modernism as a reaction to technology; Lefebvre (1974) strongly points to this conjunction.

2. Quoted in Tindall and Shi 1989:351. The quotations throughout this paragraph about the 1846 war, as well as the quotations about the "little war," are taken from Tindall and Shi 1989. There is, of course, ample bibliography which deals with the American policy in the Caribbean. David F. Trask's (1981) is still the most comprehensive analysis on the conflict; see also Beisner (1968), who handles the debate over annexation.

3. There was a call to a community through a national language, although not exactly in the same way that B. Anderson (1983) speaks about "imagined communities." At this specific time, the defense of language as national identity was closely linked to the anti–North America feeling. However, in general and in precise circumstances, I fully agree with Mary Louise Pratt (1987) when she remarks that imagined communities through national languages can be exclusionary. In a sense that was true of the imagined Latin American community, since it excluded and marginalized hundreds of Indian languages. Needless to say, the African collective was also silenced; on this point see Kubayanda 1987. I should like to stress that emancipation and anti-colonial struggle were foregrounded, and only at present are we able to recognize the shortcomings of such a project. For this reason I find Radhakrishnan's (1987) critique pertinent if limited to more contemporary identity-formation strategies, and if applied with caution to the study of the colonial liberation movements aimed at disrupting imperialism.

4. I adapt from the analysis of economic systems provided by Rex (1977:12).

5. Said (1988) underlines this point as he analyzes Yeats's poetry.

6. Berman's (1983) excellent book on modernism, modernity, and modernization regrettably sees it mainly as a European phenomenon. See the general discussion on the ideology of modernism in Eagleton 1988; Jameson 1988a; Said 1988. Said is sensitive to the relationship between modernism and decolonization. See also Lentricchia, who analyzes James in the context of imperialism (1986) and who places Wallace Stevens between the two interventions in Cuba in 1898 and 1961 (1988). It should be clear that I am approaching the ideologies of modernism, not a formalist analysis. The object of my critique is what I have called the first moments of modernists and modernness (even if some, such as Valle and Unamuno, were long-lived). For this reason, I do not hesitate to exclude Ortega, who (together with Borges) is quite well known as a modernist. See Dust, ed. 1989 for a comprehensive view of Ortega as a modernist; cf. also Zavala 1988a. In contrast, Martí, Nájera, Silva, and Casal died rather young. However, as to modernism in general, see Levin 1960; Poggioli 1968; Bradbury and McFarlane, eds. 1978; de Man 1983; Kern 1983; Chafdor, Quiñones, and Wachtel, eds. 1986; Williams 1989. For specific and complementary approaches, see Picon Garfield and Schulman 1984; Schulman 1987; Achúgar 1985; Yurkievich 1976. See also Rama (1985a, 1985b) and Ramos (1989), who interpret modernism/modernity from a different perspective. Both Pérez Firmat 1989 and G. Kirkpatrick 1989 are relevant, although their approaches are different from mine. For a persuasive complementary analysis see Larsen 1989; de Man's "Literary History Literary Modernity" (in 1983) centers on the internal contra-

dictions of literary modernity. For ample bibliographical reference see Zavala, ed. 1977, 1989; Zavala 1988a, 1989c, 1990a.

7. Barbara Johnson (1987) perceptively deconstructs Mallarmé's poetry against the background of the Panama Canal. I adapt from her the phrase "significant gaps." Her work clearly suggests that there is more than meets the eye in at least Anglo-American modernism and erasures of 1898. Lentricchia 1986 clearly discloses James's anti-imperialism at the turn of the century and the references to the Philippines, another actor in the Anglo-Spanish (and European) struggle for the Caribbean. Karnow (1989) studies this rise of American globalism in the Philippines, and provides excellent information on American behavior; they even thought that they were "Christianizing" the archipelago. The erasures of history around the French invasion of Mexico are also worth pursuing in French moderns.

8. The polemic around narratives and master narratives is best defined by Habermas 1975, 1979, 1986; Lyotard 1979, 1986–87; Jameson 1981.

9. On modernist negation, see Poggioli 1968; Bürger 1984. Poggioli suggests that novelty is the avant-garde's most important pursuit. J. Schulte-Sasse's prologue to Bürger's translation (1984) convincingly demonstrates that negation is linked to North American criticism of modernism, essentially seen as a skepticism about language. It is also known that through the new Freudianism, negation is at present understood as ambiguity. I use negation in a completely different sense, closer to Critical Theory's perspective. See also Habermas's reflections on modern culture (1975, 1979, 1986:6 passim, 1990).

10. Foucault is particularly pertinent in his analyses of discourse; see in particular 1969, 1971, 1973. Gramsci's concept of hegemony is particularly fruitful as a complement to Bakhtin's dialogical, since the former is a socio-economic theory which does not exclude the cultural, while the latter is a cultural theory which does not exclude the socio-economic. Finally, Gramsci's hegemony re-accentuates Marx's ideology from another position, not exclusively as a misrecognition. See Gramsci 1965, 1966a, 1966b. Marx's is surely a pre-Freudian or pre-psychoanalytic interpretation of the subconscious; this is not the place to develop this point further. When I use the term *subject position*, I imply not reducing heterogeneity to negotiating relations but the plural encounter of evaluative utterances that constitute subjects.

11. Modernism raises urgent questions on social theory. I agree with Merod (1987) when he stresses that intellectual work is meant not only to enrich intellectual practices but "to widen and deepen the social relevance of knowledge—to put ideas into more useful contact with democratic principles" (98). Specially and clearly if democracy is not used as an alibi.

12. I will be using *Bakhtin circle* throughout this book to refer to the work of Medvedev/Voloshinov/Bakhtin, assuming that Bakhtin had at least a "hand" in the contested texts. It is then a synecdoche. I quote from the following: Mikhail Bakhtin (V. N. Volosinov), *Freudianism: A Marxist Critique*, trans.I. R. Titunik, ed. in collaboration with Neal H. Bruss (1927; New York: Academic Press, 1976) [*FMC*]; (V. N. Volosinov), *Marxism and the Philosophy of Language*, trans. Ladislav Matejka and I. R. Titunik (1929; Cambridge: Harvard University Press, 1986) [*MPL*]; *The Dialogic Imagination: Four Essays*, ed. Michael Holquist, trans. Caryl Emerson and Michael Holquist (Austin: University of Texas Press, 1981) [*DI*]; M. M. Bakhtin, *Problems of Dostoevsky's Poetics*, ed. and trans. Caryl Emerson, intro. by Wayne C. Booth (Minneapolis: University of Minnesota Press, 1984) [*PDP*]; M. M. Bakhtin/P. M. Medvedev, *The Formal Method in Literary Scholarship: A Critical Introduction to Sociological Poetics*, foreword by Wlad Godzich, trans. Albert J. Wehrle (1928; Cambridge: Harvard University Press, 1985) [*FM*]; M. M. Bakhtin, *Speech Genres and Other Late Essays*, trans. Vern W. McGee, ed. Caryl Emerson and Michael Holquist (Austin: University of Texas Press, 1986) [*SG*]; *Art and Answerability: Early Philosophical Essays by M. M. Bakhtin*, ed. M. Holquist and Vadim Liapunov, trans. and notes Vadim Liapunov, supplement trans. Kenneth

Brostrom (Austin: University of Texas Press, 1989) [*AA*]; *Bakhtin School Papers,* ed. Ann Shukman, Russian Poetics in Translation 10 (1983) [*BSP*]. Further quotations in the text are indicated with abbreviations.

I. The Dialogical Social Imaginary and Self-Representation

1. Van Schendel has minutely analyzed the concept, to suggest aptly that it is "un effet *construit* d'une activité sociale organisée pour la production de signes [donc] *sériel et modifiable*"; see 1986/87, where he also makes interesting parallels between Bakhtin and Gramsci. The "emancipation" I refer to is very concrete, since it refers to anti-colonial struggle, and is not an unclearly defined concept which is quite prevalent. Jameson suggests that contemporary emancipatory possibilities come from a political unconscious buried under master narratives of oppositions found in texts; we will return to this. Neal H. Bruss in an appendix to *FMC* 1976 establishes relations between Voloshinov and Lacan; see also the preface to this translation.

2. On the chronotope, see Morson and Emerson 1990, which contains an excellent analysis. See also M. Holquist's lucid introduction to dialogics 1990.

3. I refer to my various developments of Bakhtin's dialogicality (1988b, 1989a, 1990b, 1991a).

4. The point is that ideology, in the mechanism of recognition, calls individuals and confers their identities. Althusser sustains that ideologies are addressed to individuals as interpellations. On ideology and Althusser, see Poulantzas, Laclau and Mouffe, and S. Hall. These last critics have argued against Althusser's argument. N. Poulantzas, T. Herbert, and E. Verón conceive two functions in ideology: metaphorical/semantic and metonymic/syntactic. Poulantzas (1971) insists that the common denominator produces the identification of the individual with the social community. See also the critique of Poulantzas and Althusser by Hall, Lumley, and McLennan (1977) and their appropriation of Gramsci. It should be noted that Freudian idioms are now common for sociological analyses, in particular the tropes used to explain the procedures of dreams—*Verdichtung* and *Verschiebung,* or "condensation" and "displacement." The idea is to state what is simultaneously both revealed and concealed. I should like to stress that when I use "connotation" I do not refer only to the association of ideas, but to "a correlation immanent in the text," or "an association made by the text-as-subject within its own system"; see Barthes 1974:8. See also Zima, ed. 1981 and *Le social, l'imaginaire, le théorique où la scène de l'idéologie,* special issue of *La Revue de Sciences Humaines* (1977).

5. This neo-Kantianism is acknowledged by Bourdieu 1982. Pêcheux (1975 [trans. 1982]) has done much work on communication and usage, and on antagonisms within discourse. He also proposes three mechanisms through which subjects may be constructed in relation to ruling ideological practices—identification, disidentification, and counteridentification. The important point is that ideologies are in struggle, what Bakhtin calls struggle for the sign. Bourdieu 1979a has an interesting critique of the symbolic in Lévi-Strauss.

6. See also Berman 1988; Jameson developed this approach in 1977, and in the *Political Unconscious.* Silverman 1983 offers a clear account of Lacan. Gayatri Spivak (1987:261–62) energetically genders Lacanian psychoanalysis as well as points to its overtly imperialistic politics. In passing, could Lyotard be using "desire" in the Lacanian sense of "lack" when he speaks about "the desire called Marx"? I hope it is clear that I base my analysis on a theory of the social subject, not on a psychoanalytical subject or the "humanist" subject. Therefore, I reactivate in a different direction the social dynamics of the imaginary. Le Goff offers a succinct definition of the imaginary; see his *La nouvelle histoire* (1988).

7. Habermas (1990:37–335) criticizes Castoriadis's central thesis. The imaginary as the site of a subject formation has reoriented different disciplines. See also Metz 1975.

Schulte-Sasse has aptly synthesized the relationship between imagination and modernity and offers ample bibliography, beginning with Kant; see 1986–87b. See also the special issue of *Critical Inquiry* (1987) on problems of representation. Leo Lowenthal (1987) has established important links between literature and consciousness: "[Literature] deals with the process of socialization, that is, the social ambiance of the private, the intimate and the individual is raised to consciousness by the artist."

8. S. Hall (1977, 1988) has a sustained rereading of Gramsci in this direction. Laclau and Mouffe have also worked with hegemony in connection with the imaginary. The reader will rightly conclude that the above-mentioned is a critique of Marx's definition of ideology as "imaginary" misrecognitions, as proposed in *The German Ideology*. The problems of mediation, reflection, and mirror are crucial, since in all disciplines the materials are mediated by discourse, and genres are split by the mediations of enunciating subjects. In a more general sense, mediation is produced by those elements of the production process that mark the objects' historicity. Some of these problems are tackled in *Sociology of Literature,* special issue of *Critical Inquiry* (1988). The best short definition I know of mediation is given by Angenot (1979:127): "instance exercé sur le devenir d'une autre instance."

9. On parallel grounds, Bourdieu proposes that from the viewpoint of the modern science of language, it is possible to approach the privileged sphere of symbolic power, of the political, as "lieu de la prévision comme prédiction prétendant à produire sa propre réalisation" (1982 passim), while new history, as described by Le Goff, conceives the imaginary as a "temps projeté," "temps de l'imagination de l'avenir" (1988:60–61). See Jameson's (1978) lucid critique of the "symbolic act" in Kenneth Burke (now in 1988b, vol. 1). My understanding of the symbolic is closer to Vattimo's (1974).

10. Myriam Díaz-Diocaretz (1985) analyzes in this direction black American women poets and their textual strategies. She has also done pathbreaking work on the dialogical enthymemic and feminist theory; see Díaz-Diocaretz 1989a, 1989b.

II. To Be Modern at the Turn of the Century

1. The wars of independence started in Haiti against the French in 1803, and then in Argentina in 1810. They culminated in the emancipation of Bolivia in 1825 and of the Dominican Republic in 1865. In 1899 the North Americans intervened in the island, and a protectorate was signed in 1907 as part of the Anglo-Spanish struggle over the Caribbean.

2. Work on the contested space of liberalism and romanticism in the Hispanic world is needed; in the meantime the interested reader can consult some of my work on the subject, and the general overview provided by S. Hall 1986 on the variants of English liberalism. I fully agree with Hall's analysis of its discursive chain of meaning and internal coherence, and also with the fact that liberalism and its cultural counterpart of romanticism were implicitly gendered. Needless to stress that modernism is also gendered; however, to disclose all its working out of the social ideology and gender constructs would require a book. Obviously, there are idioms, such as the *femme fatale,* which converge to produce a specific mode of male and female behavior.

3. See the articles in Avineri 1968. It is worth remembering that the achievement of independence by Latin American movements failed to create the basis of sustained economic growth and looked for essential resources of demand and supplies outside the new national economies, which led inevitably to dependence. There were, however, many attempts (such as under the Porfiriato) to catch up with the modernizing and industrializing Western world, which led to alignments with other modern states (e.g., Mexico and North American); see Stein and Stein 1970. It is also widely accepted that the independence movements were aimed at ending metropolitan monopoly of economic decision making; however, they hoped to maintain allegiance to embattled Spain while enjoying the right to trade directly with others (ibid. 131).

4. There is ample literature on utopian socialism; see Beecher and Bienvenu's (1971) anthology of Fourier's writing. I have done previous work on Spanish socialism, its publications, newspapers, literature, and the link between the first socialists and the serial novel; see Zavala 1971, 1972, 1989b. See also C. Rama 1982. Pratt (1988) has a detailed consideration connecting Humboldt to Bello and Sarmiento, and particularly Bello's "Silva" based on A. Rama's (1982) development of Fernando Ortiz's (1940) concept of "transculturation"; however, I find Rama's attribution rather static in comparison to Bakhtin's struggle for the sign as a contested field. It misses the lived richness of daily life.

5. The best succinct study of the reform and dissolution of colonial Iberian empires is Halperín Donghi 1985; see also the excellent synthesis of Stein and Stein 1970 on economic dependence after the wars of independence. See also Burns (1980), who echoes Marx as he analyzes "the poverty of progress" in this juncture. Beatriz González Stephan (1987) has analyzed the historiography of Latin American liberalism. My references to this complex period are meant only as background information to place the chronotope of turn-of-the-century modernism. As the reader might guess, there is a huge amount of published material on modernism, and lately much has centered on the relationships between modernism and modernity. Most of it is in Spanish (with few exceptions); I offer ample bibliographical references in several articles, and synthesize these interpretations in my studies of Darío (1989c) and Valle-Inclán (1990a), and in my book on theories of modernity (Zavala, in press). I should like to stress that I not only reposition modernism foregrounding modernity and modernness, but suggest it forms a strategic hegemonic bloc in an organic and relational whole welding together many positions, including Peninsulars, since the organic crisis of 1898 evolved around the Spanish-Anglo American War. This repositioning is based on a Bakhtinian/Gramscian reading. Other suggestive interpretations can be found in A. Rama 1970, 1985a, 1985b, grounded in the idea of a theory of dependency. See also Schulman 1987 and the readings of Ramos 1989.

6. For a good account of Gramscian hegemonic consent, see Laclau and Mouffe 1985 and S. Hall 1988. They base their interpretation of Gramscian hegemony in important distinctions regarding a field of articulatory practices. As such, an antagonism emerges when a collectivity or a collective group finds its subjectivity negated by other discourses and practices; however, the open and incomplete character of the social field is basic for every hegemonic practice. The same distinction applies to Bakhtin's dialogics. This is a major theoretical difference from the contemporary categories of otherness and difference, since different positions of struggle and resistance operate in the discourse of modernism at all moments. I fully agree with this revision of difference.

7. The reader may realize that I am offering selective examples, since I am not concerned here with literary history but with an operative concept of the modernist discursive practice, combining both Foucault and Reiss (1982), who carry on the modern episteme to the nineteenth century; therefore I mention *some* modernists who seem in a sense representative. See also Berman 1983 on modernism/modernity in general, and the pertinent pages of A. González 1983 devoted to the Latin American chronicle and modernity; the reader is reminded that Marx was also a chronicler for German and North American newspapers. Resort to this form of publication provided ways to address a wider audience as well as economic means; therefore most modernists published in newspapers and journals (Baudelaire, Verlaine, Whitman). I should like to stress that I borrow Foucaultian notions but refuse his slippages. Betances, who died in France, wrote most of his creative work in French and was pivotal in Antillean emancipation. As early as 1869 he warned his fellow Cubans about North American expansion and denounced "yanquism" on the island of Puerto Rico, from which he was exiled in 1867, along with two other important Puerto Rican moderns: Eugenio María de Hostos (who died in Chile) and Segundo Ruiz Belvis. These were the topics of most of his newspaper articles, published in New York, Mexico, and France. New York was the base

for Cuban and Puerto Rican independence, and there were two important newspapers, *La Patria* and *El Porvernir* (The Future). In 1895–98 Betances was the delegate to the Cuban Revolutionary Party in France.

8. The reader will rightly conclude that I am adapting from various sources in order to analyze turn-of-the-century modernism: the Bakhtin circle, Gramsci, Foucault, Critical Theory, Habermas. I will use the term *instrumental reason* throughout as the most appropriate term I can find to synthesize capitalism and modern technology's form of domination. However, it should be clear that it does not refer to an abstract form of domination, but to a very concrete experience.

9. I follow and adapt Foucault's suggestions in *The Archeology of Knowledge.*

10. I am drawing from Hall, Lumley, and McLennan 1977.

11. If I insist on the dialogical and heteroglossic aspect of this emergent modernity, it is to underline the fact that I am not trying to trace either Habermas's theory of communicative action in the philosophical discourse of modernity, or the Weberian discourse of rationalization which leads to "harmony." I have insisted that Latin American modernism can be understood as a responsive search for a "third" solution. Neither heteroglossia nor dialogics can be understood as a harmonious consensus or a pluralistic homogenization; see Zavala 1988b, 1989a, 1990b, 1990c, where I explain the differences between Bakhtin's other and the psychoanalytical Other of many poststructuralist theories of subject.

12. See Lauretis, Huyssen, and Woodward 1980.

13. Noble 1977, qtd. in Lauretis, Huyssen, and Woodward 1980:18.

14. On Schiller, see Habermas 1990:48–50; see also Brenkman 1987, Schulte-Sasse 1989. Schiller's and Emerson's coincide, in that culture was the site of liberty; on Emerson see Lentricchia 1986. On the English romantics see McGann 1983, 1989.

15. Modernists admired Poe and Whitman, particularly Whitman as the great poet of democracy, of modernity, and of American unity, as expressed by such poems as "Salut au Monde," "Years of the Modern," and "Song of Myself," especially a line such as "I am an acme of things accomplish'd, and I an encloser of things to be." However, they do not seem to have been aware of Whitman's defense of the Mexican invasion or his belief in the leading and messianic role of the North in the American continent. Darío mentions both poets frequently, and dedicated a poem to Whitman; his poem to Columbus is in dialogue with Whitman's "Prayer of Columbus." Unamuno quoted Whitman frequently, but he had a polymathic mind and was quite knowledgeable in many literatures and languages. When I quote Darío, I will always refer to *Poesías* (1977), unless otherwise stated. Darío also wrote an article on black poet Phillis Wheatley, "The Talent of Blacks" (El talento de los negros, 1912), and translated her poem "A Hymn to the Morning"; see Durand 1970. The interest of Latin American and Spanish poets in Whitman was constant, at least until Pablo Neruda's and Lorca's generation, for different reasons.

III. Lyric Poetry and the Constitution of the Self

1. For a deconstructive reading see González Echevarría (1985:8–12), whose approach is both different from and sometimes opposed to mine. Cândido (1980) suggests that the idea of nature and patria were linked, and these ideas compensated for the material backwardness by supervaluing regional aspects, and by upgrading eroticism to social optimism. He stresses that there was what one could call an essentialist fallacy in the idea of nature. My point of view is radically different.

2. My proposal is based on the Bakhtin circle's observations in regard to socialized language, and I adopt, with modifications, the seminal concept of carnivalesque; see *PDP, DI,* and *Rabelais.*

3. Schulman (1982) edited Martí's poetry with a lucid introduction. See also Esténger's 1971 edition.

4. The suggestion that I advance is based on an explicit combination of the Bakhtin circle's concepts of the dialogical, the enthymemic, and the situatedness of speech genres,

with some Critical Theory conceptualizations on nature, not incorporating the Weberian rationalization. It is important to note that there are interesting points of agreement between Martí and Marx's ideas on humankind and nature. Brenkman (1987:70–72) uses the "enthymemic" to analyze Marx's 1844 *Manuscripts* in the Aristotelian sense, not in the Bakhtinian sense I am suggesting. All this taken into account, I disagree with Antonio Cândido's (1980) interpretation of the *hombre natural* as a compensation for material backwardness by the supervaluing of regional aspects. To the contrary: the valorization of nature suggests a stand against useless consumption, and against colonialism which subsumes nature (subject and object) under the form of valorizable and manipulable objects.

5. All quotes from Darío refer to the edition of Ernesto Mejía Sánchez (1977). I apologize for my literal translations of great poems, and hope that they will induce a much-needed English edition of Darío's work, since the few translations are virtually inaccessible to English-speaking readers; see the information given by Kinzer 1987. See also Coester 1924. Martí's quotes come from Foner's edition. For a more thorough discussion of Darío's swan series, see Zavala 1989c, an analysis of the poems from the point of view of textual genetics and ideology.

6. It may be useful to recall that the Mexican self is frequently described as a mask, thus linking masks and myths; this metaphor is a favorite of Octavio Paz (see 1959). In *Los signos en rotación* (1983:25) he wrote: "We do not know if Mexican gods laugh or smile: they are covered by a mask" (No sabemos si los dioses de México ríen o sonríen: están cubiertos por una máscara).

7. See Kirkpatrick's 1989 reading of Lugones.

8. See the anthologies of anarchist thoughts on art, aesthetics, and the erotic in Litvak (1981, 1988), who has done important work to recuperate turn-of-the-century anarchists.

9. Martí's title refers to an obvious polyvalence of "Free Verses" in the specific canon of free verse, "free" suggesting liberated or emancipated. This book of poetry is an extended dialogue with Whitman, whom Martí admired. There are important "nocturnes," as well as poems grounded in a variety of social texts (newspaper articles, advertisements, etc.).

10. This poem to Roosevelt caused a major commotion among Latin Americans at that time, since readers compared this peaceful attitude to Darío's prior anti-imperialist stand. However, I believe that they are compatible, since Darío's subject position here is advocating not imperialism but peace. See the pertinent analysis of Stuart Hall (1988) on repositioning of subject positions, and Laclau (1988) on condensation, metaphor, and social antagonism. It should also be stressed that according to Albert (1988), Latin America was impotent during the First World War, a war which, on the other hand, disrupted international trade. Coincidentally, if the war made obvious the nature of modern economic warfare, the United States began more intense commerce, as the Panama Canal opened in 1914. Whitehead (1988) concludes that the most important regional consequence of the war was that national self-determination became a cornerstone. U.S. Marines invaded and occupied Haiti and the Dominican Republic in 1915, while imposing a military government in the Dominican Republic in 1916 (North American troops left the island in 1924) and also undertaking periodic military incursions into Mexico and occupying Veracruz in 1914. After the First World War, Latin American economic dependence on the United States became more evident.

11. In Zavala 1987 and 1989c I make reference to the intertextual dialogue between Darío's swan poems, Baudelaire, Mallarmé, and Yeats, to stress their historicity. On Baudelaire's swan poem, see Jauss 1982.

IV. The Struggle for Signs

1. It should be evident that I have in mind Marx's *Economic and Philosophical Manuscripts* (1844), where he reassesses culture and aesthetic capacity. See the lucid interpretation by Brenkman (1987:63–66) of this text.

2. On the symbolic see Bourdieu 1977, 1979a, 1982; Brenkman 1987; and from another angle, Schulte-Sasse 1986–87b.

3. Each country created its modernist periodicals; among the most influential were *El Iris* (Peru), *El año literario* (Chile), *Cosmópolis, El Cojo Ilustrado* (Venezuela), *La Lectura* (Colombia), *La Pluma* (Central America), *La Revista Moderna* (Mexico). Still the best sources for these periodicals are Henríquez Ureña 1954 and Carter 1959. Yet, much is to be done.

4. I draw, in another direction, from Johnson 1987:119.

5. See Casal's poem under that title written in 1893 (1963). See Davis (1976) on Silva's decadence. It has been suggested that Mallarmé was largely responsible for the theme of decadent voyage in art; see Grass and Risely, eds. 1979 for a collection of essays on decadence and symbolism. The theme, as I have argued, is re-accented in Latin America. Incidentally, Silva was a keen critic of the North American expansionist movement of 1898, and also wrote parodical satires of "yanquism." The reader will rightly conclude that I am polemizing with univocal understanding of modernist language.

6. This point is highly debatable, as feminists have shown for some time. The misogynism of the "pornographic" Latin American texts has been explored by Saporta Sternbach (1988). I personally find the definition of pornography rather slippery; on this issue see Feder Kittay 1984; Rubin Suleiman 1986; Kappeler 1986. There is ample bibliography. See also Silverman van Buren 1989. On erotic male fantasies see Bettelheim 1978. Ava Vargas (1986) published a collection of photographs of nudes of the Mexican belle-èpoque which point to the Parisian atmosphere of urban Mexico during the Porfiriato, after the French Maximilian empire.

7. For readings on the topics of language and nationalism, see Anderson 1983; Edwards 1985.

8. See the interesting comments of Stam (1988) on Bakhtin's cultural theory in its possible relation to Latin American literatures.

9. I am quoting from the following: *On the Genealogy of Morals and Ecce Homo* (1967) (hereafter *EH*) and *The Antichrist* from *The Portable Nietzsche* (1976). Gonzalo Sobejano's (1967) study of the reception of Nietzsche in Spain does not take into account Latin America; such a study is much needed from a less traditional perspective. However, I am not concerned here with such a reception but with underlining the Dionysian discourse in modernists.

10. See the interesting connections Renate Lachmann (1988–89) establishes between the *Doppelgänger* and Bakhtin's *Rabelais*. Julia Kristeva (1980) speaks about a "hieroglyphic spectacle," and the eccentric meaning, which Lachmann also underlines.

11. Finkelstein (1989) draws interesting conclusions on the Dionysian.

12. In quoting Ricoeur I am not suggesting that appropriation is the reader's privileged hermeneutics of understanding.

V. The Dialogical Cultural Signs

1. González Echevarría (1985) offers a slightly different interpretation of this legitimating effort, relying on Morse (1981) and his theory of this intelligentsia hegemonic power, as well as on Cândido (1980) and Melón (1979). My analysis points to different perspectives on hegemony, based on repositionings of Gramsci. Other interpretations can be found in A. Rama 1985a, 1985b; Ramos 1989. In what follows, I refer mainly to Darío and Rodó in and around 1898 (Martí died in 1896), since both represent founding discourses of modernity and are still basic in the constitution of Latin American cultures. Need I insist I am not concerned with literary history but with the emergent operative concept of modernism? It should be emphasized that there is also such a project in Catalonian modernism, which has been well studied by Cacho Viu (1984, 1988). In Spain, the sociogram of the barbaric versus the heroic was widely used in both modernist texts and popular culture; for the latter see Botrel (1982), who has

studied the structural organizing values in the *colportage* literature. See also Serrano (1982) for an analysis of regional diversities in Spain around the unpopular Cuban War.

2. Rodó wrote copiously, but *Ariel* still remains a founding discourse. All the quotes come from *Obras completas* (1967); I have translated the Spanish quotations. There is ample bibliography on Rodó. I would like to call attention to Rodó's strategy; he generates a modernist text from the position of center as he projects an oppositional political project.

3. Roberto Fernández Retamar's *Calibán* (1971; now in English translation, 1989) denounced *Ariel*'s ideology, suggesting that Latin America is "Caliban" (or the slave of Shakespeare's allegorical play); see also González Echevarría 1978. Caliban has thus become a contested idiom, and has been reappropriated, among others, by Gayatri Spivak. See Nixon 1987 for a thorough study of Caribbean and African appropriations of *The Tempest*. See also Baker 1986, linking Caliban to issues of race—a point well taken.

4. The reader will conclude that another aporia is the universal of Spanish (or European) in most modernist discursive practices, thus creating the "otherness" of Indians and blacks. Martí and Darío refer to the racial complexity of Latin America, also acknowledged by Hostos and Betances in the 1880s. Darío makes reference to his own racial mixture in many poems, as well as to his African and Indian ancestry; see his famous poem "Song to Argentina" (Canto a la Argentina, 1914), grounded on the African past. Racial differences are still a problematic blind spot in many Latin American societies.

5. I am not concerned with the autonomy of Latin American culture (or, for that matter, of any culture), since cultural realms are not autonomous but partake in commodity exchanges and the globalization of technology, especially in the modern world. I suggest that turn-of-the-century modernism projected a form of autonomous modernity, and that culture was part of the site of the problems modern theory signifies through reference to the subject. What we call literature since the early nineteenth century differs both in material form and in respect to the relations of production within which, as different practices, they are set. For example, Octavio Paz's (1974) purpose was to disclose how this modernity partakes of Western culture, but from a totally different angle.

6. From my perspective of the social imaginary as a series of projections intended to alter conditions, I am inclined to rely on a politicized hermeneutic theory which would account for the productive activation of sedimented meanings and on symbolic resistance. Therefore, neither modernism nor the imaginary (or the symbolic) is a metaphysicized essence; paraphrasing Dilthey, I could say they have histories, not essences. This is particularly relevant in the case of the simultaneous asynchronies of Latin American countries which only a reductive totalizing European and Anglo-American eye can see as a globalizing totality.

VI. Cultural Spheres and Resistance

1. I have dealt at length with this turn-of-the-century coordinated unity between anarchists, modernists, socialists, 1898 generationists, and bohemians. Ample information based on archival documentation as well as newspapers and periodicals can be found in Zavala 1974, 1986, 1990a. I am aware, however, that the name "Generation of 1898" is a Franquist construct, invented by Azorín. In Zavala, ed. 1977 there is ample information on the contacts between Hispanic modernists and the French avant-garde. Anderson (1988) does not take into consideration either Spain or Latin America in the conjunction of modernity, and the links with revolution; in contrast, Berman (1983) is right in connecting modernism/modernity with revolution, although he too silences or is unaware of Hispanic modernism. For the French alliance between the two avant-gardes, see Rebérioux 1974; Angenot 1989, 1990. See also Serrano and Salaün, eds. 1988 for a parallel yet different point of view on the Spanish turn of the century. The term

intellectual must have been coined with its present usage around 1889 and the 1890s; see Feuer (1971). However, it must be remembered that Bakunin's "intellectual proletariat" was common around 1873, and used by Ernesto Bark in 1900 with that same connotation, as I have pointed out several times elsewhere. No doubt that, after the Dreyfus affair, the term *intellectual* was more frequent in Spain; see Fox (1976), who has worked on Spanish turn-of-the-century intellectual history, Azorín and anarchism, among others. On Latin America and the Internationals, see Rama 1976, as well as his perceptive introduction to the cultural contacts between Latin America and Spain (1982).

2. It should be noted that the Ferrer case became a Western problem and drew attention from Europe as well as from Latin America, in a similar way to the Montjuich, Dreyfus, and Black Hand trials. This last one was revised in 1902, and thanks to Soledad Gustavo's energetic activities, the anarchists received national and international attention. In the Ferrer trial and execution, what was crucial were the questions on education and power Ferrer had raised through his "Modern 'Godless' Schools," which were sympathetic to anarchist ideas, although he denied any connection to the Tragic Week of 1909. Anti-clericalism was an important issue among the moderns; González Prada was concerned with the narrow and reductive concerns of Catholics in Peru. Naturally, the idioms connoting "degeneration" were part of discontent with the reductiveness of religious geopolitical hegemony.

3. The debate has been translated and edited recently by Ronald Taylor (1979). The book includes a postscript, "Reflections in Conclusion" by Jameson (196–213). I have elsewhere called attention to the fact that this debate coincides with the Bakhtin circle's polemics against formalists.

4. This is not the time to develop this point further; however, the delivered destruction of metaphysics was central to anarchists.

5. There is a wide bibliography on Spanish anarchism. Original and hitherto unknown information can be found in Lida 1972. See also Termes 1977; Kaplan 1977.

6. Much has been written on space, urbanization, and modernity. See Lefebvre 1974; Kern 1983; Olsen 1986; Harvey 1989. See the classic analysis on Latin American cities by Romero (1976); Beatriz Sarlo (1988) has analyzed the semiotics of Buenos Aires following Schorske's 1980 Vienna. See also Graña 1985.

7. Outlined in Achúgar 1981; Espino Relucé 1984. The latter has studied anarchist groups and popular anarchist culture in Peru. Much work is needed in these areas. See also Zavala, ed. 1977, where I give detailed information on Spanish anarchists and modernists. Geist (1978) has published some of Darío's chronicles on French anarchist journals. See also Fox 1976 and Litvak 1990.

8. I have made reference only to the most important journals; these modernist periodicals and newspapers and the anarchist and socialist press were published mainly in Madrid, Barcelona, Valencia, and Andalusia. The *Anthropos* 1988 special supplement offers a comprehensive list of newspapers and journals. Litvak 1990 gives ample bibliographical information on literary journals.

9. Davis 1977a is still the best account of Nordau's reception in the Hispanic world. The polemic around Nordau since 1893 is vital to understanding the conflicting and simultaneous uses of the concept of modernity and modernism. His reception in the Latin American world is wanting. See also Davis's excellent article on the reception of Oscar Wilde (1973). Litvak has done thorough descriptive work on turn-of-the-century intellectual ideas; see the latest collection of articles (1990).

10. The Sandinistas not only publicized Darío's progressiveness but popularized his anti-imperialistic position; see the recent Sandinista anthologies of his political prose (1983, 1984, and Zavala, ed. 1989). See also the anthology prepared by A. Rama (1973), devoted to the idiom of "dreams," "dreaming." From my perspective Rama missed the point. I want to thank Ivan A. Schulman, who generously provided me with a copy of Darío's recent Nicaraguan anthologies.

11. There is dispute around a set of articles on anarchism which appeared in *La Nación* (Buenos Aires) signed by Darío. It seems that they were written by Sawa as ghostwriter; see Zavala, ed. 1977. I have argued that anarchism and anarchists became popular topoi; see Dostoevsky's *The Devils,* connected to the Nechaevites. Nechaev, a former comrade of Bakunin and author of the famous *Catechism of a Revolutionary,* also appears in Valle-Inclán's *Ruedo Ibérico.* Lida (1972) connects Nechaev's text with some anarchist terrorist groups in Spain.

VII. Peninsular Moderns and the Shattered Mirror

1. I am aware that a heterogeneous set of social groups, with different objectives, are labeled as working-class.

2. "Generation of 1898" has been a contested name since Azorín fictionalized about its existence. I am using it as a strictly historical distinction, aware of its limitations.

3. I find parallels with the inception of Englishness as British hegemony disintegrates; the point is worth pursuing. See the important collective work of Colls and Dodd, eds. (1986). Américo Castro's "Spanishness" could be analyzed from this perspective.

4. The reception of Nietzsche among the anarchists was problematic; however, he was understood as an "anarchist intellectual." See Alvarez Junco 1976:145–63; Sobejano 1967. There were, however, some libertarian Nietzscheans, and a journal in Algeciras was called *The Antichrist* (El Anticristo, 1906). See also Litvak 1988, 1990.

5. I have analyzed this problem with greater detail in chapter V of my book on Valle-Inclán (1990a). The present version is oriented toward an analysis of the contending modernisms; therefore, I have incorporated new material.

6. The *Revista Blanca* had a second phase in 1923–36. There were many anarchist and socialist publications; each major city had at least one, although more were published in Barcelona, Madrid, and Seville, which show variations on the same theme. Urales (1864–1942) and Soledad Gustavo (1866–1939) contributed to many publications. They both produced fiction and theater; he adopted his pseudonym when he was set free after the Montjuich trials in 1896. Teresa Claramunt was the author of *The World Which Dies and the Newborn World* (El mundo que muere y el mundo que nace), performed in Barcelona in 1896. Federica Montseny (1905) carried on her parents' work and also wrote fictive literature. On anarchist aesthetics see Alvarez Junco 1976:65–92; Rubio Jiménez 1982:110-11, 130; special issues of *Anthropos* on Federico Urales (1987) and Urales and anarchist aesthetics (1988), see there M. Laffranque's article on Urales and the intellectuals. Litvak (1988, 1990) has produced the best informative material to date; she offers ample information on journals and periodicals. An exhaustive list of periodicals was prepared by Josep E. Adsuar for the *Anthropos* 1988 special issue. See also the special issue of *Anthropos* 1985 on Pablo Iglesias and Spanish socialism.

7. In Rubio Jiménez 1982. Many examples could be provided.

8. For a more exhaustive discussion of Valle's dialogics, simultaneity, and carnivalization, see Zavala 1990a. There I reconceptualize my work on Valle since 1969, and offer ample references and bibliography. Now I shall limit myself to the mirror metaphor.

9. The English-speaking reader can consult Zahareas, Cardona, and Greenfield, eds. 1968; Lyon 1983; Lima 1988. Regretfully, none of the most representative critics of modernism and postmodernism refer to Valle; I hope the synthesis will encourage some to read the few available translations, *Lights of Bohemia; The Pleasant Memoirs of the Marquis de Bradomin: Four Sonatas; The Tyrant: A Novel of Warm Lands; The Dragon's Head: A Fantastic Farce; The Dream Comedy; Divine Words; Wolves! Wolves! A Play of Savagery in Three Acts;* and *The Lamp of Marvels.* Some of his theatrical pieces have been represented in England, France, Germany, Italy, Norway, and Sweden (directed by Ingmar Bergman in 1950). Some of his works have also been made

into films. I wish to thank John P. Gabriele for providing me with this list of Valle's translations into English.

10. The point of repetition and history is well taken by Eagleton (1985:28). It is important to stress that, just before the Spanish Civil War, when Valle-Inclán died, the Republican front published the *Ruedo Ibérico* with a prologue by poet Antonio Machado saying that had Valle-Inclán still been alive, he would have been with the Republican cause. That is, undoubtedly, one of the best homages to the Galician writer. A few years ago, King Juan Carlos of Spain gave the title Marquisade of Bradomín to Valle's heirs, in what could be called a postmodern act of creating a title of nobility on the basis of a literary character.

11. To consider Valle as a variety of postmodernism would assume that the postmodern is textual, and not constituted by discourse on text. Valle's purpose is to reconnect an ethical violence.

12. I will concentrate here on but a few of Unamuno's dialogical practices. Interested readers can consult my other books; see Zavala 1963, 1988a, and especially the dialogue between Bakhtin and Unamuno (1991b). Most of Unamuno's main texts have been translated into English in the Bollingen Series, Princeton. I quote from Unamuno's *Obras completas*. It is rather difficult to render into English the idiom *casticismo*, an ideological unity comprising religious, ethnic, and cultural intersections. It could be argued that it became organic and left behind a sedimentation of "common sense." "Purism" is but one of its many connotations. Therefore, I have decided to leave the term in Spanish, as *casticism*.

13. I am not referring to a desocialized language which goes from the unconscious to the subject.

14. Sign here should be understood within the situated utterance of Bakhtin's social semiotics, and not in the framework of the arbitrary sign. It should also be apparent that I am repositioning Kristeva's semiotic, deaf to Bakhtin's struggle for signs. The sign to Kristeva is reductive to psychoanalytical dimensions (see 1969, 1984).

15. For a more detailed analysis of the mirror of production in Valle and Unamuno, see Zavala 1990a, 1990c, and 1991b. On mirror and the specular see Dallënbach 1977; Wright 1986; Jay 1988.

16. Foucault's article in Foucault 1984; on Nietzsche's unmaskings see Vattimo 1974.

VIII. Heterology and Popular Culture in Modernity

1. The reader will rightly understand that I am in polemic with those critics who make rigid and static distinctions around the sphere of culture, to start with Adorno. More recently, see Huyssen 1986, Bourdieu 1979b (English translation 1984). Culture is *always* contested, and there is a social dialogue as well as a dialogical interchange between literary and nonliterary, high and low culture. Stam (1988) is accurate in this point also. I follow Bakhtin's lead that social discourses interanimate each other. I adapt the term *cimarronaje cultural* from Depestre (1977:345). *Cimarrón* comes from the Spanish term for wild cattle, and *maroon* is the anglicized term for the French *maroons,* which refers to escaped or runaway slaves. Maroon power was important, and the maroons became significant actors in the Anglo-Spanish struggle over the Caribbean. Obviously, in Mexico it would be a *tequitqui,* or heterogeneous mixture of styles.

2. The reader will rightly conclude that I do not intend a musical history of these popular genres, but to suggest their link to the heterology of modernity. A sophisticated synthesis of Latin American music can be found in Pérez Fernández 1986, as well as in Moreno Fraginals, ed. 1977, the most accomplished collective work on Africa in Latin America. A wide variety of discourses emerged at this time—the Puerto Rican danza and plena, the Cuban habanera, the Portuguese *fado,* etc. I am referring to the better-known, since they have been internationalized by the mass media.

3. In other words, futurism, dada, surrealism, Russian constructivism, which I am

not considering. I should like to stress two important modernist composers who were in dialogue with popular music: Ravel and Manuel de Falla, who composed "El amor brujo" in 1915 for the dancer and singer Pastora Imperio. In Italy, texts of B. Latini, F. de Lemène, and D'Annunzio are interwoven in *Le stagioni italiche,* by G. Malipiero.

4. The gaucho absorbed by the city; by extension, the "bully."

5. I am borrowing from the collection of studies on Russian cultural history edited by Alexander D. and Alice Stone Nakhimovsky (1985) in order to indicate the semiotic system of modernist popular culture. What follows are mere suggestions, since much work is needed. The bibliography on the tango is abundant since the turn of the century, from Evaristo Carriego to Borges and Ernesto Sábato. I am using Barreiro's synthesis as well as his anthologies. See also González Ortega (1985), who has done interesting work on the lyrics and satirical dimensions of the "Tango of the Widow" (Tango del Viudo), which parodies Neruda's poetry. See also Vilariño 1965 on the lyrics of the tango; Kapschutschenko 1981; Kill 1983; Flores 1987; Campra 1988.

6. Re-accentuated in the twentieth century by Nicolás Guillén, *Motivos del son,* and Severo Sarduy's novel *De donde son los cantantes,* title of the famous *son* by Matamoros. This rhythm has traditionally been used in Cuba to critique and parody dictators; there are many documented against Batista. The Puerto Rican plena and the Dominican merengue have similar political intention.

7. I am suggesting a parallel between the bolero and the blues as narratives on experience, drawing from the fact that African culture is an ingredient of the hetero-glossic bolero. Unfortunately, the documented boleros can be found after 1911, and especially during the 1920s and 1930s, which could be called the golden years of the bolero. I have dealt with the erotic discourse of the bolero elsewhere (see Zavala 1989c), and I have written what I call a *critical fiction* on the bolero, *El bolero: Historia de un amor* (Madrid: Alianza, 1991c). See also the synthesis by Olavo Alén (1990), director of the Center for the Development of Popular Music in Cuba, and Suardiaz 1990.

8. According to music historians, the flamenco was also organized and institu-tionalized around the 1860s.

9. The Gramscian-oriented term *civic culture* and the idea of an essentialist national identity are borrowed from the excellent collection of articles on modernism and Englishness edited by Colls and Dodd (1986).

10. Espino Relucés's 1984 anthology includes texts from various cancioneros as well as from the anarchist press. See also Weinburg 1975.

IX. Other Modernist Open-ended Beginnings

1. Since the purpose of this book is not literary history, I only make reference to the emergence of Puerto Rican modernism. Betances's activities have been recorded in Godínez Sosa 1985. Various anthologies of modernism are available; see in particular Hernández Aquino 1967; Laguerre 1969; Martínez Masdeu 1977. Lisa Davis has conscientiously studied the *Revista de las Antillas* (1977b), as well as modernist prose writer Miguel Guerra Mondragón (1975), translator of Wilde.

2. I agree with Díaz Quiñones (1975) in his interpretation of Lloréns Torres as a utopian.

3. I am almost paraphrasing S. Hall's (1987) definition of "identity."

4. Glissant 1981 offers a fascinating interpretation of Caribbean culture, centered on Martinique. In 1991, while this book was in press, the Puerto Rican government passed a law to make Spanish the official language of the island.

5. Except for the second generation, the previous ones are virtually unknown. Myriam Díaz-Diocaretz (1990) has written on these last three poets as "founding discourses." See also Rosenbaum 1945, an informed thesis on some women modernists. Obviously there is major work to be done on the lesser-known women writers. Inciden-tally, Juana de Ibarborou, also called "Juana de América," appears as a general delegate

of a fascist group called La Phalange in France, whose purpose was to crush communism in 1936.

6. See Díaz-Diocaretz 1990.

7. I adapt from McHale's (1987) distinction between modernist and postmodernist.

8. Gabriela Mistral had a strong negative attitude toward sexual equality; she believed that woman's role was in the house, although she defended suffragism. See the analysis of Mistral's prose in Arrigoitia 1989.

9. See the recent reedition of two of her plays (Simón Palmer 1989). Martí wrote a strong censuring sonnet against Acuña; believing that she was Cuban, he exhorted her to come back to her roots instead of acting like a Spaniard. The incident of mistaken identity has been explained by Simón Palmer.

10. On Soledad Gustavo see Lamberet 1975. Work is wanting in these areas for Latin American cultures.

11. Salaün 1990 offers information on women artists at the turn of the century; see also Barreiro 1988, a succinct biography of Meller. She married Guatemalan modernist Gómez Carrillo in Paris, and according to Barreiro became as popular as Sarah Bernhardt, Eleanora Duse, Isadora Duncan, and Josephine Baker. Quite popular also were Galician-born "La Bella Otero," and later the Spanish actress Margarita Xirgu.

WORKS CITED

Achúgar, Hugo. "Modernización, europeización, cuestionamiento: El lirismo social en el Uruguay entre 1895–1911." *Revista Iberoamericana* 114–15 (1981):7–32.
———. *Poesía y sociedad (Uruguay 1880–1911)*. Montevideo: Arca, 1985.
Adorno, T., and Max Horkheimer. *Dialectic of the Enlightenment*. New York: Herder and Gerder, 1972.
Albert, Bill. *South America and the First World War*. Cambridge: Cambridge University Press, 1988.
Alén, Olavo. "El bolero." *El Habanero* (6 June 1990).
Althusser, Louis. *For Marx*, trans. B. Brewster. London: New Left Books, 1969.
———. *Lenin and Philosophy and Other Essays*. New York: Monthly Review Press, 1971.
Alvarez Junco, José. *La ideología política del anarquismo español (1868–1910)*. Madrid: Siglo XXI, 1976.
Anderson, Benedict. *Imagined Communities: Reflections on the Origin and Spread of Nationalism*. London: Verso, 1983.
Anderson, Perry. "Modernity and Revolution." In Nelson and Grossberg, eds. 1988, 317–34.
Angenot, Marc. *Glossaire pratique de la critique contemporaine*. Ville LaSalle, Quebec: Hurtubise, 1979.
———. *Topographie du socialisme française (1889–1890)*. Montreal: Discours social/ Social Discourse, 1989.
———. *Mille huit cent quatre-vingt neuf: un état du discours social*. Montreal: Le Préambule, 1990.
Anthropos. Núm. extraordinario. *Pablo Iglesias: El socialismo en España*. Barcelona: Anthropos, 1985.
———. Núm. extraordinario. *F. Urales: Una cultura de la acracia, ejercicio de un proyecto de libertad solidaria*. Barcelona: Anthropos, 1987.
———. Suplementos. *Pensamiento y estética anarquista: Análisis y documentación. Selección de textos de F. Urales*. Barcelona: Anthropos, 1988.
Arnold, A. James. *Modernism and Negritude: The Poetry and Poetics of Aimé Césaire*. Cambridge: Harvard University Press, 1981.
Arrigoitia, Luis. *Pensamiento y forma de la prosa de Gabriela Mistral*. Rio Piedras: Editorial de la Universidad de Puerto Rico, 1989.
Avineri, Shlomo. *Karl Marx on Colonialism and Modernization*. New York: Doubleday, 1968.
Baker, Houston, Jr. *Blues, Ideology, and Afro-American Literature: A Vernacular Theory*. Chicago: University of Chicago Press, 1984.
———. "Caliban's Triple Play." *Critical Inquiry* 13:1 (1986):182–96.
———. *Modernism and the Harlem Renaissance*. Chicago: University of Chicago Press, 1987.
Bakhtin, Mikhail M. *Rabelais and His World*, trans. H. Isowolsky. 1965; Cambridge: MIT Press, 1968.
———. [V. N. Volosinov]. *Freudianism: A Marxist Critique*, trans. I. R. Titunik, ed. in collaboration with Neal H. Bruss. 1927; New York: Academic Press, 1976.
———. *The Dialogic Imagination: Four Essays by M. M. Bakhtin*, ed. Michael Holquist, trans. Caryl Emerson and Michael Holquist. Austin: University of Texas Press, 1981.

————. "The Construction of the Utterance." In *Bakhtin School Papers,* ed. Ann Shukman. Russian Poetics in Translation, vol. 10. Oxford, 1983.

————. *Problems of Dostoevsky's Poetics,* ed. and trans Caryl Emerson, intro. by Wayne C. Booth. Minneapolis: University of Minnesota Press, 1984.

————/P. N. Medvedev. *The Formal Method in Literary Scholarship: A Critical Introduction to Sociological Poetics,* foreword by Wlad Godzich, trans. Albert J. Wehrle. 1928; Cambridge: Harvard University Press, 1985.

————. *Speech Genres and Other Late Essays,* trans. Vern W. McGee, ed. Caryl Emerson and Michael Holquist. Austin: University of Texas Press, 1986.

————. [Volosinov, V. N.] *Marxism and the Philosophy of Language,* trans. Ladislav Matejka and I. R. Titunik. Cambridge: Harvard University Press, 1986.

————. *Art and Answerability: Early Philosophical Essays by M. M. Bakhtin,* ed. Michael Holquist and Vadim Liapunov, trans. and notes Vadim Liapunov, supplement trans. Kenneth Brostrom. Austin: University of Texas Press, 1989.

Balibar, Renée, and Dominique Laporte. *Le française national: politique et pratiques de la langue nationale sous la Révolution française.* Paris: Hachette, 1974.

Barreiro, Javier. *El tango.* Madrid: Júcar, 1985.

————. *Gent Nostra: Raquel Meller.* Barcelona: Edicions de Nou Art Thor, 1988.

————. *El tango hasta Gardel.* Zaragoza: Diputación Provincial, 1989.

Barth, John. "Literature of Exhaustion." *Atlantic Monthly* 220:2 (1967).

Barthes, Roland. *Mythologies.* Paris: Seuil, 1957.

————. *Writing Degree Zero.* London: Cape, 1967.

————. *S/Z: An Essay,* trans. Richard Miller, preface by Richard Howard. 1970; New York: Hill and Wang, 1974.

————. "En sortant du Cinéma." *Communications* 23 (1975):106.

Barzun, Jacques. *Classic, Romantic and Modern.* New York: Doubleday, 1961.

Baudrillard, Jean. *Le miroir de la production: ou l'illusion critique du matérialisme historique.* Tournail: Casterman, 1973. English trans. *The Mirror of Production.* St. Louis: Telos, 1975.

Beecher, Jonathan, and Richard Bienvenu. *The Utopian Vision of Charles Fourier.* Boston: Beacon Press, 1971.

Beisner, Robert L. *Twelve against Empire: The Anti-Imperialists, 1898–1900.* New York: Macmillan, 1968.

Bénichou, Paul. *Le sacré de l'écrivain, 1750–1830.* Paris: José Corti, 1973.

————. *Le temps des prophètes: Doctrine de l'âge romantique.* Paris: Gallimard, 1977.

————. *Les mages romantiques.* Paris: Gallimard, 1989.

Benjamin, Walter. *The Origin of German Tragic Drama,* trans. John Osborne. New York: New Left Books, 1977.

Bennett, Tony. "Texts, Readings. Reading Formations." *Bulletin of the Midwestern Language Association* 16 (1983):3–17.

Bering, Dietz. *Die Intellektuellen.* Stuttgart, 1978.

Berman, Art. *From the New Criticism to Deconstruction: The Reception of Structuralism and Post-Structuralism.* Urbana: University of Illinois Press, 1988.

Berman, Marshall. *All That Is Solid Melts into the Air.* New York: Simon and Schuster, 1983.

Bettelheim, Bruno. *The Uses of Enchantment: The Meaning and Importance of Fairy Tales.* New York: Vintage Books, 1978.

Botrel, Jean F. "Nationalisme et consolation dans la littérature populaire espagnole des années 1898." In *Nationalisme et littérature en Espagne et Amérique Latine au XIXe siècle, études réunis par Claude Dumas* (Université Lille III, 1982), 63–98.

Bourdieu, Pierre. "Champ intellectuel et projet créateur." *Temps Modernes* (1966):865–906.

————. *Outline of a Theory of Practice.* Cambridge: Cambridge University Press, 1977.

————. "Symbolic Power." *Critique of Anthropology* 13/14 (1979a):78–85.

————. *La distinction*. Paris: Minuit, 1979b. English trans. *Distinction: A Social Critique of the Judgement*, trans. R. Nice. Cambridge: Harvard University Press, 1984.

————. *Ce qui parler veut dire: L'économie des échanges linguistics*. Paris: Fayard, 1982.

————. "Le Champ littéraire: Préalables critiques et principes de méthode." *Lendemains* 9:36 (1984):5–20.

————. *Choses dites*. Paris: Minuit, 1987.

Bradbury, Malcolm. "The Shock Troops of Modernism." *TLS* (Oct. 15, 1976):1297.

Bradbury, Malcolm, and James McFarlane, eds. *Modernism, 1890-1930*. London: Penguin Books, 1978.

Braudel, Ferdinand. *El mediterráneo y el mundo mediterráneo en la época de Felipe II*. 2 vols. 1949; Mexico: Fondo de Cultura Económica, 1953.

Brecht, Bertolt. "Popularity and Realism." In *Aesthetics and Politics: Debates between E. Bloch, G. Lukács, B. Brecht, Walter Benjamin, T. Adorno*, trans. and ed. Ronald Taylor. London: NLB, 1979.

Brenan, Gerald. *The Spanish Labyrinth: An Account of the Social and Political Background of the Spanish Civil War*. Cambridge: Cambridge University Press, 1978.

Brenkman, John. *Culture and Domination*. Ithaca: Cornell University Press, 1987.

Buci-Gluckmann, Christine. *La folie du voir: De l'esthétique baroque*. Paris: Galilée, 1986.

Bürger, Peter. *Theory of the Avant-Garde*, trans. Michael Shaw, foreword J. Schulte-Sasse. 1972; Manchester: Manchester University Press, 1984.

Burns, Bradford E. *The Poverty of Progress: Latin America in the Nineteenth Century*. Berkeley: University of California Press, 1980.

Cacho Viu, Vicente. *Els modernistes i el nacionalisme cultural: Antologia*. Barcelona: La Magrana, 1984.

————. "Catalonian Modernism and Cultural Nationalism" (1987), *Hispanic Issues 3, The Crisis of Institutionalized Literature in Spain*, ed. N. Spadaccini and Wlad Godzich (1988):229–50.

Calvino, Italo. *The Uses of Literature: Essays*. New York: Harvest/HBJ Book, 1986.

Campra, Rosalba. "Relaciones intertextuales en el sistema culto/popular: Poesía y tango." *Hispamérica* 17:51 (1988):19–32.

Cândido, Antonio. "Literature and Underdevelopment." In *Latin America in Its Literature*, ed. César Fernández Moreno, trans. Mary G. Berg. New York: Holmes and Meier, 1980.

Cano Ballesta, Juan. *Literatura y tecnología: Las letras españolas ante la revolución industrial (1900–1933)*. Madrid: Orígenes, 1981.

Cardona, Rodolfo, and A. N. Zahareas. *Visión del esperpento: Teoría y práctica de los esperpentos de Valle-Inclán*. Madrid: Castalia, 1970.

Carr, Raymond. *Spain, 1808-1975*. Oxford: Clarendon Press, 1982.

Carter, Boyd G. *Las revistas literarias de Hispanoamérica*. Mexico: Eds. de Andrea, 1959.

Casal, Julián del. *Poesía*. Havana: Consejo Nacional de Cultura, 1963.

————. *Prosa*. 2 vols. Havana: Letras Cubanas, 1979.

Castoriadis, Cornelius. *L'institution imaginaire de la société*. Paris: Seuil, 1981. English trans. *The Imaginary Institution of Society*. Cambridge: MIT Press, 1987.

Caudet, Francisco. " 'Las plagas sociales': nueve artículos de Felipe Trigo publicados en *El Socialista*." *Nuevo Hispanismo* 2 (1982):137–62.

Césaire, Aimé. *Discourse on Colonialism*. New York: Monthly Review Press, 1972.

Chafdor, Monique, R. Quiñones, and A. Wachtel, eds. *Modernism: Challenge and Perspectives*. Urbana: University of Illinois Press, 1986.

Charle, Christophe. *Naissance des "intellectuels" 1880–1900*. Paris: Minuit, 1990.

Chow, Rey. "Rereading Mandarin Ducks and Butterflies: A Response of Post-Modernity." *Cultural Critique,* spec. issue 5 (1986–87):69–94.

Civeira Taboada, Miguel. *Sensibilidad yucateca en la canción romántica,* vol. I. Toluca: Gobierno del Estado, 1978.

Clark, Katerina, and Michael Holquist. *Mikhail Bakhtin.* Cambridge: Harvard University Press, 1984.

Coester, Alfred L. *Anthology of the Modernista Movement in Spanish America.* Boston: Ginn and Co., 1924.

Coll, Pedro Emilio. *El castillo de Elsinor.* Caracas, 1901; rpt. Madrid: Editorial América, 1916.

Colls, Robert, and Philip Dodd, eds. *Englishness: Politics and Culture, 1880–1920.* London: Croom Helm, 1986.

Coward, Rosalind, and John Ellis. *Language and Materialism: Developments in Semiotics and the Theory of the Subject.* London: Routledge and Kegan Paul, 1977.

Dallënbach, Lucien. *Le récit speculaire.* Paris: Seuil, 1977.

Darío, Rubén. *Obras completas.* 5 vols. Madrid: Aguado, 1950–53.

———. *Poesía,* pról. Angel Rama, ed. E. Mejía Sánchez. Mexico: Fondo de Cultura Económica, 1977.

———. *Prosas políticas,* intro. by Julio Valle-Castillo, sel. and notes Jorge Eduardo Arellano. Managua: Ministerio de Cultura-Nicaragua Libre, 1983.

———. *Tantos vigores dispersos (Ideas sociales y políticas),* sel. y notas Jorge Eduardo Arellano. Managua: Distribuidora Cultural, 1984.

Davie, Donald. "The Nonconformist Contribution to English Culture." *TLS* (10 Nov. 1976):1459.

Davis, David B. "The Labyrinth of Slavery." *New York Review* (5 Nov. 1987):34–37.

Davis, Lisa. "Oscar Wilde in Spain." *Comparative Literature* XXV (1973):136–52.

———. "Guerra Mondragón como traductor de Oscar Wilde: interpretación de la estética moderna en Puerto Rico." *Sin Nombre* 6 (1975):66–81.

———. "Modernismo y decadentismo en la novela *De sobremesa,* de José Asunción Silva." In Mary Berg, Lisa Davis, et al., eds., *The Analysis of Hispanic Texts: Current Trends in Methodology* (New York: Bilingual Press, 1976), 206–20.

———. "Max Nordau, Degeneración' y la decadencia de España." *Cuadernos Hispanoamericanos* 326/327 (1977a):1–5.

———. "Revista de las Antillas: El modernismo como resistencia cultural en Puerto Rico." *Casa de las Américas* 105 (1977b):54–59.

De Diego, José. *Obras completas,* t. I: *Poesías.* San Juan: Instituto de Cultura Puertorriqueña, 1966.

De Man, Paul. "Sign and Symbol in Hegel's *Aesthetics.*" *Critical Inquiry* 8:4 (1982):761–75.

———. *Blindness and Insight: Essays on the Rhetoric of Contemporary Criticism.* Minneapolis: University of Minnesota Press, 1983.

Depestre, René. "Saludo y despedida a la negritud." In Moreno Fraginals, ed. 1977, 337–62.

Derrida, Jacques. "Limited inc. abc." *Glyph* (1977) 2:l62–254.

———. "Living On: Border-lines." In *Deconstruction and Criticism* (New York: Seabury Press, 1979), 75–176.

———. *Dissemination,* trans. Barbara Johnson. 1972; London: Athlone Press, 1981.

———. "Letter to a Japanese Friend." In *Derrida and Différance,* ed. David Wood and Robert Bernasconi (Evanston: Northwestern University Press, 1988), 1–6.

Dews, Peter. *Logics of Disintegration: Post-Structuralist Thought and the Claims of Critical Theory.* London: Verso, 1988.

Díaz, Edgardo. "Música para anunciar en la sociedad sanjuanera del siglo XIX." *Revista Musical Puertorriqueña* 1 (1987):6–13.

Díaz Alejo, Ana Elena, and Ernesto Prado Vázquez. *Indice de la Revista Azul (1894–1896)*. Mexico: Universidad Nacional Autónoma de México, 1968.

Díaz-Diocaretz, Myriam. "Black North-American Women Poets in the Semiotics of Culture." In M. Díaz-Diocaretz and I. M. Zavala, eds., *Women, Feminist Identity and Society in the 1980's* (Amsterdam: John Benjamins, 1985), 37–60.

———. "Sieving the Matriheritage of the Sociotext." In *The Difference Within: Feminism and Critical Theory,* ed. Elizabeth Meese and Alice Parker (Amsterdam: John Benjamins, 1989a), 115–47.

———. "Bakhtin, Discourse and Feminist Theories." *The Bakhtin Circle Today,* spec. issue of *Critical Studies* 1:2 (1989b):121–39.

———. " 'I will be a scandal in your boat': Women Poets and the Tradition." In Susan Bassnett, ed., *Knives and Angels: Women Writers in Latin America* (London: Zed Books, 1990), 86–109.

Díaz Quiñones, Arcadio. "La isla afortunada: sueños liberadores y utópicos de Luis Lloréns Torres." *Sin Nombre* 6:1 (1975):16–25.

Dolgoff, Sam, ed. *La anarquía según Bakunin*. Barcelona: Tusquests, 1977.

Dougherty, Dru.*Un Valle-Inclán olvidado: entrevistas y conferencias.* Madrid: Fundamentos, 1983.

Durand, René L. F. *La négritude dans l'oeuvre poétique de Rubén Darío.* Dakar: Centre de Hautes Etudes Afro-Ibéro-Américaines, 1970.

Dust, Patrick H., ed. *Ortega y Gasset and the Question of Modernity*. Hispanic Issues 5. Minneapolis: Prisma Institute, 1989.

Eagleton, Terry. *Walter Benjamin, or Towards a Revolutionary Criticism*. London: Verso, 1985.

———. *Nationalism, Colonialism and Literature. Nationalism: Irony and Commitment.* London: A Field Day Pamphlet, 1988.

Edwards, John. *Language, Society and Identity*. Oxford: Basil Blackwell, 1985.

Eisenstadt, S. N., ed. *Patterns of Modernity.* Vol. 2: *Beyond the West.* London: Pinter, 1987.

El Cancionero Revolucionario: Colección de himnos y canciones libertarias en español e italiano. Himnos revolucionarios. Buenos Aires: Librería la Escuela Moderna, n.d.

Escarpit, Robert. *La littéraire et le social: elements pour une sociologie de la littérature.* Paris: Flammarion, 1970.

Espino Relucé, Gonzalo. *La lira rebelde proletaria: Estudio y antología de la poesía obrera anarquista (1900–1926).* Lima: Tarea, 1984.

Esténger, V., ed. *José Martí: Versos.* 2 vols. New York: Anaya, 1971.

Feder Kittay, Eve. "Pornography and the Erotics of Domination." In *Beyond Domination: New Perspectives on Women and Philosophy,* ed. Carol C. Gould (Totowa, N.J.: Rowman and Allanheld, 1984), l67–80.

Fernández Retamar, Roberto. *Calibán and Other Essays,* trans. Edward Baker, foreword by Fredric Jameson. 1971; Minneapolis: University of Minnesota Press, 1989.

Fernández Valadez, Olga. *A pura guitarra y tambor.* Santiago: Editorial Oriente, 1984.

Ferris, William. *Blues from the Delta.* New York: Anchor Books, 1979.

Feuer, Lewis S. "The Political Linguistics of 'Intellectual' 1889–1918." *Survey* 16:1 (Winter 1971):156–83.

Finkelstein, Norman. "The Utopian Function and the Refunctioning of Marxism." *Diacritics* (Summer 1989):54–66.

Flores, Angel, and Kate Flores, eds. *The Defiant Muse: Hispanic Feminist Poems from the Middle Ages to the Present.* New York: The Feminist Press, 1986.

Flores, Rafael. "Los letristas del tango y su ambiente." *Cuadernos Hispanoamericanos* 445 (1987):99–105.

Foster, David William. *Para una lectura semiótica del ensayo latinoamericano.* Madrid: José Porrúa Turanzas, 1983.

Foucault, Michel. *Le mots et les choses*. Paris: Gallimard, 1966. English trans. *The Order of Things: An Archeology of the Human Sciences*. New York: Vintage, 1973.

———. *L'archeologie du savoir*. Paris: Gallimard, 1969. English trans. *The Archeology of Knowledge*. London: Tavistock, 1977.

———. *L'ordre du discours*. Paris: Gallimard, 1971.

———. *Madness and Civilization: A History of Insanity in the Age of Reason*. 1961; London: Tavistock, 1977.

———. *The History of Sexuality*. Vol. 1: *An Introduction*. London: Penguin, 1979.

———. *Power/Knowledge: Selected Interviews and Other Writings 1972–1977 by Michel Foucault*, ed. C. Gordon. Brighton: Harvester Press, 1980.

———. *The Foucault Reader*, ed. Paul Rabinow. New York: Pantheon Books, 1984.

Fox, E. Inman. "El Año de 1898 y el origen de los 'intelectuales.'" In *La crisis intelectual del 98*. Madrid: Cuadernos para el Diálogo, 1976.

Frossaert, M. *Les structures ideologiques*. Paris: Seuil, 1989.

Gadamer, Hans-Georg. *Truth and Method*, trans. J. Cumming. New York: Seabury, 1975.

Garrido, Juan S. *Historia de la música popular en México*. Mexico: Ed. Extemporáneos, 1981.

Gasché, Rudolf. *The Tain of the Mirror: Derrida and the Philosophy of Reflection*. Cambridge: Harvard University Press, 1986.

Geist, Anthony. "Colaboraciones de Rubén Darío en revistas anarquistas francesas." In *La crisis de fin de siglo: ideología y literatura*, Estudios en memoria de Rafael Pérez de la Dehesa (Barcelona: Ariel), 214–22.

Gilman, Richard. *Decadence: The Strange Life of an Epithet*. London: Secker and Warburg, 1979.

Glissant, Edouard. *Le discours antillais*. Paris: Seuil, 1981.

Godínez Sosa, Emilio. *Cuba en Betances*. Havana: Editorial de Ciencias Sociales, 1985.

Goffman, Erving. *Frame Analysis: An Essay on the Organization of Experience*. New York: Harper and Row, 1974.

González, Aníbal. *La crónica modernista hispanoamericana*. Madrid: José Porrúa Turanzas, 1983.

González Echevarría, Roberto. "Roberto Fernández Retamar: An Introduction." *Diacritics* 8:4 (1978):70–75.

———. "The Case of the Speaking Statue: *Ariel* and the Magisterial Rhetoric of the Latin American Essay." In *The Voice of the Masters: Writing and Authority in Modern Latin American Literature* (Texas: University of Texas Press, 1985), 8–33.

González Ortega, Nelson A. "La lírica en el tango o el tango en la lírica: La dimensión paródica de 'Tango del Viudo.'" *Revista de Crítica Literaria Latinamoamericana* 11:21–22 (1985):48–58.

González Stephan, Beatriz. "Todo un pueblo: Modernismo/modernidad: La crisis finisecular en Venezuela." *Escritura* (Caracas) 8:16 (l983):251–72.

———. *La historiografía literaria del liberalismo hispanoamericano del siglo XIX*. Havana: Casa de las Américas, 1987.

———. "Al filo del 900: La estética ácrata y libertaria de Pedro Emilio Coll." *Argos* (Caracas) 7 (1988):125–37.

Gramsci, Antonio. *Lettere dal carcere*. Torino: Einaudi, 1965. English trans. *Selections from Prison Notes*, ed. and trans. Quintin Hoare and Geoffrey Nowell Smith. London: Lawrence and Wishart, 1986.

———. *Socialismo e fascismo: L'Ordine nuovo 1921–1922*. Torino: Einaudi, 1966a.

———. *Gli intellettuali e l'organizzazione della cultura*. Torino: Einaudi, 1966b.

Graña, Cecilia. "La utopía como *analogon*: Sarmiento y el proyecto de una ciudad moderna." *Cuadernos Hispanoamericanos*. Los complementarios 3 (1985):59–82.

Grass, Roland, and William S. Risely, eds. *Waiting for Pegasus: Studies of the Presence of Symbolism and Decadence in Hispanic Letters*. Macomb: Western Illinois University Press, 1979.

Guillaumin, Colette. "The Idea of Race and Its Elevation to Autonomous Scientific and Legal Status." In *Sociological Theories: Race and Colonialism* (Paris: UNESCO, 1980), 37–68.

Habermas, Jürgen. *Theory and Practice,* trans. John Viertel. Boston: Beacon Press, 1974.

———. *Legitimation Crisis,* trans. Thomas McCarthy. Boston: Beacon Press, 1975.

———. "Consciousness-Raising or Redemptive Criticism: The Contemporaneity of Walter Benjamin." *New German Critique* 17 (Spring 1979):30–59.

———. *Habermas, Autonomy and Solidarity: Interviews with J. Habermas,* ed. Peter Dews. London: Verso, 1986.

———. *The Philosophical Discourse of Modernity* (1985), trans. Frederick G. Lawrence. Cambridge: MIT Press, 1990.

Hall, Edward T. *The Silent Language*. New York: Doubleday, 1959.

———. *The Hidden Dimension: Man's Use of Space in Public and Private*. London: The Bodley Head, 1966.

Hall, Stuart, Bob Lumley, and Gregor McLennan. "Politics and Ideology: Gramsci." In *On Ideology* (London: Hutchinson, 1977), 45–76.

———. "Variants of Liberalism." In *Politics and Ideology: A Reader*, ed. James Donald and S. Hall (London: Open University Press, 1986), 34–69.

———. "Minimal Selves." ICA Documents 6 *Identity*, 1987, 44–46.

———. "The Toad in the Garden: Thatcherism among the Theorists." In Nelson and Grossberg, eds. 1988, 35–74.

Halperín Donghi, Tulio. *Reforma y disolución de los imperios ibéricos 1750–1850*. Madrid: Alianza, 1985.

Harvey, David. *The Condition of Postmodernity*. London: Basil Blackwell, 1989.

Henríquez Ureña, Max. *Breve historia del modernismo*. Mexico: Fondo de Cultura Económica, 1954.

Herbert, Thomas. "Notas para una teoría general de las ideologías" (1968). *El proceso ideológico* (1971):225–50.

Hernández Aquino, Luis. *El modernismo en Puerto Rico*. San Juan: Editorial Universitaria, 1967.

———. "Nuevas reflexiones sobre el modernismo puertorriqueño." *Revista del Instituto de Literatura Puertorriqueña* 38 (1968):28–37.

Hobsbawm, Eric J. *The Age of Empire, 1875–1914*. London: Weidenfeld and Nicolson, 1987.

Holquist, Michael. *Dialogism: Bakhtin and His World*. London: Routledge, 1990.

Hutcheon, Linda. *A Theory of Parody: The Teaching of Twentieth-Century Art Forms*. London: Methuen, 1985.

Huyssen, Andreas. *After the Great Divide*. Bloomington: Indiana University Press, 1986.

Ingram, David. *Habermas and the Dialectic of Reason*. New Haven: Yale University Press, 1988.

Iturbe, Lola. *La mujer en la lucha social: La guerra civil de España*. Mexico: Editores Mexicanos Unidos, 1974.

Jameson, Fredric. "The Ideology of the Text." *Salmagundi* (1975/76):204–46.

———. "Imaginary and Symbolic in Lacan: Marxism, Psychoanalytic Criticism, and the Problem of the Subject." *Yale French Studies* 55/56 (1977):338–95.

———. "The Symbolic Inference; or, Kenneth Burke and Ideological Analysis." *Critical Inquiry* 4:3 (1978):507–23.

———. "Reflections in Conclusion." In Taylor, ed. 1979, 196–213.

———. *The Political Unconscious: Literature as a Socially Symbolic Act.* Ithaca: Cornell University Press, 1981.

———. *Nationalism, Colonialism and Literature: Modernism and Imperialism.* London: A Field Day Pamphlet, 1988a.

———. *The Ideologies of Theory: Essays, 1971–1986.* 2 vols. Foreword by Neil Larsen. Minneapolis: University of Minnesota Press, 1988b.

Jauss, Hans R. *Aesthetic Experience and Literary Hermeneutic.* Minneapolis: University of Minnesota Press, 1982.

Jay, Gregory S. "Values and Deconstruction: Derrida, Saussure, Marx." *Cultural Critique* 8 (1987–88):153–96.

Jay, Martin. "The Rise of Hermeneutics and the Crisis of Ocularcentricism." *Poetics Today* 9:2 (1988):307–26.

Jiménez, José Olivio, and Antonio R. de la Campa. *Antología crítica de la prosa modernista hispanoamericana.* New York: Eliseo Torres, 1976.

Johnson, Barbara. *A World of Difference.* Baltimore: Johns Hopkins University Press, 1987.

Kaplan, Temma. *Anarchist in Andalucia, 1868–1903.* Princeton: Princeton University Press, 1977.

Kappeler, Susanne. *The Pornography of Representation.* Minneapolis: University of Minnesota Press, 1986.

Kapschutschenko, Ludmila. "El tango: máxima expresión de un pueblo." In *Literature and Popular Culture in the Hispanic World,* ed. Rose S. Minc (Maryland: Hispamérica, 1981), 133–47.

Karnow, Stanley. *In Our Image: America's Empire in the Philippines.* New York: Random House, 1989.

Kern, Stephen. *The Culture of Time and Space, 1880-1918.* London: Weidenfeld and Nicolson, 1983.

Kill, Timothy L. "The Poetry of Moral Fragmentation in Argentine Lyrics." *Crítica Hispánica* 5:1 (1983):35–47.

Kinzer, Stephen. "Stranded by Politics and War: Nicaragua's Loved, Neglected Poet." *New York Times Book Review* (18 Jan. 1987):3.

Kirkpatrick, Gwen. *The Dissonant Legacy of Modernismo.* Berkeley: University of California Press, 1989.

Kirkpatrick, Susan. *Las Románticas: Women Writers and Subjectivity in Spain, 1835–1850.* Berkeley: University of California Press, 1989.

Kojève, Alexandre. *Introduction to the Reading of Hegel.* London, 1980.

Kramer, Lloyd S. *Threshold of a New World: Intellectuals and the Exile Experience in Paris, 1830–1848.* Ithaca: Cornell University Press, 1988.

Kristeva, Julia. *Séméiotiké, Recherches pour une sémanalyse.* Paris: Seuil, 1969.

———. *Desire in Language: A Semiotic Approach to Art and Literature* (1979), trans. Thomas Gora, Alice Jardine, and Leon S. Roudiez. New York: Columbia University Press, 1980.

———. *Revolution in Poetic Language* (1974), trans. Margaret Waller, intro. by Leon S. Roudiez. New York: Columbia University Press, 1984.

Kubayanda, Josaphat Bekunuru. "Minority Discourse and the African Collective: Some Examples from Latin American and Caribbean Literature." *Cultural Critique* 6 (1987):113–30.

Lacan, Jacques. "Of the Gaze as Object Petit a." In *The Four Fundamental Concepts of Psychoanalysis,* ed. Jacques Alain-Miller, trans. Alan Sheridan. London: Hogarth Press, 1977.

Lachmann, Renate. "Bakhtin and the Carnival: Culture as Counter-Culture." *Cultural Critique* 11 (Winter 1988–89):115–54.

Laclau, Ernesto. *Politics and Ideology in Marxist Theory*. London: New Left Books, 1977.

———. "Metaphor and Social Antagonisms." In Nelson and Grossberg, eds. 1988, 249–58.

Laclau, Ernesto, and Chantal Mouffe. *Hegemony and Socialist Strategy: Towards a Radical Democratic Politics*, trans. Winston Moore and Paul Cammack. London: Verso, 1985.

Laffranque, Marie. "Juan Montseny y los intelectuales, 1898–1905." *Anthropos* 1988:42–47.

Laguerre, Enrique A. *La poesía modernista en Puerto Rico*. San Juan: Ed. Coquí, 1969.

La lira rebelde proletaria. Lima: Federación de Motoristas y Conductores y Anexos, 1922.

Lamberet, Renée. "Soledad Gustavo, sa place dans la pensée anarchiste espagnole." *Convivium* (University of Barcelona) 44–45; I-II (1975):19–33.

Larsen, Neil. *Modernism and Hegemony: A Materialist Critique of Aesthetic Agencies*, foreword by Jaime de la Concha. Minneapolis: University of Minnesota Press, 1989.

Lauretis, Teresa de, Andreas Huyssen, and Kathleen Woodward, eds. *The Technological Imagination: Theories and Fictions*. Madison, Wis.: Coda Press, 1980.

Lazarus, Neil. "Modernism and Modernity: T. W. Adorno and Contemporary White African Literature." *Modernity and Modernism: Postmodernity and Postmodernism*, spec. issue of *Cultural Critique* 5 (1986–87):131–56.

Leenhardt, Jacques. "L'imaginaire du passé: un problème fin de siècle." In *Écrire en France au XIXe siècle (Actes du Colloque de Rome)*, ed. Graziella Pagliano and Antonio Gómez-Moriana (Montreal: Le Préambule, 1989), 159–74.

Lefebvre, Henri. *La production de l'espace*. Paris: Seuil, 1974.

Le Goff, Jacques. *La nouvelle histoire*. 1978; Paris: Complexe, 1988.

Lentricchia, Frank. "On the Ideologies of Poetic Modernism, 1890–1913: The Example of William James," in *Reconstructing American Literary History*, ed. Sacvan Bercovitch. Harvard English Studies 13 (1986):220–49.

———. *Ariel and the Police: Michel Foucault, William James, Wallace Stevens*. Madison: University of Wisconsin Press, 1988.

Levin, Harry. "What Was Modernism." *Massachusetts Review* 1 (1960):609–30.

Lichtheim, George. "Marx and the Asiatic Mode of Production.'" In Tom Bottomore, ed., *Interpretations of Marx* (Oxford/New York: Basil Blackwell, 1988), 121–38.

Lida, Clara E. *Anarquismo y revolución en la España del XIX*. Madrid: Siglo XXI, 1972.

Lima, Robert. *Valle-Inclán: The Theater of His Life*. Columbia: University of Missouri Press, 1988.

Litvak, Lily. *A Dream of Arcadia: Anti-industrialism in Spanish Literature, 1895–1905*. Austin: University of Texas Press, 1975.

———. "Latinos y anglosajones: Una polémica de la España de fin de siglo." *Revista Internacional de Sociología* (1975); rpt., *España 1900*, 155–99.

———*Erotismo fin de siglo*. Barcelona: Antonio Bosch, 1979.

———. *Musa libertaria*. Barcelona: Antonio Bosch, 1981.

———. *La mirada roja: Estética y arte del anarquismo español (1880–1913)*. Barcelona: Ediciones del Serbal, 1988.

———. *España 1900: Modernismo, anarquismo y fin de siglo*. Barcelona: Anthropos, 1990.

Lombroso, Cesare. "Lombroso on Nordau." *Review of Reviews* (New York) 12 (1894):479.

Lotman, Iurii M. "The Decembrist in Daily Life (Everyday Behavior as a Historical-Psychological Category)." In A. Nakhimovsky and Alice Stone Nakhimovsky, eds. 1985, 95–149.

Lovett, George H. "Francophobia in 19th Century Spanish Letters." *Kentucky Romance Quarterly* 19:13 (1972):290–95.

Lowenthal, Leo. "Sociology of Literature in Retrospect." *Critical Inquiry* 14:1 (1987):1–15.

Lyon, John. *The Theater of Valle-Inclán.* Oxford: Cambridge University Press, 1983.

Lyotard, Jean-F. *Discours, Figure.* Paris: Klincksiek, 1974.

———. *La condition postmoderne: Rapport sur le savoir.* Paris: Minuit, 1979. English trans. *The Postmodern Condition,* trans. G. Bennington and B. Massumi. Manchester: Manchester University Press, 1984.

———. "Rules and Paradoxes and Svelte Appendix." *Cultural Critique* 5 (1986–87):209-19.

———. "The Sublime and the Avant-Garde." *Art Forum* 22 (1984):36–43; rpt.,*The Lyotard Reader,* ed. Andrew Benjamin (Oxford: Basil Blackwell, 1989), 196–211.

McGann, Jerome. *The Romantic Ideology.* Chicago: University of Chicago Press, 1983.

———. *Towards a Literature of Knowledge.* Chicago: University of Chicago Press, 1989.

McHale, Brian. *Postmodern Fiction.* London: Methuen, 1987.

Macheray, Pierre. *Pour une théorie de la production littéraire.* Paris: François Maspero, 1966.

Maîtron, Jean. *Histoire du mouvement anarchiste en France.* 2 vols. Paris: Maspero, 1975.

Manuel, Frank. *The Prophets of Paris.* Cambridge: Harvard University Press, 1962.

Marcuse, Herbert. *Eros and Civilization: A Philosophical Inquiry into Freud.* Boston: Beacon Press, 1951.

———. *Negations: Essays in Critical Theory.* Boston: Beacon Press, 1968.

Marin, Louis. *La critique du discours: sur la "Logique de 'Port-Royal' et les Pensées" de Pascal.* Paris: Minuit, 1975.

Marrus, Michel. "Modernization and Dancing in Rural France: From 'La Bourrée' 'to Le Fox-Trot.' "In Jacques Beauroy, Marc Bertrand, and Edward T. Gargan, eds., *The Wolf and the Lamb: Popular Culture in France. From the Old Regime to the Twentieth Century* (Saratoga, Calif.: Anma Libri, 1977), 109–62.

Martí, José. *Inside the Monster: Writings on the United States and American Imperialism,* ed. with intro. and notes by Philip S. Foner, trans. Elinor Randall, with add. trans. by Luis A Baralt, Juan de Onís, and Roslyn Held Foner. New York: Monthly Review Press, 1975.

———. *Our America: Writings on Latin America and the Struggle for Cuban Independence,* ed. with intro. and notes by Philip S. Foner, trans. Elinor Randall, with add. trans. by Luis A Baralt, Juan de Onís, and Roslyn Held Foner. New York: Monthly Review Press, 1977.

———. *On Art and Literature: Critical Writings,* ed. with intro. and notes by Philip S. Foner, trans. Elinor Randall, with add. trans. by Luis A Baralt, Juan de Onís, and Roslyn Held Foner. New York: Monthly Review Press, 1982.

Martínez Masdeu, Edgar. *La crítica puertorriqueña y el modernismo en Puerto Rico.* San Juan: Instituto de Cultura Puertorriqueña, 1977.

Marx, Karl. *The Grundrisse,* ed. Martin Nicolaus. Harmondsworth: Penguin, 1973.

———. *The Capital,* intro. G. D. H. Cole. London: Everyman's Library, 1974.

———. *The Portable Karl Marx,* ed. Eugene Kamenka. London: Penguin, 1985.

Mayer, Arno. *The Persistence of the Old Regime.* New York: Pantheon, 1982.

Melón, Alfred. "Alrededor del concepto de identidad nacional." *La Gaceta de Cuba* 177 (1979):15–17.

Merod, Jim. *The Political Responsibility of the Critic.* Ithaca: Cornell University Press, 1987.

Metz, Christian. "The Imaginary Signifier." *Screen* 16:2 (1975):14–76.

Miliani, Domingo. "Utopian Socialism: Transitional Thread from Romanticism to Positivism in Spanish America." *Journal of the History of Ideas* 24:4 (1963):523–38.

Mintz, Sidney W. *Sweetness and Power: The Place of Sugar in Modern History.* London: Viking, 1985.

Moore, Barrington. *Privacy: Studies in Social and Cultural History.* New York: Sharpe, 1985.

Moreno Fraginals, Manuel, ed. *Africa en América Latina.* Mexico: Siglo XXI, 1977.

Moreno Villa, José. *Lo mexicano en las artes plásticas.* Mexico: El Colegio de México, 1948.

Moretti, Franco. "The Spell of Indecision." In Nelson and Grossberg, eds. 1988, 339–44.

Morse, George L. "Introduction." In *Degeneration*, by Max Nordau, trans. from the 2nd ed. of the German. New York: Howard Fertig, 1968.

Morse, Richard M. "La cultura política iberoamericana." *Vuelta* 58 (1981):4–16.

Morson, Gary Saul, and Caryl Emerson. *Mikhail Bakhtin: Creation of a Prosaics.* Stanford: Stanford University Press, 1990.

Mumford, Lewis. *The Pentagon of Power.* New York: Harcourt, Brace, Jovanovich, 1970.

Murray, Donald G., Miguel Seguí Aznar, presentación Oriol Bohigas. *El modernismo y su tiempo: Arquitectura y decoración en las islas.* Mallorca: José J. de Olañeta, 1989.

Nakhimovsky, Alexander D., and Alice Stone Nakhimovsky, eds. *The Semiotics of Russian Cultural History,* intro. by Boris Gasparov. Ithaca: Cornell University Press, 1985.

Nash, Mary, ed. *Mujer, familia y trabajo en España, 1875–1936.* Barcelona: Anthropos, 1983.

Náter Vázquez, Laura. "El '98 en la historiografía puertorriqueña: del político entusiasta al héroe popular." *OP. CIT. Boletín del Centro de Investigaciones Históricas* 4 (1988–89):101–22.

Nelson, Cary, and Lawrence Grossberg, eds. *Marxism and the Interpretation of Culture.* Urbana: University of Illinois Press, 1988.

Nietzsche, Friedrich. *On the Genealogy of Morals and Ecce Homo,* trans. Walter Kaufmann. New York: Random, 1967.

———. *The Portable Nietzsche,* ed. and trans. Walter Kaufmann. New York: Penguin, 1976.

Nixon, Rob. "Caribbean and African Appropriations of *The Tempest*." *Critical Inquiry* 13:3 (1987):557–78.

Norris, Christopher. *Derrida.* London: Fontana Press, 1987.

———. *Paul de Man: Deconstruction and the Critique of Aesthetic Ideology.* New York/London: Routledge, 1988.

Olsen, Donald J. *The City as Work of Art: London, Paris, Vienna.* New Haven: Yale University Press, 1986.

Orovio, Helio. *Diccionario de la música cubana: Bibliográfico y técnico.* Havana: Ed. Letras Cubanas, 1981.

Ortiz de Hadjopoulos, Theresa. *Luis Lloréns Torres: A Study of His Poetry.* New York: Plus Ultra, 1977.

Parkhurst, Ferguson, Patricia P. Desan, and W. Griswold, eds. "Mirrors, Frames, and Demons: Reflections on the Sociology of Literature." *Sociology of Literature,* spec. issue of *Critical Inquiry* 14:3 (1988):421-30.

Paz, Octavio. *El laberinto de la soledad.* Mexico: Fondo de Cultura Económica, 1959.

———. "El caracol y la sirena" (1962). In *Los signos en rotación y otros ensayos* (Madrid: Alianza, 1983), 90-104.

———. *Children of Mire: Modern Poetry from Romanticism to the Avant-Garde*, trans. Rachel Phillips. Cambridge: Harvard University Press, 1974.

Pêcheux, Michel. *Les vérités de La Palice*. Paris: Maspero, 1975. English trans. *Language, Semantics and Ideology: Stating the Obvious*, trans. Harbans Nagpal. London: Macmillan, 1982.

Pérez de la Dehesa, Rafael. *El grupo "Germinal": una clave del 98*. Madrid: Taurus, 1970.

Pérez Fernández, Rolando. *La binarización de los ritmos africanos en América Latina*. Cuba: Casa de las Américas, 1986.

Pérez Firmat, Gustavo. *The Cuban Condition: Translation and Identity in Modern Cuba*. Cambridge: Cambridge University Press, 1989.

Piaget, Jean. *The Moral Judgement of the Child*, trans. Marjorie Gabin. New York, 1965.

Picon Garfield, Evelyn, and Ivan A. Schulman. *"Las entrañas del vacío": Ensayos sobre la modernidad hispanoamericana*. Mexico: Cuadernos Americanos, 1984.

Poggioli, Renato. *The Theory of the Avant-Garde*, trans. Gerald Fitzgerald. 1962; New York: Harper and Row, 1968.

Poulantzas, N., et al. *El proceso ideológico*. Buenos Aires: Tiempo Contemporáneo, 1971.

Pratt, Mary Louise. "Linguistic Utopias." In Nigel Fabb et al., ed., *The Linguistics of Writing: Arguments between Languages and Literature* (New York: Methuen, 1987), 48–66.

———. "Humboldt y la reinvención de América." *Nuevo Texto Crítico* 1 (1988):35–54.

Proudhon, Pierre-Joseph. *Contradictions économiques*. Paris, 1875.

Radhakrishnan, R. "Ethnic Identity and Post-Structuralist Difference." *Cultural Critique* 6 (1987):199–200.

Rama, Angel. *Rubén Darío y el modernismo: circunstancia socioeconómica de un arte americano*. Caracas, Venezuela: Universidad Central de Caracas, 1970.

———. *Transculturación narrativa de América Latina*. Mexico: Siglo XXI, 1982.

———. *Las máscaras democráticas del modernismo*. Montevideo: Fundación Angel Rama, 1985a.

———. *Rubén Darío y el modernismo*. Barcelona: Alfadil, 1985b.

Rama, Angel, ed. *Rubén Darío: El mundo de los sueños*. Rio Piedras: Editorial Universitaria, Universidad de Puerto Rico, 1973.

Rama, Carlos. *Historia del movimiento obrero y social latinoamericano contemporáneo*. Barcelona: Laia, 1976.

———. *Historia de las relaciones culturales entre España y América Latina: Siglo XIX*. Mexico: Fondo de Cultura Económica, 1982.

Ramos, Julio. *Desencuentros de la modernidad en América Latina: Literatura y política en el siglo XIX*. Mexico: Fondo de Cultura Económica, 1989.

Rauch, Angelika. "The *Trauerspiel* of the Prostituted Body, or Woman as Allegory of Modernity." *Cultural Critique* 10 (1988):77–88.

Réberioux, Madeleine. "Avant-garde esthétique et avant-garde politique: le socialisme français entre 1890 et 1914." *Esthétique et marxisme*. Paris: UGE 1974.

Reiss, Timothy. *The Discourse of Modernity*. Ithaca: Cornell University Press, 1982.

Report: A Survey of Brazilian and Argentine Materials at the Internationaal Instituut voor Sociale Geschidenis in Amsterdam, ed. Eric Gordon, Michael M. Hall, and Hobart A. Spalding. *Latin American Research Review* (1973):27–70.

Rex, John. "Introduction: New Nations and Ethnic Minorities, Comparative and Theoretical Questions." In *Race and Class in Post-Colonial Society: A Study of Ethnic Group Relations in the English Speaking Caribbean, Bolivia, Chile and Mexico* (Paris: UNESCO, 1977), 11–52.

Reyes Matta, Fernando. "The 'New Song' and Its Confrontation in Latin America." In Nelson and Grossberg, eds. 1988, 447–59.

Ricoeur, Paul. *Hermeneutics and the Human Sciences,* ed. and trans. J. Thompson. Cambridge: Cambridge University Press, 1980.

Rodó, José Enrique. *Obras completas,* ed. intr. pról. y notas por Emir Rodríguez Monegal. Madrid: Aguilar, 1967.

Romano, E. "Celedonio Flores y la poesía popular." *Crisis* 8 (1973).

Romero, José Luis. *Latinoamérica: las ciudades y las ideas.* Mexico: Siglo XXI, 1976.

Rosenbaum, Sidonia Carmen. *Modern Women Poets of Spanish America. The Precursors: Delmira Agustini, Gabriela Mistral, Alfonsina Storni, Juana de Ibarborou.* New York: Hispanic Institute, 1945.

Rossi Landi, Ferruccio. *Significato, communicazione e parlare comune.* Padova: Marsilio Editore, 1961.

———. "Il linguaggio come lavoro e come mercato." *Nuova Corrente* 37 (1965):5–43.

Rubin Suleiman, Susan. "Pornography, Transgression and the Avant-Garde: Bataille's *Story of the Eye.*" In *The Poetics of Gender,* ed. Nancy K. Miller (New York: Columbia University Press, 1986), 117–36.

Rubio Jiménez, Jesús. *Ideología y teatro en España, 1890-1900.* Zaragoza: Universidad de Zaragoza, 1982.

Rudorff, Raymond. *The Belle Epoque: Paris in the Nineties.* New York: Saturday Review Press, 1973.

Said, Edward W. *Orientalism.* New York: Vintage, 1979.

———. "Permission to Narrate." *London Review of Books* (16 Feb. 1984).

———. *Nationalism, Colonialism and Literature: Yeats and Decolonization.* London: A Field Day Pamphlet, 1988.

Salaün, Serge. *El cuplé (1900–1936).* Madrid: Espasa Calpe, 1990.

Salper, Roberta. *Valle-Inclán y su mundo: Ideología y forma narrativa.* Amsterdam: Rodopi, 1988.

Saporta Sternbach, Nancy. "The Death of a Beautiful Woman: Modernismo, the Woman Writer and the Pornographic Imagination." *Ideologies and Literature* 3:1 (1988):35–60.

Sarlo, Beatriz. *Una modernidad periférica: Buenos Aires 1920 y 1930.* Buenos Aires: Nueva Visión, 1988.

Schendel, Michel van. "L'idéologème est un quasi-argument." *Théories du Texte,* spec. issue of *Texte* 5/6 (1986/87):21–132.

Schorske, C. *Fin-de-siècle Vienna: Politics and Culture.* New York: Knopf, 1980.

Schulman, Ivan A., ed. *José Martí. Ismaelillo: Versos Libres, Versos Sencillos.* Madrid: Cátedra, 1982.

———. *Nuevos asedios al modernismo.* Madrid: Taurus, 1987.

Schulte-Sasse, Jochen. "Foreword: Theory of Modernism versus Theory of the Avant-Garde." In Bürger 1984, vii-xlvii.

———. "Modernity and Modernism. Postmodernity and Postmodernism: Framing the Issue." *Cultural Critique* 5 (1986–87a):5–22.

———. "Imagination and Modernity: On the Taming of the Human Mind." *Cultural Critique* 5 (1986–87b):23–48.

———. "The Prestige of the Artist under Conditions of Modernity." *Cultural Critique* 12 (1989):83–100.

Segel, Harold B. *Turn-of-the-Century Cabaret: Paris, Barcelona, Berlin, Munich, Vienna, Cracow, Moscow, St. Petersburg, Zurich.* New York: Columbia University Press, 1987.

Serrano, Carlos. "Diversités régionales et régionalismes péninsulaires face à la guerra de Cuba (1895–1898)." In *Nationalisme et littérature* 1982, 99–120.

Serrano, Carlos, and Serge Salaün, eds. *1900 en Espagne (essai d'historie culturelle).* Bordeaux: Presses Universitaires de Bourdeaux, 1988.

Silva, José Asunción. *Obra completa,* pról. Eduardo Camacho Guizando, ed. notas y cronología E. Camacho Guizando and Gustavo Mejía. Caracas: Biblioteca Ayacucho, 1977.

Silverman, Kaja. *The Subject of Semiotics.* Oxford: Oxford University Press, 1983.

Silverman van Buren, Jane. *The Modernist Madonna: Semiotics of the Maternal Metaphor.* Bloomington: Indiana University Press, 1989.

Simón Palmer, M. del Carmen, ed. *Rosario de Acuña: Rienzi el Tribuno, El Padre Juan (Teatro).* Madrid: Castalia, 1989.

Sobejano, Gonzalo. *Nietzsche en España.* Madrid: Gredos, 1967.

Spitzer, Leo. *Essays in Historical Semantics.* New York: S. F. Vanni, 1948.

Spivak, Gayatri. *In Other Worlds: Essays in Cultural Politics.* New York/London: Methuen, 1987.

Stam, Robert. "Mikhail Bakhtin and Left Cultural Critique." In E. Ann Kaplan, ed., *Postmodernism and Its Discontents: Theories, Practices* (London: Verso, 1988), 116–45.

Stein, Stanley J., and Barbara H. Stein. *Colonial Heritage of Latin America: Essays on Economic Dependence in Perspective.* New York: Oxford University Press, 1970.

Suardiaz, Luis. "El bolero, vencedor del tiempo." *Granma* (8 June 1990):3.

Tannenbaum, Edward R. *1900: The Generation before the Great War.* New York: Anchor Press/Doubleday, 1977.

Taylor, Ronald, ed. and trans. *Aesthetics and Politics: Debates between E. Bloch, G. Lukács, B. Brecht, Walter Benjamin, T. Adorno.* London: NLB, 1979.

Termes, Josep. *Anarquismo y sindicalismo en España: La Primera Internacional (1864-1881).* Barcelona: Crítica, 1977.

Tindall, George B., and David E. Shi. *America: A Narrative History.* New York: Norton, 1989.

Todorov, Tzvetan. *Mikhail Bakhtin: The Dialogical Principle* (1981), trans. Wlad Godzich. Minneapolis: University of Minnesota Press, 1984.

Trask, David F. *The War with Spain in 1898.* New York: Macmillan, 1981.

Unamuno, Miguel de. *Obras completas.* 16 vols. Madrid: Afrodisio Aguado, 1958.

Urbina, Luis G. *Cuentos vividos y crónicas soñadas.* Mexico: Porrúa, 1971.

Urfé, Odilio. "La música y la danza en Cuba." In Moreno Fraginals, ed. 1977, 215–37.

Vargas, Ava, comp. *La Casa de Cita: Mexican Photographs from the Belle Epoque.* London: Quartet Books, 1986.

Vattimo, Gianni. *Il soggetto e la mascara. Nietzsche e il problemma della liberazione.* Milano: Bompiani, 1974.

Vilariño, Idea. *Las letras de tango: La forma, temas y motivos.* Buenos Aires: Schapire, 1965.

Watson, Stephen. "Criticism and the Closure of 'Modernism.' " *Substance* 13:1 (1984):15–30.

Weinburg, F. "Movimiento obrero y literatura utópica en la Argentina." *Caravelle* 25 (1975):7–31.

Whitebrook, Joel. "Reason and Happiness: Some Psychoanalytic Themes in Critical Theory." In *Habermas and Modernity,* ed. Richard J. Bernstein (Cambridge: MIT Press, 1985), 140–59.

Whitehead, Laurence. "Impotent Bystanders." *TLS* (19–25 Aug. 1988):904.

Williams, Raymond. *The Politics of Modernism: Against the New Conformists,* ed. Tony Pinkney. London: Verso, 1989.

Woodcock, George, and Ivan Avakumovic. *The Anarchist Prince: Peter Kropotkin.* New York: Schocken Books, 1971.

Wright, Kathleen. "Gadamer: The Speculative Structure of Language." In *Hermeneutics and Modern Philosophy,* ed. Brice R. Wachterhauser (Albany: State University of New York Press, 1986), 193–218.

Yurkievich, Saúl. *Celebración del modernismo.* Barcelona: Tusquets, 1976.

Zahareas, Antony N., Rodolfo Cardona, and S. Greenfield, eds. *Ramón del Valle-Inclán: An Appraisal of His Life and Works*. New York: Las Americas, 1968.

Zavala, Iris M. *Unamuno y su teatro de conciencia*. Salamanca: Universidad de Salamanca, 1963.

————. *Ideología y política en la novela española del siglo XIX*. Madrid: Anaya, 1971.

————. *Románticos y socialistas: Prensa española del siglo XIX*. Madrid: Siglo XXI, 1972.

————. *Fin de siglo: Modernismo, 98, bohemia*. Madrid: Cuadernos para el Diálogo, 1974.

————. "1898 Modernismo and the Latin American Revolution." *Revista Chicano-Riqueña* 3:4 (1975):43–48.

————. "Puerto Rico, siglo XIX: Literatura y sociedad." *Sin Nombre* 7:4 (1977):7–26; VIII 1 (1977):7–20.

————. "Notes on the Omniscient Reader of the Poetics of the Lyric." In *Approaches to Discourse, Poetics and Psychiatry*, ed. I. M. Zavala, Teun A. van Dijk, and Myriam Díaz-Diocaretz (Amsterdam: John Benjamins, 1987), 131–48.

————. "On the (Mis)uses of the Post-Modern: Hispanic Modernism Revisited." In T. D'Haen and E. Bertens, eds., *Postmodern: Fiction International* (Amsterdam: Rodopi, 1988a), 83–114.

————. "Bakhtin versus the Postmodern." *How to Read Bakhtin*, spec. issue of *Sociocriticism* IV:2 (1988b):51–70.

————. "Bakhtin and the Third: Communication as Response." In *The Bakhtin Circle Today*, ed. Myriam Díaz-Diocaretz, spec. issue of *Critical Studies* 1:2 (1989a):42–62.

————. *Romanticismo y costumbrismo*, T. 35, vol. 2: *Historia de España*. Madrid: Espasa Calpe, 1989b.

————. *Rubén Darío bajo el signo del cisne*. Rio Piedras: Editorial de la Universidad de Puerto Rico, 1989c.

————. "El discurso amoroso del bolero." *Los Cuadernos del Norte* 10:55 (1989d):2–8.

————. *La musa funambulesca: Poética de la carnavalización en Valle Inclán*. Madrid: Orígenes, 1990a.

————. "Bakhtin and Otherness: Social Heterogeneity." In *Bakhtin and the Epistemology of Discourse*, guest editor Clive Thomson. *Critical Studies* 2:1–2 (1990b):77–89.

————. "Metafore epistemiche del tempo e dello spazio: M. Bachtin, K. Mannheim e i Modernisti." *La genesi del senso*, spec. issue of *Idee* 13/15 (1990c):189–200.

————. *La posmodernidad y Mijail Bajtin: Una poética dialógica*. Madrid: Espasa Calpe, 1991a.

————. *Unamuno y el pensamiento dialógico*. Barcelona: Anthropos, 1991b.

————. *El bolero: Historia de un amor*. Madrid: Alianza, 1991c.

————. *Teorías de la modernidad*. Madrid: Tuero, in press.

Zavala, Iris M., ed., notes, and intro. "Estudio preliminar." In Alejandro Sawa, *Iluminaciones en la sombra*. Madrid: Alhambra, 1977; 2nd. ed. 1986.

Zavala, Iris M., ed. and intro. *Rubén Darío: El modernismo*. Madrid: Alianza, 1989.

Zavala, Iris M., and Rafael Rodríguez, eds. *Intellectual Roots of Puerto Rican Independence*. New York: Monthly Review Press, 1980.

Zima, Peter V., ed. *Semiotics and Dialectics: Ideology and the Text*. Amsterdam: John Benjamins, 1981.

Zubillaga, Carlos. *Carlos Gardel*. Prologue by Jorge Luis Borges. Madrid: Júcar, 1986.

INDEX

IRIS M. ZAVALA is Professor, and Chair of the Spanish Department at the University of Utrecht. She is the author of over ninety articles on literary history; social and political history; history of ideas; Spanish, Latin American, and Caribbean literatures and cultures; literary theory; semiotics; Bakhtin; and popular culture, and over thirty books, including *Rubén Darío bajo el signo del cisne*, which was recently awarded the Literary Prize of the Institute of Puerto Rican Culture.